GLOBAL ISSUES

CENSORSHIP

GLOBAL ISSUES

CENSORSHIP

Frank Caso

Foreword by Richard B. Collins

Director, Byron R White Center for the Study of American Constitutional Law, University of Colorado

Viva Books

New Delhi | Mumbai | Chennai | Kolkata | Bangalore | Hyderabad | Kochi | Guwahati

First Indian Edition 2010

VIVA BOOKS PRIVATE LIMITED

- 4737/23 Ansari Road, Daryaganj, New Delhi 110 002
  E-mail: vivadelhi@vivagroupindia.net, Tel. 42242200
- 76, Service Industries, Shirvane, Sector 1, Nerul, Navi Mumbai 400 706
  E-mail: vivamumbai@vivagroupindia.net, Tel. 27721273, 27721274
- Jamals Fazal Chambers, 26 Greams Road, Chennai 600 006
  E-mail: vivachennai@vivagroupindia.net, Tel. 28290304, 28294241
- B-103, Jindal Towers, 21/1A/3 Darga Road, Kolkata 700 017
  E-mail: vivakolkata@vivagroupindia.net, Tel. 22836381, 22816713
- 7, Sovereign Park Apartments, 56-58, K. R. Road, Basavanagudi, Bangalore 560 004
  E-mail: vivabangalore@vivagroupindia.net, Tel. 26607409, 26607410
- 101-102 Mughal Marc Apartments, 3-4-637 to 641, Narayanguda, Hyderabad 500 029
  E-mail: vivahyderabad@vivagroupindia.net, Tel. 27564481, 27564482
- First Floor, Beevi Towers, SRM Road, Kaloor, Kochi 682 018, Kerala
  E-mail: vivakochi@vivagroupindia.net, Tel: 0484-2403055, 2403056
- 232, GNB Road, Beside UCO Bank, Silpukhuri, Guwahati 781 003
  E-mail: vivaguwahati@vivagroupindia.net, Tel: 0361-2666386

www.vivagroupindia.com

Published by arrangement with

Facts on File, Inc.
132 West 31st Street
New York 10001
USA

ISBN 978-81-309-1415-2

Published by Vinod Vasishtha for Viva Books Private Limited, 4737/23, Ansari Road, Daryaganj, New Delhi-110 002. Printed and bound by Anand Sons, Delhi - 110 092.

CONTENTS

For Katherine and Vladimir

Foreword

Censorship suppresses human expression. Throughout recorded history, rulers and religious leaders have abused their powers to forbid speech, writing, and images they considered a threat to their authority or contrary to divine will. Censorship also means manipulating the information people are allowed to receive, including creating official messages that are thrust upon the population. A third form of censorship is secrecy; all governments label some information secret and try to prevent its publication.

Popularly elected governments were rare before the European Enlightenment. However, democracy has since become the world's dominant political ideology; even dictatorial governments now call their systems democratic. Yet censorship does not end with democratic governments. Rather, censoring power shifts from autocrats and oligarchs to popular majorities. Official messages are transmitted through public schools, libraries, and the media. Ancient Athens had a form of democracy, yet it famously condemned the philosopher Socrates because of what he said and wrote.

As the number of popularly elected governments increased, efforts to protect dissenting voices also grew. The English Bill of Rights of 1689 guaranteed freedom of speech for opposition members of Parliament. The Virginia constitution of 1776 proclaimed freedom of the press and religion and established an independent judiciary. Other American state constitutions had similar provisions. The U. S. Constitution guaranteed freedom of speech for members of Congress and created a very independent judiciary, and its ratification was achieved based on promises of a bill of rights. The first Congress honored that commitment by approving the federal Bill of Rights with First Amendment guarantees of free speech, press, and religion. Every new state constitution thereafter included similar provisions. In the 1930s and 1940s, the Supreme Court decided that the federal First Amendment also binds state governments.

CENSORSHIP

Rights to freedom of speech, press, and religion have, like democracy, become part of the dominant world ideology. In the 20th century, many nations adopted formal guarantees of free speech, press, and religion, and in 1948, the United Nations adopted the Universal Declaration of Human Rights, making these rights a matter of international law. However, these guarantees are often mere words on paper, ignored by authoritarian governments.

Technology has greatly expanded the forms of human communication, and the tools of censorship have grown with it. The printing press spread the written word far beyond the narrow world of scribes making copies by hand; censors responded by controlling publication. Later, inventors added the telegraph, telephone, photograph, film, radio, television, fax, and Internet. The censors have tried to keep up, using government ownership, licensing, jamming, and control of power supplies.

Through most of human history, the only private organizations with significant power were religious establishments; agents of censorship were either political or religious leaders. Modern democracies fostered powerful private enterprises. From the standpoint of censorship, the most important of these are print and broadcast media companies. These private enterprises form a third class of censors, whose power enables them to control information, deliver favored messages, and restrict others. However, the many competing voices in a functioning democracy greatly undercut their ability to censor. Moreover, they in turn can be independent voices that counteract government censorship.

Why do people in power want to censor others' speech and writing? The most obvious reason is to keep the power they have, in the belief that suppressing opponents' communications and criticism will help to do so. This kind of censorship has usually been done by rulers and is called political censorship. It has been common since the dawn of civilization and has been successful all too often. Religious belief is another historical reason to censor, both to maintain the power of religious leaders and to punish those whose expressions offend orthodox religious rules. It has had outward success, although human beings cannot be forced to believe in an official faith. Yet a third source of censorship is the desire of those in power to enforce social boundaries. This form of censorship shows up in measures to forbid forms of expression labeled as obscene or sometimes simply ugly. Other censorships have enforced economic orthodoxies. Many people think that political censorship is the worst form because religious, obscenity, and economic censorships are much more effective when backed by political power.

Human communication can be restricted for good reasons. Laws forbid or limit using speech or writing to cheat people, to spread malicious lies that ruin reputations, to conspire to commit murder and other crimes, to incite destructive riots, to frighten others by threats of violence, or to deface the property of others. These laws are usually not called censorship, although they literally fit the definition. Some people believe that pornography and hate speech are harmful enough to justify restricting them. An essential policy goal is to define those forms of expression that are so harmful that they should be suppressed or punished.

Censorship begins with an introduction to the topic, including examples of censorship in history and an outline of motives behind censorship, who censors, legal aspects of censorship, and methods of enforcing it. Chapter 2 then addresses the book's principal subject, censorship in the United States. Chapter 3 provides international perspective by examining censorship in four other nations: China, Egypt, Russia, and Zimbabwe. While each study begins with the country's history of censorship, it primarily focuses on how censorship is practiced today and how opponents of modern censorship fight against it. In today's world of global communication, censorship is no longer a question of domestic policy only; other nations and international organizations frequently criticize a country's censorship practices. Radio, the Internet, and other forms of electronic communication cross national boundaries and undermine censorship.

The United States led the world into modern forms of democracy and rights guarantees, evolving from the narrow electorates of 1776 to today's nearly universal suffrage. Historical examples of local censorship include suppression of the anti-slavery movement in the South before the Civil War, censoring advocacy of unions and socialism under criminal syndicalism laws, and censorship of expressions that local majorities considered obscene or blasphemous. On the national level, censorship has most commonly related to wars and national emergencies. Every war has generated some degree of censorship, mild in some, severe in others. The federal government has also suppressed obscenity, notably through its control of imported writings. After the invention of broadcast media, the federal government imposed a licensing system that allows some censorship, although it has been slight compared with that in authoritarian nations where governments own the media. Since it began to enforce the First Amendment in 1931, the Supreme Court has outlawed many forms of censorship.

Chapter 3, "Global Perspectives," begins with China, relating its long history of authoritarian rule interrupted by only a few brief periods with some degree of free expression. Two thousand years of imperial rule were succeeded by a few decades of unrest and wars until the communist victory of 1949. Since the early 1980s, there has been an increase in the freedom to pursue economic growth, but the dictatorship of the Chinese Communist Party continues to enforce its political orthodoxy. The party has adjusted its censorship methods to counteract advances in communication technology that threaten to undermine its system.

Egypt is the world's oldest civilization with a continuous identity. It has had authoritarian governments throughout its history, under pharaohs and Greek, Roman, and Arab invaders. The latter made Islam the dominant religion. The government of modern Egypt has some formal trappings of freedom but is largely an authoritarian state with many limits on freedom of expression.

The czars of Russia had powerful control over written communication and vigorously put down any form of political dissent. They were replaced by the communist dictatorship of the Union of Soviet Socialist Republics (USSR). In addition to ruthless suppression of political dissent, the Soviet state imposed a stifling orthodoxy on the arts known as Soviet Realism and adopted atheism as the official state religion. The USSR broke apart in 1991, and the new Russia enjoyed substantial freedoms of expression. More recently, the Putin government has reimposed central controls, so that today's Russia has returned to many aspects of the nation's autocratic past.

Zimbabwe, the last nation covered in chapter 3, was once under British rule where colonial laws favored European settlers over native Africans. That system had a degree of freedom of expression for the European minority but tolerated no dissent. In the 1960s British policy turned against the colonial system, and black Africans claimed majority rights, both in expression and by armed rebellion. A system of political equality was achieved in 1980, and guerilla leader Robert Mugabe was freely elected to head independent Zimbabwe. But since that time, his government has used oppressive devices to keep him in power, where he remains. The government has become steadily more authoritarian, violently suppressing all forms of political dissent.

These summaries blossom into full stories in the pages of this book. They provide a comprehensive picture of the different forms censorship can take, depending on whether its targets are political dissent or the arts and on whether the form of expression is print media, radio, television, film, or the Internet. Chapters 4 and 5 excerpt original documents relating to censorship in the five nations and international law. Other chapters include a comprehensive annotated bibliography, lists of key figures and relevant organizations, a chronology, and a glossary, providing additional tools for students who wish to research censorship.

Freedom of expression and freedom to obtain truthful information are foundations of democracy and the arts. Achieving them is a vital for everyone. Defending them is everyone's duty in a free country. This book will help you do it.

—Richard B. Collins
professor and director, Byron R. White Center
for the Study of American Constitutional Law
University of Colorado

Acknowledgments

First of all, I would like to thank Claudia Schaab for her advice, assistance, and wonderful editorial expertise. I also want to thank Richard B. Collins, director of the Byron R. White Center for the Study of American Constitutional Law, for his expert comments on the manuscript. M. Lesley Wilkins of the Harvard Law School library deserves a special mention, as do Louise Blalock, Asjad Chaudhary, Tarek Dachraoui, Augustine Hungwe, Evgeni Kiselyev, and Niel Shahroor. Lastly, I would like to thank Alexandra Simon, who I hope enjoyed reading this book as she copyedited it.

PART I

At Issue

1

Introduction

Censorship has been part of human society since ancient times. Early on, it was seen as a legitimate method of regulating society and culture, and it is still perceived that way by some. However, as societies grew more complex, better educated, and more technologically advanced, individuals became more sophisticated. This increased sophistication brought a new awareness of political rights, which in turn ushered in a better understanding of the role of speech, or, more generally, communication, in advancing or thwarting society's goals. People began to appreciate the very complexity of speech itself, its degrees of directness and symbolism, and how it can upset or critique the status quo. Thus censorship, which has always been a method of controlling the flow of information and thus the ideas of citizens, came to be used and seen as a tool for repression.

Certainly there are private citizens in the United States and throughout the world who believe that censorship remains a useful method of safeguarding society's values, but today, perhaps more than ever, censorship is primarily used by authoritarian governments, religions, democracies, and even corporations as a means of retaining power.

The examinations in this book of censorship history and current censorship in the United States, China, Egypt, Russia, and Zimbabwe reveal many of the methods by which censorship has been and continues to be implemented. They also consider the various strategies against censorship that are employed by citizens and organizations, sometimes successfully, often not.

EXAMPLES OF CENSORSHIP IN HISTORY

Ancient World

The word *censorship* derives from the Latin word *censor*. The position of censor was established in ancient Rome in 443 B.C.E., during what is known as Rome's republican period.[1] Censors were originally charged with taking the census, but they gradually acquired more power, including regulating the morals of those citizens whom they had counted. In ancient societies, with their emphasis on the prosperity of the commonwealth rather than the freedom of the individual, this type of regulation was not considered a bad thing. It was only in the Renaissance period that individual thought and action took center stage and not until the modern era, dating from the 18th century, that the rights of the individual were expanded—and even then not in all societies.

What we now consider censorship—the control of information—predated Rome's republican period. In the earliest dynasties of China and Egypt, for instance, it hardly seems thinkable that rulers, generally under threat of invasion and often propagating a belief in a divine mandate, would tolerate dissent. Since these ancient societies were structured much differently than modern ones, when factionalism did arise it led to revolts by tributary states intent on dynastic change.

The most famous case of censorship (as we understand the term) in the ancient world was the trial of the Athenian philosopher Socrates (469–399 B.C.E.). Socrates held philosophic discussions with the youth of Athens, questioning their beliefs on a wide range of topics including politics and religion. This questioning of Athens's cultural underpinnings displeased the parents of his students as well as Socrates' political enemies. He was charged with corrupting the city's youth and undermining Athens's religion. Despite an eloquent defense, as recorded by his most famous student, Plato, in the *Apology* (here *apology* means "defense"), Socrates was sentenced to die by drinking hemlock.[2] The type of censorship endured by Socrates, especially concerning his undermining of religion, would reappear in different forms over and over in many cultures, down to modern times.

China during the reign of Qin Shi Huangdi (259–210 B.C.E.) was the scene of one of the worst episodes of mass censorship in the ancient world. After ascending the throne in 221 B.C.E., Emperor Qin, in 213 B.C.E., ordered the destruction of all books of history in order that Chinese history would begin with his reign. The only books spared from the fires were those dealing with math, science, and oracles. Thus, it is likely that even the works of the most famous ancient Chinese philosopher, Confucius, were destroyed.[3]

During the Roman Empire, senators were allowed a degree of freedom of speech, as long as they did not speak against the emperor. However, the senate grew weaker as the emperor's power became more absolute. The same measure of "openness" applied to certain other public figures. By and large, the public condoned this policy, even though critics of the emperor, especially poets and other writers, faced exile, having their works burned, and, in extreme cases of sedition (speaking or writing against the government, in this case the emperor), execution.

The various peoples under Roman rule were allowed to maintain their own practices of worship as long as they included the emperor as a divinity. Jews and Christians suffered under this policy because their religions were monotheistic (belief in one God) and they considered such a directive heretical. Ironically, some historians have noted that censorship played a significant role in ancient Israel and among the early Christian leaders in maintaining solidarity among their citizens and adherents, bringing believers to a closer union with God.

In Rome itself, Judaism and Christianity were outlawed and their practitioners, particularly Christians who were the most zealous, were persecuted. After Emperor Constantine I (r. 324–37) legalized Christianity in the fourth century C.E., he ordered the destruction of certain books of Greek philosophy. This paved the way for Theodosius (r. 379–95), emperor of the East, to make Christianity the state religion. Once it became entrenched, Christianity outlasted the empire itself. The Western version, based in Rome, evolved into the Roman Catholic Church and the later Protestant denominations. The Eastern version evolved into the various Orthodox national churches as well as other independent churches such as the Armenian and Coptic Churches.

Renaissance and Early Modern Europe

Catholicism held sway in Western Europe for more than 1,000 years until the Protestant Reformation began to challenge its predominance in the 16th century. The church had become so powerful that it instituted its own prohibitions and lists of banned books. The most infamous of these lists was the *Index librorum prohibitorum*, or Index of Prohibited Books.

The mid-15th-century invention of the printing press (attributed to Johannes Gutenberg) sparked an increase in literacy in Europe. While the technology and its by-products initially worked to the advantage of the established church (as well as other political powers), the proliferation of books soon threatened Catholicism's spiritual hegemony on the continent.

The *Index librorum prohibitorum* was issued in 1559 during the reign of Pope Paul IV (r. 1555–59).[4] It banned all books that were deemed morally dangerous or incompatible with Catholic doctrine. Certain other books faced limitations, and new books had to receive prior approval before publication. Furthermore, authors of banned books faced excommunication from the Catholic Church. The 16th century was noted for its extreme degree of censorship in Europe, as the Catholic Church tried to limit the influence of the Protestant Reformation and Protestants sought to cleanse their teachings of Catholic heresies. In addition, as nations began to consolidate and choose sides in the ongoing Christian controversy, secular censorship became a popular tool for maintaining the political status quo.

The most famous case of individual censorship, after Socrates, was that of the Italian astronomer Galileo Galilei (1564–1642). Galileo was also a mathematician and a natural philosopher who did groundbreaking work in the study of motion before turning his attention to astronomy. He soon accepted the Copernican theory (named for Nicolaus Copernicus, 1473–1543) that the Sun, and not the Earth, is the center of the solar system. This directly contradicted church teaching, and, in 1616, Galileo was barred from discussing or teaching Copernican theory. However, in 1632, Galileo published *Dialogo sopra I due massimi sistemi del mondo, tolemaico e copernicano* (*Dialogue Concerning the Two Chief World Systems, Ptolemaic and Copernican*), in which two advocates of the Copernican theory demolish the argument of a supporter of the Ptolemaic system, on which the church had based its cosmology for centuries.[5] Although the book made it past the Florentine censor (Galileo was living in Florence at the time of the book's publication), it nevertheless angered Pope Urban VIII (r. 1623–44), who had been a friend of Galileo.

Galileo was summoned before the Inquisition in 1633, found guilty, sentenced to life imprisonment (which was actually house arrest), and forced to formally renounce his belief in Copernican theory. He died in 1642.[6]

In Great Britain in 1643, during the reign of Charles I (r. 1625–49), Parliament began to enforce a decree of 1637 (by the Star Chamber, a court of law which evolved from meetings of the king's royal council) requiring all published works to be registered with the Stationers' Company and to be approved by either the archbishop of Canterbury or the bishop of London before publication.[7] The following year, English poet and essayist John Milton (1608–74) wrote *Areopagitica,* which eloquently argued for an end to prepublication censorship. Unfortunately, the English Civil War was raging and Milton's tract had little effect; the law did not expire until 1694. Today, *Areopagitica* is considered a classic document of civil liberty.[8]

American Colonies

The Western Hemisphere has had its share of censorship following the arrival of Europeans. During the Spanish Conquest in the 16th century, Catholic missionaries in their zeal for conversion banned the Mayan religion and writing system. Known for its achievements in astronomy and mathematics, the Mayan civilization in Mexico and parts of Central America was at its height from the third to 11th centuries C.E. The Spanish destroyed most of the Mayan texts. Of those that survived, the most famous are the Dresden

Codex, the Paris Codex, the Madrid Codex, and the Grolier Codex (discovered in 1965). The best-known surviving Mayan text, *Popul Vuh,* the creation story, was written in the mid-16th century in the Quiché language using the Latin alphabet.[9]

After establishing its authority throughout southern North America and most of Central and South America, Spain, by the middle of the 16th century, sought ways to maintain it. One of these was the introduction of the Inquisition in Peru in 1568, during the reign of Philip II (r. 1556–98).[10] The Lima-based Inquisition was an extension of the Spanish Inquisition and took its directives from the Council of the Supreme Inquisition, which ordered its colonial counterpart to control the ideology and morality of the colony. By and large, that meant the censorship of ideas and books.

Regarding books published in Spain, censorship was twofold: Both the government and the church had the power to ban books. Moreover, all books had to be registered with the government prior to publication. Because the church controlled the importing of books, it was a more important factor than the government with regard to postpublication censorship. Inquisition officials also paid regular visits to booksellers and libraries.

The Peruvian Inquisition ordered complete running inventories from booksellers, who had to record the name of the buyer of each book. Furthermore, when evaluating private collections, booksellers had to notify authorities if any forbidden books were included.

The Peruvian Inquisition lasted until 1820, but was never as powerful as the Spanish Inquisition. It has been noted that from its inception in 1568 until 1700 not one reader of a banned book was prosecuted. However, in the 18th century, particularly after the French Revolution, the Inquisition began to crack down on the importation of forbidden material. The Peruvian Inquisition's weakness was due to a number of factors, including lack of proper staffing and internal conflicts. Nevertheless, its role in the denial of a basic human freedom to the colonists and its symbolism as a representative of the repressive bureaucracy of the Spanish crown and the Council of the Supreme Inquisition were factors in the series of revolutions that swept South America in the early 19th century.

Spanish colonials were not the only ones to suffer under censorship. Those living in the British colonies also had to abide by restrictive laws, some of which were idiosyncratic to the colonies. The Puritans, for instance, who settled and governed Massachusetts, took a much narrower view of theater than did England itself. In fact, local theater censorship was practiced to some degree throughout the 13 British colonies that eventually became the United States. The Puritans also held a narrow viewpoint concerning religious freedom, an irony (considering their own past persecution) that eventually led

Roger Williams and others in search of greater freedom to found the Rhode Island colony.

By the mid-18th century the colonies, which had enjoyed varying degrees of independence for generations, began to push back as England sought to exert more control, mainly for economic reasons.

Although it is now considered the first colonial newspaper, *Publick Occurrences, Both Foreign and Domestick,* published by Benjamin Harris (1647–1720) in 1690, ran for one issue only because it failed to comply with the Massachusetts colony's licensing act, requiring publications be licensed beforehand. This law was essentially a colonial extension of the same law that John Milton had protested in *Areopagitica* nearly 50 years earlier. In 1721, Benjamin Franklin's older brother, James Franklin (1697–1735), founded the *New England Courant,* which quickly established itself as the benchmark for colonial journalism. Unfortunately, the newspaper's success, based on lively discourse, led to its downfall. Within two years of its founding, the *New England Courant* was banned.

In 1728, Benjamin Franklin (1706–90) picked up where his brother was forced to leave off. Having moved to Philadelphia, he founded the *Pennsylvania Gazette,* which some historians consider the finest colonial newspaper. Franklin was also publisher of the renowned *Poor Richard's Almanac.*[11]

While the political atmosphere may have been somewhat lenient in Pennsylvania, that was not the situation in New York, where the most famous case of censorship in the colonies occurred in 1734, leading to the trial of New York newspaper publisher John Peter Zenger (1697–1746). Zenger was charged with printing seditious libel for criticizing Governor William Cosby and imprisoned for nine months. When Zenger was finally brought to trial in 1735 he became a cause célèbre, attracting the services of Philadelphia lawyer Andrew Hamilton, considered the best trial lawyer in the colonies. Hamilton won the case, and the Zenger decision set a precedent for a free press that resounded when the fledgling United States adopted the First Amendment to the United States Constitution (part of the Bill of Rights) more than 50 years later.[12]

Eighteenth, Nineteenth, and Twentieth Centuries

The first serious challenge to free speech and freedom of the press in the United States came during the administration of the second president, John Adams (r. 1797–1801).[13] In 1798, Congress passed, and Adams signed into law, the Alien and Sedition Acts. The Sedition Act (fourth of the four laws) called for a fine and/or imprisonment for anyone who made "false, scandalous and malicious" statements against Congress or the president, or to incite the people against the government. The Federalists (Adams's party) who proposed and backed the law felt it was a wartime necessity. Yet there was no war, only bellicose talk between the United States and France.

The Sedition Act was primarily used as a political tool to silence the opposition Republicans headed by Vice President Thomas Jefferson.[14] In fact, no Federalists were ever arrested under the law. The act expired on March 3, 1801, which coincided with Adams's final day in office. Although Congress formally repudiated the Sedition Act by repaying fines, with interest, to survivors, their heirs, or their legal representatives, a second Sedition Act was signed into law in 1918.

A few outstanding institutions of censorship in the 19th century include Russia's Foreign Censorship Board. Headquartered in Saint Petersburg, with offices in other cities throughout the Russian Empire, it was responsible for controlling all foreign printed matter that entered the country. In addition to books, magazines, and newspapers, this included maps and music. The mandate of the Foreign Censorship Board was to prevent all liberalizing influences from entering Russia.

In the first half of the 19th century in Great Britain, criminal libel laws were used to control the press. At that time, criminal libel, loosely defined as defaming the monarch, the government, or the Church of England, was divided into four categories: seditious, blasphemous, defamatory, and obscene. There were a number of sensational trials for seditious libel in Great Britain in the early 19th century, but, by the 1830s, following passage of the Reform Act of 1832, the idea of seditious libel was abandoned, at least in peacetime. The Libel Act of 1843 allowed for the truth to be considered, thus weakening the notion of sedition as well as defamatory libel. However, because of the strong hold of the Church of England and the mores of British society of the time, charges of blasphemous libel and obscene libel were brought against individuals throughout the century. In fact, with the increased importation of literature, obscenity charges were expanded.[15]

Another example of blatant, autocratic censorship during this period occurred in the Ottoman Empire, which at its peak in the 16th century stretched from southeastern Europe to the Middle East and North Africa. Centered in Turkey, the Ottoman Empire was ruled during the late 19th century by Sultan Abdűlhamid II (r. 1876–1909). A controversial figure, Abdűlhamid II attempted to modernize while at the same time cracking down on dissent. In many ways, he foreshadowed the dictators who came to power in the 20th century. He dissolved the parliament and suspended the constitution. Free speech and a free press were natural victims of this policy, which the sultan enforced through a network of secret police.[16]

The 20th century saw censorship practiced on an unprecedented scale throughout the world. The final stages of some of the monarchies of Europe and Asia fostered a crackdown on free expression while promoting a militarism that ultimately led to World War I (1914–18). The devastation of that war was a direct cause of the rise of dictatorships in Russia and its allied "republics" of the Soviet Union in the period 1918–22, and the unreasonable reparations demanded by the victors led to the rise of Nazism in Germany in the early 1930s. Other dictatorships came to power during various decades of the century in Italy, Japan, Spain, China, parts of Southeast Asia, as well as in Africa, the Middle East, Central and South America, and Cuba. In many instances, these nations blunted not only freedom of expression but exchanges of ideas between cultures.

During the 1930s and afterward, censorship in the dictatorships led not only to the banning of books and periodicals, but also religion and political ideas that did not conform to the established views of the government. In the 1930s in Germany and the Soviet Union, especially, politics and art had to conform to certain ideals, and many of those who did not conform were executed. It was also a factor in the Holocaust—the worst genocide in history.

Censorship in the 20th century was not restricted to the dictatorships. As mentioned previously, the United States enacted a second Sedition Act during World War I. U.S. censorship included films, importation of foreign literature, American literature published abroad, radio, television, magazines, and even live performances. The vast majority of cases dealt with what was perceived as obscenity. Furthermore, the states were also involved in the suppression of books and films.

In the 1980s, more and more states and municipalities in the United States enforced censorship, mostly through banning books in schools and libraries. This censorship differed from past forms in that it was often initiated by private individuals or citizens' groups and played out in state and municipal governmental bodies rather than in the federal government. These bodies ranged from local school boards to various state supreme courts. Generally, this censorship arose out of a conservative Christian agenda to eliminate what some called the "religion of secular humanism," as some parents sought to replace science textbooks that taught the theory of evolution and have creationism (a belief in the biblical account of the creation of the world) taught in public schools. The majority of those opposed to teaching evolution belonged to fundamentalist Christian sects. But they were not alone in seeking to remove ideas from the intellectual arena. Opponents of fundamentalist Christians, the so-called secular humanists, had their own agendas for censorship. These included novels (the best-known instance was Mark Twain's *The Adventures of Huckleberry Finn*) whose language was not considered politically correct.

With the widespread use of computers and the burgeoning of the Internet in the late 20th and early 21st centuries have come both a new area to censor and a means of combating repressive structures. It is very hard to curtail free speech in cyberspace; thus, the focus is on those who receive what some governments might consider illicit material rather than on those who produce it, who traditionally had been the target of censors. On the other hand, citizens of repressive countries, generally living in exile, have been able to use the Internet as a means of detailing the crimes of their governments and of offering hope to those still living under repressive regimes.

Two other areas of the Internet that governments are seeking to control are pornography and online gambling. Again, because legislation on banning any activity in cyberspace is hard to enforce, it is easier to control these activities at the points of reception, especially pornography. For this reason, Internet filters have become popular in homes and schools.

Although censorship is unlikely to ever disappear, the development of the Internet has demonstrated that people will always be determined to express themselves.

MOTIVES FOR CENSORSHIP

There are three basic reasons for censorship, which sometimes overlap. They are retention of political power, upholding of theological dogma, and maintaining community standards. Historical examples of these are the U.S. Sedition Act of 1798 (retention of power), *Index librorum prohibitorum* (upholding theological dogma), and banning books from a school system (maintaining community standards).

Retention of Political Power

In every country, the common link of censorship is the retention of power. Most obviously, this is played out on the national level for reasons that are as various as the types of government in the world. It may be because a dictator, such as Joseph Stalin in the Soviet Union or Adolf Hitler in Germany (both of whom eliminated members of their own political parties), brooks no opposition or because a president seeks reelection or to strengthen the chances of his party in an upcoming election.

Censorship to retain political power is also enforced at lower levels of government. In Russia, for example, provincial governors and mayors enjoy a degree of autonomy that they had not experienced under communism (though President Vladımir Putin has taken steps to reign in such independence) and are loathe to relinquish power. Furthermore, corruption, political and otherwise, makes criticism of the status quo in these areas difficult if not dangerous. Russia, of course, is not the only nation to suffer from provincial corruption and its ensuing censorship, but the vastness of its territory and the multitude of its national problems since the end of the Soviet Union in 1991, not to mention a tradition of censorship dating to czarist times, have made censorship an expedient and too often successful political tool. Also, in some parts of the country, the censorship battles contain political elements and power struggles.

As previously noted, censorship on the state and municipal levels in the United States generally involves private individuals or groups and, while most of this is more properly categorized as upholding theological dogma, to an extent the individuals (or groups acting on behalf of parents) are seeking to retain control of their children's religious beliefs.

A different matter altogether is military censorship. By tradition and by law, the military adheres to a different, often stricter, standard than civilian law, but it also enjoys almost carte blanche power when it comes to censorship. As a routine matter, the military classifies and/or censors documents that may be of strategic importance. However, the military (and this applies to all nations) historically has claimed this special censorship privilege in order to protect its institutional turf or personnel. Examples of military censorship in the early 21st century include the U.S. military blocking stories about abuse of Iraqi prisoners and the Russian military not only covering up investigations but harassing and threatening journalists.

Upholding of Theological Dogma

In the United States, theological dogma has not been a concern of the federal government, nor is it a concern of the central governments of China, Russia, and Zimbabwe. In the United States, individuals and organizations have sought to limit certain teachings, such as evolution, or include what has come to be known as creation science to balance what they have felt was evolution's unfair advantage in the schools. Other individuals have challenged various types of fiction (such as children's and young adult literature) on the basis of their religious beliefs. In the last century, both Soviet Russia and the People's Republic of China enacted restraints against religion. In contemporary Russia, though, the Orthodox Church has rebounded under a somewhat liberal atmosphere, enjoying more influence than it has had since the early 20th century. It has become more assertive in the courts regarding free-speech issues that challenge church dogma. This muscle-flexing by the Moscow patriarchate is a result of the favored status that the Russian Orthodox Church now enjoys over other religions (and religious organizations) in Russia.

Of the five case-study nations discussed in this book, Egypt is unique with regard to censorship for religious purposes. The Egyptian constitution is based on sharia (Islamic law), but the government tries to walk a secular line. Nevertheless, Muslim clerics play important roles in deciding Egypt's cultural trends. Their influence is felt either directly or indirectly in various genres such as literature, theater, film, and popular music.

Maintaining Community Standards

Censorship practiced to maintain community standards often overlaps with that practiced to uphold theological dogma. (Here the word *community* may range in meaning from a neighborhood to an ethnic, national, or religious group.) Generally, community standards apply to two areas: education and entertainment. In the United States, particularly, education has become a battleground as different communities exhibit different standards regarding science and religion.

Communities in the United States and elsewhere also seek to apply a kind of moral censorship on the entertainment industry to curb its excesses—both perceived and imagined. In the past, this censorship has most often applied to theater and literature (as well as some political writing), but, with all the new entertainment technologies beginning in the late 19th century, it has extended to films, television, recorded music, magazines, and the Internet.

Moral censorship seeks to protect the sensibilities of children, but often the debate centering around it is hampered by the all-or-nothing attitudes taken by proponents and opponents, which often fail to take into account the circumstances of the application. On one hand, censorship tramples on certain freedoms and rights for adults and stifles young people's ability to make their own moral decisions. On the other hand, moral censorship provides a counterweight to the upsurge in the production of pornography, especially child pornography.

IMPLEMENTATION OF CENSORSHIP

There are various means by which governments, individuals, and private and public groups implement censorship. Because modern governments as a rule do not enjoy the kind of absolute power of past monarchs and dictators and most countries' constitutions include provisions protecting free speech, modern censorship has had to become subtle. That is, people may recognize a law or an act as censorious, but it plays by the rule of law. In fact, sometimes censorship laws are passed in seeming contradiction to a country's constitution.

One way of manipulating the law is the requirement of a special license to practice journalism or broadcast on television or radio. Often, such licenses are used as political weapons against dissenters. In countries that are theocracies, or nearly such, organized religion in conjunction with the government plays the major role in censorship.

Censorship is not always done by government, religious, or military decree. Corporations may also censor employees, especially regarding union-organizing activities. Media conglomerates often practice self-censorship that pays more attention to the bottom line than to freedom of speech. Also, alleged gangsterism resulting in censorship is practiced in those parts of the world (including some of the countries examined in this book) where business activity is almost completely unregulated.

Who Censors

GOVERNMENT

By and large, government censorship emanates from the central government and/or departments of its bureaucracy—the most wide-reaching within a nation. However, provincial, state, and municipal governments also engage in censorship for many of the same political reasons. In the United States, lower governmental censorship can involve state, county, or city boards of education, libraries, state courts, and even law enforcement.

RELIGIOUS GROUPS

Religions are inherently censorious in that they admit into their canons only those texts that support their theologies or dogmas. This itself is not bad since theological and philosophical consolidation is a natural consequence of time and expansion. Nevertheless, the internal politics that decided (and continue to decide) what has been included and what has been left out of the various religious scriptures has yet to be fully explored.

A secondary, but pernicious, censorship occurs when religions and religious organizations prohibit cultural artifacts and educational information from their adherents. The usual reasons for this censorship are blasphemy and heresy. Examples of this type of censorship include the aforementioned Index of Prohibited Books, prohibitions against watching certain films, and, in the late 20th century, the Iranian fatwa against Salman Rushdie's novel, *The Satanic Verses.*

MASS MEDIA

Media companies and large corporations with media holdings have found that consolidation is more profitable. Thus, a company that owns newspapers in many markets can cut expenses by sharing various opinion pieces such as book and film reviews or even op-ed essays. Furthermore, duplication of foreign news bureaus (among the companies' holdings) can be eliminated. In the end, the losers are the newspaper readers and the public at large who receive fewer points of view. (That there may be a political undercurrent to media consolidation should not be overlooked either.) Media consolidation is not confined to newspapers and is in fact becoming a phenomenon of the global economy.

CORPORATIONS

Nonmedia corporations have also employed censorship to keep negative information about the company or its research from reaching the public and government watchdogs. Such censorship has ranged from document suppression to outright harassment and, in the most extreme cases, physical violence and murder.

Legal Aspects

FREEDOM OF SPEECH AND FREEDOM OF THE PRESS

The United States holds the distinction of having the oldest written national constitution in use in the world, and many others have been patterned after it. Yet, in its original version, the U.S. Constitution omitted guarantees for some of the most basic rights in a democracy. Foremost among these were freedom of speech and freedom of the press, which are now guaranteed after ratification of the First Amendment to the Constitution, along with the rest of the Bill of Rights, in December 1791. Although guaranteed, these rights have not always been upheld. In fact, there have been times when the legislative and executive branches of the federal government, with support from the federal judiciary and the Supreme Court, have passed and signed into law bills that have promoted censorship. The most recent example of this was the USA PATRIOT Act that quickly passed through both houses of Congress and was signed by President George W. Bush in October 2001 in reaction to the September 11, 2001, terrorist attacks in New York City and Washington, D.C., and the downed airline flight in Pennsylvania. (These First Amendment exceptions and other forms of censorship will be discussed in the case study of the United States.)

State and local governments have also been allowed to ban books from public libraries and public schools, usually on the grounds of obscenity. In some instances, states have replaced science textbooks that teach evolution with those that teach both evolution and creationism. These moves are very controversial, and the latter one contains complications that will be examined later in the case study on the United States.

The other four case study nations also have constitutions that guarantee freedom of speech and of the press. Yet their guarantees, like those of the United States, are not absolute. Some of the constitutions' wording is vague, including clauses that may be interpreted to contravene those clauses that guarantee citizens' rights. Other constitutions have censorship clauses written into them.

Where these four nations differ from the United States is in their basic form of government. Each presently has an authoritarian government and has historically been governed that way. Since the early 1980s, Hosni Mubarak and Robert Mugabe have led Egypt and Zimbabwe, respectively. In China, the Communist Party has been the single ruling party since 1949, although sometimes riven by factionalism.

Russia's authoritarianism differs from the others in that, having played the lead role in the dissolution of the Soviet Union, it initially embraced the USSR's political and economic opposites—democracy and capitalism. Throughout the 1990s, Russian newspapers and journals were free to publish their misgivings and to voice criticisms of President Boris Yeltsin, the Duma (Russia's lower house of parliament), the Federation Council (the upper house), and government ministers. The high point for post-Soviet news media, especially television, was the role it played in Yeltsin's successful reelection campaign. However, the oligarchs who owned and ran the major media outlets expected a return on their favor. A few became influential advisers to Yeltsin. In fact, they became so influential that they helped broker Yeltsin's resignation from office on December 31, 1999, and his replacement with Vladimir Putin.

Under Putin, a former KGB agent trained in the rigidly vertical structure of the Soviet system, the Russian government has become increasingly authoritarian. Elected to the presidency outright in March 2000 and reelected four years later, Putin lost no time in accruing more power to the presidency at the expense of the Duma and the regions. The Putin government also took advantage of new economic laws to reinstate an old system of government control of the media, specifically television.

PRIOR RESTRAINT

When writers must have approval of the government before publishing, the practice is called prior restraint. Licensing laws, which require registration of writers and publications, are an example of prior restraint, as the purpose of such laws is to weed out dissent before it occurs.

Prior restraint has also been used when official censors decide what scenes or dialogue are unacceptable in a film.

POSTPUBLICATION

The most common postpublication censorship involves the banning of books, newspapers, periodicals, films, and music. A less common form of postpublication censorship is the rewriting of texts in order to delete licentious or politically charged material. This method, popular in the 19th century, is known as bowdlerizing and is named for Thomas Bowdler who first practiced it when he published his *Family Shakespeare*, an abridged edition of Shakespeare's works that omitted passages Bowdler considered unsuitable for family reading.

The film ratings system in the United States is an example of industry self-censorship that shifts the responsibility of enforcement from government to theater management and parents. In the United States, ratings are also used for primetime broadcast programs and popular music.

Enforcement

POLICE AND SECURITY AGENCIES

Police and other security forces, including the military and militias, have historically been the primary enforcers of censorship and continue to be so. Generally, the censorship they enforce is legal, although methods of enforcement—smashing printing presses, illegally confiscating computers or hard drives, physical violence—can overstep official bounds. In the United States, these tactics are mostly a thing of the past. The 2001 USA PATRIOT Act has empowered security agencies to not only examine any person's computer files, but also enabled them to issue nonjudicial gag orders.

TECHNOLOGY

Jamming, or electronically blocking, television and radio broadcasts was a common censorship technique for years, but satellite technology has made that more difficult. However, technological advances in communication have also brought new means of censorship in their wake. Television has a V-chip, which allows parents to block programs they do not want their children to watch. Internet service providers offer filters to block computers from visiting Web sites deemed inappropriate. The filter option is generally for parents, but public libraries also use it on their public-use computers to block pornography, as do companies with employees' computers.

Public libraries' blocking of Web sites is a form of governmental censorship, in this instance municipal government. National governments, such as

China and Zimbabwe, are also seeking ways to block Internet sites, as well as other forms of communication such as cell phones and blogs. Whereas the usual method of Internet censorship is to filter out the site at the point of reception, the computer, that would be impossible in nationwide Internet censorship. Instead, search engines have become the target. This has led to controversial deals between popular search engines, such as Google, and some countries, including China and India.

GOVERNMENT CONTROL OF THE MEDIA

While national governments are loosening their grip on the media in some countries, they are tightening it in others. Media control by the government generally takes two forms. The method used in the United States, and the one that is least censorious, is for government agencies to issue licenses with the power of revocation. A more insidious form is outright government ownership of the media. In the countries described in this book, outright government ownership occurs in China, Egypt, Russia, and Zimbabwe. A third option is for media owners to ally themselves with the government in such a way that censorship, under the appearance of divergent viewpoints, is actually the norm. This is a method practiced in both the United States and in Russia with varying degrees of success in each country.

CENSORSHIP ENFORCED BY COURTS

The judicial system can play a role in either resisting censorship or enforcing it. In Russia, the judicial system has taken an active enforcement role. In 2005, courts in Russia ruled that certain texts were "extremist materials," that is, likely to instigate ethnic or religious strife within the Russian Federation. A 2006 presidential decree charged Russia's Federal Registration Service with keeping records on such material and to regularly publish it. The first list of so-called extremist material was published in the newspaper *Rossiyskaya Gazeta* on July 14, 2007.

RELIGIOUS HIERARCHIES

Religious leaders have always held the power to expel or excommunicate adherents as a mandate to enforce censorship against those they consider heretics or blasphemers. In theocratic societies, their power extends to the civil courts. This extension occurs as well in certain secular societies where religious law provides the underpinning of civil law. Egypt is one such country where clerics influence civil law.

The following case studies consider each country's history as it relates to censorship and look at current censorship practices as well as counterstrategies being taken to neutralize those censorship practices, whether successful or not. In the case studies on Russia, China, Egypt, and Zimbabwe, comparisons and contrasts will be made to practices and counterstrategies in the United States.

---

[1] This period of Rome's history wasn't republican in the modern sense. It lasted nearly five centuries and bridged the gap between Rome's kingdom and its empire.

[2] Garth Kemmerling. "Socrates (469–399 B.C.E.)." Available online. URL: http://www.philosophypages.com/ph/socr.htm. Downloaded August 3, 2006.

[3] Ancient Civilizations. "Censorship." Available online. URL: http://library.thinkquest.org/C004203/political/political05.htm. Downloaded August 3, 2006.

[4] *New Advent Catholic Encyclopedia.* "Index of Prohibited Books." Available online. URL: http://www.newadvent.org/cathen/07721a.htm. Downloaded August 4, 2006.

[5] Claudius Ptolemaeus, or Klaudios Ptolemaios, lived c. 87–150 C.E. His system of the cosmos placed the Earth at the center of the solar system. Despite this, he was able to predict the motions of the known planets accurately.

[6] *New Advent Catholic Encyclopedia.* "Index of Prohibited Books." Available online. URL: http://www.newadvent.org/cathen/07721a.htm. Downloaded August 4, 2006

[7] The Star Chamber was the name given to the court that evolved from the king's royal council. The name came from the original meeting room, which had stars painted on the ceiling. Over time, kings expanded its power so that it came to be despised. It was abolished in 1641.

[8] See Douglas Bush, ed. *The Portable Milton.* New York: Viking Press, 1969, pp. 8, 151–205.

[9] "Mayan Civilization." Available online. URL: http://www.indians.org/welker/maya.htm. Downloaded August 7, 2006.

[10] Pedro Guibovich. "The Lima Inquisition and Book Censorship, 1570–1820: Study and Annotated Bibliography." Available online. URL: http://www.beaconforfreedom.org/about_database/peru.html. Downloaded August 11, 2006.

[11] Mark Canada. *Colonial America, 1607–1783.* "Journalism." Available online. URL: http://www.geocities.com/markcanada_uncp/period.html. Downloaded August 11, 2006.

[12] Douglas Linder. "The Zenger Trial: An Account." Available online. URL: http://www.law.umkc.edu/faculty/projects/ftrials/zenger/zenger.html. Downloaded August 5, 2006.

[13] David McCullough. *John Adams.* New York: Simon & Schuster, 2001.

[14] Also known as the Democratic-Republican Party, it was the forerunner of the present-day Democratic Party.

[15] Jean O'Grady. "Laws of Public Worship, Speech, and the Press," in *Victorian Britain, An Encyclopedia,* ed. by Sally Mitchell. New York, London: Garland Publishing, Inc., 1988, pp. 440–441.

[16] *Encyclopedia of World History, 2001.* Available online. URL: http://www.bartleby.com/67/1345.html#c5p02637. Downloaded August 20, 2006.

2

Focus on the United States

Despite the guarantees of First Amendment freedoms, censorship has had a long, infamous history in the United States. Federal curtailment of citizens' free speech rights has come most often during wartime or those times the president and Congress (and often the public) have perceived as dangerous, such as the cold war or the post–September 11 war on terrorism. During peacetime, federal government censorship has usually focused on obscenity. In this area, federal censorship has moved from direct action such as mail seizures to threats of direct action that forced the various entertainment industries to practice self-censorship. While Supreme Court decisions concerning obscenity, artistic license, and citizens' freedoms in the latter half of the 20th century paved the way for a more relaxed atmosphere, the federal government, in the form of the Federal Communications Commission, continued to hold the power of direct action, which could include fines or revocation of broadcasting licenses.

States and municipalities have their own long histories of censorship, and the censorship battles waged in the late 20th and early 21st centuries by special interest groups and politicians with similar views were fully within that tradition. These battles most often involve school curricula and textbooks, and the battlegrounds are boards of education, city and state legislatures, and even state supreme courts.

CENSORSHIP HISTORY

Alien and Sedition Acts (1798)

The United States Constitution, written in 1787 and ratified by the original 13 states between 1787 and 1790, established a federal republic, granting certain powers to the national government while reserving other powers to the states. It was opposed by the so-called anti-Federalists who objected to the centralization of power; their demand for specific limitations on the power of the federal government was fulfilled with the ratification in 1791 of the first 10 amendments to the Constitution, collectively called the Bill of Rights. These amendments, together with bills of rights in state constitutions, established the basic rights of (most) people living within the United States, including freedom of speech, freedom of the press, freedom of religion, and the right to assemble—all mentioned in the First Amendment.

The earliest abrogation of the First Amendment was the Alien and Sedition Acts of 1798. Anticipating war with France, Congress passed, and President John Adams signed, the Alien Enemies Act in July 1798, by which citizens of a country with which the United States is at war could be detained, imprisoned, or deported. This act remains in effect today. The Alien Friends Act was enacted in June 1798 and stated that any noncitizen could be deported or detained at the president's discretion. This act expired in 1800. The other two laws making up the Alien and Sedition Acts were the Naturalization Act enacted in June 1798 and the Sedition Act enacted in July of that same year.

The Sedition Act, which made it unlawful to combine with others to oppose measures of the government and to defame the government, expired on the last day of Adams's presidency in 1801. The Sedition Act stifled dissent and free speech among citizenry and in Congress too. In fact, the first person imprisoned under the Sedition Act was Congressman Matthew Lyon (1750–1822) of Vermont.

So vehement was Lyon's opposition to the Federalists and the Sedition Act that he founded a magazine with the unwieldy title of *Scourge of Aristocracy and Repository of Important Political Truths.* In it he wrote, "[M]easures which I opposed [in Congress] as injurious and ruinous to the liberty and interest of this country . . . you cannot expect me to advocate at home."[1] Lyon was indicted under the Sedition Act on October 5, 1798. As his own attorney, Lyon argued that the Sedition Act was unconstitutional. He was found guilty and sentenced to four months in prison with a fine of $1,000 plus court costs. He was released on February 9, 1799.

Many others were imprisoned under the Sedition Act, including influential Republican newspaper editors.[2] All were pardoned by Thomas Jefferson (r. 1801–09), who defeated Adams in the 1800 presidential election. The imminent war with France, the supposed rationale for the Alien and Sedition Acts, never happened.

There is little doubt that the Sedition Act was used as a political weapon and intended as such by Adams and the Federalists. Since the act did not mention the vice president, it was not illegal to speak or publish "scandalous and malicious writing or writings" against Jefferson, vice president at the time, and not a single Federalist was indicted under the act despite their attacks on him.

Wars of the Nineteenth Century

Censorship was a benign issue in the United States during the first half of the 19th century, which was dominated by two wars and the issue of slavery in the western territories. The South did practice a form of censorship in that the vast majority of slaves were not allowed to learn to read, but the primary issue for abolitionists was their enslavement, not their lack of education. Censorship was not imposed by the federal government to any extent during either of the two wars the United States fought during this period—the War of 1812 (1812–14) and the Mexican War (1846–48).[3] In fact, during the former, Federalist politicians and the press in New England were so opposed to the war that there was talk of secession. By the time of the Mexican War, the Federalist Party had ceased to exist and its successor, the Whig Party, was irresolute in its opposition, partly because the two leading generals in the war were Whigs.

In this era, censorship was more often imposed by state governments. For instance, in 1821, Massachusetts banned John Cleland's 1750 novel, *Memoirs of a Woman of Pleasure* (commonly known as *Fanny Hill*) as obscene.[4] And in the years preceding the Civil War (1861–65), Virginia and North Carolina outlawed pamphlets and speech that advocated abolition.[5]

During the Civil War, President Abraham Lincoln (r. 1861–65) suspended habeas corpus in the border states of Delaware, Maryland, and Pennsylvania, as well as in Washington, D.C., as an antiterrorist measure and for anyone "guilty of any disloyal practice." The suspension tempered criticism of the war but did not extinguish it. There were other cases of censorship during the Civil War, the most egregious were perpetrated by the army and often were an embarrassment to Lincoln.

Two in particular came under the jurisdiction of General Ambrose Burnside who, in his capacity as commander of the Department of Ohio (an administrative military district that included all or parts of six states), issued General Order No. 38 in April 1863, declaring martial law and outlawing expression of sympathy for the Confederacy in his jurisdiction.

The first to challenge the order was a former Democratic congressman, Clement Vallandigham (1820–72). At the April 1863 Ohio Democratic convention, Vallandigham spoke against the war and against what he viewed as federal usurpation of state powers. Burnside promptly ordered Vallandigham's arrest. He was tried by a military commission and found guilty. As expected, there was an outcry in the Democratic press. One of the Democratic newspapers, the *Chicago Times*, was so vehement in its criticism of the Vallandigham affair and the Lincoln administration in general, that

General Burnside ordered it closed down. Burnside was denounced by the Illinois state legislature, and a bipartisan crowd gathered in Chicago to protest the newspaper's closing. When word reached Lincoln, he ordered Secretary of War Stanton to write Burnside and have him rescind the closure order.

Vallandigham was another matter. His arrest and conviction were upheld, but, instead of serving his sentence in prison, Lincoln exiled him to the Confederacy. All in all, and despite his suspension of habeas corpus, historians have judged Lincoln's conduct regarding censorship during the Civil War as generally exemplary, noting the vast amount of criticism he faced from Democrats and the public.[6]

From the carnage of the Civil War came three amendments, all of which dealt directly with the recent plight of African Americans. The Thirteenth Amendment abolished slavery, and the Fifteenth Amendment extended voting rights to male citizens regardless of "race, color, or previous condition of servitude." But it was the Fourteenth Amendment, ratified on July 9, 1868, that had the most wide-ranging effect. The Supreme Court has interpreted the amendment as extending First Amendment guarantees and holding state and municipal governments to the same standard as the federal government with regard to free speech, a free press, and the establishment of a state religion—or favoring any religion.

Comstock Act (1873)

While war may seem the most likely time for the federal government to clamp down on free speech, one of the worst assaults on the First Amendment occurred during peacetime. On March 3, 1873, Congress passed the Act for the Suppression of Trade in, and Circulation of, Obscene Literature and Articles for Immoral Use, better known as the Comstock Act after its chief supporter, Anthony Comstock. The act was signed into law by President Ulysses S. Grant (r. 1869–77).

No figure in U.S. history personifies censorship the way Comstock does. He was a member of the Young Men's Christian Association and he cofounded the New York Society for the Suppression of Vice (SSV). Comstock started his antivice crusade by shutting down saloons that stayed open after legal closing hours and by confiscating racy postcards. He was also influential in lobbying the New York legislature for an antiobscenity law.

Since the Comstock Act was a federal law, its mandate to suppress trade and circulation of obscene material had to be enforced by the U.S. Postal Service. Comstock had himself appointed as a special postal inspector which, combined with his leadership role in the SSV, gave him great power to confiscate and destroy material. He led the SSV and served as a postal inspector until his death in 1915. During the course of his career, Comstock seized approximately 160 tons of printed material, photographs, and plates and prosecuted people such as political activists Victoria Woodhull and Emma Goldman, playwright George Bernard Shaw, and Margaret Sanger, cofounder of the Planned Parenthood Foundation.

Comstock's definition of obscenity was so broad that it not only included pornography but also works of literature, reproductions of paintings, and social information. Margaret Sanger ran afoul of the Comstock Act for sending birth control information through the mail. The charges against her were dropped after Comstock's death, but the kind of censorship Comstock practiced did not end with his death. The federal law against using the mail to transmit obscenity remains on the books to this day. It has been amended over the years and various judicial rulings have narrowed the definition of obscenity from Comstock's broad version. Many states passed prohibitions on what could be distributed within their borders. Collectively, these federal and state restrictions are known as the Comstock laws.

In 1936, the law was changed to allow birth control material to pass through the mail. Nevertheless, Comstock's legacy lingered for decades. It took a 1933 court fight before James Joyce's novel *Ulysses* was allowed into the United States. In fact, much of modern literature had to undergo a litmus test either directly in the American courts or indirectly after court decisions were handed down. This includes the work of D. H. Lawrence and, most famously, Henry Miller's *Tropic of Cancer.* That book endured litigation in a number of states before the Supreme Court finally deemed it worthy for the American reading public in 1964. Two years later, the Supreme Court ruled that the so-called notorious novel, *Memoirs of a Woman of Pleasure,* was not obscene—145 years after it had first been declared so.[7]

By 1915, the government was less concerned with upholding Comstock's version of morality than with the war in Europe. In another two years, the United States would enter World War I and a whole new form of censorship would take hold.

World War I (1914–1918) and the Red Scare (1919–1920)

In 1915, the passenger liner *Lusitania* was sunk by a German U-boat. One hundred twenty-eight American passengers drowned, approximately 10 percent of the total fatalities. Although some in and out of government began agitating for action, President Woodrow Wilson (r. 1913–21) maintained official neutrality, while at the same time initiating rearmament. Wilson was reelected in 1916 with the campaign slogan "He kept us out of the war," but

U.S. neutrality came to an end after Germany resumed its submarine campaign against U.S. (and other neutral countries') shipping. Congress declared war on April 6, 1917.

A little over two months after the United States entered the war, Congress, at Wilson's instigation, passed the Espionage Act of 1917. The original bill's three provisions dealt with censorship of the press, disloyalty, and "nonmailability," but the bill that eventually passed was less harsh than the one proposed by the Wilson administration. Much of the debate centered on the issue of press censorship with representatives and senators on both sides of the argument vehement over their positions. President Wilson even interjected himself into the congressional debate, declaring the necessity for press censorship during wartime. In the end, the House of Representatives voted against the press censorship portion of the bill 184 to 144.

Although the House of Representatives had voted down the section of the Espionage Act dealing with press censorship, the disloyalty section of the bill, which defined disloyalty as "cause or attempt to cause insubordination, disloyalty, mutiny, or refusal of duty, in the military or naval forces of the United States," would serve to dampen the enthusiasm of antiwar writers, editors, and publishers. The nonmailability provision attacked the press from another angle. Even though Congress had insisted on more precise language than originally proposed, the postmaster general, and later the courts, interpreted the law broadly. The nonmailability section actually had a working precedent in the federal Comstock Act, which also gave the U.S. Postal Service discretionary powers. However, in the Espionage Act of 1917, political rather than obscene material was the focus of censorship.[8]

One of the first journals to run afoul of the nonmailability provision of the Espionage Act of 1917 was a socialist magazine called *The Masses.* In addition to its political journalism, it published poetry and fiction as well as high-quality illustrations. After the United States entered World War I, *The Masses* immediately took an antiwar stand. Postmaster General Albert Burleson, exercising his authority under the Espionage Act, excluded the magazine's August 1917 issue from the mails, claiming four cartoons and four texts in the issue violated the Espionage Act.[9]

Judge Learned Hand, one of the few jurists in the United States willing to ensure that the Espionage Act was not taken to extremes, granted an injunction that prohibited *The Masses* from being barred from the mails. It was quickly reversed in an appeals court. *The Masses* soon went out of business because it could not reach its subscribers (nor gain new ones), and seven staff members were indicted for conspiracy to violate the Espionage Act. They endured two trials that ended in hung juries before their cases were dismissed.

More than 2,000 dissenters were tried under the Espionage Act during World War I, and no one knows how many more people were stifled out of fear of prison. Among those imprisoned were the anarchists Emma Goldman and Alexander Berkman and the five-time Socialist candidate for president, Eugene Debs. While the tone for the arrests was set by the Justice Department under Attorney General Thomas Gregory, the tone of the various trials was set by a federal judiciary that was more than willing to broadly interpret dissent as a sign of disloyalty. Though the Supreme Court was more circumspect than the lower courts, it never struck down the Espionage Act of 1917 or the Sedition Act of 1918 as unconstitutional. In fact, in *Schenck v. United States*, the Court voted unanimously, in 1919, to uphold the conviction of defendants for conspiring to block recruiting and enlistment by circulating a pamphlet that urged people to protest the draft by writing their congressional representative. In writing for the entire Court, Justice Oliver Wendell Holmes wrote what has become one of the best-known American legal opinions. In an often quoted (and misquoted) passage Justice Holmes wrote, "The most stringent protection of free speech would not protect a man in falsely shouting fire in a crowded theater, and causing a panic . . ."[10] Essentially, Holmes declared that the circumstances surrounding an action define the nature of the action. Thus, there are certain limitations to free speech. In the ensuing years, Justice Holmes would move away from that position, influenced by Judge Learned Hand and fellow Supreme Court justice Louis Brandeis.

The other piece of federal legislation passed during this period that affected First Amendment rights was the Sedition Act of 1918. The Sedition Act was not a new law, but an amendment to section 3 of the Espionage Act of 1917. The original draft of the Sedition Act of 1918 was introduced by the Justice Department, but was actually made stricter by the Senate. As its name suggests, it dealt specifically with criticism of the war, the federal government, the Constitution, the flag, and the armed forces, including their uniforms. The Senate voted in favor of the Sedition Act, 48 to 26, and the House of Representatives approved it by a nearly unanimous vote, 293 to 1. President Wilson signed it into law on May 16, 1918.[11]

Fewer people were actually prosecuted during the war under the Sedition Act than under the Espionage Act. But the Sedition Act of 1918 was destined to play a greater role in stifling dissent during the next couple of years of peace.

In January 1919, a general strike by Seattle workers, in sympathy with that city's shipyard workers, was declared a Communist plot by the mayor of Seattle. This was the beginning of the Red Scare hysteria. It was reinforced in late April 1919 when a bomb was sent to the mayor's office, followed by an exploded bomb in the Atlanta home of a former U.S. senator, and the discovery of 34 bombs in the New York post office, addressed to various financiers, cabinet members, and others in the federal government.

The day after the New York post office discovery was May 1—May Day—and riots occurred in a number of cities, including New York and Boston, as bystanders, aided by police, fought with radicals. In June, bombs exploded in eight cities around the United States. There were more strikes in the fall of 1919, including police and miners, but by then Attorney General A. Mitchell Palmer had set the Justice Department on a path of suppression of radicalism. Earlier state and federal legislative hearings had convened to deal with the problem, but it was the Palmer Raids, as the crackdown came to be known, that set the tone of reaction to the strikes and the violence.

With the Espionage and Sedition Acts as justification, the Palmer Raids were a widespread roundup of radicals, many of whom were deported. The raids further stifled antigovernment speech, of both the revolutionary and nonrevolutionary kind, as well as language that should in no way be considered seditious, such as strike talk. The raids waned partly because of their early success and partly because the public had grown tired of the climate of fear brought on first by the war and then the Red Scare. The scare itself and the raids ended in 1920, and on December 13, 1920, Congress repealed the Sedition Act of 1918.[12]

The Scopes Trial (1925)

The most famous court battle concerning a state's power of censorship occurred in Dayton, Tennessee, in 1925 when John T. Scopes went on trial for teaching the theory of evolution.[13] On March 13 of that year, the state legislature of Tennessee had passed a statute known formally as the Tennessee Anti-Evolution Act, also known as the Butler Act after John Washington Butler who had sponsored it. It prohibited "the teaching of the Evolution Theory in all the Universities, Normals and all other public schools of Tennessee, which are supported in whole or in part by the public school funds of the State, and to provide penalties for the violations thereof." Fifteen other states had antievolution laws pending at the time. For the American Civil Liberties Union (ACLU), this was reason enough to challenge the Tennessee law in a test case. The Scopes trial might have remained a small town legal battle had not the prosecution enlisted the aid of William Jennings Bryan (1860–1925). Bryan was a three-time Democratic candidate for president and secretary of state during Woodrow Wilson's first term. Clarence Darrow (1857–1938), the most famous trial lawyer of the era, whose résumé included numerous high-profile cases in which he had taken a progressive stand, volunteered his services for the defense. With these two famous men opposing each other in the courtroom, the national press latched onto the story, thus, in a sense, making the trial a test case for the nation: Would the United States embrace modernism or would it retain its 19th-century evangelical outlook? In fact, that question had such deep-rooted ramifications that it has lingered into the 21st century.

The ACLU's defense was to focus on the constitutionality of the law, but Darrow gradually shifted the strategy to a debate between science and religion. The trial judge, John T. Raulston, was determined to counteract Darrow's strategy by excluding from the proceedings and the record anything that touched on the debate between evolution and religion. His concern was to stick to the charge for which Scopes had been indicted, violating the Butler Act by teaching evolution. What was lost in all of that was the fact that Scopes had used the state-mandated textbook, which included a section on evolution.

The defense team, having relinquished its constitutionality case, actually had no defense and so declined a summation. Scopes was found guilty, and Judge Raulston fined him $100. Bryan offered to pay the fine.[14]

The ACLU appealed the verdict to the Tennessee Supreme Court and based the appeal on four points: that evolution was a broad term; that the Butler Act denied due process as guaranteed by the Fourteenth Amendment to the U.S. Constitution; that it violated Tennessee's constitution which stated, "It shall be the duty of the General Assembly in all future periods of this government, to cherish literature and science"; and that it violated the First Amendment of the Constitution by establishing a religion.[15] The Tennessee Supreme Court sustained the validity of the statute but overturned the verdict on a technicality: Fines of $100 or more had to be set by the jury not the judge. The prosecution did not retry the case.

Tennessee repealed the Butler Act in 1967. In 1968, in *Epperson v. Arkansas*, the Supreme Court decided that according to the First Amendment states cannot design school curricula so as to support or defend a religion.[16] The battle between evolution and religion was not decided by the Scopes trial, nor by the Supreme Court decision 43 years later. While evolution has come to be acknowledged as the leading theory of human (as well as plant and animal) development, the battle still rages in many states where Christian fundamentalism has enjoyed resurgence since the 1980s. Since then, questions of censorship have again risen, but it is the fundamentalists often making the charges.

Hollywood and Entertainment Censorship

In the late 1910s and early 1920s, Hollywood was hit by a number of scandals that tarnished the filmmaking industry's image. To set things right, or at least give the appearance of such, studio bosses created the Motion Picture Producers and Distributors of America (MPPDA) in 1922 and asked Postmaster General Will Hays to serve as the organization's first president. Hays, an Indiana politician, had served as chairman of the Republican National Committee before his appointment to President Warren Harding's (r. 1921–23) cabinet. As postmaster general, Hays's priority was to block obscenity from the mails, which made him the right man, symbolically at least, to "clean up" Hollywood.

During the first years of his tenure, Hays's duties were primarily to run the film industry's business affairs and act as a communications liaison. But, as the 1920s wore on and Hollywood films, as well as films imported from Europe, became racier, a public outcry was raised, along with a threat of congressional interference and public boycott. In 1927, the Hays Office (as the MPPDA was also known) issued a list of "Don'ts" and "Be Carefuls," but this had little effect on the actual content of Hollywood films. As a result, in 1930, the Hays Office devised a production code of standards, which films had to meet in order to receive the MPPDA seal of approval.[17]

The Production Code (also known as the Hays Code) was virtually unenforced until 1934 when the Production Code Administration (PCA), part of the MPPDA, was formed. Not coincidentally, in 1933, U.S. Roman Catholic bishops formed the Catholic Legion of Decency. The Legion advised Roman Catholics on which movies to boycott as immoral; the lists it drew up were not unlike a 20th-century version of the *Index librorum prohibitorum* of the Middle Ages. In 1934, the organization changed its name to the National Legion of Decency in order to reflect the ecumenical makeup of its membership. The pressure that the National Legion of Decency applied on Hollywood served as a wake-up call for the MPPDA, which began to enforce the Production Code.

Under this form of self-censorship, Hollywood was probably stricter than the federal government would have been. Certainly, there was no recourse in the courts for independent-minded screenwriters and directors who wanted to defy the Hays Code. Over the years, there were various revisions to the Production Code that essentially added to its restrictions or made it less vague. Among the on-screen matters that the Code took into account were the presentation of crimes, sex, vulgarity, obscenity, profanity, costumes (which could not be too revealing), dances (banned if they were suggestive), religion, locations, national feelings, titles (as in title cards for silent films, which were still being made in 1930), and repellent subjects.[18]

There were subcategories to most of these general subjects and some of the subcategories had a second level of subcategories. Essentially, the Production Code took into account anything that might be deemed offensive.

Some of the items described in the first- and second-level subcategories were prohibited, others were restricted. The Code was at its most powerful during the years 1934–45 when the studio system itself was in its heyday.

Hays retired in 1945, the year the MPPDA changed its name to the Motion Picture Association of America (MPAA). Meanwhile, postwar changes in society began to erode the Code's sway over the film industry. The decline in the Code's censorship power actually began in the 1950s, as the studios' control of the American entertainment business came under attack. An antitrust suit forced the studios to sell off the movie theaters they owned, opening the door for foreign films that did not have to adhere to the Production Code. However, cultural historians agree that the mass introduction of television that began in the late 1940s was the single most important factor in the decline of the Hollywood studio system. Television had its own strict code of production standards, but it was far more convenient for viewers.

Another challenge to the Production Code came from directors who had grown tired of its restrictions. Foremost among these in the 1950s was Otto Preminger (1906–86). In the 1950s, Preminger directed three successful films that dealt with subjects and language considered taboo by the Code: *The Moon Is Blue* (1953), *The Man with the Golden Arm* (1955), and *Anatomy of a Murder* (1959). *The Man with the Golden Arm,* about drug addiction, was especially troublesome for the Hollywood censors. When the MPAA refused to give it its seal of approval, Preminger and the film's producers decided to release it anyway. The next year, the Code was relaxed a bit and drug addiction became a permissible subject in Hollywood films.

By the mid-1960s, both the studio system and the Production Code seemed like relics of the past, and the Legion of Decency was no longer as powerful as it had been 20 or 30 years earlier. In 1968, the Code was scrapped entirely for a ratings system, which has continued with some modification to the present day.

A side effect of the Production Code was that it spawned similar codes of self-censorship in the television and comics industries. The comics code was instituted in 1954. A year earlier, a psychiatrist named Fredric Wertham published a critique of the comic book industry, *Seduction of the Innocent,* in which he complained about the possible effects of crime and horror comics on children. Dr. Wertham's complaints soon gained the attention of the U.S. Senate, and the Senate Judiciary Committee formed the Subcommittee to Investigate Juvenile Delinquency. As the subcommittee looked into various reasons for the cause of juvenile delinquency, the comics industry decided to head off the government by following Hollywood's path of self-censorship. Comics publishers formed the Comics Magazine Association of America (CMAA), which in turn devised the Comics Code Authority (CCA). The

CCA was patterned after Hollywood's Production Code with additional bans and restrictions concerning what advertising the comics publishers might accept (for instance, alcohol, tobacco, and fireworks ads were prohibited).[19] A direct result of the Comics Code Authority was that a number of publishers went bankrupt. Writers and artists subsequently left the field because of the censorship imposed on them. By the 1980s, the CCA's grip on the comics industry was loosened as more and more publishers ceased to participate in its voluntary self-censorship. By the early 21st century only two publishers followed the CCA's restrictions.

Television was an altogether different story, as licenses to broadcast were (and are) issued by the Federal Communications Commission (FCC). Still, it took the prodding of a House of Representatives committee investigation in 1952 before the major networks initiated their own code of standards. The television code was patterned after the one for radio established in the 1930s but with obvious alterations for the new medium—both codes were concerned with advertising as well as program content. The networks also developed internal divisions of standards and practices, commonly known as the network censors. In addition, the FCC has its own regulations that have been updated over the years to keep up with technological developments.[20]

By the late 1960s and early 1970s, the power of the voluntary television code had begun to erode, especially concerning content and language, as producers sought more artistic freedom for their programs. In the 1980s, deregulation also led to laxness in enforcing FCC regulations. However, in the early 2000s, the FCC began a zero tolerance policy regarding obscenity, indecency, and profanity on television and radio, levying fines whenever possible.

Radio censorship has also fluctuated between times of severity and times of laxness. The rise and subsequent popularity of the shock jocks (Howard Stern and his imitators) and talk radio hosts in the 1980s have tested the boundaries of censorship. With increased FCC enforcement of regulations in the early 21st century, not to mention larger monopolies controlling more stations nationwide, censorship has again become either a problem or a reassurance, depending on one's point of view.

Senator Joseph McCarthy, HUAC, and the Federal Loyalty Hearings (1947–1955)

At the close of World War II (1939–45), the United States and the Soviet Union (USSR) were the two most powerful nations on Earth. However, the one-time allies began to draw apart as a result of broken promises and new strategic military alliances that more or less divided Europe. Each of the "superpowers," as they came to be known, had its own sphere of influence. The United States was the main partner in Western Europe, while the USSR controlled Eastern Europe. Each also had spheres of influence in Asia and Africa. This was the beginning of what became known as the cold war, which lasted until the breakup of the Soviet Union in 1991.

In the United States, anticommunist sentiment that had been restrained during the wartime alliance began to be unleashed. During the course of the 10 years following World War II, domestic and international events not only escalated the cold war but contributed to First Amendment repression in the United States. One of the major differences between the post–World War II Red Scare and the earlier one of 1919–20 was the use of blacklists by private industry, federal and state governments, and universities to block people from working who were considered communist or sympathetic to communism.

When President Franklin D. Roosevelt (r. 1933–45) died suddenly on April 12, 1945, he was succeeded by Vice President Harry S. Truman (r. 1945–53). After the war, when the joyous flush of victory and homecoming had receded, the bipartisan effort between Democrats and Republicans to win the conflict was set aside. In their effort to regain control of Congress, Republicans made anticommunism the focal point of their political attack. The mainstream Democrats, on the other hand, had to battle not only the Republicans but also a resurgent progressive movement within their own party. In fact, this brief postwar flourishing of progressivism spawned the Progressive Party in 1948 led by Henry Wallace (1888–1965), Roosevelt's vice president during his third term and Truman's former secretary of commerce.

In the 1946 elections, the Republicans won majorities in both houses of Congress. The following year, Congress passed the Labor-Management Relations Act, also known as the Taft-Hartley Act. Truman vetoed the bill, but Congress overrode his veto. The act came on the heels of labor unrest in the railroad and mining industries, which big business—rightly or wrongly—blamed on communist agitation. Imposing many new restrictions on labor unions, Taft-Hartley had a crippling effect on organized labor across the United States. Among other things, it required labor leaders to sign affidavits that they were not members of the Communist Party.

Having lost Congress to his political opposition, President Truman decided to take a harder line against communism than the Republicans. In 1947, he issued what has become known as the Truman Doctrine, which vowed to fight communism at home and abroad. He also branded opponents of this doctrine as disloyal. By doing so, he hoped to co-opt the Progressives.

Meanwhile, the House Un-American Activities Committee (HUAC), which had been formed in 1938 to investigate political subversion, had passed to Republican control under Chairman J. Parnell Thomas.[21] In 1947, HUAC decided to investigate communist influence in Hollywood. Over the course of nine days, a number of witnesses were called to testify, many were "friendly" witnesses who answered the committee members' questions, but a group of "unfriendly" witnesses refused to answer. Known as the Hollywood Ten, they were jailed for contempt of Congress and blacklisted from working in Hollywood. As witnesses were pressured to reveal more names, the blacklist grew until more than 300 performers, writers, and directors were banned from working in film, television, and radio. Some individuals, such as Charlie Chaplin, playwright Bertholt Brecht, and film director Jules Dassin, left the country to pursue their careers elsewhere. Most were not so fortunate. The blacklisting was not a result of a government order, but rather a reaction to the climate of fear that was beginning to engulf the country. Thus, citizens were deprived of freedom of expression by private industry acting in accordance with the tone set by the federal government. In a sense, the Taft-Hartley Act was extended to Hollywood.[22]

Not to be outdone, Truman called for a loyalty program for civilian employees of the federal government; every employee was to be investigated by the FBI. On March 21, 1947, he signed Executive Order No. 9835 establishing the Federal Employees Loyalty and Security Program.[23] Within four years, more than 3 million federal employees were investigated. Of that number, a few thousand resigned and 212 were fired for having "questionable loyalty." However, none of these people were indicted for espionage.[24]

The announcement of the loyalty program was followed by the publication of a list of subversive organizations compiled by the Department of Justice. Called the Attorney General's List of Subversive Organizations (AGLOSO), it named the Nazi Party, the Ku Klux Klan, and numerous alleged communist front groups, most of which were leftist political parties or workers' organizations.[25] In July and August 1948, former Communists Elizabeth Bentley and Whittaker Chambers testified before HUAC, charging that various former government employees were members of the Communist Party. Their testimonies led to the imprisonment of five people for perjury, the most prominent being Alger Hiss (1904–66). Hiss had worked in the State Department during the Roosevelt administration and had been present at the Yalta Conference of Roosevelt, Churchill, and Stalin. In 1948, he was president of the Carnegie Endowment for International Peace. His appearances before HUAC turned into a cause célèbre, which was debated for years afterward.[26]

Despite the HUAC revelations, Truman was reelected in 1948 and the Democratic Party again took control of Congress. However, the next year two major international events further increased the country's anxiety over communism. First, the Soviet Union exploded an atom bomb on August 29, 1949. Then on October 1, 1949, the People's Republic of China was formally established, led by the Chinese Communist Party with Mao Zedong (1893–1976) as its chairman. With communism now stretching from Central Europe to the Pacific Ocean, many Americans felt that the communist takeover was well on its way to becoming a reality.

Under this new heightened anxiety, the various government agencies created loyalty boards to investigate employees. Where it was thought warranted, the FBI did full field investigations of individuals. The loyalty board hearings were remarkable because they judged people not only on their own beliefs but on the beliefs of their friends or associates. The phrase *guilt by association* became a popular one in this era, helping to fan the flames of paranoia that swept the country.

Since the anticommunist crusade was a bipartisan affair, the First Amendment rights of all citizens were essentially restricted, with regard to speaking or writing positively about communism or anything that others might construe as communist. Americans, whether they wanted to or not, had to be wary of what they said or wrote for fear of being thought communists.

While the loyalty boards were busy investigating federal workers, HUAC focused on Communist Party members, labor leaders, academics, and assorted progressives. In the two years alone when J. Parnell Thomas was committee chairman, HUAC compiled thousands of dossiers on organizations and people. The committee also had its own list of more than 300,000 individuals who, the committee intimated, were fellow travelers or at least somewhat sympathetic to the communist cause. After the Democratic sweep of Congress in the 1948 elections, Thomas, a Republican, was no longer HUAC chairman, and he was soon replaced in the public's mind by another Republican—Senator Joseph McCarthy.

On February 9, 1950, Joseph McCarthy (1908–57) was a little-known first-term senator from Wisconsin when he claimed in a speech given in Wheeling, West Virginia, to have a list with the names of 205 employees of the State Department who were members of the Communist Party. The accusations rocketed McCarthy to national prominence, although a departmental investigation proved him wrong. Nevertheless, McCarthy continued to make accusations in the Senate chamber and on the radio. His accusations were without merit, sometimes outright lies, but in the spirit of the times his bullying technique made him a powerful and popular figure among America's right-wing politicians, many of whom cynically hoped to ride his success to election in 1952.

In 1953, Senator McCarthy was at the peak of his power. In 1952, the Republicans had recaptured both houses of Congress and the Republican candidate, Dwight D. Eisenhower (r. 1953–61), was elected president. McCarthy, himself, was reelected to a second term. With the Republicans in charge of the Senate again, McCarthy was named chairman of the Committee on Operations and of the Permanent Subcommittee on Investigations. From the latter position, he set out to investigate the Voice of America, which he accused of being infiltrated with communists.

Voice of America (VOA) had been established during World War II to promote the United States. Its main component was worldwide radio broadcasting, but it also published magazines, distributed newsreels (news reports on film), and maintained libraries. As an agency within the State Department, VOA was a logical target for McCarthy. Uncovering communist influence at VOA would justify his earlier accusations against the State Department. McCarthy's investigation discovered that VOA had more than 30,000 books in its facilities that were written by people whom he deemed communists and fellow travelers; he revealed this during the televised hearing of his subcommittee. As a result, an already rattled State Department banned those books, music, and art that were produced by so-called communists from VOA facilities. This was an ironic decision given that VOA was set up to project an image of a country that upheld the basic rights of its citizens.[27]

McCarthy's downfall came when he tried to prove that communists had infiltrated the U.S. Army. The 1954 Army-McCarthy hearings, as they were called, began behind closed doors but were later televised, showing the American public the true nature of McCarthy's personality and tactics. Even before the hearings were televised, McCarthy had come under attack from newspaper editorials objecting to the way he had browbeaten and insulted a highly decorated general. After the Democrats recaptured control of the Senate in the 1954 midterm elections, that chamber voted to condemn McCarthy for his tactics. In 1955, McCarthy had to relinquish his chairmanships to the Democrats and thereafter he was ineffective. He died in 1957.[28]

Depending on the political mood of the country, HUAC, Senator McCarthy, and President Truman's loyalty program each has undergone widely differing evaluations. Regarding their assaults on the First Amendment, however, there can be little doubt. McCarthy was directly responsible for the banning of thousands of books and other works of art because the authors did not share his political views. All three, in the course of ruining reputations, also served notice that particular ideas were "un-American" and therefore unacceptable and that to hold such ideas and profess them in speech or print was a punishable offense. Furthermore, it was never the possessor of the ideas who was allowed to define their value; there was never a debate, always an inquisition. Unlike the situation for the dissenters who were charged with violating the Espionage and Sedition Acts during World War I and the postwar Red Scare of 1919–20 where the courts, for the most part, held the final say, the hearings before the loyalty boards, HUAC, and McCarthy's Permanent Subcommittee on Investigations gave Congress and federal agencies a power over people's ability to digest competing ideas. The hysteria of the times, fanned by the media, expanded that power so that it extended not only over those who had come under scrutiny, but over the general population as well.

The Turbulent 1960s

The Vietnam War (1961–75), the assassinations of President John F. Kennedy (1963), the Reverend Martin Luther King Jr. (1968), and Senator Robert F. Kennedy (1968), and the Civil Rights and antiwar movements are the events that define the 1960s for most people. But one particular event, often overlooked in history books, came amid the Civil Rights movement and played an important role in later press coverage of the Vietnam War. It was the First Amendment decision regarding freedom of the press handed down in 1964 by the Supreme Court in *New York Times Company v. Sullivan.*

On March 29, 1960, a full-page advertisement appeared in the *New York Times,* titled "Heed Their Rising Voices." The ad was paid for by an organization known as the Committee to Defend Martin Luther King and the Struggle for Freedom in the South and contained 10 paragraphs that outlined harassment of Reverend King and racial confrontations in various communities of the South. The ad's third paragraph discussed an incident at Alabama State College in Montgomery, Alabama, in which "truckloads of police armed with shotguns and tear-gas ringed the Alabama State College Campus." (*sic*) The ad's sixth paragraph read in part: "They have arrested him [Dr. King] seven times—for 'speeding,' 'loitering' and similar 'offenses.' And now they have charged him with 'perjury'—a felony under which they could imprison him for ten years. . . ."

Following the ad's publication a lawsuit was initiated by L. B. Sullivan, a Montgomery commissioner who supervised the police department. Sullivan contended that he was defamed by the use of the word "police" since his position made him synonymous with the department—even though his name was never mentioned in the advertisement. Sullivan won his lawsuit, and the circuit court awarded him $500,000 in damages. On appeal, the Alabama Supreme Court upheld the decision.

The U.S. Supreme Court heard the case in January 1964. The New York Times Company based its argument on the freedom of press issue, urging reversal of the lower court decision, and received assistance from the Washington Post Company, the (Chicago) Tribune Company, and the American Civil Liberties Union (ACLU) which all filed friend-of-the-court briefs. The Court voted 9-0 to reverse the decision of the Alabama circuit court. In his opinion for the Court, Justice William Brennan pointed out that Alabama's state libel law had made it almost impossible to criticize public officials. He reasoned that the Alabama Supreme Court's decision equating criticism of a government department or agency with attacks on the department head made any government criticism potentially libelous.[29]

New York Times Company v. Sullivan has influenced lower court decisions regarding freedom of the press ever since. For the American press, the decision helped usher in an era that mirrored and contributed to the skepticism and rebelliousness of the decade. It marked a timely convergence with the Civil Rights movement and especially the Vietnam War, so that the war and the politicians and generals who carried it out were eventually subjected to greater scrutiny and criticism than during any previous conflict since the Civil War.

Despite the passage of landmark Civil Rights legislation in 1964, the lives of most African Americans had not gotten noticeably better. By the end of 1966, a number of cities around the United States had suffered through race riots, born of African Americans' frustration at the slow pace of change and a government that seemed determined to ignore the demands of leaders such as Martin Luther King. Intent on seeking change for the African-American community at whatever cost, in October 1966, six men in Oakland, California, led by Huey P. Newton and Bobby Seale, formed the Black Panther Party of Self-Defense, later shortened to the Black Panther Party.[30]

Because of the Black Panthers' willingness to accept violence, coupled with the country's lingering racism, FBI Director J. Edgar Hoover made their destruction a top priority. The Panthers advocated revolution, but they also set up social programs within communities; they soon had chapters in many U.S. cities. Their quick growth concerned city, state, and federal officials already worried by the increasingly radical behavior of the antiwar movement, some of which was in imitation of the Panthers' boldness. The suppression in various municipalities of the Black Panther Party newspaper *The Black Panther*, was just one of the violations of their First Amendment rights. FBI raids on various chapter headquarters also kept the Panthers on the defensive, in a sense justifying their original name. Although for a time they were the FBI's primary target, the Panthers' actions were generally localized and their battles were mostly with municipal police.

African-American radicalism was one aspect of 1960s culture that grew out of the Civil Rights movement of the late 1950s and early 1960s. Another, even more divisive, aspect was the antiwar movement. Taking its cue from the Black Panthers and other Black nationalists such as Malcolm X (1925–65), the antiwar movement began to divide between hardline radicals and more cautious liberals. While this was particularly evident by 1968, during the Lyndon Johnson administration (1963–69), two antiwar-related trials took place that had important free speech implications. The first was the trial of David Paul O'Brien who, along with three others, was arrested in Boston in 1966 for publicly burning his draft card during an antiwar protest. The other was the conspiracy trial of the Boston Five.

O'Brien was arrested for knowingly violating a 1965 law that prevented willful destruction of draft cards. At his trial, O'Brien claimed that his action was done with the intention of influencing others who were eligible for the draft or who might support the Vietnam War. Thus, O'Brien claimed his action was symbolic and that draft card burning was an aspect of free speech. O'Brien was subsequently convicted.

The case was appealed to the U.S. Supreme Court, which, in 1968, upheld O'Brien's conviction. In the opinion for the Court, Chief Justice Warren held that the law preventing draft card burning was not a restriction of freedom of speech, even if the burning was intended as a protest of the war.

In 1968, the Justice Department took advantage of conspiracy laws to convict four men (the fifth was acquitted), including famed pediatrician Dr. Benjamin Spock and Yale chaplain, the Reverend William Sloane Coffin, of conspiring to advocate refusal to obey the draft law for military service. The convictions of the Boston Five were later overturned and they were not retried. Nevertheless, the conspiracy law under which they were prosecuted remained on the books; in fact, Congress tightened it later in 1968. As written into the federal Riot Act, it became illegal to cross state lines "with the intent to incite, organize, promote, encourage, participate in or carry on a riot."[31]

During the presidency of Lyndon Johnson's successor, Richard Nixon (r. 1969–74), numerous conspiracy trials of antiwar radicals took place, including the most famous of all the antiwar conspiracy trials, and probably the best-known trial in the United States during the 1960s—that of the Chicago Seven. Originally, eight men were indicted by a grand jury on March 20, 1969, for conspiracy to cross state lines to incite a riot and for crossing state lines to incite a riot. The riot that this case referred to was a mass demonstration held in Chicago during the Democratic Convention in August 1968 to protest the war. The city was well armed with police and reinforcements from the National Guard and the FBI. Army troops were stationed in the suburbs. Although it was dubbed the "Battle of Chicago," it was really a one-sided affair. Not only were the protestors beaten and arrested, but so were innocent bystanders, people returning to their homes, and even journalists. The eight men indicted were Jerry Rubin and Abbie Hoffman, leaders of the Youth International Party (Yippie for short); Students for a Democratic Society (SDS) leaders Tom Hayden and Rennie Davis; college professors John Froines and Lee Weiner; David Dellinger; and Black Panther Party chairman Bobby Seale. Seale actually did not take part in planning the protests, arriving in Chicago two days after the convention had begun. In fact, early in the trial, Judge Julius Hoffman (no relation to Abbie Hoffman) declared a mistrial for Seale, and then sentenced him to a four-year term for contempt of court. Seale had shown his disdain for the judge and the judicial system when Hoffman denied Seale's motion to delay the trial so that his attorney could recover from surgery. The remaining defendants were dubbed the Chicago Seven.

The free speech issue was actually incidental to the trial since the trial centered on the conspiracy charges. But underlying it was the right of the defendants to advocate civil disobedience—not whether it was lawful to do so, but whether at that time in the United States and under the circumstances of nationwide dissent during wartime it would be tolerated by the government. The prosecution charged that the defendants had conspired to incite a riot; the defense countered that the riot had been started by the police. It was clear even before Seale was sentenced that there was no respect between the defendants and the judge. The former turned the trial into political theater while Judge Hoffman countered by piling contempt of court charges on them.

After four and a half months, the jury found the defendants not guilty on the conspiracy charges, but found five of the seven—Dellinger, Hoffman, Rubin, Hayden, and Davis—guilty of inciting a riot. All the sentences were overturned on appeal because of Judge Hoffman's antagonism toward the seven. The defendants were never retried on the original charges, though some (and their lawyers) were retried on contempt charges and found guilty on 13 of the counts, but never sentenced.

The Pentagon Papers (1967–1971)

About nine months before the Chicago Seven trial got underway, the final work was being done on a report that would have broad implications for freedom of the press and public sentiment toward the war in Vietnam.

Commissioned by Secretary of Defense Robert McNamara, the secret report, later known as the Pentagon Papers, traced the history of American involvement in Vietnam from Word War II to May 1968. The more than 7,000 pages in 47 volumes revealed major disparities between declared government policies and the real intentions of American leaders.

The Pentagon Papers were leaked to *New York Times* reporter Neil Sheehan in March 1971 by Daniel Ellsberg, a former Pentagon and State Department employee who later worked as an analyst for the Rand Corporation (a think tank). Realizing the grave risk to the newspaper of publishing the documents, a *Times* editorial team spent more than two months secretly conferring with the newspaper's attorneys and analyzing the material before running it. The decision was made to run the articles and facsimiles of some of the documents in 10 installments beginning June 13, 1971.

The evening after the second installment had been published, Attorney General John Mitchell notified the newspaper that it was in violation of the Espionage Act of 1917, asking that the *Times* stop publication of further installments and hand over the documents to the Department of Defense. The *Times* declined. On June 15, the U.S. Department of Justice sought to prevent the further publication of the Pentagon Papers. Judge Murray Gurfein granted a four-day restraining order that put a halt to the *Times*'s series on the report.

Meanwhile, Ellsberg had gone into hiding and was the subject of an intense FBI search. When the *Times* chose to obey the temporary restraining order, he decided to offer the documents to the *Washington Post.* The *Post* could not afford to mull over the papers the way the *Times* had and decided to publish articles based on the papers. The first article came out in some of the June 18, 1971, editions of the paper. Again, the Justice Department served the same notice on the *Post* as it had on the *Times,* with the same results. The Justice Department sought another restraining order, but this time was refused. Judge Gerhard Gesell cited the First Amendment in his ruling. He also cited the fact that the Espionage Act of 1917 had no provision for barring the press from publishing sensitive material. Lastly, Judge Gesell pointed out that the government had not made a case that publication of the papers would be harmful.

Meanwhile, on June 19, Judge Gurfein ruled in favor of the *New York Times,* citing the same reason as Judge Gesell. The difference between the two judges was that Gurfein extended the restraining order to give the government time to appeal. The Justice Department, in fact, appealed both decisions, receiving a temporary restraining order against the *Washington Post.*[32]

The two courts of appeals handed down somewhat conflicting decisions. In Washington, D.C., the district court ruling (for the *Post*) was upheld, while in New York the court of appeals ordered the case sent back for another hearing. The *New York Times* petitioned the Supreme Court against this ruling; the Justice Department did the same against the ruling of the Washington, D.C., court of appeals. The Supreme Court decided to combine both cases and heard them on June 26. The case is known as *New York Times Company v. United States.*[33]

Because the government's argument that publication of the papers violated the Espionage Act of 1917 had been rebuked, the Justice Department instead argued in favor of presidential powers. As commander in chief of the armed forces and the person who determines the nation's foreign policy, the president should be able to forbid the publication of military secrets, the Justice Department argued. The newspaper argued its First Amendment rights, which, thanks to Congress, not even the Espionage Act of 1917 had abridged. The Court ruled 6-3 in favor of the New York Times Company. Each of the six justices who voted in the majority handed down a separate opinion. The three minority justices also produced three separate opinions. Despite the ruling in favor of the newspapers, the issue of prior restraint was not really decided. Three of the six justices who voted in the majority mentioned in their opinions that prior restraint would be acceptable if the government could prove imminent danger to the country or its policies because of publication. Nevertheless, the burden of proof was placed on the government.

Grenada (1983)

In 1983, the federal government practiced a more imaginative, yet simple, manner of prior restraint: It barred the press from covering the invasion of Grenada, a tiny island nation in the Caribbean Sea.[34] The pretext for the invasion was to rescue American medical students on the island following a coup that overthrew, and executed, Prime Minister Maurice Bishop (r. 1979–83). Bishop, who himself had come to power in a 1979 coup, was a Marxist. He was overthrown by hardliners led by Deputy Prime Minister Bernard Coard.

The United States, under President Ronald Reagan (r. 1981–89), adamantly opposed any Marxist government on the island and seized on the island's political instability following the coup as an opportunity to install a government favorable to American policy in the region. It was also a chance to reinstill pride in America's military—two days earlier more than 200 troops had been killed in a bomb explosion in Beirut, Lebanon. Although the success of the invasion, dubbed Operation Urgent Fury, was practically a foregone conclusion, the federal government and the military decided they did not want a repeat of the Vietnam War press coverage and chose to emulate British military procedure in its brief Falkland Islands conflict by barring the press from accompanying the invasion. This was an effective veiled attack on the First Amendment. In the next 20 years, the press would make compromises with the military to ensure its wartime coverage.

Censorship in the 1980s and 1990s

BOOK BANNING

Book banning in the United States enjoys a long, inglorious history that actually predates Anthony Comstock and his Society for the Suppression of Vice and extends well past his time. However, there is a big difference between Comstock's quasi-official role and many of the people who took it upon themselves to act as censors in the last quarter of the 20th century. Beginning in the 1980s, many important censorship battles were fought on state and municipal levels rather than in the federal government. That decade saw a resurgence of Christian fundamentalism as the country shifted rightward politically following the election of Ronald Reagan as president. Later in the decade, another form of extremism evolved in response to fundamentalist attacks on multiculturalism. Just as fundamentalism symbolized the most radical form of conservatism in the United States, so did political correctness become the radical watchdog of liberalism. The censorship battles mainly revolved around classroom textbooks and books that were either banned or restricted in public and school libraries.

Of the banned books, the most famous was Mark Twain's *The Adventures of Huckleberry Finn,* considered by many to be America's greatest work of fiction. Censorship of *The Adventures of Huckleberry Finn* dates back to 1885, the year it was published. While language was always a controversial aspect (in England the book was criticized for one of the characters' anti-monarchy views), a lot of the early censorship dealt with the influence of the rebellious Huckleberry Finn on the minds of young readers. This same criticism was used against Twain's earlier book *The Adventures of Tom Sawyer.* By the 1980s, criticism from the political left of *The Adventures of Huckleberry Finn* focused on the book's language and on the portrayal of the runaway slave, Jim, which critics considered demeaning and thus harmful to young readers.[35] Some felt that the book's complexity made it suitable for teaching only in colleges and universities on the graduate level.

TEXTBOOK CENSORSHIP

From a Christian fundamentalist standpoint, textbook censorship in the 1980s primarily centered on sex education and secular humanism. Religious beliefs were a motivating factor for peoples' opposition to certain classroom topics or books, but sex education was also seen as a usurpation of parental authority. In fact, parental authority played a role in all of the textbook controversies, since various school districts were advocating the teaching of ideas that fundamentalist parents opposed, thus potentially setting them at odds with their children.

Secular humanism is a term used by conservative Christians to describe a worldview that examines the world and human actions without the mediation of God and, in the eyes of its critics, elevates humanity itself to the position of God. Christian fundamentalists thus consider secular humanism a religion; consequently, fundamentalists contend, the teaching of it (primarily the teaching of evolution) in public schools is a violation of the First Amendment. This argument eventually found its way into the courts; local fundamentalists were supported by national organizations such as the American Family Association, Concerned Women for America, Eagle Forum, the National Association of Christian Educators, and the National Legal Foundation. Those opposing censorship were supported by the American Civil Liberties Union and People for the American Way. Although fundamentalists lost many of the cases that went to trial, one of the outcomes was that the textbook publishers began practicing self-censorship in order to appease the marketplace.

The initial plan of those opposing the teaching of evolution in some school districts was for evolution to be replaced by creation science, an idea that holds close to the biblical account of the creation as told in the book of Genesis. Other plans called for creation science to be taught along with evolution or as an option for those students who did not want to study evolution. Creation scientists argue that modern scientific methods can prove the biblical account of creation to be correct. In the 1970s an organization called the Institute for Creation Research (ICR) decided to use state legislatures to implement creation science in school curricula. ICR lawyers drafted a prototype bill titled the Balanced Treatment for Creation-Science and Evolution-Science Act. With this act as a model, Arkansas enacted a bill in 1981 calling for the teaching of creation science alongside evolution.

Opponents of the new law, including Methodist, Episcopal, Roman Catholic, and African Methodist Episcopal clergy, filed a lawsuit in federal district court charging that it violated the First Amendment. The law's proponents argued that evolution was part of the religion of secular humanism (and therefore a First Amendment violation in its own right), and therefore the teaching of creationism would balance the school curricula. *McLean v. Arkansas Board of Education* was decided by the U.S. District Court for the Eastern District of Arkansas on January 5, 1982. The court ruled against the law, deciding that creationism is religion and evolution science. The ICR and the Moral Majority (a fundamentalist conservative political action group founded in 1979 by the Reverend Jerry Falwell [1933–2007] and dissolved in 1989) took this defeat as a temporary setback and urged the Arkansas attorney general not to appeal. Another case was looming in Louisiana, which had passed a similar Balanced Treatment law the previous summer. ICR lawyers reasoned that upholding of the district court's decision on appeal could jeopardize their defense of the Louisiana law.[36]

There were actually two lawsuits filed involving the Louisiana version of the Balanced Treatment Act. The first was filed by proponents of the law against the Louisiana Department of Education. It argued that the department had failed to implement the new law in the state's school system. The main purpose of the suit was to have the law declared constitutional. The U.S. District Court for the Middle District of Louisiana dismissed *Keith v. Louisiana Department of Education* because the constitutionality of the law had not been challenged and therefore the court could not make a decision.

The second lawsuit, *Aguillard v. Edwards* (Aguillard was the first name listed on the plaintiff list and Edwin W. Edwards was the governor of Louisiana), was a battle between the Creation Science Legal Defense Fund (CSLDF), the legal arm of the ICR, and the ACLU. The difference between this lawsuit and the one in Arkansas was that the Louisiana law was not written as narrowly as the Arkansas law had been. Despite this, the U.S. District Court for the Eastern District of Louisiana ruled that the state's Balanced Treatment law was unconstitutional. The appeals court upheld this decision and the CSLDF petitioned the Supreme Court to hear the case, where it was named *Edwards v. Aguillard.* On June 19, 1987, the Supreme Court affirmed the judgment of the Court of Appeals by a 7-2 vote. In the final paragraph of his majority opinion, Justice Brennan wrote: "The Act violates the Establishment clause of the First Amendment because it seeks to employ the symbolic and financial support of government to achieve a religious purpose."[37]

The debate between evolution and creationism continues into the 21st century. On one side, the evolutionists declare that creationism is not science, while creationists declare that evolution is an aspect of secular humanism, itself a religion. In other words, each has been trying to exclude the other from school curricula on First Amendment grounds that government cannot favor a religion. Fundamentalists have also claimed that censorship has been practiced against a particular idea—that of biblical revelation. While true insofar as censorship is concerned, the establishment clause of the First Amendment justifies the banning of such teaching in public schools.

An important underlying issue is parental control versus that of the school boards to decide what children shall be taught. Most often, since the 1980s, the courts have decided in favor of the city or state boards of education. As a result, the battleground has somewhat shifted in that fundamentalists have tried to gain majorities on these boards.

CHALLENGES TO LIBRARY BOOKS

Libraries have been another battleground for censorship. In the years 1990–2000, there were 6,364 challenges to books either reported to or recorded by the Office for Intellectual Freedom of the American Library Association.[38] Many more challenges went unreported, and the ALA estimated that there could have been between 25,000 and 30,000 challenges during that period. Most of the challenges were aimed at books for children and young adults. The reasons for the challenges ranged from sexual themes (mostly for sex education books), same-sex relationships, language, inappropriate depiction of minorities, and antireligious themes. The latter category usually involved fantasy books. Three of the 10 most challenged books for that period were adult classics: Maya Angelou's *I Know Why the Caged Bird Sings* (#3), *The Adventures of Huckleberry Finn* (#5), and *Of Mice and Men* (#6) by John Steinbeck.

POPULAR MUSIC

Another area where parents, fundamentalist or not, have sought to exert greater control over their children is popular music. Music censorship in the United States predates rock and roll, but throughout the 1950s, 1960s, and 1970s, lyrics were altered because of their suggestiveness or their political content, radio stations refused to play certain records, or music companies dropped acts altogether. None of that had changed by the 1980s, but a new twist was added—the RIAA (Recording Industry Association of America) universal parental warning sticker.

In the mid-1980s, rock lyrics became a concern for more and more parents. One of the better-known organizations for parental advocacy was the Parents Music Resource Center (PMRC), one of whose founders was Tipper Gore, wife of then Senator Al Gore. Founded in 1985, PMRC advocated ratings for albums and concerts, a media watch, and opposition to performers whose performances were deemed violent or sexually explicit. The organization quickly gained prominence. In September 1985, PMRC representatives testified before the Senate Committee on Commerce, Science, and Transportation in support of music regulation. They were opposed by musicians Frank Zappa, John Denver, and Dee Snider. The battle continued for three-and-a-half years, and, in March 1989, RIAA universal parental warning stickers were placed on albums. Parents now had guidelines for popular music similar to movie ratings.[39]

THE INTERNET

With the growing popularity of the Internet throughout the 1990s came other issues that made music lyrics seem tame by comparison. In the United States, the most pressing problems having to do with the Internet were children's access to pornography and child pornography. Internet filters and close supervision on computers at home and schools were the main solution in preventing children from accessing pornography. However, the issue of child pornography, a major concern even before the rise of the Internet, has remained a societal problem, despite the fact that no court upheld it as constitutionally protected under the First Amendment. Court-ordered fines and jail sentences for those discovered possessing child pornography, whether in standard print or electronic form, are the only recourse. As a rule, Web sites have come under little scrutiny and have remained generally free of U.S. censorship.

CURRENT FORMS OF CENSORSHIP IN THE UNITED STATES

There are numerous forms of censorship in the United States in the early 21st century. Some of the more common ones are ratings systems, the television V-chip, and the Internet filter parents and guardians may employ in their homes to block television programs and Web sites. However, these are rather benign as they still allow the individual a choice.

The United States prides itself on being a nation that adheres to the rule of law and, whenever the federal government has sought to override the Constitution, it has, for the most part, done so with laws.[40] Today, two of the most important laws that may contravene the First Amendment are the Espionage Act of 1917 and the USA PATRIOT Act of 2001. (The official name is the Uniting and Strengthening America by Providing Appropriate Tools Required to Intercept and Obstruct Terrorism Act.) Because of Supreme Court rulings in the decades subsequent to the enactment of the Espionage Act of 1917, and because of the changes in both the political culture of the United States and in society in general, the Espionage Act poses less of a danger to free speech and a free press. Although it remains on the books, enforcement is unlikely, though always a possibility. Of more immediate concern is the USA PATRIOT Act.

USA PATRIOT Act (2001)

This law was passed in record time following the terrorist attacks of September 11, 2001, with far less congressional discussion than over the Espionage

Act. The bill was introduced in the House of Representatives on October 23, 2001; voted on by the House, which passed it passed it 357-66, on October 24; passed by the Senate with a 98-1 vote on October 25, 2001; and signed into law by President George W. Bush on October 26, 2001.

Some of the main concerns over the PATRIOT Act, which is really a series of changes throughout the U.S. Civil Code, are: Political organizations can be subjected to surveillance, which could have the effect of hampering freedom of speech; law enforcement agencies have increased power of telephone and Internet surveillance, which also could hamper freedom of speech; noncitizens can be jailed or denied entry into the country based on what they have said or written (e.g., criticism of the government or its policies). In addition to threatening rights guaranteed by the First (freedom of speech, the press, religion, and the right to assemble) and Fourteenth (noncitizens entitled to due process) Amendments, those guaranteed by the Fourth (freedom from unreasonable search and seizure), Fifth (due process of law), Sixth (right to a speedy trial), and Eighth (no excessive bail or cruel and unusual punishment) Amendments are also in danger.

One of the more chilling aspects of the PATRIOT Act is the national security letter (NSL) delivered by the FBI. The power of the NSL is twofold: It can demand private information without prior court approval of the order, and it places a gag order on the letter's recipient, which means that the recipient cannot tell anyone (including his or her spouse or partner) that he or she has even received the letter. Furthermore, the PATRIOT Act gives authorities expanded search powers.

Even people not under suspicion can be the subjects of searches. Because of the gag order, it is unclear how many NSLs have been delivered to people, but the *Washington Post* has estimated the number at 30,000 a year in the years just after the law was signed. One NSL in particular managed to catch the attention of the press in 2005 because of an FBI slipup. In Connecticut, an NSL was served on four librarians in charge of computer services for a library consortium. The letter sought Internet information on a particular library computer user, but requested all the information for users of that library's computer for that day—February 15, 2005. The NSL also made it clear the librarians were under a gag order and could not relate the request to anyone—a clear infringement of the librarians' First Amendment rights to freedom of speech.[41]

Casting such a wide net—where FBI agents can request private information of innocent people—leads directly to censorship, because it affects the things people read, write, and speak. Even more chilling, innocent people can be caught up in McCarthyesque "guilt by association" traps in which correspondence with certain organizations on the government's terrorist list (unbeknownst to the correspondents) can incorrectly identify them as terrorists.

Of the 16 major provisions of the USA PATRIOT Act, 14 had "sunset provisions." That is, the provisions were set to expire on March 10, 2006, if Congress did not vote to renew them. On March 9, 2006, President Bush signed the USA PATRIOT Improvement and Reauthorization Act of 2005. Reauthorization of the PATRIOT Act extended certain provisions that were set to expire and tightened loopholes in other provisions.

Challenges to Library Books

Rather than declining in the 21st century, challenges to books in libraries and schools have increased—by about 10 percent since the 1980s according to the American Library Association. Parents initiate most of the challenges, usually for the same dogmatic and ideological reasons they had in the past. Through 2005, seven of the 10 most challenged books had appeared in the top 10 list of the previous decade. One of the newcomers was the Harry Potter series by J. K. Rowling, young adult fantasy books that focus on the plight of a young wizard and his friends. Fantasy books are considered by some to be anti-Christian either because the protagonists or the antagonists (or both) possess Godlike powers or because of the focus on demons. They are also considered to promote a pagan lifestyle.

In October 2006, a challenge in a suburban Georgia county was made to the Harry Potter books that had a slightly different twist. Instead of charging that the books violated a particular religion's teachings, or were Satanic, the challenge charged that the books were actually an attempt to indoctrinate, or at the very least teach, children about the Wicca religion. Wicca, or modern-day witchcraft, is a neopagan, Earthbound religion. By arguing that it is a religion and that the Potter books taught it, the challenge sought to have them removed from school libraries and classrooms for violating the establishment (of a state religion) clause in the First Amendment. In December 2006, the Georgia Board of Education ruled that having the Potter books in public schools does not constitute advocacy of a religion.

Press Censorship

In the 21st century, the press has faced obstacles both new and old—in fact as old as the Zenger trial. Reporters have been threatened with imprisonment for contempt of court for not revealing sources. In 2005, a *New York Times* reporter was jailed for refusing to reveal the source of her information regarding a CIA spy. And, in 2006, two *San Francisco Chronicle* sportswriters were threatened with jail for refusing to reveal who leaked grand jury testimony to them. While this is not direct censorship (since the newspaper or magazine article has usually been printed), it is impossible to tell how many others have been intimidated into not digging hard enough for a story for fear that they might either have to reveal their sources or go to jail. Reporters are loathe to reveal their sources because in most cases the information the sources leak is confidential, and the source may face prison time for leaking the information. Also, the reporter would be regarded as untrustworthy, and his or her sources would dry up. Nevertheless, the issue is not so cut and dry. The examples mentioned above, for instance, strike at our national security and our judicial system.

A revived obstacle to press freedom is military censorship. In a compromise between banning the press from the frontlines, as was done during the Grenada invasion, and allowing the highly critical stories that became prevalent in the latter stages of the Vietnam War, reporters who have covered the wars in Iraq and Afghanistan have been embedded with the U.S. military. Because journalists are "embedded," the press is more likely to face military censorship. Military censorship is not new; its function is to make the press passive and less likely to criticize military tactics and political motives.

The newest obstacle to press freedom comes from the press itself. Media consolidation for corporate profit (and political ends) has led to a diminishing number of voices in the press.

Lastly, an overlooked form of censorship is that of school—usually high school—newspapers. In this matter, school administrations and city, county, and state boards of education have wide latitude in decision making. This type of censorship generally comes under the classification of maintaining community standards. The problem is that the community whose standards are being maintained is that of adults (parents, faculty, and administration), while the community for whom the censored paper is produced, and which produces it, is students.

COUNTERSTRATEGIES TO CENSORSHIP

There are various organizations in the United States that are dedicated to opposing censorship. These include the American Civil Liberties Union (ACLU), the American Library Association (ALA), People for the American Way (PFAW), PEN America, the Freedom Forum, and the Electronic Frontier Foundation. Internationally there are such organizations as Reporters Without Borders, Index for Free Expression, and Article 19, which takes its name from Article 19 of the Declaration of Human Rights. These organizations perform various tasks or counterstrategies in their ongoing battle against censorship. PEN America sponsors a Freedom to Write Program whose (international) mission is "to protect the freedom of the written word wherever it is imperiled. [The program] defends writers and journalists from all over the world who are imprisoned, threatened, persecuted, or attacked in the course of carrying out their profession. In the United States it protests book-bannings in schools and counters legal challenges to the First Amendment."[42] In 2005 and 2006, PEN America initiated legal action on behalf of writers and scholars who were denied visas to the United States. The denials were based on the misapplication of a specific provision of the USA PATRIOT Act that bars from entering the United States those who either "endorse or espouse terrorist activity" or "persuade others to endorse or espouse terrorist activity." Many were barred simply because they were Muslim or had criticized certain U.S. policies.

Another example of counterstrategy is the ALA-sponsored Banned Books Week that occurs every fall. Coordinated with the beginning of the academic year, Banned Books Week keeps the spotlight on those books that for whatever reason have been challenged and/or removed from library and school shelves.

More important, the ALA, through its Office for Intellectual Freedom, provides a resources guide to assist librarians in not only making the public more aware of the censorship crisis and other First Amendment challenges, but providing strategies for dealing with such challenges. The strategies include advice on how to conduct a challenge hearing, effective one-on-one communication, effective listening techniques, and dealing with the media. There are also strategies to help librarians develop a solid selection policy that will successfully withstand challenges.

Providing legal assistance in censorship cases remains one of the main duties of these organizations. In the case of the Connecticut librarians, for example, an ACLU lawyer was lead attorney for their case. Because of the gag order, the four librarians were known collectively as John Doe. The suit that the ACLU filed on behalf of "John Doe" in August 2005 charged that the NSL violated the First, Fourth, and Fifth Amendments. Of particular importance was the gag order because Congress at that time was debating whether or not to renew the USA PATRIOT Act, and the librarians had proof, contrary to administration denials, that NSLs were being served on libraries (or at least one library). The courts ruled to keep the gag order in place, but it was eventually lifted by the FBI, after the congressional debates had concluded. The lawsuit at least served the purpose of defending the rights of the librarians, the libraries, and the library patrons, and this defense was not an insignificant matter. It also showed that win or lose, the courts remain the most effective counterstrategy to censorship in the United States. The ACLU also assists libraries in presenting a stronger lobby to resist censorship.

Cities and states, at the urging of residents, have taken up opposition to the federal USA PATRIOT Act. On May 2, 2002, just a little more than six months after President George W. Bush signed the PATRIOT Act into law, the Northampton, Massachusetts, city council unanimously passed a resolution "to defend the Bill of Rights." Within a year, more than 100 communities had passed resolutions declaring their city or town a safe haven for the Bill of Rights. Arcata, California, took the extreme move of passing a city ordinance barring the city administration from voluntarily cooperating "'with investigations, interrogations, or arrest procedures, public or clandestine' that would violate the Constitution." That same month, April 2003, Hawaii became the first state in the Union to pass a resolution defending the Bill of Rights. Alaska and New Mexico followed suit.[43]

The press, despite the economic forces that are working against it, is still a bulwark against censorship. One notable instance occurred just 10 days after the September 11 terrorist attacks, and it briefly carried implications of a return to McCarthyism. The Voice of America radio network, which Senator McCarthy had victimized in the early 1950s, was stopped temporarily from broadcasting a news story that contained an interview with then Taliban leader Mullah Mohammad Omar. The U.S. State Department attempted to suppress the interview (because of the Taliban's close ties to al-Qaeda), but in the end VOA defied the order.[44]

Points of view may be shrinking in number, but overall the American press still spans the entire political spectrum. With accompanying Web sites, many newspapers, newsweeklies, and magazines, not to mention television and radio news, can now reach more people worldwide. Press censorship stories are reported widely. For example, the story of the jailed *New York Times* reporter became an issue as big as the outing of the CIA agent about which the reporter had information.

The Internet is also a medium for countering censorship, though in the United States its role is less active than the role it plays in free speech issues in other countries, including the other four case study nations in this book. Many of the organizations that actively oppose censorship in the United States use the Internet to track ongoing issues and court cases, probably none more so than the Electronic Frontier Foundation (EFF). The EFF was founded in July 1990 as a proactive watchdog organization that advises and litigates on free speech and privacy issues involving the Internet. One of

EFF's initiatives is FLAG (FOIA Litigation for Accountable Government) whose goal, as described on the EFF Web site, is "to expose the government's expanding use of new technologies that invade Americans' privacy. Through Freedom of Information Act (FOIA) requests, the project will help protect individual liberties and hold the government accountable."[45] Bloggers also keep censorship issues before the public eye, and the EFF has published a Legal Guide for Bloggers (living in the United States).[46]

Blogging is the 21st-century electronic version of the New Journalism popularized in the 1960s and 1970s. *Blogs* (the word is a contraction of Web logs) run the gamut from highly subjective to a traditional style of journalistic objectivity—in fact many journalists write blogs to include information that does not get into the traditional media. By 2006, blogs had somewhat lost their rebel cachet as the mainstream began to capitalize on the phenomenon. Yet, like the Internet in which it operates, blogging is too immense to be controlled. With each passing year, bloggers are becoming a more viable alternative to traditional, or corporate, news media and they present the best hope of keeping free speech alive when legal guarantees have been contravened.

---

[1] Geoffrey R. Stone. *Perilous Times: Free Speech in Wartime, From the Sedition Act of 1798 to the War on Terrorism.* New York, London: W. W. Norton & Company, 2004. For a different slant on Adams and his critics, see: David McCullough. *John Adams.* New York: Simon & Schuster, 2001, p. 49.

[2] Stone, pp. 61–66.

[3] An exception to this was General Andrew Jackson's suspension of habeas corpus prior to and after the Battle of New Orleans at the close of the War of 1812. Jackson acted unilaterally and without orders from the federal government.

[4] William Lasser. "A Book Named Fanny Hill." *Historic U.S. Court Cases, 1690–1990: An Encyclopedia,* John W. Johnson, ed. New York, London: Garland Publishing, 1992, p. 590.

[5] Stone, p. 95. The U.S. Postal Service also suppressed abolitionist materials.

[6] Stone, pp. 94–120.

[7] E. R. Hutchison. *Tropic of Cancer on Trial: A Case History of Censorship.* New York: Grove Press, 1968. For the Supreme Court's Grove Press decision, see FindLaw for Legal Professionals. *Grove Press v. Gerstein* 378 U.S. 577 (1964). Available online. URL: http://caselaw.lp.findlaw.com/scripts/getcase.pl?court=us&vol=378&invol=577. Downloaded August 25, 2006. For the Jacobellis decision, see FindLaw for Legal Professionals. *Jacobellis v. Ohio* 378 U.S. 184 (1964). Available online. URL: http://caselaw.lp.findlaw.com/scripts/getcase.pl?court=us&vol=378&invol=184. Downloaded August 25, 2006. For *Fanny Hill,* see FindLaw for Legal Professionals. *Memoirs v. Massachusetts,* 383 U.S. 413 (1966). Available online. URL: http://caselaw.lp.findlaw.com/scripts/getcase.pl?court=us&vol=383&invol=413. Downloaded August 25, 2006. See also Lasser, pp. 590–591 for an analysis of *Memoirs.*

[8] Stone, pp. 146–182.

[9] Stone, p. 164.

[10] FindLaw for Legal Professionals. *Schenk v. U.S.* 249 U.S. 47 (1919). Available online. URL: http://caselaw.lp.findlaw.com/scripts/getcase.pl?court=us&vol=249&invol=47. Downloaded August 28, 2006.

[11] Stone, pp. 184–191.

[12] Stone, pp. 220–226.

[13] The Scopes trial was actually a test case to try and overturn the law. Scopes knew what he was getting into beforehand.

[14] Famous Trials in American History. "Tennessee v. John T. Scopes: The 'Monkey Trial' 1925." Available online. URL: http://www.law.umkc.edu/faculty/projects/FTrials/scopes/scopes.htm. Downloaded August 28, 2006.

[15] This was the ACLU's strategy all along. The Scopes trial was a test case to get the Tennessee Supreme Court to decide the law.

[16] Jonathon Green and Nicholas J. Karolides (reviser). "*Epperson v. Arkansas.*" *Encyclopedia of Censorship, New Edition.* New York: Facts on File, 2005, p. 167. See also FindLaw for Legal Professionals. *Epperson v. Arkansas* 393 U.S. 97 (1968). Available online. URL: http://caselaw.lp.findlaw.com/scripts/getcase.pl?court=us&vol=393&invol=97. Downloaded August 28, 2006.

[17] Answers.com. "Production Code." Available online. URL: http://www.answers.com/topic/production-code. Downloaded August 30, 2006.

[18] ArtsReformation.com. "The Motion Picture Production Code of 1930." Available online. URL: http://www.artsreformation.com/a001/hays-code.html. Downloaded August 29, 2006.

[19] Comic Books in the 50s. "The Comics Code Authority." Available online. URL: http://ublib.buffalo.edu/libraries/projects/comics/cca.html. Downloaded August 30, 2006. See also Answers.com. "Comics Code Authority." Available online. URL: http://www.answers.com/topic/comics-code-authority. Downloaded August 30, 2006.

[20] The Museum of Broadcast Communications. "Ethics and Television." Available online. URL: http://www.museum.tv/archives/etv/E/htmlE/ethicsandte/ethicsandte.htm. Downloaded August 30, 2006. See also "'The Shadow of Incipient Censorship': The Creation of the Television Code of 1952." Available online. URL: http://www.historymatters.gmu.edu/d/6558/. Downloaded August 30, 2006.

[21] HUAC was originally a select committee; it became a standing (or permanent) committee in 1945. It was dissolved in 1975.

[22] Green and Karolides, pp. 240–242.

[23] In his memoirs, Truman seemed to have lamented this program, since it was a factor in unleashing the later McCarthy witch hunts for communists in the government and the military. See Harry S. Truman. *Memoirs.* 2 vols. Garden City, N.Y.: Doubleday & Co., 1955, Volume 2, *Years of Trial and Hope*, pp. 278–290, covers the loyalty program.

[24] David McCullough. *Truman.* New York: Simon & Schuster, 1992.

[25] AGLOSO remained in effect until 1974.

[26] Green and Karolides, pp. 240–242.

[27] Stone, pp. 382–383.

[28] Green and Karolides, pp. 344–345; Stone, pp. 386–390.

[29] FindLaw for Legal Professionals. *New York Times Co. v. Sullivan,* 367 U.S. 254 (1964). Available online. URL: http://caselaw.lp.findlaw.com/scripts/getcase.pl?court=us&vol=376&invol=254. Downloaded September 8, 2006. See also Susan Duffy. "Public Officials, Libel, and a Free Press." *Historic U.S. Court Cases, 1690–1990: An Encyclopedia,* John W. Johnson, ed. New York, London: Garland Publishing, 1992, pp. 538–540.

[30] "What Was the Black Panther Party?" Available online. URL: http://www.blackpanther.org/legacynew.htm. Downloaded September 1, 2006.

[31] Stone, p. 484.

[32] Stone, pp. 500–516.

[33] Edwin E. Moise. "The Pentagon Papers." *Historic U.S. Court Cases, 1690–1990: An Encyclopedia.* New York, London: Garland Press, 1992, pp. 726–732.

[34] Michael Kernan. "Grenada: The Reaction to the Invasion; On TV, Picturing the Invasion." *Washington Post.* October 26, 1983, p. B1.

[35] For a brief discussion opposing censorship to *The Adventures of Huckleberry Finn,* see Joan Delfattore. *What Johnny Shouldn't Read: Textbook Censorship in America.* New Haven, London: Yale University Press, p. 132.

[36] Joan Delfattore. *What Johnny Shouldn't Read: Textbook Censorship in America.* New Haven, London: Yale University Press, pp. 93–95.

[37] Delfattore, pp. 97–98.

[38] ALA-American Library Association. "The 100 Most Frequently Challenged Books, 1990–2000." Available online. URL: http://www.ala.org/ala/oif/bannedbooksweek/bbwlinks/100mostfrequently.htm. Downloaded September 4, 2006.

[39] Eric Nuzum. "A Brief History of Banned Music in the United States." Available online. URL: http://ericnuzum.com/banned/. Downloaded September 5, 2006.

[40] Lincoln's suspension of habeas corpus and invoking martial law is an exception to this, as are a few other instances. In 1866, with the Civil War over and President Lincoln dead, the Supreme Court took up the question of the legality of suspending habeas corpus in *Ex parte Milligan.* The Court unanimously agreed (though two opinions were written, reflecting some dissent among the justices) that Milligan ought to be freed on his petition of habeas corpus and that a military commission had no judicial power in Indiana even during wartime. See Thomas D. Morris. "The Constitution: A Law for Rulers in War and Peace?" *Historic U.S. Court Cases, 1690–1990: An Encyclopedia,* John W. Johnson, ed. New York, London: Garland Publishing, 1992, pp. 665–668.

[41] June Sandra Neal. "A Patriotic Act." *NE* Sunday magazine, *Hartford Courant,* September 24, 2006, pp. 4–5.

[42] PEN American Center. "Freedom to Write." Available online. URL: http://www.pen.org/page.php/prmID/172. Downloaded September 28, 2006.

[43] Nat Hentoff. *The War on the Bill of Rights and the Gathering Resistance.* New York: Seven Stories Press, 2003, pp. 88, 131, 143.

[44] Ellen Nakashima. "Broadcast with Afghan Leader Halted; State Department Pressures Voice of America Not to Air 'Voice of the Taliban.'" *Washington Post*, September 23, 2001, p. A9. Felicity Barringer. "A Nation Challenged: The Broadcast; State Dept. Protests Move by U.S. Radio." *New York Times*, September 26, 2001, p. B3.

[45] FOIA Litigation for Accountable Government (FLAG) Project. Electronic Frontier Foundation. Available online. URL: http://www.eff.org/flag/. Downloaded September 25, 2006.

[46] EFF: Legal Guide for Bloggers. Electronic Frontier Foundation. Available online. URL: http://www.eff.org/bloggers/lg/. Downloaded September 25, 2006.

3

Global Perspectives

CHINA

Censorship has a long and complicated history in China. The earliest recorded instance of censorship in China dates back to the Qin dynasty (221–206 B.C.E.), the first dynasty to unite much of the territory of what is now modern-day China. Subsequent dynasties imposed their own legal codes, and, of these, the Tang, Ming, and Qing codes are the best known. While each of these codes included censorship provisions, they more properly fit into the category of regulating society. Throughout most of China's history, Confucianism—the philosophy of Confucius—provided the framework for society. Self-censorship became an ingrained cultural attitude.

After the fall of the final dynasty, the Qing, in the early 20th century, power struggles led to the rise of regional warlords, who imposed their own laws over the territories they ruled. Most of the warlords were defeated by the Nationalists under Chiang Kai-shek, whose own rule turned out to be autocratic and tumultuous. Civil war and World War II not only devastated China in the 1930s and 1940s, but left little room in the political landscape for the basic human freedoms. After the Communists under Mao Zedong declared the People's Republic of China (PRC) in 1949, they maintained that tradition of censorship. Government censorship in the PRC has been practiced for the three classic reasons: to retain power, to maintain community standards, and to protect dogma—in this case Maoist dogma. Although the latter reason has gone out of fashion since Mao's death, Mao's ideas have not been entirely discredited. Since the 1980s, the PRC has been moving toward what Deng Xiaoping termed a "socialist market economy." However, the PRC is still an authoritarian, single-party state.

Historical Overview

EARLY DYNASTIES

China's pre-1911 history is divided into 17 dynasties, many of them with subdivisions and periods. The earliest was the prehistoric Xia civilization. Xia ruins date from c. 2000 B.C.E. to c. 1500 B.C.E. Since no written record of the Xia exists, much of what historians know about them is inferred from archaeological sites and ancient historical tales.

The most important of the early dynasties was the Zhou, which historians have divided into Western Zhou (1027–771 B.C.E.) and Eastern Zhou (770–221 B.C.E.). It was the Zhou who developed the notion of the mandate from heaven for their rulers, which has loomed important in China's history.

The Eastern Zhou period is further divided into two subperiods: the Spring and Autumn Period and the Warring States Period. Overlapping and bridging these subperiods was a golden age known as the Hundred Schools of Thought. Foremost among the myriad philosophies of the time was the Confucian school, founded by Confucius, or Kong Fuzi[1] (551–479 B.C.E.). Like Socrates in the West, Confucius's teachings were written down as a series of dialogues after his death called *Lunyu* (*Analects*). Essentially, Confucius espoused an ethics that looked back on the reign of the early Zhou dynasty as the ideal, in which people's places in society were set from birth. "Let the ruler be a ruler, and the subject be a subject" is one of his most famous quotes. The Confucian ideal was *junzi,* the "superior man," literally "son of a prince." However, for Confucius, the prince was superior not because of his high birth but because of his learning and culture; he was a person who placed duty and integrity above the small interests of life.

The second most important contributor to Confucianism was Mencius (Meng Zi, 372–289 B.C.E.). His philosophy was based on the belief that humans are innately good and have a natural disposition to do the right thing. Mencius gave practical applications to Confucianism that enabled it to become the state philosophy under the Han dynasty (206 B.C.E.–220 C.E.) and remained so under all subsequent dynasties.

The third major exponent of Confucianism was Xun Zi (c. 300–237 B.C.E.), who espoused a philosophy that was the exact opposite of Mencius: He believed humans were innately evil, that goodness was gained through education, and that the best government was the authoritarian one. As developed by his disciple Han Feizi (c. 280–233 B.C.E.), this philosophy became the Legalist school. The ideas of the centralized authoritarian government along with strict adherence to the code of law advocated by the Legalist school formed the basis for the imperial dynasties that ruled China for two millennia.

Another significant school of thought was Taoism, traditionally thought to be founded by Laozi (n.d.). The opposite of Confucianism, it stressed detachment from the affairs of the world and taught the importance of harmony with nature and the constantly changing universe.

THE IMPERIAL DYNASTIES

The First Imperial Period is notable for three things. A good amount of what is now China was consolidated for the first time after the state of Qin (also Ch'in, from which the name China is taken) defeated its rival states, and the Great Wall of China was built.[2] Finally, one of the worst-known incidents of censorship in the ancient world took place during this period. In 221 B.C.E., Ying Zheng (259–210 B.C.E.) proclaimed himself emperor, taking the title of Qin Shi Huangdi, First Emperor of the Qin (221–207 B.C.E.). During the Warring States Period, the Qin kings, who favored the Legalist school, executed many Confucians and burned their books. After Ying Zheng proclaimed himself emperor, he decided the only way to maintain unity was to destroy the books of the other philosophic schools,[3] leaving the Legalist school as the basis of government. The Qin dynasty ended four years after Shi Huangdi's death, but the imperial system lasted for 2,000 years. With the fall of the Qin, the Chinese states were thrust into civil war until the Han emerged victorious.

The Han dynasty (206 B.C.E.–220 C.E., with a brief interruption 9–24 C.E.) introduced a tributary system by which non-Chinese states remained autonomous in exchange for Han overlordship. Under the Han, expansion continued westward, the Silk Route was established, and culture again flourished. Most important, Emperor Wu Di (141–86 B.C.E.) made Confucianism the state philosophy and the basis for education.

THE MIDDLE DYNASTIES

Confucianism was firmly entrenched by the time of the Tang dynasty (618–907 C.E.). Thus, the Tang Code, a set of laws promulgated in the early seventh century, reflects a synthesis of Confucianism and Legalism. The Code was divided into 12 volumes and consisted of more than 500 articles plus subsections. In the mid-ninth century, during the reign of Emperor Wen Zong, an edict was added to the Code that "prohibited the unauthorized reproduction of . . . items that might be used for prognostication."[4] Later, it was extended to prohibit the unauthorized reproduction of government documents, Buddhist and Taoist texts, and certain books. The ban on the religious texts and books also applied to possession and distribution. After the Tang dynasty fell, five smaller dynasties emerged in the north, while in the south 10 kingdoms filled the power vacuum. This disunity lasted until the emergence of the Song dynasty in 960,[5] which controlled most of China.

Historians divide the Song dynasty into two periods: the Northern Song (960–1127) and the Southern Song (1127–1279). The Song also promulgated a law code. Under the Song Code, prior restraint became a legal fact. Not only was prepublication review adopted, but also registration since printers (block printing was employed at this time) were required to submit text to local officials. Prohibited works included government and military documents, the classics, writings that inappropriately used the names of members or ancestors of the royal family, and pornography.[6] The Song Code also limited religious freedom and public speech with regard to religion.[7]

The Song thrived until the middle of the 13th century, when they came under attack from the north by the Mongols, led by Kublai Khan, grandson of Genghis Khan. The Mongols defeated the Song in 1279 and established the Yuan dynasty (1279–1368). Under the Yuan, Confucianism was revived in the north, but Taoism was persecuted.

THE LATE DYNASTIES

The Ming dynasty (1368–1644) was the final ethnic Chinese dynasty, and the Ming emperors presided over a period of relative stability. That stability was in part dependent on the rule of law: The Ming, like some of their predecessors, established a law code. The Ming Code contained more than 400 articles that embraced many of the aspects of life in the different strata of Chinese society, including Buddhist and Taoist clerical behavior in certain matters. There was even an article that prohibited publicly joking about committing a robbery.[8]

In its turn, the Ming dynasty suffered from corruption and inner decay that made it ripe for a Manchu invasion from the north. With the assistance of a Ming general, the Manchu captured Beijing and established the Qing dynasty (1644–1912).

The Qing promoted culture—literature and history especially flourished during their rule—but also censored and persecuted intellectuals and banned or destroyed books and other cultural artifacts of which the rulers disapproved. The Qing Code, grounded in Confucian thought, was much more detailed than previous dynastic law codes, running to more than 1,900 articles.

In the 19th century, Qing rule was challenged by secret societies and by Western powers that had long sought to gain a foothold in the empire. Until the 1830s, China had maintained a tribute system whereby foreign countries wanting to conduct trade first had to submit to Chinese suzerainty. But, during that decade, British merchants in China began importing cotton and opium from India, although the latter was prohibited by law. In 1839, China enacted more stringent laws against the opium trade, and that same year a special commissioner seized illegal opium owned by Chinese and British nationals in Guangzhou (Canton). This triggered the disastrous First Opium War (1839–42) with Britain, which marked the beginning of the end of the Qing dynasty.

In the late 1800s, incursions by Great Britain, France, Russia, Japan, Germany, and Belgium resulted in territorial transfers, usually of the border countries that had submitted to China as their overlord. Russia took present-day Turkmenistan, France colonized Vietnam, and Britain gained control over Burma and wrangled a 99-year lease for Hong Kong.[9] In 1899, the United States, which had been left out in the cold, proposed what became known as the Open Door Policy: All foreign nations would have equal rights and privileges in all Chinese treaty ports. This proposal was quickly agreed to by all countries involved except Russia.

In early June 1898, Emperor Guangxu set in motion a set of reforms with the intention of changing China's ruling infrastructure and its society. Modernization of agricultural techniques was at the top of the list, as was the substitution of practical studies for neo-Confucianism. The reform movement lasted a little over 100 days. By late September 1898, the emperor found himself the victim of a coup engineered by the Empress Dowager Cixi, who ruled as regent.[10] The resurgence of the Manchu conservatives was a boon for the various secret societies that at the time were building a wide-front anti-foreign and anti-Christian movement. These societies, called Yihetuan or Societies of Righteous, and Harmonious Fists, were collectively known in the West as the Boxers.[11] In what became known as the Boxer Rebellion, they eventually turned their attacks on foreigners, especially missionaries, and Chinese Christians. The rebellion lasted from November 1899 to September 7, 1901, when it was crushed by an alliance of foreign forces. The subsequent peace treaty, known as the Boxer Protocol, called for foreign troops to be stationed in China.

During the first decade of the 20th century, discontent with the Qing dynasty manifested itself in protests and various local uprisings. Despite a bow toward democracy with the establishment of the National Assembly, by 1911 the stage was set for a full-scale revolution.

THE REPUBLIC

The leader of the Chinese revolutionaries was Sun Yat-sen (1866–1925), cofounder of the Tongmeng Hui (United League) in 1905. Sun's political philosophy was based on what he called the Three Principles of the People: nationalism, democracy, and people's livelihood. The Tongmeng Hui was by no means the only Chinese revolutionary movement at this time, but the force of Sun's popularity made it the most powerful. Sun was inaugurated as president on January 1, 1912, but resigned the following month in favor of the commander in chief of the imperial army, General Yuan Shikai, as part of a deal that called for the abdication of the Qing dynasty.

Over the course of the next few years, political divisions arose in the new government. The Guomindang (Kuomintang), a nationalist party comprised of revolutionaries, won a huge majority in the National Assembly and opposed many of Yuan's policies, as the president became more and more autocratic. On January 10, 1914, Yuan dissolved the National Assembly, severely limiting freedom of speech only two years after the fall of the Qing dynasty. By 1916, many of Yuan's allies had abandoned him; he died of natural causes later that year.

In 1917, Sun Yat-sen, who had been in exile, became leader of a military government centered in Guangzhou that had made alliances with southern warlords. Two years later, he reestablished the Guomindang as the main political opposition to the government in Beijing. All of this took place in a brief era of China that has become known as the New Cultural Movement. It lasted from 1917–23, sparking not only an intellectual boom, a flourishing of cultural periodicals, and the birth of modern Chinese literature, but a rise in political consciousness in China. The latter was best exhibited by the May Fourth Movement, named for a student demonstration that took place on May 4, 1919, in Beijing's Tiananmen Square. Many of the students had recently returned to China from abroad with new political ideas. The students demonstrated against the Beijing government, which had made a secret agreement with Japan during World War I to award all of Germany's former concessions in China to Japan. The apex of this golden age of free expression came in 1922 when the Western powers and Japan recognized China's independence and sovereignty. While it was Sun's dream to unify China under a republican government, he never achieved it. Sun died of cancer in March 1925.

After Sun's death, Chiang Kai-shek (1887–1975), Sun's brother-in-law, became the leader of the Guomindang and in June 1926 commander in chief of the National Revolutionary Army, a force that exceeded 100,000 men. With support from the Chinese Communist Party (CCP), the National Revolutionary Army on July 1, 1926, launched the Northern Expedition to unify China. By March 1927, Chiang's forces had control of most of the north. Following his success, Chiang irrevocably split with the left-wing of the Guomindang and the CCP, whose party apparatus he tried to destroy. The de facto leader of a fractious China, Chiang, except for a brief retirement, spent the next 22 years fighting warlords, the Japanese invaders, or the CCP, now led by Mao.

As Chiang pursued his anti-Communist policy in the early 1930s, Mao Zedong (1893–1976) was beginning to dominate the CCP. The incident that propelled Mao to the forefront was the Long March, a nearly year-long evacuation of CCP cadres and some 100,000 supporters to escape extermination at the hands of the Nationalist army. The Long March covered more than 4,000 miles and relocated the remnants of the CCP to an area outside of Chiang's direct control. Although it cost the lives of some 90,000 people, it also drew many new followers to the Communist cause.[12]

In 1937, the Guomindang and the Communists agreed to suspend their hostilities in order to make common cause against Japan. However, by 1938, Nationalists and Communists sporadically clashed in areas not under Japanese control. At the time of Japan's defeat in 1945, the Nationalists had approximately 2.7 million troops and the Communists counted nearly 1 million.[13] Hostilities between the Guomindang and the Communists soon became an all-out war that ended with the Communist victory in 1949.

On October 1, 1949, Mao proclaimed the People's Republic of China (PRC) with Beijing as its capital. Chiang and the Guomindang remnants escaped to the island of Taiwan where, with U.S. assistance, they set up the Republic of China. Chiang served as the ROC president until his death in 1975.

THE PEOPLE'S REPUBLIC OF CHINA

The first nation to recognize the PRC was the Soviet Union, which did so on October 2, 1949. Yet, despite this friendly overture and Mao's earlier proclamation that China was "leaning to one side," meaning political alignment with the Marxist countries, there was tough negotiating on both sides before the PRC and the Soviet Union signed the 30-year Treaty of Friendship, Alliance and Mutual Assistance in February 1950.

The government's first task was to reign in inflation and implement a program of industrialization and land reform, as well as political reforms. Mao declared that it was the duty of the new government, the People's Democratic Dictatorship, to "deprive the reactionaries of the right to speak." He stated "the people alone have that right."[14] In time, the definition of who was a reactionary would shift dramatically in the PRC.

In February 1951, just three months after entering the Korean War, the government issued the Regulations for the Suppression of Counterrevolutionaries, by which the police were empowered to take action against dissidents and political opponents. Furthermore, the government, simultaneous to land redistribution policies, launched a class war that was followed by even harsher censorship. Intellectuals, especially university professors, had to undergo Communist reeducation and "self-criticism." The work of writers, artists, composers, actors, film directors, and other "culture workers" was specifically delineated to reflect proletarian values. In a sense they were to produce a Chinese version of socialist realism.

Films, literary criticism, and scholarship all fell afoul of the Party for one reason or another, usually because they failed to develop a class sensibility that conformed with the Party dicta. And these were becoming more radical with each passing year. For instance, by the mid-1950s, it was no longer enough to portray a reformist in a heroic light, because reform would not lead to revolution.[15] By spring 1956, persecutions of intellectuals had begun to ease, and the party began the Hundred Flowers Campaign.

HUNDRED FLOWERS CAMPAIGN (1956–1957)

During this campaign, Mao urged coexistence between Communists and nonparty members in China and the broadening of China's outlook by taking into account certain foreign views. He even urged the study of foreign languages. The Hundred Flowers Campaign took its name from one of his major speeches of 1956 in which he poetically challenged Party members to "let a hundred flowers bloom" and "a hundred schools of thought contend." The first quote referred to culture, the second to science and technology; it was also a nod to the ancient golden age known as the Hundred Schools of Thought.

China seemed to be entering a period of free speech that would eclipse even the New Cultural Movement of the late 1910s and early 1920s. Intellectuals responded by criticizing the Communist Party and the structures of government, previous mass campaigns, Party control over thought and speech, in short just about every aspect of society in which censorship and Party corruption had twisted the ideals of the revolution. University students also took part in the criticism. Criticisms also pointed out Party mismanagement. Unfortunately by June 1957, the brief period of freedom was over.

Repression began in the provinces, where party bosses were less likely to accept reforms. They were backed by the Beijing hardliners who had never supported the Hundred Flowers Campaign but had not had the political strength to take on Mao. Now, with criticisms of the Party raging throughout the country and provincial leaders showing their discontent with the campaign, they were again emboldened. Mao quickly saw which way the wind was blowing and switched sides in the argument. Almost overnight what seemed like a clear signal for public criticism of CCP policy was turned into a mass denunciation by Mao and other leaders. It has been estimated that Mao's turnabout affected "over 300,000 intellectuals" in China.[16] Labeled rightists and counterrevolutionaries, their careers were shattered. Some were sent to prison, some were executed, and others were driven to suicide by constant harassment. There has been a great deal of speculation that Mao orchestrated the Hundred Flowers Campaign and its turnaround to weed out so-called "rightists" among the intellectuals and in the Party. Whether true or not, the wilting of the Hundred Flowers was a dark foreshadowing of the Cultural Revolution, which China's leaders unleashed in the next decade.

GREAT LEAP FORWARD (1958–1960)

The campaign that followed the Hundred Flowers was called the Great Leap Forward, an attempt at ensuring that China would not remain economically dependent on the Soviet Union. In the countryside, the Great Leap Forward was a mobilization of the peasants into communes about the size of small villages. In the cities, it was an urban renewal that, like a great deal of city planning throughout the world—especially the Communist world—during this period, sacrificed the aesthetics of a cityscape for function. By everyone's reckoning, the Great Leap Forward was a failure right from the beginning, and its legacy was a famine responsible for the deaths of at least 20 million people between 1959 and 1962. It cost Mao his position as chairman of the People's Republic, although he retained his position as Communist Party chairman. Mao's successor as PRC chairman was Liu Shaoqi.

By the early 1960s, numerous program failures and the growing importance of his rivals as well as his protégés within the CCP had made Mao's position somewhat tenuous. As chairman of the CCP, however, he still retained the power to put down a political revolt should any occur. In fact he took steps to reinforce his position by naming Lin Biao, a Mao loyalist, as minister of defense. Over the next few years, Lin gave the People's Liberation Army (PLA) a thorough indoctrination in Mao Zedong thought.

THE CULTURAL REVOLUTION (1966–1976)

The Cultural Revolution affected China like no other event since World War II. It was a decade-long era of chaos and repression. It was initially aimed at members of the Communist Party who seemed (to Mao and his allies) to have veered politically rightward, that is away from Mao thought. It was also a way to reinvigorate the arts with Mao thought. The Cultural Revolution was preceded by the Poisonous Weeds campaign, headed by Jiang Qing (1914–97), Mao's third wife, that resulted in the banning of approximately 400 Chinese films. By the time the Cultural Revolution came along, no films had been produced in China for two years and none would be produced until 1971. The Chinese music industry fared no better during the Cultural Revolution. Western music was still unavailable in the mid-1960s, and Chinese pop and classical music were replaced by "revolutionary operas."

In 1960, the Third Congress of Artistic and Literary Workers proclaimed that art in the PRC was to serve the ongoing revolution and the class struggle "in the victory of Marxist-Leninist principles." These rules were reinforced by the Cultural Revolution. Literature and publishing in general suffered greatly and "all academic journals vanished for at least six years." Works that were published had to have an ideological purity that heroicized the peasants, workers, and Party leaders. Such content inevitably led to stylistic numbness.[17]

The initial stages of the Cultural Revolution moved pretty rapidly. First, members of the Ministry of Culture were purged, and writers and critics persecuted. The revolution quickly spread to China's university students and radicalized professors via Beijing University. From Beijing University, the revolution spread to the capital's secondary schools. High school students, dubbed the Red Guards, were the shock troops of the cataclysm.

August 1966 was a pivotal month for the Cultural Revolution. It began with the Central Committee (now fully embracing Mao's tactic) issuing a 16-point manifesto and ended with Mao enhancing his cult of personality in Tiananmen Square as thousands of Red Guards paraded past.[18] This was the era of the little red book of Mao's collected sayings, and censorship enforced by cadres of Red Guards. Over the next year, violence and killings intensified, children denounced their parents and grandparents, and gangs of Red Guards fought against the police and against each other. The Cultural Revolution leaders urged on the fanatical Red Guards. All education was halted, buildings were demolished, art objects, books, and newspapers were destroyed. Those who opposed the Cultural Revolution soon found their positions precarious. Among the leaders who were purged at this time were Liu Shaoqi and Deng Xiaoping.

Intellectuals were singled out for special persecution. Ironically, some destroyed their own libraries to avoid Red Guard abuse. Many committed suicide, including, in probably the most poignant irony of the madness, the writer Lao She whose 1932 novel, *Cat Country,* described the Chinese turning on each other.

The Cultural Revolution reached a frenzied peak in January 1967 when Red Guard cadres inflamed with radical fervor attempted to reclaim the CCP apparatus from the old guard. China quickly ignited with hot spots where varying degrees of success were claimed. The most successful, though, was in Shanghai, where the theoretical groundwork for the Cultural Revolution had first been laid. Here, workers and not students were the most radicalized—each group of workers claiming to be more radical than the next. The workers demanded pay raises and permanent jobs, but their positions were soon deemed rightist (actually "economism" was the term used).

Shanghai became paralyzed by worker and student actions, both against the establishment and against each other. Transportation and communication lines were disrupted and sometimes halted altogether. Finally, Zhang Chunqiao, a colleague of Jiang Qing, backed by the PLA, put an end to the chaos in the city. By that time, the PLA was the only organization capable of reigning in the Red Guards. Though it had been indoctrinated with Mao thought, Lin Biao had managed to keep the army free from the madness that had swept the younger generation and the workers. From the time the PLA suppressed the chaos in Shanghai to the end of 1967, China came to the edge of civil war, with the PLA engaging in frequent battles with the Red Guard. However, Jiang Qing's praise of the PLA and condemnation of the radicals were clear signals which way the leadership had swung.

The end of the clashes between the Red Guard and the PLA signaled the end of the most violent phase of the Cultural Revolution. The period of upheaval, itself, would conclude only with the death of Mao in 1976, although during the last five years of his life he played less and less of a role on the Chinese political stage. However, in February 1972, he met with President Richard M. Nixon in Beijing. The warmer relations between the United States and China that evolved from the meeting gave China more leverage in its ongoing dispute with the Soviet Union. That same year, relations were finally normalized with Japan. The 1971 death of PLA chief Lin Biao and the subsequent purging of his supporters in the CCP and the PLA paved the way for a less political, more professional army and signaled the rehabilitations of some of those who had been disgraced during the harshest period of the Cultural Revolution.

The most important of those rehabilitated was Deng Xiaoping (1904–97). He was reinstated as vice premier in April 1973 and, from then until 1976, he and Premier Zhou Enlai (1898–1976) were the two main forces in the government. In August 1973, Deng was named to the central committee of the CCP. In the next couple of years, Deng acquired more power. In 1975, he became vice chairman of the CCP (Mao retained the post of chairman), was named to the Party's political bureau, and became the first civilian to lead the PLA's general staff department.[19] Then, in April 1976, Deng was removed from all his posts by party radicals, allegedly on Mao's order.

THE EARLY POST-MAO ERA (1976–1989)

During the power struggle that followed the deaths of Mao and Premier Zhou Enlai in 1976 the Maoists were dislodged by the moderates led by Hua Guofeng. On October 6, less than a month after Mao's death, the CCP ordered the arrests of Mao's widow, Jiang Qing, and three other leaders of the Cultural Revolution: Wang Hongwen, Zhang Chunqiao, and Yao

Wenyuan—collectively known as the Gang of Four. Their arrests have been viewed as the end of the Cultural Revolution.

In the late 1970s, a cult of personality began to build around Hua, but, by 1981, he was out of power, removed by the machinations of his former rival, Deng Xiaoping, who had been rehabilitated for a second time in 1977. With Deng in charge, China in the 1980s took its first major steps toward modernity and economic prosperity. It also experienced its most infamous case of public censorship in decades.

As China's leaders sought to modernize and strengthen the economy, others, notably students, writers, artists, and intellectuals, sought to reform China's strict censorship policy. Their tactics included Communist Party criticism and demands to open up the political process. To further their demands, students took to public demonstrations throughout the country in 1986. The result was a crackdown by officials and demotion for those who failed to foresee the demonstrations. One of those demoted was Hu Yaobang (1917–89), who became something of a martyr figure among Chinese students.

When the news of Hu's death on April 15, 1989, was made public, student leaders began a pro-Hu demonstration in Tiananmen Square, ostensibly to have Hu posthumously rehabilitated, but also to protest for political reforms. Initially, the demonstrations involved students from People's University in Beijing, some of whom were Party members or the children of Party members. They were soon joined by students from Beijing University and other campuses in the capital. Students also held sit-ins at the Great Hall of the People, Party headquarters, and in front of the residences of senior Party leaders.[20]

The demonstrations stretched into May, and the now emboldened students began calling for Deng Xiaoping's dismissal. Events began their tragic turn on May 20 when the government declared martial law and called in the PLA to clear Tiananmen Square. During the next two weeks the students were joined by workers who used various means to slow down the military's advance. The embarrassed government was split in its decision on how to handle the situation, but Deng held to a hard-line position and eventually more experienced troops were brought in to take care of the situation.

On the night of June 3, 1989, these troops moved to suppress the demonstrators. Backed by tanks and other armored vehicles, they fired into the crowd, killing protesters and members of the PLA alike, and tanks rolled over protesters who tried to block their paths. Early on June 4, the troops blocked off all of the streets leading to the square and turned off the lights, which left the protesters more helpless. After hours of discussion, the protesters gave up and left the square. Hundreds had died and thousands were wounded. The attack brought worldwide condemnation, but no diplomatic relations were broken off. By the end of 1989, Deng had relinquished his post on the Military Affairs Commission, but remained a powerful figure in Chinese politics until his death in 1997 as China's modernization continued. In 1992, he proclaimed that China was on the path toward a "socialist market economy."

LATE TWENTIETH-CENTURY POLICIES

China in the years since the Tiananmen Square massacre has experienced phenomenal economic growth. Its reacquisition of Hong Kong in 1997 also served to open an economic window to Japan and the West. Despite this growth, the PRC experienced continued protests in the years 1990–2007. These protests have occurred in both urban and rural areas. Many of the protests have been carried out by workers and farmers who have been alienated from China's new economy, whether through unemployment and inflation in the cities or unfair (in many cases illegal) land distribution and the lack of "nonagricultural opportunities" in the rural areas. Other protests have centered around human rights for individuals and groups, such as the Falun Gong religious sect, founded in 1992.[21] In July 1999, Falun Gong adherents were arrested and the group was banned. The arrests were apparent reprisals for an April 25, 1999, demonstration in which 10,000 Falun Gong practitioners gathered in Beijing outside the leadership compound to protest violence against Falun Gong members and a ban on publishing Falun Gong material. It was the largest antigovernment demonstration in China since the student protests in Tiananmen Square 10 years earlier.[22]

Following Deng Xioping's death in 1997, Jiang Zemin (b. 1926), who had been elected chairman of the Central Military Commission in 1989 and president of the PRC in 1993, was confirmed as president and party leader.[23]

Throughout the 1990s and up to 2003, Jiang worked closely with Zhu Rongzhi (b. 1928), who was first deputy premier and then premier of the PRC. Both men were protégés of Deng and both had been mayor of Shanghai. Zhu's main portfolio was the country's economy, in which he continued Deng's modernization and was mainly responsible for China's growth at the end of the 20th century. Jiang passed on leadership of the CCP in 2002 to Hu Jintao (b. 1942), and in 2003 Hu was elected president of the PRC.

By the 21st century, the PRC was a much different place than that which Mao had envisioned, although politically it retained the one-party system he and his cohorts had installed. The economy was radically changed. With its entry into the World Trade Organization in 2001, the PRC seemed one step closer to realizing Deng's goal of a socialist market economy. One feature of Chinese life that Mao would recognize, however, is censorship, although even in that area technological advances in communications since 1976 (the year of Mao's death), notably the Internet, have made control of information harder to accomplish, while at the same time more necessary for an authoritarian government.

Legal Aspects of Censorship

The current constitution of China was adopted on December 4, 1982, and amended in 1988, 1993, 1999, and 2004. It provides guarantees of citizens' rights under the tenets of socialism. The following articles in the Chinese constitution (none of which have been amended) deal with such rights.

- Article 35: Citizens of the People's Republic of China enjoy freedom of speech, of the press, of assembly, of association, of procession and of demonstration.
- Article 36: Citizens of the People's Republic of China enjoy freedom of religious belief.
- Article 40: The freedom and privacy of correspondence of citizens of the People's Republic of China are protected by law.
- Article 41: Citizens of the People's Republic of China have the right to criticize and make suggestions to any state organ or functionary.
- Article 47: Citizens of the People's Republic of China have the freedom to engage in scientific research, literary and artistic creation and other cultural pursuits. The state encourages and assists creative endeavors conducive to the interests of the people made by citizens engaged in education, science, technology, literature, art and other cultural work.

Despite such assurances, censorship still exists in China. Within the constitution itself exist articles that can be interpreted to contradict the guarantees of freedom. Two of these articles are:

- Article 22: The state promotes the development of literature and art, the press, broadcasting and television undertakings, publishing and distribution services, libraries, museums, cultural centers and other cultural undertakings, that serve the people and socialism, and sponsors mass cultural activities. . . .
- Article 51: The exercise by citizens of the People's Republic of China of their freedoms and rights may not infringe upon the interests of the state, of society and of the collective, or upon the lawful freedoms and rights of other citizens.

At face value, Article 22 sounds positive, but actually it limits the viewpoint of the media ("that serve the people and socialism") and the wide range of "cultural undertakings." Article 51 has the power to make any and all dissent unlawful. When the interests of the state and society clash with the legitimate interests of the individual(s), the former take precedence according to this article. Thus, all public criticism of the government can be interpreted, along with Article 22, as not serving the cause of socialism and therefore seditious.

Current Forms of Censorship

PRESS AND BROADCAST MEDIA

The CCP controls China's press and broadcast media. In January 2001, President Jiang Zemin declared "the news media are the spokespeople of the Party and the people and . . . they have the duty to educate and propagate the spirit of the Party."[24] Thus, while the press is not free, it is not suppressed. It is hard to gauge to what degree Chinese journalists take Jiang's formulation to heart because of the culture of self-censorship. Two of the most widely read newspapers in China are *The People's Daily* and *Red Flag*, both popular with CCP members. Other newspapers, whether national, provincial, or municipal, also adhere to Party guidelines.

There are two official news agencies in the PRC: the China News Service and the Xinhua news agency, also known as the New China news agency. Both serve the Party and state as filters of what Chinese citizens can read and what others, including Chinese abroad, can read about the PRC. In January 1996, new controls were placed on foreign financial news agencies working in the PRC, such as Reuters and Dow Jones. These agencies were ordered "to submit to control by the Communist Party's New China news agency (Xinhua) and threatened to punish them if they released information within the country that 'slanders or jeopardizes the national interest of China.'"[25] As part of the controls, foreign agencies had to register with Xinhua, which would act as an intermediary between Chinese companies and government departments and the agencies. Xinhua also controlled subscription rates. On September 10, 2006, the PRC further tightened its control of foreign news dissemination in China by decreeing that "Xinhua news agency has the right to select the news and information released by foreign news agencies in China and shall delete any materials mentioned [in its itemized list]." Xinhua now had the power to ban news reports "that disrupt 'China's economic and social order or undermine China's social stability, national unity, sovereignty, and territorial integrity. . . . endanger China's national security, reputation, and interests,' violate 'China's religious policies or preach evil cults or superstition,' or incite hatred and discrimination among ethnic groups."[26] Material banned by previous law continued to be banned.

The move was viewed not only as a way of controlling the flow of information, but as an attempt to boost Xinhua's financial, sports, and photo desks in the world market. It was also noted at the time that "President Hu Jintao's leadership has sought to rein in state-controlled media that have strayed from party dictates in search of profits and market share. Journalists and editors have been fired and arrested."[27]

ARTS

The Party has yet to relinquish its control over the arts. While the severity of censorship is far less than that practiced during the Cultural Revolution, if press controls are an indication, then more tightening can be anticipated as the first decade of the 21st century winds down. Among the books that have been banned in the PRC for political and/or moral reasons since 2000 are: *Chinese Painting,* by Wang Yue-Chen; *Waiting,* by Ha Jin; *Shanghai Baby,* by Zhou Weihui; and *We Are Still Looking at the Starry Sky,* by He Qinghan.[28] Of all the arts, music probably enjoys the most freedom of expression in the PRC, especially rock. However, even the Rolling Stones have been forced to submit to prior restraint censorship during live performances.

INTERNET

The September 2006 laws restricting news dissemination notwithstanding, China has focused a great deal of its censorship efforts on the Internet. The country's first Internet laws were implemented in 1997. Those laws made it a criminal act "to defame government agencies, divulge state secrets, or promote separatist movements on the Internet." The final provision seemed aimed at dissidents and Tibetan separatists.

In 2002, the PRC took a different Internet censorship path when it launched a campaign for self-censorship titled the "Public Pledge on Self-Discipline for China's Internet Industry." At the same time, it continued to ban certain types of information outright. On August 1, 2002, the PRC implemented the law "Interim Regulations on Management of Internet Publishing," which foreshadowed the foreign news agency laws of 2006. The 2002 Internet regulations banned items that "harm national unity, sovereignty, or territorial integrity, or damage national honor or interests, disturb the social order or damage social stability," or "advocate cults." The last seemed aimed at Falun Gong.[29]

In December 2002, a Harvard Law School study concluded that the Chinese government was most frequently blocking Web sites pertaining to Tibet, Taiwan, and democracy. The study checked more than 200,000 Web sites between May 2002 and November 2002 by using Chinese Internet service providers and, after these were blocked, 50 Chinese proxies (proxy servers reroute connections through a third computer).[30]

The 1997 and 2002 laws were anything but idle threats. In 2002, Amnesty International published a List of People Detained for Internet-related Offences in China.[31] The offenses of the 33 people listed ranged from "printing pro-democracy material from the Internet" to "downloading material from Falun Gong Web sites" to "subversion." "'Subverting state power,' 'endangering state security,' and disseminating reactionary documents via the Internet" were other accusations against the prisoners.[32] Not all of the fates of these prisoners were known when the list was compiled, but at least two people, both of whom were Falun Gong practitioners, died in custody. By February 2006, the number of those imprisoned for criticizing the PRC on the Internet had increased to 49 "cyberdissidents" and 32 journalists.[33]

On September 25, 2005, the PRC promulgated a new set of regulations covering the Internet that in some areas reaffirmed existing rules and added new restrictions. Some of the new rules applied to major search engines and portals, which had to replace their own commentary articles with government-approved pieces. Also, private individuals and groups had to register as so-called news organizations in order to disseminate news or commentary via e-mail.[34] Of course, these would all be empty laws if China did not possess the technology to block search engines and Web sites. Basically, these two provisions ensured the dissemination of government propaganda while aiding censors in weeding out dissent before it reached Chinese Internet users, who numbered approximately 100 million at the time.

As of 2005, there were also rules requiring Internet cafes to register the names of customers, record their online activity, and store the information for 60 days.[35] All of this combined—the censorship, the registrations of online users and online newsgroups and e-mailers, the requirements for search engines, and the most sophisticated blocking technology in the world—has come to be known as the Great Firewall of China.

In early 2006, three of the most popular Western search engines—Google, Yahoo!, and Microsoft—decided to alter their search engines in order to do business in China. The companies were heavily criticized for collaborating with the regime's censorship, and their decision seemed to most a setback in the fight to gain free speech and a free press in the PRC.

Counterstrategies to Censorship

As of late 2006, counterstrategies for censorship in China were few and not very strong. This was due to a major crackdown by the government on media liberalization and its success in insulating China inside its own corner of cyberspace. Ironically, the best hope for free speech, a free press, and freedom of religion exists in cyberspace. Government firewalls cannot remain leak proof forever, just as laws can change with the country's economic circumstances.

Watchdog groups such as Reporters Without Borders, PEN International, and the International Federation of Library Associations and Institutions continue to apply pressure, albeit indirectly. These groups monitor the censorship situation in the PRC and pressure Western governments and those companies that comply with the censorship laws in order to do business in the PRC. The mainstream media in the West also serve as watchdogs in China, though a weak one. Interestingly, one of the companies that has set up a Web site in the PRC, Google, saw its move as a new kind of electronic open door policy in China.

A Google senior policy counsel who posted a blog on January 27, 2006, wrote about the company's decision to launch a Chinese Web site. "Launching a Google domain that restricts information in any way isn't a step we took lightly. . . . Filtering our search results clearly compromises our mission. Failing to offer Google search at all to a fifth of the world's population, however, does so far more severely. . . . We are convinced that the Internet, and its continued development through the efforts of companies like Google, will effectively contribute to openness and prosperity in the world. . . . Our launch of google.cn, though filtered, is a necessary first step toward achieving a productive presence in a rapidly changing country that will be one of the world's most important and dynamic for decades to come. . . ."[36]

The increased media crackdown of September 2006 seems to dispel the hopeful rationalizations of Google and, perhaps, those of other Internet service providers doing business in China. Pressure from Western governments will only gain so much (and that very little). Ultimately, cracks in the Great Firewall will come from within. The increasing number of people imprisoned for violating the censorship laws show that the largest population in the world will not remain acquiescent in the face of such repression. The internal cracks will be not only technological but political, just as the PRC's economic fortune changed through an altered political policy that veered from orthodox Maoism.

EGYPT

Like most ancient societies, Egypt in the pre–Common Era most likely practiced a form of censorship that would not then have been recognized as such. In all likelihood, any censorship would have been viewed by most citizens as benefiting society.

Some of the earliest nonpolitical censorship might have been between Sunni and Shia Muslims, depending on which group controlled the Egyptian throne. Foreign control of Egypt, by the Ottoman, French, and British Empires, also engendered censorship to various degrees. Modern censorship in Egypt began with Gamal Abdel Nasser and has continued under his successors, Anwar Sadat and Hosni Mubarak. These three men have ruled Egypt for more than 50 years, the majority of that time under a declared state of emergency. They countered modern advances in communication technology with laws that were sometimes harsh, sometimes ambiguous, but generally designed to stifle dissent.

Historical Overview

EARLY DYNASTIES

Like China, the civilization of Egypt dates back to antiquity. Its earliest dynasty began c. 3100–3000 B.C.E. and is shrouded in myth. Many have ascribed the pharaonic line as beginning with Menes (the commonly used Greek name of the Egyptian king Mni). Menes united Upper and Lower Egypt and is thought to have founded the city of Memphis as his capital.

The 31 pharaonic dynasties lasted until 332 B.C.E. Historians have divided these dynasties into various ruling periods: the Early Period (2950–2575 B.C.E.), the Old Kingdom (2575–2150 B.C.E.), the First Intermediate Period (2125–1975 B.C.E.), the Middle Kingdom (1975–1640 B.C.E.), the Second Intermediate Period (1630–1520 B.C.E.), the New Kingdom (1539–1075 B.C.E.), the Third Intermediate Period (1075–715 B.C.E.), and the Late Kingdom (715–332 B.C.E.), during which Egypt was a province of the Persian Empire.[37] Most of the famous pyramids, as well as the Sphinx, date from the Old Kingdom.

The regular dynastic rule was replaced by Greek rule, the Ptolemaic dynasty, when Alexander the Great (356–323 B.C.E.) conquered Egypt in 332 B.C.E. and proclaimed himself pharaoh. Alexander founded the city of Alexandria, but never actually ruled Egypt. He died in Babylon a few years later. Alexander's generals divided the empire after his death and Egypt was thus claimed by Ptolemy, who ruled as Ptolemy I Soter (c. 367–282 B.C.E.). Under the Ptolemies, Egypt experienced a cultural rebirth. Aside from the lighthouse at Pharos, the most notable achievement of the Ptolemaic dynasty was the library at Alexandria, the most magnificent in the ancient world. Alexandria became a truly cosmopolitan Mediterranean city and the country as a whole benefited from the intermingling of Greek and Egyptian culture. The Ptolemies assumed the classic pharaonic trappings, including mummification and burial in sarcophagi. The Ptolemaic line lasted until 30 B.C.E., the last ruler being Cleopatra VII (69–30 B.C.E.).

The stories of Cleopatra consorting with Julius Caesar (100–44 B.C.E.) and then Marc Antony (c. 83–30 B.C.E.) are well known, but it was Caesar's nephew, Octavian (later Augustus Caesar, 63 B.C.E.–14 C.E.), who brought Egypt into the Roman Empire when he defeated the combined forces of Antony and the Egyptian navy at the Battle of Actium in 31 B.C.E. Like their Greek predecessors, the Romans in Egypt absorbed many trappings of Egyptian culture, which by then had become greatly Hellenized. However, while the Ptolemies established a dynasty in Egypt, the Romans ruled Egypt as simply another province of their empire—Egypt became its granary. Because of their absence, the Roman emperors never had the allegiance of the Egyptians, although the Roman military ensured there was no large-scale rebellion. Eventually, Roman rule in Egypt morphed into Byzantine rule, which came to Egypt before the fall of Rome in the mid-fifth century.

With the exception of religious strife—initially persecution of the Coptic Christians and later a schism between the Copts and the Orthodox Church—Byzantine rule in Egypt was peaceful and Alexandria continued to thrive as a capital. That all came to an end when the Arab armies during the Umayyad dynasty defeated the Byzantine army in 636; Alexandria fell in 642. These military victories ushered in the Islamic period of rule over Egypt.

THE ISLAMIC PERIOD

The Islamic period lasted for approximately 1,150 years and is divided into subperiods or dynasties: the Abbasid, who defeated the Umayyad dynasty; the Fatimid; the Ayyubid; Mamluk; and Ottoman Turk. The Fatimid period introduced Shia Islam to Egypt; the Shiites believe that rule should come from the line of the prophet Muhammad, and the first Fatimid rulers were grandsons of Muhammad's youngest daughter, Fatima.[38] The end of Fatimid rule coincided with losses to the Crusaders from Europe and a strange alliance between the Fatimids and the Franks (a Germanic tribe) to preserve their remaining holdings from other European invaders. However, the alliance proved the downfall of the Fatimids as the Seljuk sultan, Nur al-Din (1118–74), angered over the alliance, sent General Shurkuh and Shurkuh's nephew to defeat the Crusaders and the Fatimids, capture Alexandria, and establish Seljuk rule. This they did, and the sultan appointed Shurkuh vizier of Egypt. Shurkuh died soon after and his nephew took over as ruler of Egypt, establishing the Ayyubid dynasty.

That nephew, Salah al-Din Yusif al-Ayyubi, known in Europe as Saladin (1137–93), became one of Islam's most revered figures. One of his first acts was to replace Shiite Islam with Sunni Islam, which rejects the belief that religious leadership should descend from the prophet Muhammed, as the official religion in Egypt. He fortified Cairo and initiated the moves that turned it into a magnificent city and a center of Sunni scholarship. Saladin also brought in mamluks, Turkic slaves who were trained to become members of an elite army. In all, Saladin remained in Egypt for eight years before turning over the throne to his brother and setting off to fight (and defeat) the invading Crusaders, for which he gained worldwide fame.

In one of the greatest ironies in world history, the mamluks eventually seized control of the central administration in 1250 and became the rulers of Egypt. The Bahri Mamluks stopped the Mongol expansion into Syria, eventually driving them out. Their 180-year reign was bloody, but less so than that of their successors, the Burgi (or Circassian) Mamluks.[39] The Burgi Mamluks also had to deal with a Mongol invasion, this one by Tamerlane, but, overall, their rule was one of heavy taxation and brutality toward the population.

The Ottoman Turks, who succeeded the Mamluks, made Egypt a province of their vast empire and ruled it from Istanbul through a succession of pashas. Although the Ottomans overthrew Mamluk rule, they continued to use Circassian Mamluks in the army to enforce tax collection, suppress Egyptian revolts, and defend the province. By the end of the 18th century, however, the Mamluks and, therefore, the Ottomans, were unable to defend Egypt against the onslaught of the French army under Napoléon Bonaparte (1769–1821).

MEHMET ALI PASHA AND BRITISH RULE

Napoleon ruled Egypt for three years but in the end failed as an administrator. After his departure, the British and Ottomans formed an alliance to drive the French out of Egypt. A British fleet under Admiral Nelson destroyed the French fleet at Alexandria while the Ottomans captured Cairo. One of the Ottoman officers, an Albanian named Mehmet Ali (1769–1849), enlisted the help of the Mamluks to drive out the British. After this success, he then turned the Ottoman forces on the Mamluks. In gratitude, the Ottoman caliph named him khedive, or viceroy, of Egypt. Mehmet Ali ruled from 1802–49, and by the end of his reign he was in control of a great deal of the Ottoman Empire, though he always deferred to the caliph. The dynasty of Mehmet Ali Pasha lasted until the British reestablished their authority in Egypt in 1882, and its most notable achievement was the design and completion of the Suez Canal.

Egypt became a province of the British Empire at the outbreak of World War I, in response to the Ottoman Empire's aligning with the Central Powers of Germany and Austria-Hungary. Although the British were in charge, the descendants of Mehmet Ali continued their nominal rule of Egypt. During the war, the nationalists, led by Saad Zaghlul (c. 1860–1927), became more outspoken; attacks against British soldiers occurred after the Armistice was signed on November 11, 1918. Egypt gained sovereignty in 1922, and Sultan Fuad (1868–1936) was proclaimed king, but the country remained under British "protection." In 1923, Egypt's first constitution went into effect. It mandated a parliamentary form of government, though the king had the right to dissolve the legislature. The constitution remained in effect until 1952, with the exception of the years 1930–35.

Britain's protection of Egypt included control of the Suez Canal Zone, where the British maintained troops as per an Anglo-Egyptian Treaty signed in 1936. British control of Egypt lasted until after World War II, by which time Fuad's son, Faruq (1920–65), was king.

GAMAL ABDEL NASSER

When World War II ended, Egyptians, especially those in the nationalist Wafd Party and the Muslim Brotherhood, a fundamentalist movement dedicated to restoring the institutions of Islam, expected complete independence from Great Britain as gratitude for supporting the allies during the war. It took two years before Britain, under nationalist pressure, withdrew troops from the Suez Canal Zone and Alexandria. The next year, 1948, Egypt and other Arab states suffered an embarrassing military defeat at the hands of a much smaller, though better trained Israeli army, following their attack on the new nation. This defeat would trigger a series of events within the military that had important ramifications for Egyptian politics.

In 1952, when Prime Minister Mustafa al-Nahhas (1879–1965) voided the 1936 Anglo-Egyptian Treaty, King Faruq dismissed him from the government. The dismissal caused anti-British riots among the nationalists that were finally put down by the army. What resulted from this action was a coup d'état led by a group of officers known as the Free Officers. They forced King Faruq to abdicate and placed General Muhammad Naguib (1901–84) nominally in charge of the nation as prime minister and commander of the armed forces. However, the real leader was Colonel Gamal Abdel Nasser (1918–70), who led the nine-member Revolutionary Command Council (RCC). Under Nasser, the RCC abolished the monarchy, banned all political parties, and nullified the 1923 Constitution. Nasser moved swiftly to consolidate his power. In 1953, the RCC declared the Arab Republic of Egypt. In 1954, Nasser became acting head of state, and in 1956 he officially became president of Egypt, whereupon he declared that Egypt was a single-party socialist country whose official religion was Islam.[40]

Nasser's domestic policies were a double-edged sword. He sought to better the lot of the average citizen, but at the same time he severely curtailed their rights. Nasser's regime established wide-scale censorship, engaged in tapping the telephones of opponents, and arrested political opponents. Yet, his foreign policy and the adulation he received from Arabs everywhere made him a figure almost beyond reproach.

Nasser's political strength derived from his anti-Israel stance, his ability to maneuver among larger cold war players, and his pan-Arabic dreams. Nasser understood Egypt's significance in a world becoming increasingly dependent on oil. Egypt may have lacked that resource, but it had the canal, and Nasser leveraged it in his game of cat and mouse with the two cold war superpowers. In 1957, he nationalized the Suez Canal Company, which precipitated a military crisis between Egypt and, at first, Israel, then Britain and France. Pressure from the United Nations, with backroom negotiations by the United States and the Soviet Union, helped resolve the conflict—the tripartite Israeli, British, and French force withdrew from Egypt. Nasser was also the driving force behind the United Arab Republic—the union of Egypt and Syria (for a time it seemed as though Iraq would also join). However, the United Arab Republic lasted only until 1961. When it ended, Nasser's pan-Arab dream began to fade.

Using Israel as a focal point of Arab hostility, Nasser never completely gave up hope for pan-Arabism until he launched the disastrous Six-Day War against Israel in June 1967. Egypt's defeat was more decisive than the earlier 1948 defeat: Israel claimed the Sinai Peninsula as a buffer zone. Nevertheless, Nasser's prestige remained intact. He died of a heart attack in 1970, and was succeeded by Anwar Sadat (1918–81).

POST-NASSER RULE

Sadat was among the original group of officers who had engineered the coup against King Faruq. At the time of Nasser's death, he was Egypt's vice president and Nasser's chosen successor. Under Sadat's early rule, Egypt remained in the forefront of Arab policy toward Israel that led to the Yom Kippur War in 1973. That war ended in a stalemate, but Sadat gained in prestige among Egyptians. It also gave Egypt leverage in negotiations with Israel. His newly won esteem enabled Sadat to carry out domestic and international programs that veered from Nasser's: He moved Egypt's economy away from socialism just as he began to turn its foreign policy toward the West. Sadat also relaxed the domestic repression that had existed in Egypt for decades.

By the late 1970s, Sadat had come to the conclusion that the series of useless wars with Israel had nearly ruined Egypt's economy. On November 19, 1977, he did the unthinkable when he traveled to Israel bearing the olive branch of peace. The actual negotiations were held in the United States and concluded in 1979 in what came to be known as the Camp David accords. Sadat's goal of a negotiated peace between the two countries was achieved.[41] Egypt became the first Arab nation to recognize Israel. Sadat was a hero in the West, but in the Arab countries, including Egypt, he was viewed as a traitor; and Egypt lost its position as first among the Arab nations. The negotiations more or less sealed Sadat's fate; he was assassinated in October 1981 while viewing a military parade.

In the years between the Camp David accords and Sadat's death, the Muslim Brotherhood, among others, had grown bolder in its criticism of his policies—many called for his ouster. As a result, Sadat became inflexible toward his rivals. The period of limited freedoms that he had allowed came to an end, further isolating him from his fellow citizens. In 1980, two laws were passed that greatly restricted freedom of speech and of the press. These were the Press Law and the Law on Protecting Values from Shameful Conduct. The latter gave the government even greater powers of censorship, but essentially both laws prohibited criticizing the state religion, Sunni Islam, and the government.[42] Then, in September 1981, Sadat ordered the mass arrests of opponents and critics. By the time of his assassination by members of the Islamic Jihad organization the following month, Sadat was beginning to be viewed as unsatisfactory in the West as he was in the Arab world.

Vice President Hosni Mubarak (b. 1928) became president upon Sadat's assassination. While some thought he would renounce the Camp David accords, he did not, instead focusing on regaining Egypt's position in the Arab world while maintaining good relations with the United States. To a large extent, he spent the final two decades of the 20th century achieving and maintaining that continually precarious balance, but his domestic critics have not been few.

During his rule, Mubarak has had to deal with the rise of Islamic fundamentalism and domestic terrorism. Although he declared a state of emergency immediately after Sadat's death, Mubarak attempted to restore some political rights to the Egyptians early on. However, by the end of the 1980s, the state of emergency had been extended, and, in the mid- and late-1990s, Mubarak had, like his predecessors, resorted to government repression of opposition groups. The repression was to counter violence by militants, but it nevertheless extended to any group that opposed Mubarak's policies. Throughout his time in office, Mubarak has had an uneasy relationship with the Muslim Brotherhood. In 2005, the Brotherhood was barred from participating in parliamentary elections, though some of its candidates won seats running as independents.

Legal Aspects of Censorship in Egypt

The current constitution was adopted on September 11, 1971, at the beginning of Sadat's presidency and nearly 20 years after the coup d'état that brought Nasser to power. Like most other national constitutions, it spells out specific guarantees concerning the rights of Egyptians to free speech, freedom of religion, and a free press. The articles in the Egyptian constitution guaranteeing the freedoms of speech, religion, and the press are:

- Article 46: The state shall guarantee the freedom of belief and the freedom of practicing religious rites.
- Article 47: Freedom of opinion shall be guaranteed. Every individual shall have the right to express his opinion and to publicize it verbally, in writing, by photography or by other means of expression within the limits of the law. Self-criticism and constructive criticism shall guarantee the safety of the national structure.
- Article 48: Liberty of the press, printing, publication and mass media shall be guaranteed. Censorship on newspapers shall be forbidden as well as notifying, suspending or canceling them by administrative methods. In a state of emergency or in time of war, a limited censorship may be imposed on the newspapers, publications and mass media in matters related to public safety or for purposes of national security in accordance with the law.
- Article 49: The State shall guarantee for citizens the freedom of scientific research and literary, artistic and cultural creativity and provide the necessary means for encouraging their realization.

A close reading of Article 47 shows that it not only buttresses Article 46 (concerning religion), but that it guarantees freedom of political expression as well as criticism of the government. However the final sentence of the article puts limits on these freedoms. "Self-criticism and constructive criticism" are code words for, or at the very least pathways to, censorship. Additionally, the article does not mention who or what organization would provide the constructive criticism.

Article 48 is more forthright as it actually sets up a situation where censorship would be constitutionally legal. The problem is that no one can predict beforehand what the limits of a "limited censorship" would be, especially during time of war. The experience of the United States during World War I serves as a good example of increasing wartime hysteria leading to increasing censorship. Furthermore, the censorship clause of Article 48, if taken in conjunction with the previous article's mention of self- and constructive criticism, may lead to more than state censorship during times of emergency or war. Private individuals and groups are certainly more likely to take it upon themselves to squelch speech or publications that dissent from the official line, and they would feel justified in doing so. One can assume that the guarantees of all four of these articles would be jeopardized during times of emergency or war.

The basis of the Egyptian constitution is sharia, or Islamic law. This is stated in Article 2 of the Egyptian constitution: "Islamic jurisprudence is the principal source of legislation." Westerners are familiar with sharia only from its most extreme punishments such as flogging, stoning, and caning and for its oppressive rules regarding women. In Egpyt, sharia is most influential when it comes to personal laws such as marriage and divorce, yet sharia, as interpreted by Islamic clerics, is also responsible for censorship. The most infamous case of recent censorship attributed to sharia was that of Salman Rushdie's novel *The Satanic Verses,* which was even pulled briefly from American bookstore shelves. In 1988, Ayatollah Ruhollah Khomeini, spiritual leader of Iran, issued a fatwa that effectively called for Rushdie's death. Rushdie was forced into hiding for more than a decade. Egypt has had its own notorious case of sharia-imposed censorship. In 1995, Nasr Abu Zayd, a university professor, was declared an apostate by an Islamic cleric for his unorthodox views of the Quran. Because Islamic law does not allow a Muslim woman to remain married to an apostate (who, as a result of his heresy, is declared a non-Muslim), Zayd and his wife were forced to flee to the Netherlands. Eventually, the declaration against Zayd was lifted.

Two well-known laws that legalize censorship are the Law on Protecting Values from Shameful Conduct, passed in 1980, and the Press and Publication Law 96 of 1996. The "Shameful Conduct" law was passed during Sadat's rule but has been extended under Mubarak. As the *Encyclopedia of Censorship* points out, the law's first article declares, "it is the duty of each citizen to uphold the basic social values and that any departure therefrom represents shameful conduct, justifying a prosecution."[43] The Press and Publication Law 96 prescribes imprisonment and financial penalties for journalists convicted of defamation, "inciting hatred," "violating public morality," "harming the national economy," or "offending a foreign head of state."[44]

Current Censorship in Egypt

Following the assassination of Anwar Sadat in October 1981, his successor, Hosni Mubarak, declared a state of emergency. As detailed in Article 48 of the Egyptian constitution, this state of emergency effectively nullified those laws that outlawed censorship. The state of emergency was renewed in 1988 and remained in effect through 2007. During the more than 25 years of Mubarak's rule, every facet of Egyptian life has experienced censorship. The vast majority of the censorship has been initiated by government agencies, though some has come as a result of religious rulings.

Anti-Mubarak, anti-Islamic, and overtly sexual are the most common reasons for censorship. The Ministry of Culture has censorship powers regarding books, films, music, theater, and art, and it exercises its authority regularly. Other Egyptian government agencies responsible for censorship are the Ministry of the Interior, which suppresses criticism of the government and is also in charge of confiscating foreign newspapers, and the Ministry of Defense, which has censorship powers regarding security issues. Lastly, the Council of Ministers may also ban anything it judges offensive, antireligious, or simply likely to create a disturbance.[45]

In addition, there is the Islamic Research Council (IRC) that operates out of al-Azhar University. Since the 1990s, the Ministry of Culture has ceded more and more censorship power to the al-Azhar Islamic Research Council, which has applied a fundamentalist interpretation to works of art.

PRESS

The most notable censorship taking place in Egypt is that of the press. Press laws passed in 1980 and 1996 define the role of the press in Egyptian society and the punishment, usually prison, for journalists convicted under Egypt's censorship laws.[46] Furthermore, the government controls the three most influential daily newspapers in the country, *al-Ahram, al-Akhbar,* and *al-Gomhouriya.* Here, censorship is more insidious, as the editorial policies set by the newspapers mirror the government's wishes. Prior restraint is imposed on those Egyptian journals not controlled directly by the government. They are required to obtain licenses, and these licenses can be withheld or revoked if the publishers and editors fall out of favor.

During the early years of Mubarak's rule, numerous "unlicensed publications flourished despite the law," but "in early 1987 the authorities purged many of these."[47] Also, printers are only allowed to print licensed publications. Almost as a backup to all of this, the government's control of newspaper distribution further limits the political opposition.

Like China, Egypt is one of the world's most serious offenders when it comes to imprisoning journalists. In addition to prison time, journalists may be fined according to the provisions of the Press Law. The length of a prison sentence and the amount of a fine vary according to the crime.

Foreign-language publications are not exempt from the law, although it is thought that they are not dealt with as harshly. However, one English-language magazine, *Cairo,* founded in early 2005, was temporarily taken off the newsstands three times in its first six months of publication. The magazine's offenses included a report on a constitutional convention, an editorial cartoon, and a cover photograph that showed security forces as they were about to attack prodemocracy demonstrators.[48] This last offense occurred in August 2005, one month prior to Egypt's presidential election, which Mubarak won.

BOOKS

In 2000, the Islamic Research Council banned one of Nasr Abu Zayd's books, *Discourse and Interpretation,* which examines, among other things, sheikhs' public bearing as a way to add gravitas to their pronouncements. Although the number of books al-Azhar bans is small, the council's rulings occasionally contradict secular rulings, as happened in 2003 when the Islamic Research Council banned *Commandments for Loving Women.* The book was restored by the government after one day, which explained that the ban had been merely an advisement.[49] In August 2004, the council banned *The Responsibility for the Failure of the Islamic State,* by Gama al-Banna. The book discusses ways for Muslims to better integrate into non-Islamic societies and argues for reform of sharia.[50]

At the time his book was banned, al-Banna was a fairly well-known figure among Egypt's intelligentsia for having published *Towards a New Jurisprudence,* a three-volume work that set forth his reformist principles. Even the Nobel Prize–winning novelist Naguib Mahfouz has had to face censorship. His book *Children of the Alley* (also published in English as *Children of Gebelawi*) was charged as blasphemous by Islamic scholars in 1959 and banned. In January 2006, Mahfouz, then 94 years old, petitioned to finally have the book published; he died seven months later.[51]

A 2005 Human Rights Watch report declared that academic freedom in Egypt is so stunted that professors and students practice self-censorship. Furthermore, the report pointed out that all appointments and promotions are controlled by the government, another reason for academic self-censorship.[52]

FILMS, THEATER, AND MUSIC

While bans on such foreign films as *The Matrix Reloaded* (for its handling of human existence and creation) and *Bruce Almighty* (for infringing on God's sacredness) have resulted because of the rise of fundamentalist Islam in Egypt, intimidation of film directors and actors has also risen under Mubarak.[53] One director in particular, Inas al-Degheidy, received anonymous death threats in 2006. In July of that year, Egyptian legislators demanded that gay love scenes be cut from Marwan Hamed's film version of Alaa Al Aswany's best-selling 2002 novel, *The Yacoubian Building.*[54]

Theater also comes under close scrutiny. When Eve Ensler's *The Vagina Monologues* was performed in February 2004 at the American University in Cairo, the performance had neither the university's sanction nor was it open to the public. The audience came by invitation only. To have either the university's approval or a public performance would have invited the censors to close down the play.[55]

In 2002 and 2003, one of Egypt's most popular singers, Shaaban Abdel Rahim, was censored from the airwaves by the Ministry of Information, which operates Egyptian television and radio stations.[56] Rahim's most popular song was "I Hate Israel." Released in 2000, it was subtitled "But I Love Amr Moussa" (the head of the Arab League and former foreign minister, sometimes seen as Mubarak's rival and successor).[57] A second song, "Bin Bin Bin Bin Laden," was also banned from broadcast for promoting militant Islam. However, prior to the U.S. invasion of Iraq, Rahim had a hit with his antiwar song, "The Attack on Iraq."[58]

Music videos and concert performances are also often either censored or banned outright. In 2005, Egyptian authorities banned 20 music videos "which featured sexual connotations and females barely dressed." The censors also claimed the videos' song lyrics were meaningless. In early 2006, a music video by the Tunisian singer Najla was banned from the Egyptian music station Mazzika for being pornographic.[59] A year earlier, she had been refused reentry into Egypt after visiting her homeland. As with much of its censorship actions, the government has the support of fundamentalist Muslims. Although it is often the target of censorship itself, the Muslim Brotherhood has vowed it would continue to censor videos and end free concerts should it come to power.

Counterstrategies to Censorship in Egypt

Egyptians employ various measures to get around censorship. People resort to tactics such as inviting audiences to private theater performances, publicizing the censorship, demonstrating against the government's practices, and violating the bans. All of these methods are used in Egypt, but whether in isolation or collectively they have had little effect. If anything, censorship has gotten stricter since the early 1990s with the rise of Islamic fundamentalism in Egypt.

Like many other countries facing such problems, technology-savvy Egyptians have turned to the Internet. As elsewhere, bloggers are the driving force behind this counterstrategy to censorship. Many of the bloggers, however, write in English, which gives them a wider readership worldwide but restricts the number of readers where it most counts. By late 2005, the political bloggers in Egypt had evolved into "a tightly-knit group" but their readership numbered "no more than a few hundred."[60] On the other hand, English-language blogging in Egypt is subject to less censorship than Arabic blogging. Some opposition organizations such as Kifaya ("enough" in Arabic) also do their organizing through blogging networks. Though it appears bloggers are less scrutinized than mainstream journalists and writers, they are not immune from retribution, and many have been imprisoned, some even tortured. However, Egyptian expatriate bloggers in the United States, Western Europe, and elsewhere are beyond the reach of the authorities, and they provide information that is bypassed in the mainstream Egyptian media outlets.

Political discussions and organizing are not the only things Egyptian writers are posting on the Internet. Fiction writers and poets, many of whom have turned to a more personal literature, have been posting their work on the Web since the early 2000s. One advantage this has over the print media—other than not having to submit to a prepublication review—is that when the authorities close down a particular Web site, a new one can take its place and the offending material can remain online.[61]

Lastly, organizations fighting for democracy and an end to censorship in Egypt manage to keep the pressure on the government and the problem before the international community. Kifaya is a loose-knit confederation, though very popular.[62] Other organizations working for change, or at least seeking to protect their constituents who have run afoul of the censorship laws, include the Egyptian Syndicate of Journalists, the International Freedom of Expression Exchange (IFEX), the Arab Press Freedom Watch, Reporters Without Borders, and PEN International. All of these organizations have Web sites in which they post the latest censorship news and impending (legal) actions.

RUSSIA

For decades, Russia has been a nation synonymous with censorship. While that is not as true now as it was in the mid-20th century—the high point of the Soviet Union—the terrible lessons of Russia's past have had occasion to play out in its present.

All autocrats practice censorship to an extent but modern Russian censorship and political repression can be traced to Czar Nicholas I. Yet ironically, Russian literature experienced its Golden Age during his reign. The three czars who followed him employed censorship and repression in varying degrees. Nicholas's son, Alexander II, was a moderate who freed the serfs, while his son, Alexander III, chose to revert to his grandfather's harsher style of rule.

Censorship and repression were practiced on a massive and nearly complete scale during the Soviet period (1917–91). This era was infamous for its denunciations, show trials, purges, gulags, and stultifying official literature and art. However, as in the Golden Age, Russians (and other Soviet citizens) managed to transcend censorship and repression. Now, in the post-Soviet era, democracy and capitalism struggle to take root in a soil whose richness has been depleted, and the once promising free press has all but been co-opted by the government.

Historical Overview

PRE-ROMANOV RULERS

In the ninth century, Scandinavian tribes swept into Eastern Europe, conquering and settling into established cities from the Baltic to the Black Seas. In the territory of what is now Russia, the semi-legendary Rurik, leader of the Varangians, founded the first dynasty in the city of Novgorod in 862. Although Rurik's existence has been called into question, he is named in the *Primary Chronicle*, the earliest history of Kievan Rus', as the pre-Russian state came to be called. Rurik's successor, Oleg, expanded southward and, in 882, gained control of Kiev (a fifth-century Slavic city and the present capital of Ukraine). Oleg also signed a commercial treaty with the Byzantine Empire that elevated the status of Kiev.[63] It was during this period that the Cyrillic alphabet was developed.[64]

At the beginning of the 10th century, the push for unity had made Kiev the center of eastern Slavic culture. By the end of the 10th century, Kievan Rus' was a small regional power. Oleg's great-grandson Vladimir I began the process of institutionalizing that power by choosing Greek Orthodoxy as the state religion. This had the advantage of allying his kingdom with the Byzantine Empire.

The decline of Kievan Rus' in the late 12th century can be attributed to a number of factors: the various principalities that sprang up diluted power from the center; the sack of Constantinople in the Fourth Crusade weakened formerly attractive trade routes; the transfer of the seat of the Orthodox Church from Kiev to Vladimir, northeast of Moscow; and, most important of all, the sack of Kiev itself by the Mongols in 1240. For the next two centuries, the Slavs of Kievan Rus' would be heavily taxed under the domination of the Golden Horde, as those Mongols who settled around the lower Volga River region were known. The only city in the area to escape Mongol attack was Novgorod in the north, but the Mongols exacted tribute from it too. At that time, Moscow was little more than a remote trading post in the Vladimir-Suzdal principality.

Moscow's rise was an unintended consequence of the Mongol overlordship. Situated farther north and away from the immediate reach of the

Golden Horde in the southeast, Moscow began to emerge as an important city and the region a principality in its own right in the early 14th century. The earliest princes of Muscovy, as the principality was called, paid tribute to the Mongols by collecting taxes and seeking their permission to organize as a principality. Soon Moscow's superior location for trade enabled it to surpass its rival northern city, Tver. When the Orthodox Church transferred the patriarchate to Moscow in 1327, the city gained even more prestige. In 1380, Dmitry Donskoi, a Muscovite prince, attacked and defeated the Mongols. This victory signaled the beginning of the end of Mongol power in Russia, although it would take another century to complete its decline.[65]

It was Grand Duke Ivan III (Ivan the Great, 1462–1505) who presided over Muscovy's greatest rise to power during this period. He first conquered one of Moscow's northern rivals, Novgorod, then annulled the Mongol overlordship of the Russian lands in 1480. Five years later, he conquered the city of Tver. Ivan III was the first Russian ruler to claim the title of czar and "Ruler of all Rus."[66]

Despite Ivan III's grand titles, Russia was not yet a unified state. The aristocracy, known as boyars, still ruled many individual principalities. It was under Ivan's great grandson, Ivan IV, better known as Ivan the Terrible (1533–84), that Russia became unified. He conquered what remained of the Golden Horde, extending Russia as far south as the Volga River city Astrakhan, and smashed the autonomous power of the boyars. It was also during his reign that Russia first began to extend into Siberia.[67]

One of the most notorious instances of censorship in Russia during its premodern times had to do with the Russian Orthodox Church. Seeking to correct deviations that had crept into the liturgy, Patriarch Nikon (1608–81) proposed standardizing church ritual to bring it into line with established Greek practice. The resistance against this was fierce, and those who opposed the reforms were called Old Believers. Nikon had the power of the state behind him, however, and Old Believers were persecuted. Their leader, Avvakum, was executed. Nevertheless, the Old Believers persisted, and a schism in the Russian Orthodox Church came about in 1667.

THE ROMANOV DYNASTY

After the death of Ivan the Terrible in 1584, a weak czar (Ivan's son Fyodor), the lack of qualified administrators, palace intrigue, and murder led to the Time of Troubles (1604–13) in which two false pretenders to the throne vied with one another, while Polish and Lithuanian armies made frequent invasions.[68] The Time of Troubles ended when the boyars came to Ipatievsky Monastery in Kostroma, where young Mikhail Romanov had taken refuge from an invading Polish army. They offered him the crown, he accepted, and was installed as czar in Moscow. The Romanov dynasty lasted until 1917.

The most influential of the early Romanov czars, and one of the most important of all Russian rulers, was Peter I (Peter the Great, 1672–1725), who came to power in 1682. Peter's reign was marked by many notable reforms: He built a modern navy, Westernized Russia, simplified the Cyrillic alphabet, placed the Orthodox clergy under a Holy Synod, changed the calendar, and established technical schools. Peter also began military conscription, since he was often at war, first with the Ottoman Empire, then with the Swedes, and then with the Ottoman Empire again. His wars with the Ottomans pretty much ended in a stalemate, but his Swedish war gained new territory that gave Russia access to the Baltic Sea. For this reason, Peter also assumed the title of emperor. The state of Muscovy, originally a principality under Mongol control, was now the Russian Empire.[69]

Peter's most ambitious project was the construction of the city of Saint Petersburg on the Gulf of Finland and the transfer of the Russian capital to there from Moscow, a city he disliked.

Except for sentimental monarchists, Peter's legacy has been debated by historians and Russian citizens alike. On one hand, he set in motion the changes that were to make Russia a powerful modern state. But those changes came at a great price, and by and large that price was paid by the peasants who fell into serfdom and the common people who became further removed from the aristocracy.

Peter died in 1725 and for the next 37 years a succession of men and women wore the crown of Russia, each to no great distinction. That run of mediocre and bad rulers came to an end in June 1762 when a former German princess ascended the throne as Catherine II, though history knows her as Catherine the Great (1729–96).

Catherine came to power as a result of a coup against her husband, Peter III.[70] Catherine not only continued the reforms of Peter the Great, but in many instances she saw them through. Like Peter, she carried out wars against the Ottoman Empire on two occasions that resulted in territorial expansion to the south. This expansion included the Crimea and the establishment of Odessa as a Black Sea port for the Russian navy. Russia also expanded westward during Catherine's reign.

She introduced major provincial reforms that left the nobles less beholden to the center. As with Peter the Great, however, the reforms left the peasants and common folk further estranged from the ruling and upper classes. It was also during Catherine's reign that the Pale of Settlement was established. This was an area in the western part of the Russian Empire where Jews were forced to live. It was a mass segregation that set the tone for later anti-Semitic pogroms in Russia.

Under Catherine's influence, there was a general push toward Western enlightenment. She collected art (and founded the Hermitage Museum), corresponded with the French encyclopedists, and founded numerous academies. The beneficiaries of this largess were the royal family, the nobles, and the Russian intelligentsia (often the last two groups overlapped). But with enlightenment came a new freedom that Catherine had not anticipated: the freedom to question the status quo.[71] One result of this freedom was perhaps the most important case of censorship in Russia during the 18th century. It was important because it was a defiant criticism of an economic and social institution.

In 1790, Alexander Radishchev published *A Journey from Saint Petersburg to Moscow.* This book was an indictment of the institution of serfdom that caused consternation among the nobles. Catherine, herself, was dismayed over the book, and, though Radishchev was actually a noble, she pronounced him "a rebel worse than Pugachev."[72] Taking its cue from the empress, a court tried Radishchev and sentenced him to death. Catherine must have had second thoughts, because she commuted the sentence to 10 years' exile in Siberia.[73] The plight of the serfs continued until the 1860s.

Catherine's son, Paul I, succeeded her, but he reigned for only five years before he was assassinated. He in turn was succeeded by his son, Alexander I (1777–1825). Alexander had actually been his grandmother's choice to succeed her and so learned statecraft at an early age. During the first half of his reign, which lasted until his death in 1825, he continued the reformist tradition, but he grew more conservative and suspicious after 1812, the year French emperor Napoléon I invaded Russia.

The most notable feat of his reign, chronicled decades later by Lev Tolstoy in his novel *War and Peace,* was the part Russia played in the alliance to defeat Napoléon, and Alexander's victory tour of Europe afterward. For a brief time, he managed to play both sides of the Napoleonic Wars. Initially allied with Great Britain and Austria against France, Alexander, after suffering losses against Napoléon at Austerlitz and Friedland, signed a treaty of alliance with France in 1807—which allowed him to take Finland from the Swedes. When Alexander repudiated the treaty rather than engage in a continental blockade of Britain, the infamous French invasion of Russia ensued. Although the French army was far superior numerically, the Russians eventually turned the tide and drove Napoléon back to Paris where he was defeated and sent into exile. Alexander was regarded as the savior of Europe. Such high esteem enabled him to create the Quadruple Alliance of Russia, Great Britain, Austria, and Prussia in 1814.[74]

Alexander was succeeded by his younger brother, Nicholas I (1796–1855), in 1825. In December of that year, a number of army officers, hoping to bring about democratic reform, carried out a brief uprising that was quickly crushed. Many of the Decembrists, as they became known, were killed and the others exiled to Siberia.[75] Nicholas, in turn, was scarred by their action and proved to be a far more autocratic ruler than his predecessors.

Nicholas's reaction to the Decembrists was to make full use of the Russian secret police, known as the Third Section. Furthermore, his reign marks the beginning of censorship in the modern Russian state, extending into the Soviet Union in the 20th century. "The government exercised censorship and other controls over education, publishing, and all manifestations of public life."[76] In addition, Nicholas exported reactionaryism to continental Europe by helping to suppress revolts.

Despite heavy censorship during Nicholas's reign, Russia experienced its Golden Age of literature. Alexander Pushkin, Mikhail Lermontov, and Nikolai Gogol were among the many poets and writers who flourished. Yet even the most famous could not escape censorship, especially Gogol.[77] In particular, his satirical play *The Inspector General,* at first warmly received by the czar and the nobles, was later banned at the request of the reactionary upper class, which it satirized. In 1852, the writer Ivan Turgenev was jailed simply for praising Gogol in print.[78]

Journals and newspapers were also banned. Much of what was censored centered on political activity, reformist ideas, or both. Because of Nicholas's extremely reactionary policies, many political activists and avowed revolutionaries were imprisoned, and some were executed. The overall effect of Nicholas's reign was actually to spur on those forces he had been dedicated to eliminating.

Nicholas was succeeded by his son, Alexander II (1818–81). Compared to his father, the conservative Alexander was a true reformer. In 1861, he freed the approximately 20 million serfs from their bondage.[79] Unfortunately, the new freedom did not radically improve their lives. Alexander also initiated a number of governmental reforms in response to the times. Judicial reform—with "Western-style courts" that included jury trials—was carried out in 1864. Alexander also eased some of the censorship laws, but reversed course in 1866 after an unsuccessful assassination attempt. In 1870, elected councils were established at the local level, though again reform was thwarted by landlords who tended to dominate the councils.[80]

There were numerous other reforms in banking and investment, in education, and in the military, but these were either slow or thwarted by reactionaries within the government or other institutions. Furthermore, despite the less harsh censorship under Alexander (or perhaps as a result of it), many radical political thinkers gained prominence, including those who advocated terrorism and revolution. One such group, which called itself the People's Will, assassinated Alexander in 1881. He was succeeded by his son, Alexander III (1845–94).[81]

Alexander III reverted to the harsh autocracy of his grandfather, Nicholas. One of his most significant counterreforms was to strengthen the powers of the secret police, which he renamed the Okhrana. Restrictions were placed on the local councils and religious censorship was revived—the Russian Orthodox Church again flexed its muscles as the state religion. Yet, once again reactionary measures proved counterproductive. Radical political organizations continued to sprout up and grow in influence. The works of foreign radicals, particularly Karl Marx and Friedrich Engels, also gained influence during this time.

Alexander was succeeded by his son, Nicholas II (1868–1918), in 1894. Compared to most of his predecessors, Nicholas was a weak ruler who reigned during a period when calls for political change in Russia were beginning to accelerate. For the first nine years of his rule, Nicholas was advised by strong-willed men, notably Finance Minister Sergei Witte. Witte was responsible for programs that ranged from conversion to the gold standard to heavy taxation of the peasantry, to industrial development and the Trans-Siberian Railroad, all of which were designed to modernize Russia. By 1903, though, the country was deeply in debt and Witte was dismissed.[82]

The following year, Russia stumbled into the disastrous Russo-Japanese War (1904–05), which exposed the country's military and economic weaknesses. This war was essentially the beginning of the end for czarist rule. In January 1905, a peaceful workers' march in Saint Petersburg led by a Russian Orthodox priest was fired upon by troops. Commemorated as Bloody Sunday, the event sparked what came to be known as the Revolution of 1905.[83] Worker strikes were called and a workers' council was formed in Saint Petersburg. Witte, who still had the czar's ear, persuaded Nicholas to issue the October Manifesto. The manifesto granted a constitution, guaranteed civil rights, and instituted a ministerial form of government that was answerable to the czar. It also included a national assembly called the Duma. Witte was named the first prime minister of the government that was to take office in 1906. However, the political scene changed in Nicholas's favor, and he dismissed Witte and replaced him with Petr Stolypin.[84]

The conservative Stolypin clashed with the more progressive Duma so much that he dissolved the Second Duma in 1907. The Third Duma, while more orderly, also refused to be a rubber stamp, and the Fourth Duma was slightly more progressive. Stolypin's boldest reform involved the breakup of peasant communes that would have allowed peasants to purchase land or work in the cities if they so chose. But even this failed—Russia was becoming too radicalized for such measures. In 1911, Stolypin was assassinated, and for the next three years the government became more and more isolated from the people. Whatever opportunity the czar and his ministers had had for establishing a constitutional government had slipped through their fingers. After the death of Stolypin, political censorship and other repressions increased, though history repeated itself as political radicals gained influence among the citizenry. Many of the radical leaders had opposed the October Manifesto as another fraud perpetrated on the people.

Because of Russia's various alliances with the Balkan countries and England and France, it was drawn into World War I. Though numerically superior to its primary opponents, Germany and Austria-Hungary (the Ottoman Empire was the other opponent), Russia's military was poorly equipped. By 1916, the military defeats had begun to have a ripple effect on Russia's domestic situation as one crisis after another brought the country closer to revolution. Finally, in February 1917, a more or less spontaneous uprising occurred in the capital city of Petrograd.[85] This led to the overthrow of the monarchy—Nicholas abdicated on February 17, 1917, in favor of his brother, Michael, who renounced his claim to the throne the next day. The Duma then set up a Provisional Government, led first by Prince Georgi Lvov and then by Alexander Kerensky. The Provisional Government never had the support of the radical left because it maintained the wartime alliance. For this reason, as the months wore on, the Bolsheviks chipped away at any backing the government had with the people, who were tired of the deprivations of war. On October 25, 1917, the Bolsheviks overthrew the Kerensky government, and Vladimir Lenin (1870–1924) took charge as premier of the Council of People's Commissars.[86] In December 1917, the Soviet government recognized the independence of Finland. Four months later, the Communist government (as the Bolsheviks became known) signed the Treaty of Brest-Litovsk with Germany. It was a humiliating defeat, but Lenin had kept his promise of extracting Russia from the war. The Communists also returned the capital to Moscow during their first months of rule.

COMMUNIST RULE

For the next two years, 1918–20, Russia was embroiled in a civil war between the Communists, known as the Reds, and an alliance of anti-Communists consisting of socialists, monarchists, and democrats—known collectively as the Whites—and their foreign allies, Great Britain and the United States. By 1920, the Red Army led by Leon Trotsky (1879–1940) had prevailed decisively, but it was another two years before the Union of Soviet Socialist

Republics (USSR) was formed with Lenin as its leader. At its height, the Soviet Union consisted of 15 republics.[87]

The 1920s were a golden age for Soviet arts as the avant-garde flourished. One of the men most responsible for this was Anatoli Lunacharsky. In 1917, Lenin appointed him commissar of enlightenment, in which he oversaw educational and cultural matters. By Soviet standards, Lunacharsky was a moderate who increased the literacy rate in the USSR by introducing universal, free education for the first time in the country's history while taking a generally hands-off approach to writers and artists; however, anti-Soviet ideas were not tolerated. Joseph Stalin (1879–1953) removed Lunacharsky from his post in 1929.

Despite this freedom of expression, censorship did take hold. During the Civil War, the Soviet secret police was the All-Russian Extraordinary Committee for Combating Counter-Revolution, Profiteering, and Corruption, commonly known as the Cheka.[88] It was headed by Felix Dzerzhinsky who was also Commissar for Internal Affairs. The Cheka was originally an investigative organization but quickly gained powers of arrest and, as its name states, was used against enemies of the regime. It also instigated the Red Terror following an assassination attempt against Lenin. The Red Terror was by its very nature a form of censorship that took the lives of thousands.

In early 1922, the duties of the Cheka were transferred to the State Political Directorate (GPU), which became the Unified State Political Directorate (OGPU) after the USSR was formed.[89] Early on, the OGPU's powers were fairly moderate, but, after Lenin's death and especially as Stalin acquired more power, the OGPU became very powerful.

Lenin's death in 1924 was followed by a four-year power struggle among the high-ranking members of the Communist Party (CP). The two principal figures of this struggle were Trotsky and Stalin.[90] By 1928, Stalin had managed to outmaneuver first Trotsky then his other opponents to become the undisputed Soviet leader, which he remained until his death in 1953. Once he had consolidated his power, he expelled Trotsky from the Soviet Union.[91]

By the 1930s, art, literature, and political thought in the Soviet Union had been subverted not only to the cause of socialism but to the growing cult of Stalin. From the mid-1930s until Stalin's death in 1953, Soviet life was marked by domestic terror and war. From 1936 until the German military invasion of the Soviet Union in 1941, Communist Party members and top military personnel whom Stalin viewed as his enemies or political opponents were caught up in what came to be known as the Great Purge. It has been estimated that more than one-third of Communist Party members were purged between 1936 (the year of the first show trial in Moscow) and 1938 (the year of the third and final show trial).

In addition, many of the writers, artists, filmmakers, songwriters, composers, dancers, and theater people who blossomed in the decade following the October Revolution were either silenced, imprisoned, or executed. (And many of those imprisoned died in prison, while others committed suicide). Much of the art and literature that was produced subscribed to the official theory of socialist realism, which sought to uplift the masses while at the same time paying homage to Communist achievements, particularly those of Lenin and Stalin. A great amount of non-Russian literature, art, film, and music from the West was generally not made available to the average person.[92] The Orthodox Church had made its peace with the Communist Party, but even it had to endure certain restrictions and persecutions. During the Stalin era, the Soviets perfected the art of censorship, going as far as expunging all references to purged Party members and other "non-persons," including photographic evidence. The photos remained but technicians airbrushed the "offensive" person out of the pictorial record. Sometimes the person was replaced with an architectural or landscape feature, sometimes the space was left empty—an obviously gaping hole in the record arrogantly left that way because no one would dare question it.[93]

As there was after Lenin's death nearly 30 years earlier, a Kremlin power struggle occurred following Stalin's death, from which Nikita Khrushchev (1894–1971) emerged as the Soviet leader. Although Soviet censorship was not abolished, it was somewhat abated during this time, especially after Khrushchev's "secret speech" at the Twentieth Party Congress in 1956 in which he denounced the cult of personality that had arisen around Stalin. With regard to freedom of speech, Khrushchev's era is known as the "thaw." Novelists and poets in particular were somewhat freer to go beyond the tired genre of socialist realism. However, it was during this period that Soviet censorship was broadcasted to the world when Boris Pasternak, known primarily for his poetry, was awarded the 1958 Nobel Prize in Literature for *Dr. Zhivago,* a novel that was only published abroad until 1988. Convinced the award was given to embarrass them, Soviet authorities not only denounced the Swedish judges, they forced Pasternak to refuse the award, expelled him from the Soviet Writers Union, and stripped him of the title of "Soviet writer."[94]

Despite this incident, the so-called "thaw" occurred during the next six years in which writers were somewhat freer to publish work that was a bit more daring. This brief period came to an abrupt end when Khrushchev was deposed in 1964 and replaced by Leonid Brezhnev (1906–82) and Alexei Kosygin. Eventually, Brezhnev became the sole leader of the USSR and remained so until his death in 1982. Brezhnev was a neo-Stalinist (although without his own cult of personality) who took a more hard-line approach to both foreign and domestic policies. The domestic crackdown was made clear to all in 1966 when writers Andrei Sinyavsky (1925–98) and Yuli Daniel (1925–88) were put on trial for violating the section of the Soviet criminal code that dealt with "agitation or propaganda carried out with the purpose of subverting or weakening the Soviet regime ... dissemination for the said purposes of slanderous inventions defamatory to the Soviet political and social system ..."[95] In other words, they were charged with sedition even though their work was only published abroad. Both were found guilty: Sinyavsky was sentenced to seven years in a labor camp and Daniel received a five-year sentence.[96] While the vast majority of their peers denounced the trial and the verdict, the outcry made no difference. One result of the trial was the onset of samizdat. Samizdat (literally, self-publishing house) was an underground publishing network that managed to bypass the official channels. Distributed by individuals or groups, sometimes in handwritten copies, sometimes using mimeograph and, later, photocopy machines, it produced literary, political, scientific, or any writing the regime might consider seditious or subversive. It lasted right up until the end of the Soviet Union.[97]

In the 1970s and 1980s, samizdat had its correlate among musicians and music aficionados—*magnitizdat. Magnitizdat* was the underground distribution of folk, rock, and jazz, all forbidden by the authorities. Two beneficiaries of the *magnitizdat* movement were the Dylanesque bards Vladimir Vysotsky and Bulat Okhudzhava, both of whom are now considered cultural heroes of that era.[98]

Other notable instances of censorship during the Brezhnev era included those of dissident Andrei Sakharov, who was sentenced to internal exile in the city of Gorky (now Nizhny Novgorod), Alexander Solzhenitsyn, who was forced to immigrate to the West, and Natan Sharansky, another dissident who was eventually allowed to immigrate to Israel. Other than returning the country to a more closed system, the Brezhnev era is also known as a period of economic stagnation.

Brezhnev's successor was Yuri Andropov, the former head of the KGB, the successor organization to the NKVD. He died suddenly in February 1984, less than 15 months after assuming power. His successor was Konstantin Chernenko, who died in March 1985. Chernenko was the last of the Soviet gerontocrats to rule the country. He was succeeded by Mikhail Gorbachev (b. 1931), the first and only Soviet leader born after the October Revolution.

What Gorbachev inherited was a country staggering under the weight of a political and economic system that at best had been mismanaged and at worst was simply political gangsterism. As part of his reform program, he initiated perestroika (an economic restructuring plan) and glasnost (openness), the latter allowing for a greater degree of freedom of speech. After the dissolution of the Soviet Union in 1991, many hardliners blamed these two programs, especially glasnost, for the downfall and the succeeding hard times, but the reality was the USSR was falling apart.

POST-COMMUNIST RULE

As president of the Russian Federation, Boris Yeltsin (1931–2007) convinced the leaders of Ukraine and Belarus to join him in declaring independence from the USSR. Other republics within the USSR soon followed Russia's lead, and Gorbachev had no choice but to dissolve the Union of Soviet Socialist Republics on December 25, 1991. Yeltsin was now president of an independent Russian Federation.

The 1990s were chaotic for Russia. The country endured a near total economic collapse. The foreign monetary assistance that was meant to ease the abrupt transition from a planned economy to a free market system disappeared without any accountability. As a result of the economic hardship and lack of governmental oversight, crime increased just about everywhere. State-owned resources were nearly all sold off well below market value to insiders and those best able to take advantage of the new system. Some of these people grew so wealthy that they were later dubbed the "oligarchs," and a few of the best-placed oligarchs became Yeltsin's closest advisers during his last years in office in an informal kitchen cabinet known as The Family.

Yet, for a brief time, there was again a golden era for freedom of speech and of the press in Russia. New magazines and newspapers sprang up, offering vastly different points of view, while some of the older journals retooled themselves editorially. Television, too, offered new opinions and began to present the news in a somewhat unbiased manner. A multitude of political ideas (and parties) now flooded the country; literature, art, music, theater, and film all reaped the benefits of this explosion of expression.

After years of enduring the country's official atheism, the Russian Orthodox Church enjoyed a renaissance of sorts, as did a handful of other religions that were historically part of Russia: Judaism, Islam, and Buddhism among them. However, the Orthodox Church's history and the many who at least paid lip service to its authority combined to make it once again the dominant religion of Russia. As such, it too would find itself again in a position to enforce censorship.

All of this free speech did not come without a price. Some of the oligarchs were quick to move into the media sector, further consolidating their power; bookstores and kiosks were flooded with second- and third-rate foreign literature; and pornography was ubiquitous. Politically, the freedom extended to criticism of the president, especially his economic policy and his handling of the First Chechen War (1994–96). Yeltsin endured the criticism and made no move to ban newspapers and journals or imprison writers for their words.

However, although the Yeltsin administration refrained from censorship, other powers were less tolerant. One young reporter, Dmitri Kholodov, was blown up by a bomb in a suitcase in late 1994 while investigating the military. In early 1995, television journalist Vladislav Listyev was murdered in the entryway to his apartment building. Listyev had just become head of the state-run television network and was about to reorganize the company. The killers of both men were never convicted.

Yeltsin won reelection in 1996, but, as the decade and the century wound down, he relied more and more on The Family, which in turn sought a way to protect itself in the post-Yeltsin years. By late 1999, Yeltsin appointed the sixth and final prime minister of his administration—Vladimir Putin (b. 1952).[99] The former head of the FSB or Federal Security Service, the successor organization to the KGB, Putin served as prime minister for less than half a year, but in that time managed to make himself indispensable not just to Yeltsin but to the Moscow power brokers.[100] To the electorate he seemed the man who would restore lost glory by defeating the Chechen rebels and bandits once and for all.[101]

On December 31, 1999, Yeltsin shocked his countrymen and the world when he announced on television that he was resigning as president of Russia, effective the next day. As prime minister, Putin then became acting president, and the presidential election were pushed up from June to March as per the Russian constitution. Putin handily won election in his own right and set about distancing himself from the Yeltsin administration. By the time he won reelection in 2004, Putin enjoyed an enormous popularity despite the ongoing Chechen conflict and the erosion of personal freedoms that had occurred under his more authoritarian style. By 2006, Putin had accrued far more power than Yeltsin had had and probably more than even Gorbachev had enjoyed in his final years in power. The following year, he began making public pronouncements that hinted he would remain a powerful figure in Russian politics after his second term expired on May 7, 2008. He also began taking steps to ensure this. He joined the United Russia Party; he replaced his prime minister; and he announced his support for Gazprom chairman and First Deputy Prime Minister Dmitry Medvedev as United Russia's candidate for president, who received his party's nomination on

December 17, 2007. It was understood that Putin would become prime minister if Medvedev were elected, both being foregone conclusions.

Legal Aspects of Censorship

After the collapse of the Union of Soviet Socialist Republics, the new constitution of a democratic Russia, ratified on December 12, 1993, included the following articles and clauses to ensure freedom of religion, speech, and the press:

- Article 28: Everyone shall be guaranteed the right to freedom of conscience, to freedom of religious worship, including the right to profess, individually or jointly with others, any religion, or to profess no religion, to freely choose, possess and disseminate religious or other beliefs, and to act in conformity with them.
- Article 29, Section 1 (first sentence): Everyone shall have the right to freedom of thought and speech. . . .

  Section 4: Everyone shall have the right to seek, get, transfer, produce and disseminate information by any lawful means.
- Article 29, Section 5: The freedom of the mass media shall be guaranteed. Censorship shall be prohibited.

Despite the high-toned guarantees, Russia has not been free of censorship in the years since the ratification of its constitution. The new Russia is generally not as heavy-handed as the Soviet Union was, and various social and economic forces are at work that make censorship a more complicated issue than it was previously. Some of the methods of censorship in Russia in the late 20th and early 21st centuries include government and corporate takeover of media outlets and intimidation. Various economic laws have been invoked to silence and even shut down some outlets or imprison those deemed a threat. Military whistle-blowers have been imprisoned for treason, presumably in violation of the vague second sentence of Article 29, Section 4, that states: "The list of information constituting the state secrets shall be established by the federal law." Lastly, the Russian Orthodox Church has gained quite a bit of political influence in Russia since the fall of the Soviet Union and in some cases has used its new-found power to ensure that public criticism of the church is kept in check.

Censorship in Contemporary Russia

Russian censorship in the 21st century is not nearly as all-encompassing as the Communist version was. The Writers Union no longer intimidates individuals into subscribing to a single artistic viewpoint and art, music, film, dance, and theater are also free from the burden of socialist realism. The marketplace, including an influx of foreign literature and music, has taken its toll on the indigenous arts, although the Russian film industry has been making a comeback after years of neglect.

Although censorship of the press is not as heavy-handed as it was in the Soviet Union, the government takeover of media enterprises nevertheless amounts to censorship. Contemporary press censorship in Russia more closely resembles its Communist past than it does media conglomeration in the United States. Intimidation is also a factor Russian journalists must deal with.

OLIGARCHS V. THE GOVERNMENT

Through the use of new economic laws, the government has managed to either take over independent channels or put them out of business. The seeds of this censorship in contemporary Russia were planted early in Boris Yeltsin's tenure as president when oligarchs like Vladimir Gusinsky and Boris Berezovsky made various media outlets part of their business interests. Both men played important roles in Yeltsin's 1996 reelection campaign, and both expected the favor to be returned. Prior to the election, Gusinsky had been a critic of Yeltsin, and his television station, NTV, had not only been critical of the First Chechen War but had dared to broadcast images of the war that the state-run stations would not. Like Gusinsky, Berezovsky saw Yeltsin as a far better option than his Communist opponent in the 1996 election.[102] After the election, he too invested in media and quickly ingratiated himself to Yeltsin, becoming one of his close advisers in The Family.[103] Those oligarchs who were members of The Family and others continued to do business in a high-handed way without fear of government prosecution.

After Yeltsin resigned, Vladimir Putin was not beholden to the oligarchs in the way they had expected he would be. Furthermore, Putin was eager to show the Russian political establishment that he was his own man and not merely a creation of the Yeltsin regime as most suspected.

Although he paid lip service to the ideals of a free press, Putin almost immediately set about establishing a presidency that was more authoritarian than Yeltsin's had been, and thus less open to criticism. When radio journalist Andrei Babitsky began reporting critical stories about the war in Chechnya, he was arrested and charged with spying for the rebels in January 2000.[104] The charges against him were eventually dropped. By executive order, journalists covering the war had to be accredited, and even these were accompanied by the military. Thus Russian journalists were embedded with the military three years before their American counterparts in Iraq.

With the Duma already under his control after the 1999 election, Putin reined in the provincial governors (which in itself was not a bad thing given the fact that corruption in the provinces was rampant) and set about silencing his political opponents. These included not only the leaders of various factions but, more important, those oligarchs whom he viewed as disloyal to his program. The first of these was Vladimir Gusinsky.

Gusinsky was the owner of Media-Most, a media and banking empire whose enterprises included a daily Moscow newspaper, *Sevodnya* (Today); a magazine, *Itogi*; the NTV television channel; and a radio station, Ekho Moskvy (Echo of Moscow).[105] During the December 1999 Duma and March 2000 presidential elections, he had supported Putin's opponents. Gusinsky's empire began to unravel just four days after Putin's inauguration in May 2000 when police raided the headquarters of his holding company. Gusinsky was arrested for financial impropriety the following month. Sensing their turn might be next, other oligarchs came to Gusinsky's defense, as did the Western media, which viewed Gusinsky's imprisonment as blatant censorship. Gusinsky was soon released from prison, but it turned out to be only a temporary reprieve.

Gusinsky had made a deal in which he would sell his Media-Most company to the state-run gas monopoly, Gazprom. More accurately, it was to be sold to Gazprom-Media, the company's subsidiary which already owned dozens of newspapers. After he was released from jail, Gusinsky reneged on the deal and made it public, hoping to turn the tide in his favor. But all that tactic did was buy him a few more months. In the end, Gazprom, which by April 2001 owned 46 percent of NTV, took control of the station.[106] Those journalists most critical of the government were then purged from the station, among them Evgeni Kiselyev, perhaps the best-known television journalist in Russia. Gazprom also tried, but failed, to take over Ekho Moskvy. Meanwhile Gusinsky sold his magazine and newspaper. The former, *Itogi*, was revived minus those journalists critical of Putin's policies; but the newspaper, *Sevodnya*, closed down.[107] In the end, Gusinsky went into exile in Spain.

Next in Putin's sights was Boris Berezovsky. Berezovsky had been Gusinsky's rival, but he came to his defense when the Media-Most boss was jailed. Soon after that event, Berezovsky, himself, became a critic of Putin. After Gusinsky's empire fragmented, the more independent-minded NTV journalists, led by Kiselyev, moved to TV-6, owned by Berezovsky. (Berezovsky's other media holdings included a stake in the government television channel, ORT, which he was forced to sell; the business newspaper *Kommersant*; and the daily *Nezavisimaya gazeta.*) Berezovsky's background was shady, and the prosecutor general had no trouble bringing fraud charges against him. Like Gusinsky, Berezovsky fled Russia for Western Europe, eventually obtaining political asylum in Great Britain.

As for the fate of Berezovsky's empire, an "obscure financial law" was used to shutter TV-6, the "only time this legislation was used."[108] The Russian Arbitration Court upheld the ruling that closed down the station and Kiselyev and the others were again homeless in Moscow's journalistic world—criticism of the Second Chechen War and the government diminished even more.[109] The channel itself morphed into an all-sports station.

JOURNALISM AND ORGANIZED CRIME

Russian journalists continue to have to deal with intimidation, usually from anonymous sources that most feel are tied to criminal organizations. It is impossible to assess how much self-censorship occurs in the Russian media due to intimidation, but, according to the Committee to Protect Journalists, 44 journalists in Russia have died from unnatural causes since the dissolution of the Soviet Union; 14 were killed between 2000 and 2006. These are the (confirmed) figures for those whose deaths were connected to their jobs. There have also been 19 deaths from 1992–2006 that remain unconfirmed as to whether they were job related. Among the most recent murders were those of reporter Anna Politkovskaya in October 2006 and the American editor of the Russian edition of *Forbes,* Paul Klebnikov, in 2004.[110] Both of these crimes, like the majority of the killings of journalists in Russia, remain unsolved.

OTHER FORMS OF CENSORSHIP

In the provinces, many of the governors or presidents (some of Russia's regions are autonomous republics) continue to rule like overlords of fiefdoms, paying homage to the central government but ignoring the needs of the people. In turn, they exert controls over the local media that are seldom discussed outside of their districts—unless a journalist is murdered.

Lastly, the Russian Orthodox Church has gained in stature and influence since the collapse of the Soviet Union, and it occasionally wields its power. In 2003, an exhibition titled "Caution—Religion" at the Andrei Sakharov Museum and Public Center in Moscow was vandalized by two angry churchgoers. This in itself did not constitute censorship, but it did move church officials to condemn the exhibition as blasphemy and to urge prosecutors to move against the museum curator, a colleague, and one of the exhibition's artists. Subsequently, they were indicted for inciting religious hatred; their trial lasted from June 2004 to March 2005 when the two museum curators were found guilty and fined.

A *New York Times* article quoted Duma member Alexander V. Chuyev, who was one of the lawmakers who urged criminal charges be brought against the museum workers: "The people and the authorities now understand that religion and the feelings of believers should not be touched on. They should understand that their rights end where the other person's begin."

In April 2006, President Putin signed into law a bill that gave the government stricter regulatory power over nongovernmental organizations (NGOs)—including the power to deny registration (all NGOs in Russia must be registered). While the law itself is not a direct vehicle for censorship, its wording is vague enough to be used for that purpose.

Counterstrategies to Censorship

Except for delaying tactics in the courts, there is no counterstrategy to the Russian government's takeover of a media outlet by legal means, especially when the owners of the targeted outlet have engaged in questionable financial activities. The motives both for the prosecution and defense become blurred under such circumstances, and the public ends up the biggest loser because each time the result is a further loss of independent voices.

There are, however, counterstrategies to the expanding monolithic viewpoint of the Russian news media and to the regional controls on a free press and free speech. Foremost are the independent outlets that remain. Although their collective influence may have been reduced since the Yeltsin years (the point is debatable), they still reach an important segment of the public. Anna Politkovskaya, the journalist murdered in October 2006, worked for one of these outlets, *Novaya gazeta*. Another counterstrategy has to be the solidifying of the rule of law—and not merely the laws opposing censorship, but the basic civil laws of society. Many of the murders of journalists, especially in Russia's provinces, have been attributed to criminal organizations. The murdered journalists were often working to uncover financial or governmental improprieties.

The foreign press has in the past and continuing into the present presented opposition to censorship in Russia. The uproar of the foreign press contributed to Vladimir Gusinsky's release from prison, but its influence too has declined since the Yeltsin years. Foreign organizations also have some ability to limit censorship: the Committee to Protect Journalists, Reporters Without Borders, and the International Federation of Journalists maintain focus on the worsening situation for working journalists in Russia.[111]

As with many other countries, the most important Russian counterstrategy to censorship lies with the Internet. For Russians, the Internet is the

21st-century version of samizdat—the material in cyberspace is there for everyone to read. Not only do blogs serve useful informational purposes, but there are official Web sites such as gazeta.ru and polit.ru. For whatever reason, Russia has yet to implement the type of Internet controls that China has. And it is less likely that it would be able to do so effectively. Many Russians are able to read the foreign press via the Internet, whether at home or in Internet cafes.

ZIMBABWE

The history of Zimbabwe over the last 150 years has been one of political repression for the population at the hands of a colonial government, a white minority government, and, since 1980, an autocratic African dictator. The colonial government was actually a corporate enterprise that set itself up to rule over a country it had all but enslaved. When Southern Rhodesia (as Zimbabwe was then called) gained autonomy within the British Empire, it established a 60-year oligarchy of minority white rule. Political and economic repression of Africans continued, and, from the 1950s until 1979, African political agitation increased exponentially. Draconian laws against the majority were answered with guerrilla warfare and terrorism.

Independence in 1980 did little to lessen the plight of the majority of citizens. The new president, Robert Mugabe, based his rule on the traditions of censorship and repression that had characterized the white government. In fact, for many years he retained some of the old Rhodesian laws restricting freedoms and, when those laws became obsolete, they were replaced by harsher ones.

Historical Overview

The archaeological record of the area of what is now Zimbabwe indicates Paleolithic culture dating as far back as 500,000 B.C.E. In c. 350 C.E., the area was settled by Shona farmers seeking to escape the deadly sleeping sickness carried by the tsetse fly.[112] By c. 1100, Great Zimbabwe was the center of an extensive trading empire. At its peak, Great Zimbabwe proper may have contained as many as 18,000 inhabitants who traded gold, copper, tin, ivory, cowrie shells, and cattle for such exotic items as Syrian glassware or ceramics from Persia and China.

The Great Zimbabwe civilization fell into decline after 1450. There is speculation that a decline in the gold trade may have been a factor (Spain's thriving gold trade from the New World began in the early 16th century). In the wake of Great Zimbabwe, the fractured Shona tribes created the Rozwi (or Urozwi) state. Although it had neither the influence nor the trade network of its predecessor, Rozwi remained viable until the early 19th century when it was invaded by the Ndebele, who ruled the greater portion of the area and in some cases enslaved the Shona.[113]

COLONIZATION AND AUTONOMY

While it was the Scottish explorer David Livingstone (1813–73) who, in the mid-1800s, prepared the way for European expansion into the interior of southeastern Africa, it was the founder of the South African diamond-mining cartel De Beers, Cecil Rhodes (1853–1902), who effected that expansion. Earlier Portuguese traders had confined themselves to working the coastal areas and had not had much contact inland. But after Livingstone and his father-in-law, Robert Moffat, who set up the first European mission in the area, the British sought to head off Portuguese and Boer (Dutch South African) expansion. The prime mover in the effort was Rhodes, who headed the South Africa Company and who had made a fortune with De Beers.[114]

In 1888, Rhodes sent his emissaries to negotiate mineral rights treaties with local chiefs in Matabeleland and Mashonaland. The treaties were so one-sided that later that year the entire area came under the British sphere of protection. The following year, the South Africa Company received a royal charter and was renamed the British South Africa Company (BSAC), and in 1890 the territorial capital of Salisbury (now the city of Harare) was founded. After five years of exploitation by the British during which time the overall map of south and south-central Africa was redrawn with little or no regard to indigenous claims, the Shona and Ndebele became increasingly disenchanted and dissatisfied. The latter initiated a brief insurrection in 1893 that ended when the Ndebele king, Lobengula, died under mysterious circumstances.[115] Continued abuses led to a second rebellion in 1896 that lasted nearly a year, but ended with the defeat of the Shona and the Ndebele. By then, the area was generally called Rhodesia and divided into Northern and Southern Rhodesia.

With their defeat in the rebellions of the 1890s "the Africans ceased to count politically."[116] They were moved into separate "tribal reserves" and their former lands were allotted to white settlers. British settlers and BSAC officials enjoyed carte blanche power over the Shona and Ndebele, whose only status in Rhodesian society was as laborers, primarily in the mines. With such disenfranchisement came de facto censorship.

Southern Rhodesia in fact was a "company state" until 1923, when the white settlers voted for independence as part of the British Commonwealth. The 1923 constitution, known as the Responsible Government constitution, stipulated that Southern Rhodesia not only elect its own legislature, but have its own military and civil services. Nevertheless, the government in London "retained the right to intervene" in Rhodesia's internal affairs, "particularly in matters affecting Africans," who otherwise had no recourse to protection of the law.[117] The constitution went into effect on October 1, 1923. As for Northern Rhodesia (which ultimately became the country of Zambia), the United Kingdom made it a British protectorate in April 1924.

Despite its move toward Responsible Government (as opposed to a company-supervised state), Southern Rhodesia was essentially a segregated one-party state for the first 30 years after the constitution was ratified. Even as other political parties gained power, they merely reflected different opinions within the white minority. In 1953, at the urging of the London government, Southern Rhodesia, Northern Rhodesia, and Nyasaland (Malawi) formed the Central African Federation (CAF). However the CAF disbanded in 1963 after Nyasaland and Northern Rhodesia withdrew. During its brief history, the government was in Southern Rhodesia, which realized economic benefits that the other two countries did not.

In the late 1950s and early 1960s, African nationalist parties began making headway in both Northern Rhodesia, and Nyasaland. In Southern Rhodesia, the African majority also gained a few concessions in 1957 under the United Federal Party and Prime Minister Reginald Stephen Garfield Todd (1908–2002). However, when Todd tried to increase the percentage of the African electorate, he was forced out of office and replaced as prime minister in February 1958.[118] In 1962, the United Federal Party lost the general election to the Rhodesia Front, whose main goal was to preserve white minority rule in Southern Rhodesia.[119]

When Ian Smith (also of the Rhodesia Front Party) became prime minister in 1964, Rhodesia's former CAF partners were on the verge of independence. Northern Rhodesia and Nyasaland became the independent republics of, respectively, Zambia and Malawi within the British Commonwealth. Soon after, Southern Rhodesia changed its name to Rhodesia and pushed for its own independence.[120] The London government was loathe to grant independence to Rhodesia because the white minority refused to accept majority rule. By that time, political consciousness among the Africans in Rhodesia was moving beyond its first phase. Like their brethren in the other two states of the CAF, Africans in Rhodesia had begun forming political parties in the late 1950s: The Southern Rhodesian African National Congress (SRANC) was led by Joshua Nkomo (1917–99), who in the early 1960s became head of the National Democratic Party (NDP) after the government banned the ANC. When the NDP was banned, Nkomo formed the Zimbabwe African People's Union (ZAPU). Meanwhile, Robert Mugabe (b. 1924) helped form the Zimbabwe African National Union (ZANU) in 1963. ZAPU primarily represented the Ndebele and ZANU the Shona.

THE STRUGGLE FOR INDEPENDENCE

In 1965, under Prime Minister Ian Smith (b. 1919), Rhodesia issued a Unilateral Declaration of Independence (UDI), which London immediately rejected. The UDI was received poorly not only in London but just about everywhere else in the world. Rhodesia's only allies were its neighbor to the south, the Republic of South Africa, itself run by a white minority government, and Portugal. It was condemned by the United Nations Security Council, which on December 16, 1965, imposed sanctions on Rhodesia that were broadened in May 1968. These were more extensive than the sanctions imposed on Rhodesia by Great Britain that had largely been ignored. By the early 1970s, isolation and external pressures were beginning to take their toll as the Smith government struggled with internal pressures.

With regard to domestic problems, the Smith government early in its tenure sought to end the violence of the African nationalist resistance by further repressions. Many of the leaders were arrested and placed in internal exile and the nationalist newspaper, *Daily News*, was banned. ZAPU and ZANU were declared illegal.[121] Instead of putting an end to the African nationalist sentiments and the violence, guerrilla activity increased. In 1974, ZAPU and ZANU joined forces in a Patriotic Front that began striking deeper into the heart of Rhodesia's white-owned farmland from their bases outside the country. By 1976, even Smith realized that Rhodesia's battle to retain minority rule was a lost cause.

That year Smith agreed to meet with nationalist leaders in Geneva, Switzerland, in order to hammer out a new policy of majority rule. The meeting between Smith, Nkomo, Mugabe, Bishop Abel Muzorewa (b. 1925) of the United African National Council, and a former ZANU leader, the Reverend Nadabaningi Sithole (1920–2000), ultimately failed because of the nationalists' disunity and Smith's intransigence, which may have been strengthened by the others' failure to forge a common political bond.[122] After continued prodding by the United Kingdom and the United States, Smith agreed not only to majority rule, but, among other provisions, to new elections that would serve to provide an interim government as Rhodesia moved toward independence. Joining Smith in signing this agreement in March 1978 were Bishop Muzorewa, Reverend Sithole, and Chief Jeremiah Chirau, a leader of the Zimbabwe United People's Organization (ZUPO). Later, in 1978, the government agreed to end all discrimination against Africans. Elections were held in April 1979, and the UANC won a majority after Mugabe and Nkomo boycotted the election. Bishop Muzorewa took office as prime minister on

June 1, 1979. However, effective control over the army, police, and civil service remained in the hands of Smith and the white minority.

Both ZAPU and ZANU-PF (Patriotic Front) saw the agreement as an effort to preserve the major elements of white privilege in the country, and neither Nkomo nor Mugabe was willing to end the guerrilla warfare that, by the time of Bishop Muzorewa's election, had cost the lives of more than 20,000 people. ZANU-PF, especially, was dedicated to a radical socialist revolution. A few months prior to the signing of the agreement, Mugabe publicly referred to the nationalist "internal" leaders (as opposed to the "external" leaders, Mugabe and Nkomo) as "renegade and quisling Sithole, stooge Muzorewa, and puppet Chirau."[123]

Throughout Muzorewa's brief turn as prime minister, the guerrilla war continued. In September 1979, negotiations for Rhodesian independence began at Lancaster House in London. The negotiations lasted three months and involved all parties, including Mugabe and Nkomo. The Lancaster House Agreement was signed on December 21, 1979. It brokered a cease-fire, called for general elections, a new constitution, British transitional rule (which had already begun), and a name change from Rhodesia to Zimbabwe upon independence. As a result of the agreement, the United Kingdom, the United States, and the United Nations lifted their sanctions against Rhodesia.[124]

The general elections were held in February 1980 with nine political parties contesting the 80 legislative seats. ZAPU and ZANU-PF threatened to disrupt the elections, but Nkomo backed out of his threat and, at any rate, the British had sent enough troops to ensure the smooth running of the polls. In the month prior to the elections, ZANU-PF violations of the cease-fire nearly caused the British governor to ban the party and Mugabe from the elections.[125] ZANU-PF won an outright majority with 57 of the 80 seats allowed to African delegates. ZAPU won 20 seats and UANC won 3 seats. Twenty more seats were reserved for the white minority, and these were won by the Republican Front (RF), formerly the Rhodesia Front.[126] Independence was gained on April 18, 1980, and Rhodesia formally became Zimbabwe. That same day, the United States was the first country to open an embassy in the newly independent nation. The Zimbabwean parliament met for the first time on May 13, 1980, with Mugabe as prime minister. Zimbabwe joined the United Nations on August 25, 1980.

MUGABE'S REIGN

From independence to the present, Zimbabwe has had only one leader—Robert Mugabe. In the beginning, Mugabe remained committed to his Marxist revolutionary platform, but, as the years wore on, he jettisoned

Marxism, declaring that it was no longer the program Zimbabwe needed. Soon after taking office, he issued a general amnesty to all those who had taken part in the guerrilla conflict; he also successfully completed the integration of ZANU, ZAPU, and government military forces into a unified military. Within two years, though, the violence renewed itself—not all guerrillas had surrendered their weapons. In 1982, ZAPU dissidents were accused of plotting a coup d'état. This was counteracted by a largely Shona military brigade that embarked on its own atrocities in Matabeleland, where ZAPU had its strongest support. Although the ZAPU rebels were never directly linked to Nkomo, Mugabe nevertheless reduced his rank in the government cabinet.

In the 1985 parliamentary elections, ZANU-PF gained an even bigger majority. Prior to the election, the party had embraced a policy that would push Zimbabwe to a single-party socialist state, and after the election Mugabe and Nkomo entered negotiations to further that end. Mugabe also abolished the 20 parliamentary seats reserved for whites. In 1986, the formerly all-white Republican Front renamed itself the Conservative Alliance of Zimbabwe and became a biracial political party. Ian Smith, the RF leader and parliamentary opposition leader, went into retirement.

In 1987, Mugabe and Nkomo agreed to merge ZANU-PF and ZAPU; the agreement was ratified in 1988. Mugabe became the leader of the new ZANU while Nkomo was named as one of two vice presidents. Mugabe also issued another general amnesty for all those involved in the armed clashes since he had gained power, in which an estimated 10,000 more lives were lost. In 1987, the post of prime minister was combined with the position of president, who was now chief of state, head of government, and commander in chief of the military without constitutional limits on tenure.

Trouble soon arose within the ranks of the new ZANU. Dissident Edgar Tekere formed the Zimbabwe Unity Movement (ZUM) in 1989, drawing political strength from disaffected city dwellers. Meanwhile antigovernment student protests began to intensify in 1989 and 1990.

In 1990, Mugabe accepted assistance from the World Bank to put a new, five-year economic plan into action. He also gave up on his idea of a one-party state (although not until after the idea was voted down by the ZANU Central Committee).[127] That year, ZANU-PF again won a majority in parliamentary elections, 117 of the 120 seats, and Mugabe won the presidential election over Tekere with approximately 78 percent of the vote. Tekere went into political retirement following his defeat, causing many critics to theorize that he was merely a "straw opponent" whose purpose was to make a show of democracy to the world. In 2006, Tekere came out of retirement and rejoined ZANU-PF.

During the 1990s, Mugabe embarked on a series of land seizures that ostensibly were supposed to redistribute land to the African majority at the expense of the white farmers who held most of the arable land. The reality was a land grab by Mugabe's associates. Nevertheless, this policy, among other things, helped propel Mugabe to another victory in the 1996 Zimbabwe presidential election.

In 1999, opposition politicians, labor leaders, academics, and others launched the most important challenge thus far to Mugabe and ZANU-PF's hold on the government—the Movement for Democratic Change (MDC). The following year, MDC held its first party congress and participated in the parliamentary elections where it nearly succeeded in capturing a majority of the seats, winning 57 of the 120 seats (ZANU-PF won 62 seats). Eventually, the MDC opposition became splintered into factions.

Despite domestic and foreign outcries concerning his dictatorial policies, Mugabe won reelection once again in 2002. By 2006, there was a grassroots idea being floated among Mugabe loyalists in ZANU to name him president for life. In January 2008, Mugabe announced by proclamation that national elections would take place on March 29, 2008. He also dissolved the Zimbabwean parliament, which was in recess. The announcement angered the opposition MDC, which had called for constitutional and electoral changes and the pushing back of the election by a few months. The leaders of the MDC feared that once again opposition candidates would be barred and/or harassed during their campaigns.

Legal Aspects of Censorship

The Zimbabwean constitution of 1979 underwent numerous changes in its first 25 years. Mugabe's political philosophy also developed from its initial anticolonialist socialism to despotism. While the Zimbabwean constitution does guarantee freedom of speech it limits this right in an unusual way:

> Article 20: Protection of freedom of expression
> (1) Except with his own consent or by way of parental discipline, no person shall be hindered in the enjoyment of his freedom of expression, that is to say, freedom to hold opinions and to receive and impart ideas and information without interference, and freedom from interference with his correspondence.

While subsection one upholds the family unit (as well as school and tribal authorities) with its reference to parental discipline, it is hard to imagine a legitimate situation in a democratic society where a person would consent to the hindrance of "the enjoyment of his freedom of expression." Furthermore, subsection two lays out the reasons for depriving an individual or an organization of protection of freedom of expression:

> (2) Nothing contained in or done under the authority of any law shall be held to be in contravention of subsection (1) to the extent that the law in question makes provision—
> (a) in the interests of defence, public safety, public order, the economic interests of the State, public morality or public health;
> (b) for the purpose of—
> (i) protecting the reputations, rights and freedoms of other persons or the private lives of persons concerned in legal proceedings;
> (ii) preventing the disclosure of information received in confidence;
> (iii) maintaining the authority and independence of the courts or tribunals or the Senate or the House of Assembly;
> (iv) regulating the technical administration, technical operation or general efficiency of telephony, telegraphy, posts, wireless broadcasting or television or creating or regulating any monopoly in these fields;
> (v) in the case of correspondence, preventing the unlawful dispatch therewith of other matter;
> or,
> (c) that imposes restrictions upon public officers; except so far as that provision or, as the case may be, the thing done under the authority thereof is shown not to be reasonably justifiable in a democratic society.

Thus, according to subsection two, freedom of expression can be limited or even revoked entirely for reasons of morality or to maintain public safety and order (which itself limits dissent). Nor can one criticize the "economic interests of the state." This itself is critical in a country that as of mid-2006 had an unemployment rate of approximately 80 percent. It also appears that criticism of political and legal authority can be considered unlawful, although there is no mention of criticism of the executive, President Mugabe, in the constitution. (However, the Public Order and Security Act (POSA) of 2002 made it a crime to "undermine the authority of or insult the President" (Sec. 16).)

Nowhere in the Zimbabwean constitution is there mention of the rights of the press or of writers and artists. It can be assumed then that Article 20 covers them. Regarding the media, though, various forms of mass media (except print and the Internet) seem to be included under regulations that subsection two (of Article 20) grants as "not contravening" the freedom of expression guarantee. Furthermore, subsection six states: "The provisions of subsection (1) shall not be held to confer on any person a right to exercise his freedom of expression in or on any road, street, lane, path, pavement, sidewalk, thoroughfare or similar place which exists for the free passage of persons or vehicles." This in effect prohibits public demonstrations, unless the government waives this subsection.

Article 21 deals with the citizens' freedom of assembly; this right, too, is guaranteed by the article's first subsection, only to have that freedom chipped away in the following subsections in terms that, at first glance, may read as valid exceptions but can be broadly interpreted by a government intent on stifling dissent.

> Article 21: Protection of freedom of assembly and association
> (1) Except with his own consent or by way of parental discipline, no person shall be hindered in his freedom of assembly and association, that is to say, his right to assemble freely and associate with other persons and in particular to form or belong to political parties or trade unions or other associations for the protection of his interests.
> (3) Nothing contained in or done under the authority of any law shall be held to be in contravention of subsection (1) to the extent that the law in question makes provision—
> (a) in the interests of defence, public safety, public order, public morality or public health;
> (b) for the purpose of protecting the rights or freedom of other persons;
> (c) for the registration of companies, partnerships, societies or other associations of persons, other than political parties, trade unions or employers' organisations; or
> (d) that imposes restrictions upon public officers;
> except so far as that provision or, as the case may be, the thing done under the authority thereof is shown not to be reasonably justifiable in a democratic society.
> (4) The provisions of subsection (1) shall not be held to confer on any person a right to exercise his freedom of assembly or association in or on any road, street, lane, path, pavement, side-walk, thoroughfare or similar place which exists for the free passage of persons or vehicles.

In 2002, prior to and after the presidential election, the government of Zimbabwe passed two highly controversial laws that restricted the freedoms of speech and association. These laws were the Public Order and Security Act (POSA) and the Access to Information and Protection of Privacy Act (AIPPA).

Censorship in Contemporary Zimbabwe

Since independence from Great Britain, Zimbabwe has come to resemble more the Stalin-era Soviet Union than the multiparty democracy it professes to be. Under the rule of Robert Mugabe, Zimbabwe has been marred by factional violence, ruinous economic policies, and a burdening censorship that has crippled dissent within the country. Zimbabwe's censorship begins and ends with the Mugabe government, but it also stems from a loose interpretation of the country's constitution by Mugabe loyalists. Thus, other laws have been promulgated that strengthen the government's hold over the media and curtail the freedoms of the constitution.

Following Mugabe's reelection in 2002, the Access to Information and Protection of Privacy Act (AIPPA) became law. Among the act's original provisions were requiring registration of media companies (the high registration fee can be prohibitive to some companies), tightening of accreditation rules for journalists, and criminalizing of the publishing of falsehoods whether or not publication is intentional. The term falsehood is vague enough to be "open to interpretation abuse."[128] The penalty for such publication is a fine and/or a prison sentence.

In 2003, the Zimbabwe Supreme Court overturned that section of AIPPA (Section 80) that dealt with the publication of falsehoods. Stemming from a case in which a story was published that was later found to be untrue and was retracted by the journalists with an apology, the Supreme Court's decision was that Section 80 violated Article 20 of the Zimbabwe constitution.[129]

The other law affecting freedom of speech passed in 2002 prior to AIPPA was the Public Order and Security Act (POSA), a set of sedition laws. It replaced the Law and Order Maintenance Act of 1960. Provisions in Part II of the law make it a crime to "cause disaffection among Police Force or Defence Force" (Sec. 12), "publish or communicate false statements prejudicial to the State" (Sec. 15), or "undermine the authority of or insult the President" (Sec. 16). Parts III and IV of the law deal with Offences Against Public Order and Offences Against Public Gatherings, respectively.[130]

These laws have been used to disrupt political meetings and arrest scores of politicians, journalists, and citizens protesting the government. That number included more than 150 members of the organization Women of Zimbabwe Arise (WOZA), who were arrested in November 2006 for holding an antigovernment demonstration.[131] Just a few weeks later, on December 1, 2006, four street actors in Bulawayo, Zimbabwe's second largest city, were beaten by police and arrested for satirizing the country's economy with a play titled *Indlala* (Hunger). They were arrested under the POSA law for criticizing Mugabe, but the actors were also accused of being MDC agents looking to incite a revolt.[132]

POSA and AIPPA are not the only restrictive laws that contravene the spirit of Zimbabwe's constitution. The 2001 Broadcasting Services Act limits the point of view broadcast on television and radio. While it allows for one independent television and radio broadcaster, the reality is that at the end of 2006 there were no independent stations in either medium.[133] The Censorship and Entertainments Control Act provides for a board of censors to control content of films and books, though its concerns are less of a political nature than a moralistic one.[134]

In 2006, the government introduced two draft laws to further stifle freedom of speech. The Suppression of Foreign and International Terrorism Act enables the government to define which group is terrorist, thus putting the political opposition to ZANU-PF further at risk. The Interception of Communications Act would allow the government to legally monitor e-mail and other forms of electronic communication, further curbing free speech and stifling political opposition.[135]

Counterstrategies to Censorship

Zimbabweans and others employ extensive methods to counter the various censorship tactics of the Mugabe government, among them open demonstration, though the demonstrators risk arrest and beatings. Occasional court challenges to the more repressive provisions of such laws as AIPPA and POSA have proven fruitful in a limited context. Radio broadcasts from South Africa and Voice of America have managed to crack the barrier set up by the Broadcasting Services Act, although both of these stations' broadcasts have been jammed.

Like others whose countries are under the shadow of heavy censorship (and even those whose countries are not), the Internet has become the main counterstrategy to censorship in Zimbabwe. Three important Web sites are ZimOnline.com, New Zimbabwe.com, and ZimDaily.com, the Web site of Zimbabwe's best-known newspaper and therefore the most vulnerable. These Web sites publish economic and political news articles that would otherwise be censored. The drawback is that they are not generally read by the average citizen, too poor to own a computer. Nevertheless, the facts of daily life in Harare, Bulawayo, and elsewhere in Zimbabwe are made known to the world. The Web sites allow expatriate Zimbabweans in South Africa, Western Europe, the United States, and elsewhere to keep abreast of what is happening in their country and at the same time to plan strategy. Zim Net radio on the Internet enables listeners to bypass government-sponsored broadcast stations or even those outside Zimbabwe subject to jamming.

International organizations such as the Committee to Protect Journalists, Reporters Without Borders, Amnesty International, PEN International, and the International Crisis Group regularly monitor Zimbabwe's political scene, noting censorship and other rights infringements. These groups regularly urge the governments of developed countries to pressure the Mugabe government to uphold the Zimbabwean constitution.

In September 2006, ZimOnline published the comprehensive "Zimbabwe: An Opposition Strategy" by the International Crisis Group that detailed recommendations and strategies for public demonstrations, internal dissent within the ruling party, strikes, public discourse, and sanctions from foreign governments. It also examined the factionalism with the main opposition group, MDC, and the effect of sanctions.

In 2007, Robert Mugabe was 83 years old, and moves that year to extend his term and make him president for life suggest that when he passes from the scene a power vacuum will occur in Zimbabwe. If so, the short-range outlook for the lifting of censorship in that country is not good. In a worst-case scenario, the power vacuum will be filled by another strongman with no inclination to brook criticism or dissent. In the best case, freedom of speech in all its manifestations may follow a pattern similar to the one set by post-Soviet Russia.

---

[1] Translates as Master Kong.

[2] At this time, the Great Wall was actually four separate walls.

[3] It was also a way of rewriting history. Books from the other schools of philosophy that were in the royal Qin library were spared.

[4] Peter K. Yu. "The Sweet and Sour Story of Chinese Intellectual Property Rights." Available online. URL: http://72.14.209.104/search?q=cache:_wBxxCL3jbsJ:www.peteryu.com/sweetsour.pdf+%22Tang+Code%22+censorship&hl=en&gl=us&ct=clnk&cd=6. Downloaded September 14, 2006. The quote is actually from William Alford, *To Steal a Book Is an Elegant Offense.*

[5] China wasn't completely reunified under the Song. The Liao, Western Xia, and Jin managed to retain territory throughout most of the Song dynasty.

[6] Peter K. Yu. "The Sweet and Sour Story of Chinese Intellectual Property Rights." Available online. URL: http://72.14.209.104/search?q=cache:_wBxxCL3jbsJ:www.peteryu.com/sweetsour.pdf+%22Tang+Code%22+censorship&hl=en&gl=us&ct=clnk&cd=6. Downloaded September 14, 2006.

[7] Tanya Storch. "The Past Explains the Present: Law and Religious Freedom in Medieval China." American Oriental Society, Abstracts from the Two Hundred Thirteenth Meeting, Nashville, Tenn. Available online. URL: http://72.14.209.104/search?q=cache:fpKsJfbckoUJ:

www.umich.edu/~aos/2003/aosabstracts2003.pdf+%22Code+of+the+Song+dynasty%22&hl=en&gl=us&ct=clnk&cd=1. Downloaded September 14, 2006.

[8] Comparable to the federal crime in the United States about joking about bombs at airports or on passenger jets.

[9] Hong Kong was returned to China in 1997.

[10] Although the emperor did not abdicate the throne, power was in the hands of the empress dowager.

[11] From a previous name, Yihequan—Fists of Righteous Harmony.

[12] There are many published accounts and descriptions of the Long March. For a concise description, see Jonathan D. Spence. *The Search for Modern China*. New York, London: W. W. Norton and Company, 1990.

[13] Jonathan D. Spence. *The Search for Modern China*. New York, London: W. W. Norton and Company, 1990, p. 485.

[14] Quoted in Spence, p. 514.

[15] This thinking was akin to V. I. Lenin's formulation in the early 20th century that Bolshevism not unionization was the true workers' movement, as the latter would merely result in the continuance of capitalism.

[16] Spence, p. 572.

[17] Jonathon Green and Nicholas Karolides (reviser). *Encyclopedia of Censorship*, New Edition. New York: Facts On File, 2005, pp. 103–106.

[18] The Mao cult received a boost when Nikita Khrushchev was ousted as Soviet premier and replaced by neo-Stalinists. See also Spence, p. 605, for a further description of this demonstration.

[19] The Cultural Revolution Decade, 1966–76, "End of the Era of Mao Zedong, 1972–76." Available online. URL: http://www-chaos.umd.edu/history/prc3.html. Downloaded October 10, 2006.

[20] Spence, p. 739.

[21] China-Profile, Timeline: Details 1990–2006. Available online. URL: http://www.china-profile.com/history/indepth/id_121.htm. Downloaded October 5, 2006.

[22] Green and Karolides, p. 107. See also "Information on the Situation in China." Falun Dafa. Available online. URL: http://www.falundafa.org/eng/faq.htm. Downloaded October 1, 2006.

[23] *People's Daily*. "Jiang Zemin." *People's Daily* Online. Available online. URL: http://english.people.com.cn/data/people/jiangzemin.shtml. Downloaded October 1, 2006.

[24] Green and Karolides, p. 102.

[25] Steven Mufson. "Chinese Impose Strict Controls Over Financial News Agencies." *Washington Post*, January 17, 1996, p. 2.

[26] Elaine Kurtenbach. "China Tightens Controls on Foreign News." September 10, 2006. Boston.com. Available online. URL: http://www.boston.com/news/world/asia/articles/2006/09/10/china_tightens_controls_on_foreign_news/. Downloaded September 30, 2006.

[27] Kurtenbach.

[28] Green and Karolides, p. 104.

[29] Green and Karolides, p. 106.

[30] CBS News. "China's Internet Censorship." December 3, 2002. CBSNEWS.com. Available online. URL: http://www.cbsnews.com/stories/2002/12/03/tech/main531567.shtml. Downloaded October 2, 2006.

[31] Amnesty International. "List of People Detained for Internet-related Offences in China." November 2002. Available online. URL: http://web.amnesty.org/web/content.nsf/pages/gbrimages7/$FILE/China_internet_list.pdf. Downloaded October 2, 2006.

[32] Amnesty International. In some instances it is unclear if Amnesty International is paraphrasing the accusation.

[33] Rebecca MacKinnon. "Yahoo! Helped Jail Another Chinese Cyberdissident." February 8, 2006. RConversation. Available online. URL: http://rconversation.blogs.com/rconversation/2006/02/yahoo_helped_ja.html. Downloaded October 2, 2006.

[34] Joseph Kahn. "China Tightens Its Restrictions for News Media on the Internet." *New York Times*, September 26, 2005, p. 9.

[35] Dave Belt. "Chinese Government Cracks Down on Internet Free Speech." Newshour Extra. Available online. URL: http://www.pbs.org/newshour/extra/features/july-dec05/china_10-19.pdf. Downloaded October 3, 2006.

[36] Andrew McLaughlin. "Google in China." January 27, 2006. Google Blog. Available online. URL: http://googleblog.blogspot.com/2006/01/google-in-china.html. Downloaded October 10, 2006.

[37] Time Line of Ancient Egypt in "Egypt: Secrets of an Ancient World." NationalGeographic.com URL: http://www.nationalgeographic.com/pyramids/timeline.html. Downloaded October 31, 2006. The dates, of course, are approximations; other scholars place the Early Period later.

[38] The initial political difference grew into a theological schism.

[39] The Bahri Mamluks were named for their barracks, while the Burgi Mamluks were named for the Citadel tower from which they ruled. Since most originally came from the Caucasus, they are also called the Circassian Mamluks. Circassians are people from the northwest Caucasus.

[40] CNN Cold War. "Gamal Abdel Nasser." Available online. URL: http://www.cnn.com/SPECIALS/cold.war/kbank/profiles/nasser/. Downloaded October 28, 2006.

[41] Sadat and Israeli prime minister Menachem Begin shared the 1978 Nobel Peace Prize.

[42] Green and Karolides, p. 162.

[43] Green and Karolides, p. 162.

[44] Green and Karolides, p. 164.

[45] Green and Karolides, p. 164.

[46] Green and Karolides, p. 164.

[47] Green and Karolides, p. 163.

[48] Brian Whitaker. "Egyptian Censors Block Magazine." *The Guardian* (London), August 12, 2005, p. 13.

[49] Gabrielle Menezes. "Cairo Sheikhs Find Book Bans Tougher." *Christian Science Monitor*, December 10, 2003, p. 16.

[50] Paul Schemm. "Book Banning in Egypt Targets a Muslim Moderate." *Christian Science Monitor*, September 22, 2004, p. 11. See also Green and Karolides, p. 163.

[51] David Hardaker. "Egypt's Nobel Winner Asks Islamists to Approve Book." *The Independent* (London), January 28, 2006, p. 34. See also an interview with Mahfouz by Mohamed Salmawy published in *Al-Ahram Weekly On-line*. Available online. URL: http://weekly.ahram.org.eg/2006/779/op6.htm.

[52] "Academics Apply Self-Censorship." *The Independent* (London), June 9, 2005, p. 33.

[53] "Carrey's *Bruce Almighty* banned in Egypt." *The Globe and Mail* (Canada), November 10, 2003, p. R5; "Matrix Refused." *Herald Sun* (Melbourne), June 12, 2003, p. 31.

[54] Jack Epstein. "Fundamentalism Fears: Egyptian Artists Worry about Growing Islamic Fervor in a Nation Long Known for Being a Cultural and Secular Center in the Arab World." *San Francisco Chronicle*, July 15, 2006, p. E1.

[55] Jacqueline Tuinstra. "V-Day Comes to Cairo—Very Carefully." *The Globe and Mail* (Canada), February 19, 2004, p. R1.

[56] The Ministry of Information is also responsible for "reviewing and censoring foreign publications" through its Print and Press Office. See Green and Karolides, p. 164.

[57] Guy Saville. "Egypt Draws Veil Over Top Pop Star; Egypt's Favourite Pop Star Banned." *The Independent* (London), January 14, 2002, p. 11.

[58] Philip Smucker. "Anti-War Song Tops the Arab Hit Parade." *The Daily Telegraph* (London), March 12, 2003, p. 15.

[59] FREEMUSE: Freedom of Musical Expression. "Egypt: State Censorship Committee Bans Music Videos." Available online. URL: http://www.freemuse.org/sw9979.asp. Downloaded November 2, 2006.

[60] John R. Bradley. "Tuning in to the Bloggers' Wavelength." The *Straits Times* (Singapore), September 6, 2005. See also Charles Levinson. "Egypt's Growing Blogger Community Pushes Limit of Dissent." *Christian Science Monitor*, August 24, 2005, p. 7.

[61] Emily Wax. "Literary Agents of Change: A New Generation Finds Power in Prose, Poetry." *Washington Post*, May 14, 2003, p. C1.

[62] Opposition to the regime of Hosni Mubarak doesn't always translate into anticensorship activity.

[63] "Ancient Russia." History and Culture of Russia. Available online. URL: http://www.geographia.com/russia/rushis02.htm. Downloaded October 27, 2006.

[64] The Cyrillic alphabet is named for its inventor, Saint Cyril (827–869), who, along with his brother Saint Methodius (826–885), translated the Gospels and other Christian liturgical books into Slavonic.

[65] "The Mongols and the Emergence of Moscow." History and Culture of Russia. Available online. URL: http://www.geographia.com/russia/rushis03.htm. Downloaded October 27,

2006. See also "The Rise of Muscovy." Available online. URL: http://www.russiansabroad.com/russian_history_23.html. Downloaded October 28, 2006.

[66] The word "czar," like the German emperor's title, "kaiser," is derived from "caesar."

[67] "The Mongols and the Emergence of Moscow." History and Culture of Russia. Available online. URL: http://www.geographia.com/russia/rushis03.htm. Downloaded October 27, 2006. See also "The Rise of Muscovy." Available online. URL: http://www.russiansabroad.com/russian_history_23.html. Downloaded October 28, 2006.

[68] Some place the beginning of the Time of Troubles in 1598. See "Ivan IV." RussiansAbroad.com. Available online. URL: http://www.russiansabroad.com/russian_history_25.html. Downloaded October 28, 2006.

[69] "Peter the Great and the Russian Empire." RussiansAbroad.com. Available online. URL: http://www.russiansabroad.com/russian_history_30.html. Downloaded October 28, 2006. See also "The Romanovs." History and Culture of Russia. Available online. URL: http://www.geographia.com/russia/rushis04.htm. Downloaded October 27, 2006.

[70] Catherine left nothing to chance. Peter III died a week after his abdication.

[71] "Imperial Expansion and Maturation: Catherine II." RussiansAbroad.com. Available online. URL: http://www.russiansabroad.com/russian_history_32.html. Downloaded October 28, 2006. "The Romanovs." History and Culture of Russia. Avaliable online. URL: http://www.geographia.com/russia/rushis04.htm. Downloaded October 27, 2006.

[72] Emel'yan Pugachev was a Don Cossack who led a brief rebellion against Catherine in southern Russia in 1773–1774.

[73] "Alexander Radishchev, Journey from Saint Petersburg to Moscow. 1790." Documents in Russian History. Seton Hall University. Available online. URL: http://artsci.shu.edu/reesp/documents/radishchev.htm. Downloaded October 30, 2006.

[74] "War and Peace, 1796–1825." RussiansAbroad.com. Available online. URL: http://www.russiansabroad.com/russian_history_34.html. Downloaded October 28, 2006.

[75] "War and Peace."

[76] "Reaction under Nicholas I." RussiansAbroad.com. Available online. URL: http://www.russiansabroad.com/russian_history_35.html. Downloaded October 28, 2006.

[77] Alexander Nikitenko. *Diary of a Russian Censor,* tr. by Helen Saltz Jacobson. Amherst, Mass.: The University of Massachusetts Press, 1975, pp. xix, 48, 376. The English translation is an edited and abridged version of Nikitenko's complete diaries.

[78] Nikitenko, p. 128.

[79] This was more than a year prior to President Lincoln's issuing the Emancipation Proclamation freeing the slaves in the United States.

[80] "Reforms and Their Limits, 1855–1892." RussiansAbroad.com. Available online. URL: http://www.russiansabroad.com/russian_history_38.html. Downloaded October 28, 2006.

[81] In 1887, there was a failed assassination attempt against Alexander III by Alexander Ul'yanov, the older brother of V. I. Lenin, the future leader of the Bolsheviks and first leader of the Soviet Union.

[82] "Witte and Accelerated Industrialization." Russians Abraod.com. Available online. URL: http://www.russiansabroad.com/russian_history_41.html. Downloaded October 28, 2006.

[83] This is considered the first Russian revolution.

[84] "Revolution and Counterrevolution, 1905–07." RussiansAbroad.com. Available online. URL: http://www.russiansabroad.com/russian_history_45.html. Downloaded October 28, 2006.

[85] One result of wartime anti-German feeling was that the name of the city of Saint Petersburg was changed to the more Russian Petrograd.

[86] Prior to the Bolshevik Revolution, Russia was on the Julian calendar, which was 13 days behind the Georgian calendar used by the rest of the world. Dates for this period are often given as Old Style (Julian calendar) and New Style (Georgian calendar). The Communists reformed the calendar, but the name October Revolution remained although the anniversary was celebrated on November 7. Also, Nicholas II abdicated March 2, New Style.

[87] The USSR consisted of: Russia, Ukraine, Belarus, Georgia, Armenia, Azerbaijan, Kazhakstan, Uzbekistan, Moldova, Turkmenistan, Tadzhikistan, Kirgizstan, Lithuania, Latvia, and Estonia. The last three were annexed in 1940.

[88] Founded in 1917, it was originally known as the All-Russian Extraordinary Committee for Combating Counter-Revolution and Sabotage. Cheka is an abbreviation of the first letters of the Russian words for Extraordinary Committee—*chrezvychainaia komissiia.*

[89] "Soviet Predecessor [Intelligence] Organizations, 1917–54." FAS Intelligence Resource Program. Available online. URL: http://www.fas.org/irp/world/russia/intro/su0510.htm. Downloaded October 29, 2006.

[90] These were their revolutionary names. Their real names were, respectively, Lev Bronstein and Josef Dzhugashvili.

[91] Trotsky was murdered in Mexico City in 1940.

[92] Certain Western classics of literature and music already had a high reputation in the Soviet Union, and the Hermitage contained one of the world's great art collections.

[93] David King. *The Commissar Vanishes.* New York: Metropolitan Books, 1997.

[94] Green and Karolides, pp. 151–153.

[95] Green and Karolides, p. 513.

[96] Sinyavsky was the better known of the two. He wrote under the pen name Abram Tertz. Daniel wrote under the name Nikolai Arzhak.

[97] Green and Karolides, pp. 491–492.

[98] "Music." RussiansAbroad.com. Available online. URL: http://www.russiansabroad.com/russian_history_146.html. Downloaded October 29, 2006.

[99] For an interesting analysis and speculation of how the relatively unknown Putin came to be appointed prime minister, see Lilia Shevtsova. *Putin's Russia.* Washington, D.C.: Carnegie Endowment for International Peace, 2003, pp. 7–68.

[100] In Russian, the initials FSB mean *Federalnaya Sluzhba Bezopasnosti* or Federal Security Service. KGB means *Komitet Gosudarstvennoy Bezopasnosti*—Committee for State Security.

[101] The Second Chechen War was begun in 1999 while Putin was prime minister.

[102] The Communists held the most seats in the Duma at that time and were seen as a viable alternative to Yeltsin.

[103] The closest figure to Yeltsin at this time was his daughter, Tatiana Dyachneko.

[104] Lilia Shevtsova. *Putin's Russia*. Washington, D.C.: Carnegie Endowment for International Peace, 2003, pp. 83–84. See also Robert Coalson. "Babitsky's 'Crime' and Punishment." CPJ Special Reports from around the World. Available online. URL: http://www.cpj.org/Briefings/2000/Babitsky/main.html. Downloaded October 30, 2006.

[105] Gusinsky's bank was called Most Bank. *Most* means "bridge" in Russian.

[106] In the 1990s, Gazprom had guaranteed Gusinsky's loans from the state and Western banks.

[107] Shevtsova, pp. 106–108, 176–177.

[108] Author interview with Evgeni Kiselyev, Hartford, Conn., November 8, 2006.

[109] Kiselyev subsequently served a stint as editor of *Moskovskie Novosti.*

[110] "Journalists Killed: Statistics and Archives." Committee to Protect Journalists. Available online. URL: http://www.cpj.org/killed/killed_archives/stats.html. Downloaded November 10, 2006.

[111] According to CPJ, Russia stands third behind Iraq and Algeria as the country with the most journalist deaths from 1992–2006. See "Journalists Killed: Statistics and Archives." Committee to Protect Journalists. Available online. URL: http://www.cpj.org/killed/killed_archives/stats.html. Downloaded November 10, 2006.

[112] Manu Ampin. "Great Zimbabwe: A History Almost Forgotten." Available online. URL: http://www.manuampim.com/ZIMBABWE.html. Downloaded October 12, 2006.

[113] "The History of Zimbabwe." Bulawayo1872.Com. Available online. URL: http://www.bulawayo1872.com/history/zimhistory.htm. Downloaded October 12, 2006. The Ndebele had broken away from Zulu domination.

[114] "Zimbabwe." Encyclopedia of the Nations. Available online. URL: http://www.nationsencyclopedia.com/Africa/Zimbabwe-HISTORY.html. Downloaded October 11, 2006.

[115] It was never established how Lobengula died. See Robert Blake. *A History of Rhodesia*. New York: Alfred A. Knopf, 1978, p. 111.

[116] Blake, p. 155.

[117] "History of Zimbabwe." Available online. URL: http://www.historyofnations.net/africa/zimbabwe.html. Downloaded October 11, 2006.

[118] He was replaced by Edgar Whitehead, also a member of the United Federal Party.

[119] A very small minority of the African population was allowed to vote in an electoral system that divided voting lists into "A" and "B" rolls.

[120] The name change was unilateral—Great Britain continued to refer to it as Southern Rhodesia.

[121] Blake, p. 363.

[122] "History of Zimbabwe." Available online. URL: http://www.historyofnations.net/africa/zimbabwe.html. Downloaded October 11, 2006.

[123] M. Tamarkin. *The Making of Zimbabwe: Decolonization in Regional and International Politics.* London: Frank Cass & Co. Ltd., 1990, p. 220. The quote is actually from the *Zimbabwe News,* January 1, 1978, p. 55.

[124] "History of Zimbabwe." Available online. URL: http://www.historyofnations.net/africa/zimbabwe.html. Downloaded October 11, 2006.

[125] Stephan Chan. *Robert Mugabe: A Life of Power and Violence.* Ann Arbor, Mich.: University of Michigan Press, 2003, p. 16.

[126] "Europeans Chronology." Available online. URL: http://www.cidcm.umd.edu/inscr/mar/data/zimeurchro.htm. Downloaded November 18, 2006. ZANU thus held 57 of the total 100 seats.

[127] In reality, Zimbabwe was a one-party state since ZANU-PF won huge majorities in the parliamentary elections. Mugabe's goal was to make the one-party state a part of the legal structure.

[128] Green and Karolides, p. 668.

[129] "Zimbabwe: Supreme Court Strikes down Repressive Media Legislation." Committee to Protect Journalists. May 7, 2003. Available online. URL: http://www.cpj.org/news/2003/Zim07may03na.html. Downloaded November 2, 2006.

[130] "Public Order and Security Act (POSA), Sokwanele Comment: 20 August 2004." Sokwanele Civic Action Support Group. Available online. URL: http://www.sokwanele.com/articles/sokwanele/POSA_20aug2004.html. Downloaded November 2, 2006. See also Green and Karolides, pp. 668–669.

[131] Savious Kwinika. "Over 150 Women Charged under Draconian Law of POSA in Zimbabwe." African News Dimension, November 7, 2006. Available online. URL: http://www.andnetwork.com/index?service=direct/0/Feed/story&sp=l55498. Downloaded November 11, 2006.

[132] "Street Actors Beaten Up for Satirising Crisis." ZimOnline. URL: http://www.zimonline.co.za/Article.aspx?ArticleId=553. Downloaded December 1, 2006.

[133] Green and Karolides, p. 669. See also "Zimbabwe: An Opposition Strategy." International Crisis Group. ZimOnline, September 14, 2006. Available online. URL: http://www.zimonline.co.za/Article.aspx?ArticleId=96. Downloaded December 1, 2006.

[134] Green and Karolides, p. 669.

[135] "Zimbabwe: An Opposition Strategy." International Crisis Group. ZimOnline, September 14, 2006. Available online. URL: http://www.zimonline.co.za/Article.aspx?ArticleId=96. Downloaded December 1, 2006.

PART II

Primary Sources

4

United States Documents

The following primary sources are presented chronologically from the colonial period to the 21st century. The documents themselves are court transcripts, laws (some of which were subsequently repealed), presidential decrees, and opinions of various Supreme Court justices. Taken together, they present the evolution of thought in all three branches of the federal government regarding censorship.

The Zenger Affair

The best-known incident of colonial censorship was the trial of publisher John Peter Zenger, a German immigrant who was publisher of the New York Weekly Journal. *Zenger was imprisoned for nine months in 1734–35 for the crime of publishing "seditious libel"—an anonymously written article that criticized Governor William Cosby. Zenger's jury acquittal set the precedent for press freedoms in the United States (and elsewhere) that continues to this day.*

Below are some of the documents related to the Zenger case. These include: the order to burn certain issues of the New York Weekly Journal, *Zenger's arrest warrant, and excerpts of Zenger's own account of the trial, published in 1736. In the trial account, Zenger's attorney, Andrew Hamilton, makes the case for truth as a defense against libel.*

Order for the Public Burning of Zenger's Journals Order of Governor William Cosby (October 22, 1734)

Whereas by an order of this Council some of John Peter Zenger's journals, entitled *The New York Weekly Journal*, Nos. 7, 47, 48, 49, were ordered to be burned by the hands of the common hangman or whipper near the pillory in this city on Wednesday the 6th between the hours of 11 and 12 in the forenoon, as containing in them many things tending to sedition and faction, to bring His Majesty's government into contempt, and to disturb the peace thereof, and containing in them likewise not only reflections upon His Excellency the Governor in particular, and the legislature in general, but also upon the most considerable persons in the most distinguished stations in this Province;

It is therefore ordered that the mayor and magistrates (aldermen sitting in their judicial capacities as Justices of the Peace) of this city do attend at the burning of the several papers or journals aforesaid, numbered as above mentioned.

Bench Warrant for Arrest of John Peter Zenger (November 2, 1734)

At a Council held at Fort George in New York, November 2, 1734. Present: His Excellency William Cosby, Captain General and Governor in Chief, Mr. Clarke, Mr. Harison, Mr. Livingston, Mr. Kennedy, the Chief Justice [DeLancey], Mr. Cortland, Mr. Lane, Mr. Horsmanden.

It is ordered that the sheriff for the City of New York do forthwith take and apprehend John Peter Zenger for printing and publishing several seditious libels dispersed throughout his journals or newspapers, entitled *The New York Weekly Journal*; as having in them many things tending to raise factions and tumults among the people of this Province, inflaming their minds with contempt of His Majesty's government, and greatly disturbing the peace thereof. And upon his taking the said John Peter Zenger, to commit him to the prison or common jail of the said city and county.

John Peter Zenger, "A Brief Narrative of the Case and Trial of John Peter Zenger" (1736) (excerpt)

Before James DeLancey, Chief Justice of the Province of New York, and Frederick Philipse, Associate Justice, my trial began on August 4, 1735, upon an information for printing and publishing two newspapers which were called libels against our Governor and his administration. . . .

Case for the Prosecution

MR. ATTORNEY. May it please Your Honors and you, Gentlemen of the Jury. The information now before the Court, and to which the defendant, Zenger, has pleaded 'Not guilty,' is an information for printing and publishing a false, scandalous, and seditious libel in which His Excellency, the Governor of this Province, who is the king's immediate representative here, is greatly and unjustly scandalized as a person that has no regard to law or justice; with much more, as will appear upon reading the information. . . .

These words are to the great disturbance of the peace of the said Province of New York, to the great scandal of the king, of His Excellency the Governor, and of all others concerned in the administration of the government of the Province, and against the peace of the king, his crown, and his dignity.

Whereupon the said Attorney General of the king prays the advisement of the Court here, in the premises, and the due process of law against the said John Peter Zenger. To this information the defendant has pleaded not guilty, but we are ready to prove [Zenger's guilt].

MR. HAMILTON. . . . I shall save Mr. Attorney the trouble of examining his witnesses to that point. I do (for my client) confess that he both printed and published the . . . newspapers set forth in the information—and I hope that in so doing he has committed no crime. . . .

MR. CHIEF JUSTICE. Well, Mr. Attorney, will you proceed?

MR. ATTORNEY. Indeed, Sir, as Mr. Hamilton has confessed the printing and publishing of these libels, I think the jury must find a verdict for the king. For supposing they were true, the law says that they are not the less libelous for that. Nay, indeed the law says their being true is an aggravation of the crime.

MR. HAMILTON. Not so neither, Mr. Attorney. There are two words to that bargain. I hope it is not our bare printing and publishing a paper that will make it a libel. You will have something more to do before you make my client a libeler. For the words themselves must be libelous that is, false, scandalous, and seditious or else we are not guilty.

Case for the Defense

MR. HAMILTON. May it please Your Honor, I agree with Mr. Attorney that government is a sacred thing, but I differ widely from him when he would insinuate that the just complaints of a number of men who suffer under a bad administration is libeling that administration. Had I believed that to be law, I should not have given the Court the trouble of hearing anything that I could say in this cause. . . .

Is it not surprising to see a subject, upon receiving a commission from the king to be a governor of a Colony in America, immediately imagining himself to be vested with all the prerogatives belonging to the sacred person of his princes? . . . Is it so hard a matter to distinguish between the majesty of our sovereign and the power of a governor of The Plantations? Is not this making very free with our prince, to apply that regard, obedience, and allegiance to a subject, which is due only to our sovereign?

And yet in all the cases which Mr. Attorney has cited to show the duty and obedience we owe to the supreme magistrate, it is the king that is there meant and understood, although Mr. Attorney is pleased to urge them as authorities to prove the heinousness of Mr. Zenger's offense against the Governor of New York. . . .

MR. ATTORNEY. . . . The case before the Court is whether Mr. Zenger is guilty of libeling His Excellency the Governor of New York, and indeed the whole administration of the government. Mr. Hamilton has confessed the printing and publishing, and I think nothing is plainer than that the words in the information are "scandalous, and tend to sedition, and to disquiet the minds of the people of this Province." If such papers are not libels, I think it may be said that there can be no such thing as a libel.

MR. HAMILTON. May it please Your Honor, I cannot agree with Mr. Attorney. For although I freely acknowledge that there are such things as libels, yet I must insist at the same time that what my client is charged with is not a libel. And I observed just now that Mr. Attorney, in defining a libel, made use of the words "scandalous, seditious, and tend to disquiet the people." But, whether with design or not I will not say, he omitted the word "false."

MR. ATTORNEY. I think that I did not omit the word "false." But it has been said already that it may be a libel notwithstanding that it may be true.

MR. HAMILTON. In this I must still differ with Mr. Attorney. For I depend upon it that we are to be tried upon this information now before the Court and the jury, and to which we have pleaded "Not guilty." By it we are charged with printing and publishing "a certain false, malicious, seditious, and scandalous libel." This word "false" must have some meaning, or else how came it there? . . .

MR. CHIEF JUSTICE. You cannot be admitted, Mr. Hamilton, to give the truth of a libel in evidence. A libel is not to be justified; for it is nevertheless a libel that it is true.

MR. HAMILTON. I am sorry the Court has so soon resolved upon that piece of law. I expected first to have been heard to that point. I have not, in all my reading, met with an authority that says we cannot be admitted to give the truth in evidence upon an information for libel.

MR. CHIEF JUSTICE. The law is clear that you cannot justify a libel.

MR. HAMILTON. I own that, may it please Your Honor, to be so. But, with submission, I understand the word "justify" there to be a justification by plea, as it is in the case upon an indictment for murder or an assault and battery.

MR. CHIEF JUSTICE. I pray, show that you can give the truth of a libel in evidence.

MR. HAMILTON. How shall it be known whether the words are libelous, that is, true or false, but by admitting us to prove them true, since Mr. Attorney will not undertake to prove them false? Besides, is it not against common sense that a man should be punished in the same degree for a true libel, if any such thing could be, as for a false one? . . .

MR. CHIEF JUSTICE. Mr. Attorney, you have heard what Mr. Hamilton has said, and the cases he has cited, for having his witnesses examined to prove the truth of the several facts contained in the papers set forth in the information. What do you say to it?

MR. ATTORNEY. The law, in my opinion, is very clear. They cannot be admitted to justify a libel, for . . . it is not the less a libel because it is true. I think I need not trouble the Court over again. The thing seems to be very plain, and I submit it to the Court.

MR. CHIEF JUSTICE. Mr. Hamilton, the Court is of the opinion that you ought not to be permitted to prove the facts in the papers. . . .

MR. HAMILTON. . . . Then, Gentlemen of the Jury, it is to you that we must now appeal for witnesses to the truth of the facts we have offered, and are denied the liberty to prove. Let it not seem strange that I apply myself to you in this manner. I am warranted by both law and reason. . . .

But of this I can have no apprehension. You are citizens of New York. You are really what the law supposes you to be, honest and lawful men; and according to my brief, the facts which we offer to prove were not committed in a corner. They are notoriously known to be true. Therefore in your justice lies our safety. And as we are denied the liberty of giving evidence to prove the truth of what we have published, I will beg leave to lay it down as a standing rule in such cases that the suppressing of evidence ought always to be taken for the strongest evidence; and I hope it will have that weight with you.

But since we are not admitted to examine our witnesses, I will endeavor to shorten the dispute with Mr. Attorney, and to that end I desire he would favor us with some standard definition of a libel by which it may be certainly known whether a writing be a libel, yes or no.

MR. ATTORNEY. The books, I think, have given a very full definition of libel.

MR. HAMILTON. Ay, Mr. Attorney, but what standard rule have the books laid down by which we can certainly know whether the words or signs are malicious? Whether they are defamatory? Whether they tend to the breach of the peace, and are a sufficient ground to provoke a man, his family, or his friends to acts of revenge: especially the ironical sort of words? What rule have you to know when I write ironically? I think it would be hard when I say, "Such a man is a very worthy honest gentleman, and of fine understanding," that therefore I mean, He is a knave or a fool.

MR. ATTORNEY. I think the books are very full. It is said in Hawkins . . . , "Such scandal as is expressed in a scoffing and ironical manner makes a writing as properly a libel as that which is expressed in direct terms. I think nothing can be plainer or more full than these words." . . .

MR. CHIEF JUSTICE. Mr. Hamilton, do you think it so hard to know when words are ironical or spoken in a scoffing manner?

MR. HAMILTON. I own it may be known. But I insist that the only rule by which to know is as I do or can understand them. I have no other rule to go by but as I understand them.

MR. CHIEF JUSTICE. That is certain. All words are libelous or not as they are understood. Those who are to judge of the words must judge whether they are scandalous, or ironical, or tend to the breach of the peace, or are seditious. There can be no doubt of it.

MR. HAMILTON. I thank Your Honor. I am glad to find the Court of this opinion. [T]hen it follows that these twelve men must understand the words in the information to be scandalous—that is to say, false. For I think it is not pretended they are of the ironical sort. And [only] when they understand the words to be so, they will say that we are guilty of publishing a false libel, and not otherwise.

MR. CHIEF JUSTICE. No, Mr. Hamilton, the jury may find that Zenger printed and published those papers, and leave it to the Court to judge whether they are libelous. You know this is very common. It is in the nature of a special verdict, where the jury leave the matter of the law to the court.

MR. HAMILTON. I know, may it please Your Honor, the jury may do so. But I do likewise know that they may do otherwise. I know that they have the right beyond all dispute to determine both the law and the fact; and where they do not doubt of the law, they ought to do so. Leaving it to judgment of the court whether the words are libelous or not in effect renders juries useless (to say no worse) in many cases. But this I shall have occasion to speak to by and by. . . .

But when a ruler of a people brings his personal failings, but much more his vices, into his administration, and the people find themselves affected by them either in their liberties or properties, that will alter the case mightily; and all the things that are said in favor of rulers and of dignitaries, and upon the side of power, will not be able to stop people's mouths when they feel themselves oppressed. I mean, in a free government.

MR. ATTORNEY. Pray, Mr. Hamilton, have a care what you say, don't go too far. I don't like those liberties. . . .

Hamilton's Summation for Zenger

May it please Your Honor, I was saying that notwithstanding all the duty and reverence claimed by Mr. Attorney to men in authority, they are not exempt from observing the rules of common justice either in their private or public capacities. . . .

And has it not often been seen—I hope it will always be seen that when the representatives of a free people are by just representations or remonstrances made sensible of the sufferings of their fellow subjects, by the abuse of power in the hands of a governor, that they have declared (and loudly too) that they were not obliged by any law to support a governor who goes about to destroy a Province or Colony, or their privileges, which by His Majesty he was appointed, and by the law he is bound, to protect and encourage? But I pray that it may be considered—of what use is this mighty privilege if every man that suffers is silent? And if a man must be taken up as a libeler for telling his sufferings to his neighbor? . . .

I will go farther, it is a right, which all free men claim, that they are entitled to complain when they are hurt. They have a right publicly to remonstrate against the abuses of power in the strongest terms, to put their neighbors upon their guard against the craft or open violence of men in authority, and to assert with courage the sense they have of the blessings of liberty, the value they put upon it, and their resolution at all hazards to preserve it as one of the greatest blessings heaven can bestow. . . .

I beg leave to insist that the right of complaining or remonstrating is natural; that the restraint upon this natural right is the law only; and that those restraints can only extend to what is false. For as it is truth alone that can excuse or justify any man for complaining of a bad administration, I as frankly agree that nothing ought to excuse a man who raises a false charge or accusation even against a private person, and that no manner of allowance ought to be made to him who does so against a public magistrate. . . .

It is agreed upon by all men that this is a reign of liberty. While men keep within the bounds of truth I hope they may with safety both speak and write their sentiments of the conduct of men in power, I mean of that part of their conduct only which affects the liberty or property of the people under their administration. Were this to be denied, then the next step may make them slaves; for what notions can be entertained of slavery beyond that of suffering the greatest injuries and oppressions without the liberty of complaining, or if they do, to be destroyed, body and estate, for so doing?

If a libel is understood in the large and unlimited sense urged by Mr. Attorney, there is scarce a writing I know that may not be called a libel, or scarce a person safe from being called to an account as a libeler.

Gentlemen: The danger is great in proportion to the mischief that may happen through our too great credulity. A proper confidence in a court is commendable, but as the verdict, whatever it is, will be yours, you ought to refer no part of your duty to the discretion of other persons. If you should be of the opinion that there is no falsehood in Mr. Zenger's papers, you will, nay pardon me for the expression, you ought, to say so—because you do not know whether others—I mean the Court—may be of that opinion. It is your right to do so, and there is much depending upon your resolution as well as upon your integrity.

The loss of liberty, to a generous mind, is worse than death. And yet we know that there have been those in all ages who for the sake of preferment, or some imaginary honor, have freely lent a helping hand to oppress, nay to destroy, their country. . . .

Source: Famous American Trials. "John Peter Zenger Trial, 1735." Available online. URL: http://www.law.umkc.edu/faculty/projects/ftrials/zenger/zenger.html. Downloaded November 15, 2006.

The Sedition Act of 1798 (excerpt)

The Constitution of the United States of America, ratified in 1788, replaced the Articles of Confederation that had been the governing document for the 13 loosely unified states since 1781. However, abuses committed by the British during the Revolutionary War were still fairly fresh in most citizens' memories, and the Zenger affair was still within recent historical memory. Many worried that the Constitution did not provide enough guarantees for basic rights, so the first Congress proposed 12 articles to be ratified by the states—the first two of which were not ratified.

The Bill of Rights was proposed when two-thirds of both houses of Congress (as required by Article V of the Constitution) voted to send the amendments to the states for ratification. The first 10 amendments to the Constitution, or the Bill of Rights, took effect on December 15, 1791, when Virginia became the 10th state to ratify articles 3 through 12.

Thus, with a precedent to lean on, not to mention any number of newspapers and periodicals that were critical of King George III and Parliament during the revolution, freedom of speech and of the press were guaranteed in the First Amendment. In full it reads: Congress shall make no law respecting an establishment of religion, or prohibiting the free exercise thereof; or abridging the freedom of speech, or of the press; or the right of the people peaceably to assemble, and to petition the government for a redress of grievances.

More than anything else, those 45 words are the backbone of democracy in the United States, yet even they have come under fire, been ignored, or simply contravened. There has also been discussion on whether the amendment's language actually means what it says ("Congress shall make no law"), and whether that language is pertinent to contemporary security problems.

The first laws to contravene the First Amendment were the Alien and Sedition Acts, promulgated during the administration of John Adams. While the Alien Acts were xenophobic laws designed to restrict the political activities of noncitizens within the United States, the Sedition Act was directed at U.S. citizens. More particularly, it affected those members of the American political class who opposed the policies of Adams and the Federalists. The act makes no mention of the unlawfulness of defaming or maligning the vice president—Adams's main political opponent, Thomas Jefferson. The act's final section (Section 4, not included) had a sunset provision by which the law expired on the final day of President Adams's term of office, March 3, 1801.

> SECT. 2. *And be it further enacted,* That if any person shall write, print, utter, or publish, or shall cause or procure to be written, printed, uttered, or published, or shall knowingly and willingly assist or aid in writing, printing, uttering, or publishing any false, scandalous and malicious writing or writings against the government of the United States, or either House of the Congress of the United States, or the President of the United States, with intent to defame the said government, or either House of the said Congress, or the said President, or to bring them, or either of them, into contempt or disrepute; or to excite against them, or either or any of them, the hatred of the good people of the United States, or to stir up sedition within the United States; or to excite any unlawful combinations therein, for opposing or resisting any law of the United States, or any act of the President of the United States, done in pursuance of any such law, or of the powers in him vested by the Constitution of the United States; or to resist, oppose, or defeat any such law or act; or to aid, encourage or abet any hostile designs of any foreign nation against the United States, their people or government, then such person, being thereof convicted before any court of the United States having jurisdiction thereof, shall be punished by a fine not exceeding two thousand dollars, and by imprisonment not exceeding two years.

> SECT. 3. *And be it further enacted and declared,* That if any person shall be prosecuted under this act for the writing or publishing any libel aforesaid, it shall be lawful for the defendant, upon the trial of the cause, to give in

evidence in his defence, the truth of the matter contained in the publication charged as a libel. And the jury who shall try the cause shall have a right to determine the law and the fact, under the direction of the court, as in other cases. (338)

Source: "Sedition Act." Available online. URL: http://www.constitution.org/rf/sedition_1798.htm. Downloaded November 15, 2006.

President Abraham Lincoln's Third Suspension of Habeas Corpus (September 24, 1862)

On September 24, 1862, nearly 18 months into the Civil War and with the Union forces having suffered a number of losses and Confederate sympathizers in the border states (notably Maryland) and elsewhere committing acts of terrorism or voicing secession in other states where Democrats were strong, President Abraham Lincoln suspended habeas corpus for the third time since the outbreak of war. He was the first president in the history of the Republic to suspend the writ.

Habeas corpus, literally "you shall have the body," is the right of a citizen who has been arrested to appear before a judge who then decides if the detainment is legal, and if so to set bail. By suspending habeas corpus prisoners could be held indefinitely. Lincoln's suspension of this protection was ruled illegal because the United States Constitution, in Article 1, Section 9, grants the power to suspend habeas corpus to Congress. The war Congress promptly gave Lincoln the power. The writ was restored throughout the Union after the war.

The suspension of habeas corpus was not a direct infringement on the First Amendment, but the idea that one could be arrested for voicing sympathy toward the Confederacy or criticism of Lincoln's handling of the war and not appear before a judge who could determine whether the arrest was lawful was itself a form of censorship.

BY THE PRESIDENT OF THE UNITED STATES OF AMERICA:
A PROCLAMATION

Whereas, it has become necessary to call into service not only volunteers but also portions of the militia of the States by draft in order to suppress the insurrection existing in the United States, and disloyal persons are not adequately restrained by the ordinary processes of law from hindering this measure and from giving aid and comfort in various ways to the insurrection; Now, therefore, be it ordered, first, that during the existing insurrection and as a necessary measure for suppressing the same, all Rebels and Insurgents, their aiders and abettors within the United States, and all persons discouraging volunteer enlistments, resisting militia drafts, or guilty of any disloyal practice, affording aid and comfort to Rebels against the authority of United States, shall be subject to martial law and liable to trial and punishment by Courts Martial or Military Commission:

Second. That the Writ of Habeas Corpus is suspended in respect to all persons arrested, or who are now, or hereafter during the rebellion shall be, imprisoned in any fort, camp, arsenal, military prison, or other place of confinement by any military authority or by the sentence of any Court Martial or Military Commission.

In witness whereof, I have hereunto set my hand, and caused the seal of the United States to be affixed.

Done at the City of Washington this twenty-fourth day of September, in the year of our Lord one thousand eight hundred and sixty-two, and of the Independence of the United States the 87th.

ABRAHAM LINCOLN
By the President:
WILLIAM H. SEWARD, Secretary of State.

Source: TeachingAmericanHistory.org, "Proclamation Suspending the Writ of Habeas Corpus." Available online. URL: http://teachingamericanhistory.org/library/index.asp?document=425. Downloaded November 17, 2006.

The Comstock Act (1873) (excerpts)

At the urging of, most prominently, Anthony Comstock, the head of the New York Society for the Suppression of Vice, Congress passed the Act for the Suppression of Trade in, and Circulation of, Obscene Literature and Articles for Immoral Use *in 1873. This law's more familiar name is the Comstock Act. As its title suggests the law makes it illegal to circulate or sell obscene material and "articles for immoral use." However it does not define such terms, which gave Comstock and others wide latitude in confiscating birth control pamphlets and devices, literature, and art. As a postal inspector (unpaid during most of his tenure), Comstock seized tons of material and took the lead in defining obscenity for more than three generations of Americans; he was the author of a book titled* Morals Versus Art. *Various 20th-century court decisions and amendments eventually whittled away at the broad interpretations of the Comstock Act, and changing mores in society also served to nullify it a great deal. The law, however, still exists.*

Act for the Suppression of Trade in, and Circulation of, Obscene Literature and Articles for Immoral Use

Be it enacted . . . That whoever, within the District of Columbia or any of the Territories of the United States . . . shall sell . . . or shall offer to sell, or to lend, or to give away, or in any manner to exhibit, or shall otherwise publish or offer to publish in any manner, or shall have in his possession, for any such purpose or purposes, an obscene book, pamphlet, paper, writing, advertisement, circular, print, picture, drawing or other representation, figure, or image on or of paper of other material, or any cast instrument, or other article of an immoral nature, or any drug or medicine, or any article whatever, for the prevention of conception, or for causing unlawful abortion, or shall advertise the same for sale, or shall write or print, or cause to be written or printed, any card, circular, book, pamphlet, advertisement, or notice of any king, stating when, where, how, or of whom, or by what means, any of the articles in this section . . . can be purchased or obtained, or shall manufacture, draw, or print, or in any wise make any of such articles, shall be deemed guilty of a misdemeanor, and on conviction thereof in any court of the United States . . . he shall be imprisoned at hard labor in the penitentiary for not less than six months nor more than five years for each offense, or fined not less than one hundred dollars nor more than twc thousand dollars, with costs of court. . . .

Source: "Comstock Act." Available online. URL: http://shs.westport.k12.ct.us/jwb/AP/TLdocs/comstock.htm. Downloaded November 19, 2006.

The Espionage Act (June 15, 1917) (excerpts)

The actual title of the Espionage Act of 1917 is "An Act to punish acts of interference with the foreign relations, the neutrality, and the foreign commerce of the United States, to punish espionage, and better to enforce the criminal laws of the United States, and for other purposes." While the first two sections of the act deal with espionage, the third section takes into account the "other purposes," in terms that can be used to punish dissent. Its opening clause, revealing the heightened state of emergency after the United States entered World War I, echoes the previous sections, but the second clause takes a whole different turn. By making it illegal to "willfully cause or attempt to cause insubordination . . . refusal of duty in the military . . ." the section in effect gives the government wide latitude in prosecuting dissent or even criticism of the war effort.

The Espionage Act came about at the behest of President Woodrow Wilson; the Justice Department wrote the original draft, but Congress had misgivings: The bill's restrictions on the press were too radical, and some of the wording was too vague. The changes made didn't please Wilson, who indeed equated criticism of the government at war with disloyalty, but nevertheless were used to stifle dissent. The Espionage Act was enacted June 15, 1917.

Be it enacted by the Senate and House of Representatives of the United States of America in Congress assembled . . .

Section 3

Whoever, when the United States is at war, shall willfully make or convey false reports or false statements with intent to interfere with the operation or success of the military or naval forces of the United States or to promote the success of its enemies and whoever when the United States is at war, shall willfully cause or attempt to cause insubordination, disloyalty, mutiny, refusal of duty, in the military or naval forces of the United States, or shall willfully obstruct the recruiting or enlistment service of the United States, to the injury of the service or of the United States, shall be punished by a fine of not more than $10,000 or imprisonment for not more than twenty years, or both.

Section 4

If two or more persons conspire to violate the provisions of section two or three of this title, and one or more of such persons does any act to effect the object of the conspiracy, each of the parties to such conspiracy shall be punished as in said sections provided in the case of the doing of the act the accomplishment of which is the object of such conspiracy. Except as above provided conspiracies to commit offences under this title shall be punished as provided by section thirty-seven of the Act to codify, revise, and amend the penal laws of the United States approved March fourth, nineteen hundred and nine.

Source: Third World Traveler. "The Espionage Act – June 15, 1917." Available online. URL: http://www.thirdworldtraveler.com/Civil_Liberties/Espionage_Act_1917.html. Downloaded November 19, 2006.

The Sedition Act of 1918

The Sedition Act of 1918 was an amendment to Section 3 of the Espionage Act of 1917. The new act expanded on the language of the previous. After the Sedi-

tion Act of 1918 was passed on March 16, 1918, it became illegal to criticize not only the war or the war effort but the form of government of the United States, the Constitution, the flag, the military, and, strangely, the uniforms of the military.

In a foreshadowing of what was to come 30 years later, federal employees were liable to dismissal from their jobs for uttering or writing "unpatriotic or disloyal" language, or even criticizing the government in a fit of anger.

During wartime fewer persons were prosecuted under the Sedition Act because it was enacted so late—the Armistice occurred less than six months later. However, it was used to punish Communists, Socialists, fellow travelers, anarchists, and other dissenters during the Red Scare of 1919–20. Congress repealed the Sedition Act of 1918 on March 3, 1921.

Be it enacted by the Senate and House of Representatives of the United States of America in Congress assembled, That section three of title one of the Act entitled "An Act to punish acts of interference with the foreign relations, the neutrality, and the foreign commerce of the United States, to punish espionage, and better to enforce the criminal laws of the United States, and for other purposes," approved June fifteenth, nineteen hundred and seventeen, be, and the same is hereby, amended so as to read as follows:

Sec. 3. Whoever, when the United States is at war, shall willfully make or convey false reports or false statements with intent to interfere with the operation or success of the military or naval forces of the United States, or to promote the success of its enemies, or shall willfully make or convey false reports or false statements, or say or do anything except by way of bona fide and not disloyal advice to an investor or investors, with intent to obstruct the sale by the United States of bonds or other securities of the United States or the making of loans by or to the United States, and whoever, when the United States is at war, shall willfully cause or attempt to cause, or incite or attempt to incite, insubordination, disloyalty, mutiny, or refusal of duty, in the military or naval forces of the United States, or shall willfully obstruct or attempt to obstruct the recruiting or enlistment service of the United States, and whoever, when the United States is at war, shall willfully utter, print, write, or publish any disloyal, profane, scurrilous, or abusive language about the form of government of the United States, or the Constitution of the United States, or the military or naval forces of the United States, or the flag of the United States, or the uniform of the Army or Navy of the United States, or any language intended to bring the form of government of the United States, or the Constitution of the United States, or the military or naval forces of the United States, or the flag of the United States, or the uniform of the Army or Navy of the United States into contempt, scorn, contumely, or disrepute, or shall willfully utter, print, write, or publish any language intended to incite, provoke, or encourage resistance to the United States, or to promote the cause of its enemies, or shall willfully display the flag of any foreign enemy, or shall willfully by utterance, writing, printing, publication, or language spoken, urge, incite, or advocate any curtailment of production in this country of any thing or things, product or products, necessary or essential to the prosecution of the war in which the United States may be engaged, with intent by such curtailment to cripple or hinder the United States in the prosecution of the war, and whoever shall willfully advocate, teach, defend, or suggest the doing of any of the acts or things in this section enumerated, and whoever shall by word or act support or favor the cause of any country with which the United States is at war or by word or act oppose the cause of the United States therein, shall be punished by a fine of not more than $10,000 or imprisonment for not more than twenty years, or both: Provided, That any employee or official of the United States Government who commits any disloyal act or utters any unpatriotic or disloyal language, or who, in an abusive and violent manner criticizes the Army or Navy or the flag of the United States shall be at once dismissed from the service. Any such employee shall be dismissed by the head of the department in which the employee may be engaged, and any such official shall be dismissed by the authority having power to appoint a successor to the dismissed official.

Source: Dangerous Citizen. "Espionage and Sedition Act." Available online. URL: http://www.dangerouscitizen.com/Articles/525.aspx. Downloaded November 19, 2006.

Opinion of Justice Oliver Wendell Holmes in *Schenck v. United States* (March 3, 1917) (excerpts)

Charles Schenck, a Socialist, was convicted of conspiracy to obstruct military recruitment after he was arrested for circulating pamphlets that equated the draft to involuntary servitude. The anticonscription pamphlet cited the Thirteenth Amendment to make its case. Schenck was charged under the Espionage Act of 1917 and convicted. He also lost on appeal.

In January 1919, his case was heard by the United States Supreme Court, which unanimously decided on March 3, 1919, that Schenck's conviction was constitutional. Justice Oliver Wendell Holmes was assigned the task of writing the opinion for the Court, with which the other justices all concurred. In his opinion, Justice Holmes set out the "clear and present danger" test for deciding whether or not speech is constitutionally protected. Schenck v. United States *is considered the Supreme Court's first important free speech decision.*

Note: With the exception of deleted material between the first two paragraphs (explained in brackets) all ellipses refer to case references.

This is an indictment in three counts. The first charges a conspiracy to violate the Espionage Act of June 15, 1917 . . . by causing and attempting . . . to cause insubordination, &c., in the military and naval forces of the United States, and to obstruct the recruiting and enlistment service of the United States, when the United States was at war with the German Empire, to-wit, that the defendant wilfully conspired to have printed and circulated to men who had been called and accepted for military service under the Act of May 18, 1917, c. 15, 40 Stat. 76 . . . , a document set forth and alleged to be calculated to cause such insubordination and obstruction. The count alleges overt acts in pursuance of the conspiracy, ending in the distribution of the document set forth. The second count alleges a conspiracy to commit an offense against the United States, to-wit, to use the mails for the transmission of matter declared to be non-mailable by title 12, 2, of the Act of June 15, 1917 . . . , to-wit, the above mentioned document, with an averment of the same overt acts. The third count charges an unlawful use of the mails for the transmission of the same matter and otherwise as above. The defendants were found guilty on all the counts. They set up the First Amendment to the Constitution forbidding Congress to make any law abridging the freedom of speech, or of the press, and bringing the case here on that ground have argued some other points also of which we must dispose. . . . [Justice Holmes first dealt with the non-free speech portion of *Schenck*'s argument.]

. . . It well may be that the prohibition of laws abridging the freedom of speech is not confined to previous restraints, although to prevent them may have been the . . . main purpose, as intimated in *Patterson v. Colorado*. . . . We admit that in many places and in ordinary times the defendants in saying all that was said in the circular would have been within their constitutional rights. But the character of every act depends upon the circumstances in which it is done. . . . The most stringent protection of free speech would not protect a man in falsely shouting fire in a theatre and causing a panic. It does not even protect a man from an injunction against uttering words that may have all the effect of force. . . . The question in every case is whether

> the words used are used in such circumstances and are of such a nature as to create a clear and present danger that they will bring about the substantive evils that Congress has a right to prevent. It is a question of proximity and degree. When a nation is at war many things that might be said in time of peace are such a hindrance to its effort that their utterance will not be endured so long as men fight and that no Court could regard them as protected by any constitutional right. It seems to be admitted that if an actual obstruction of the recruiting service were proved, liability for words that produced that effect might be enforced. The statute of 1917 in section 4 . . . punishes conspiracies to obstruct as well as actual obstruction. If the act (speaking, or circulating a paper), its tendency and the intent with which it is done are the same, we perceive no ground for saying that success alone warrants making the act a crime. . . . Indeed that case might be said to dispose of the present contention if the precedent covers all media concludendi. But as the right to free speech was not referred to specially, we have thought fit to add a few words.
>
> It was not argued that a conspiracy to obstruct the draft was not within the words of the Act of 1917. The . . . words are 'obstruct the recruiting or enlistment service,' and it might be suggested that they refer only to making it hard to get volunteers. Recruiting heretofore usually having been accomplished by getting volunteers the word is apt to call up that method only in our minds. But recruiting is gaining fresh supplies for the forces, as well by draft as otherwise. It is put as an alternative to enlistment or voluntary enrollment in this act. The fact that the Act of 1917 was enlarged by the amending Act of May 16, 1918, c. 75, 40 Stat. 553, of course, does not affect the present indictment and would not, even if the former act had been repealed. . . . Judgments affirmed.

Source: Findlaw for Legal Professionals. "U.S. Supreme Court, *Schenck v. U.S.*, 249 U.S. 49 (1919)." Available online. URL: http://caselaw.lp.findlaw.com/scripts/getcase.pl?court=us&vol=249&invol=47. Downloaded November 21, 2006.

The Smith Act (June 28, 1940)

A little more than nine months after World War II broke out in Europe, Congress, perhaps anticipating the United States's entry into the conflict, sought to revise the Immigration Act of 1917. In doing so, it also returned somewhat to the war atmosphere of late 1910s. The Alien Registration Act of 1940 is commonly known as the Smith Act, after Virginia representative Howard W. Smith who authored the act's antisedition portion. Revealing congressional priorities at the time, the antisedition portion includes the act's first five sections. In many ways, the Smith Act of 1940 echoes the Espionage and Sedition acts of 1917–18, and in fact its primary use was to prosecute Communists and war dissenters during World War II and the first decade of the cold war. The most famous of these prosecutions was that of Eugene Dennis and 11 other members of the Communist Party USA, who were arrested in 1948 and subsequently convicted. Their convictions were upheld by the Supreme Court on a 6-2 vote in 1951. The act was approved on June 28, 1940, and subsequently amended.

AN ACT
To prohibit certain subversive activities; to amend certain provisions of law with respect to the admission and deportation of aliens; to require the fingerprinting and registration of aliens; and for other purposes.

Be it enacted by the Senate and House of Representatives of the United States of America in Congress assembled,

TITLE I
Section 1. (a) It shall be unlawful for any person, with intent to interfere with, impair, or influence the loyalty, morale, or discipline of the military or naval forces of the United States—

(1) to advise, counsel, urge, or in any manner cause insubordination, disloyalty, mutiny, or refusal of duty by any member of the military or naval forces of the United States; or

(2) to distribute any written or printed matter which advises, counsels, or urges insubordination, disloyalty, mutiny, or refusal of duty by any member of the military or naval forces of the United States.

(b) For the purposes of this section, the term "military or naval forces of the United States" includes the Army of the United States, as defined in section 1 of the National Defense Act of June 3, 1916, as amended (48 Stat. 153; U.S.C., title 10, sec. 2), the Navy, Marine Corps, Coast Guard, Naval Reserve, and Marine Corps Reserve of the United States; and, when any merchant vessel is commissioned in the Navy or is in the service of the Army or the Navy, includes the master, officers, and crew of such vessel.

Sec. 2. (a) It shall be unlawful for any person—

(1) to knowingly or willfully advocate, abet, advise, or teach the duty, necessity, desirability, or propriety of overthrowing or destroying any government in the United States by force or violence, or by the assassination of any officer of any such government;

(2) with the intent to cause the overthrow or destruction of any government in the United States, to print, publish, edit, issue, circulate, sell, distribute, or publicly display any written or printed matter advocating, advising, or teaching the duty, necessity, desirability, or propriety of overthrowing or destroying any government in the United States by force or violence.

(3) to organize or help to organize any society, group, or assembly of persons who teach, advocate, or encourage the overthrow or destruction of any government in the United States by force or violence; or to be or become a member of, or affiliate with, any such society, group, or assembly of persons, knowing the purposes thereof.

(b) For the purposes of this section, the term "government in the United States" means the Government of the United States, the government of any State, Territory, or possession of the United States, the government of the District of Columbia, or the government of any political subdivision of any of them.

Sec. 3. It shall be unlawful for any person to attempt to commit, or to conspire to commit, any of the acts prohibited by the provisions of this title.

Sec. 4. Any written or printed matter of the character described in section 1 or section 2 of this Act, which is intended for use in violation of this Act, may be taken from any house or other place in which it may be found, or from any person in whose possession it may be, under a search warrant issued pursuant to the provisions of title XI of the Act entitled "An Act to punish acts of interference with the foreign relations, the neutrality and the foreign commerce of the United States, to punish espionage, and better to enforce the criminal laws of the United States, and for other purposes," approved June 15, 1917 (40 Stat. 228; U.S.C., title 18, ch. 18).

Sec. 5. (a) Any person who violates any of the provisions of this title shall, upon conviction thereof, be fined not more than $10,000 or imprisoned for not more than ten years, or both.

(b) No person convicted of violating any of the provisions of this title shall, during the five years next following his conviction, be eligible for employment by the United States, or by any department or agency thereof (including any corporation the Stock of which is wholly owned by the United States).

The amended Alien Registration Act of 1940 reads as follows:

§ 2385. Advocating Overthrow of Government.
Whoever knowingly or willfully advocates, abets, advises, or teaches the duty, necessity, desirability, or propriety of overthrowing or destroying the government of the United States or the government of any State, Territory, District or Possession thereof, or the government of any political subdivision therein, by force or violence, or by the assassination of any officer of any such government; or

Whoever, with intent to cause the overthrow or destruction of any such government, prints, publishes, edits, issues, circulates, sells, distributes, or publicly displays any written or printed matter advocating, advising, or teaching the duty, necessity, desirability, or propriety of overthrowing or destroying any government in the United States by force or violence, or attempts to do so; or

Whoever organizes or helps or attempts to organize any society, group, or assembly of persons who teach, advocate, or encourage the overthrow or destruction of any such government by force or violence; or becomes or is a member of, or affiliates with, any such society, group, or assembly of persons, knowing the purposes thereof—

Shall be fined under this title or imprisoned not more than twenty years, or both, and shall be ineligible for employment by the United States or any department or agency thereof, for the five years next following his conviction.

If two or more persons conspire to commit any offense named in this section, each shall be fined under this title or imprisoned not more than twenty years, or both, and shall be ineligible for employment by the United States or any department or agency thereof, for the five years next following his conviction.

As used in this section, the terms "organizes" "and "organize", with respect to any society, group, or assembly of persons, include the recruiting of new members, the forming of new units, and the regrouping or expansion of existing clubs, classes, and other units of such society, group, or assembly of persons.

Source: Documents of American History II. "1940s: Alien Registration Act of 1940." Available online. URL: http://tucnak.fsv.cuni.cz/~calda/Documents/1940s/Alien%20Registration%20Act%20of%201940.html. Downloaded November 22, 2006. "Smith Act of 1940," [Amended]. Available online. URL: http://www.bc.edu/bc_org/avp/cas/comm/free_speech/smithactof1940.html. Downloaded November 22, 2006.

Executive Order 9835 Issued by President Harry S. Truman (March 21, 1947) (excerpts)

On March 21, 1947, President Harry S. Truman issued Executive Order No. 9835, which instituted the loyalty program for federal employees in the executive branch of the government. Following a Democratic defeat in the previous November's midterm elections in which the Republicans captured both houses of Congress by taking a hard stance against Communism, the president felt pushed into a political corner. In January 1947, after Republican-controlled HUAC began investigating Communist influence in Hollywood, Truman signed the executive order in part to fend off assertions that he was soft on Communism.

Executive Order No. 9835 consisted of an introduction and six main parts, each with accompanying sections and subsections. The six main parts dealt with investigation of applicants for federal positions, investigation of employees, responsibilities of the civil service commission, security measures of the investigations, standards by which a person could be refused employment or whose employment could be terminated, and miscellaneous details such as coordination, and when the order would go into effect.

By 1951, more than 3 million people had been investigated, a few thousand had resigned their federal positions, and 212 were fired, but no one was indicted for espionage. In his memoirs President Truman regretted the federal loyalty program, claiming it helped create the atmosphere that led to McCarthyism.

PART I—INVESTIGATION OF APPLICANTS

1. There shall be a loyalty investigation of every person entering the civilian employment of any department or agency of the executive branch of the Federal Government.
   a. Investigations of persons entering the competitive service shall be conducted by the Civil Service Commission, except in such cases as

are covered by a special agreement between the Commission and any given department or agency.

b. Investigations of persons other than those entering the competitive service shall be conducted by the employing department or agency. Departments and agencies without investigative organizations shall utilize the investigative facilities of the Civil Service Commission.

2. The investigations of persons entering the employ of the executive branch may be conducted after any such person enters upon actual employment therein, but in any such case the appointment of such person shall be conditioned upon a favorable determination with respect to his loyalty.

   a. Investigations of persons entering the competitive service shall be conducted as expeditiously as possible; provided, however, that if any such investigation is not completed within 18 months from the date on which a person enters actual employment, the condition that his employment is subject to investigation shall expire, except in a case in which the Civil Service Commission has made an initial adjudication of disloyalty and the case continues to be active by reason of an appeal, and it shall then be the responsibility of the employing department or agency to conclude such investigation and make a final determination concerning the loyalty of such person.

3. An investigation shall be made of all applicants at all available pertinent sources of information and shall include reference to:

   a. Federal Bureau of Investigation files
   b. Civil Service Commission files
   c. Military and naval intelligence files
   d. The files of any other appropriate government investigative or intelligence agency
   e. House Committee on un-American Activities files
   f. Local law-enforcement files at the place of residence and employment of the applicant, including municipal, county, and State law-enforcement files
   g. Schools and colleges attended by applicant
   h. Former employers of applicant
   i. References given by applicant
   j. Any other appropriate source

4. Whenever derogatory information with respect to loyalty of an applicant is revealed a full investigation shall be conducted. A full field investigation

shall also be conducted of those applicants, or of applicants for particular positions, as may be designated by the head of the employing department or agency, such designations to be based on the determination by any such head of the best interests of national security.

PART II—INVESTIGATION OF EMPLOYEES

1. The head of each department and agency in the executive branch of the Government shall be personally responsible for an effective program to assure that disloyal civilian officers or employees are not retained in employment in his department or agency.
   a. He shall be responsible for prescribing and supervising the loyalty determination procedures of his department or agency, in accordance with the provisions of this order, which shall be considered as providing minimum requirements.
   b. The head of a department or agency which does not have an investigative organization shall utilize the investigative facilities of the Civil Service Commission.

2. The head of each department and agency shall appoint one or more loyalty boards, each composed of not less than three representatives of the department or agency concerned, for the purpose of hearing loyalty cases arising within such department or agency and making recommendations with respect to the removal of any officer or employee of such department or agency on grounds relating to loyalty, and he shall prescribe regulations for the conduct of the proceedings before such boards.
   a. An officer or employee who is charged with being disloyal shall have a right to an administrative hearing before a loyalty board in the employing department or agency. He may appear before such board personally, accompanied by counsel or representative of his own choosing, and present evidence on his own behalf, through witnesses or by affidavit.
   b. The officer or employee shall be served with a written notice of such hearing in sufficient time, and shall be informed therein of the nature of the charges against him in sufficient detail, so that he will be enabled to prepare his defense. The charges shall be stated as specifically and completely as, in the discretion of the employing department or agency, security considerations permit, and the officer or employee shall be informed in the notice (1) of his right to reply to such charges in writing within a specified reasonable period of time, (2) of his right to an administrative hearing on such charges before a

loyalty board, and (3) of his right to appear before such board personally, to be accompanied by counsel or representative of his own choosing, and to present evidence on his behalf, through witness or by affidavit.

3. A recommendation of removal by a loyalty board shall be subject to appeal by the officer or employee affected, prior to his removal, to the head of the employing department or agency or to such person or persons as may be designated by such head, under such regulations as may be prescribed by him, and the decision of the department or agency concerned shall be subject to appeal to the Civil Service Commission's Loyalty Review Board, hereinafter provided for, for an advisory recommendation.

4. The rights of hearing, notice thereof, and appeal therefrom shall be accorded to every officer or employee prior to his removal on grounds of disloyalty, irrespective of tenure, or of manner, method, or nature of appointment, but the head of the employing department or agency may suspend any officer or employee at any time pending a determination with respect to loyalty.

5. The loyalty boards of the various departments and agencies shall furnish to the Loyalty Review Board, hereinafter provided for, such reports as may be requested concerning the operation of the loyalty program in any such department or agency. . . .

PART IV—SECURITY MEASURES IN INVESTIGATIONS

1. At the request of the head of any department or agency of the executive branch an investigative agency shall make available to such head, personally, all investigative material and information collected by the investigative agency concerning any employee or prospective employee of the requesting department or agency, or shall make such material and information available to any officer or officers designated by such head and approved by the investigative agency.

2. Notwithstanding the foregoing requirement, however, the investigative agency may refuse to disclose the names of confidential informants, provided it furnishes sufficient information about such informants on the basis of which the requesting department or agency can make an adequate evaluation of the information furnished by them, and provided it advises the requesting department or agency in writing that it is

essential to the protection of the informants or to the investigation of other cases that the identity of the informants not be revealed. Investigative agencies shall not use this discretion to decline to reveal sources of information where such action is not essential.

3. Each department and agency of the executive branch should develop and maintain, for the collection and analysis of information relating to the loyalty of its employees and prospective employees, a staff specially trained in security techniques, and an effective security control system for protecting such information generally and for protecting confidential sources of such information particularly.

Source: TeachingAmericanHistory.org. "Executive Order 9835." Available online. URL: http://teachingamericanhistory.org/library/index.asp?document=930. Downloaded November 22, 2006.

Joseph McCarthy, Speech in Wheeling, West Virginia (February 9, 1950) (excerpts)

As the cold war dawned, Senator Joseph McCarthy was a first-term Republican senator from Wisconsin who had yet to make his mark in the capital. On the advice of a friend, and noting the temper of the times, he decided to make anti-Communism his primary issue. Specifically, he sought to expose Communists in the United States.

Senator McCarthy's opening salvo came on February 9, 1950, during a speech in Wheeling, West Virginia. In the speech, McCarthy began by noting the occasion on which he was invited to speak—a celebration of Abraham Lincoln's birthday—but quickly moved toward cold war rhetoric. He compared population shifts under Communist and democratic governments and used the numbers to determine the "odds."

Senator McCarthy eventually segued to the point of his speech—exposing Communists in the State Department. This was the speech in which he made his claim to have a list containing the names of 205 Communists, a number he later amended downward but which never proved credible.

Ladies and gentlemen . . .

Five years after a world war has been won, men's hearts should anticipate a long peace—and men's minds should be free from the heavy weight that comes with war. But this is not such a period—for this is not a period of peace. This is a time of "the cold war." This is a time when all the world is split into two vast, increasingly hostile armed camps—a time of a great armament race.

Today we can almost physically hear the mutterings and rumblings of an invigorated god of war. You can see it, feel it, and hear it all the way from the Indochina hills, from the shores of Formosa, right over into the very heart of Europe itself.

The one encouraging thing is that the "mad moment" has not yet arrived for the firing of the gun or the exploding of the bomb which will set civilization about the final task of destroying itself. There is still a hope for peace if we finally decide that no longer can we safely blind our eyes and close our ears to those facts which are shaping up more and more clearly . . . and that is that we are now engaged in a show-down fight . . . not the usual war between nations for land areas or other material gains, but a war between two diametrically opposed ideologies. . . . Today we are engaged in a final, all-out battle between communistic atheism and Christianity. The modern champions of communism have selected this as the time, and ladies and gentlemen, the chips are down—they are truly down.

Lest there be any doubt that the time has been chosen, let us go directly to the leader of communism today—Joseph Stalin. Here is what he said—not back in 1928, not before the war, not during the war—but 2 years after the last war was ended: "To think that the Communist revolution can be carried out peacefully, within the framework of a Christian democracy, means one has either gone out of one's mind and lost all normal understanding, or has grossly and openly repudiated the Communist revolution." . . .

Ladies and gentlemen, can there be anyone tonight who is so blind as to say that the war is not on? Can there be anyone who fails to realize that the Communist world has said the time is now? . . . Unless we face this fact, we shall pay the price that must be paid by those who wait too long.

Six years ago, . . . there was within the Soviet orbit, 180,000,000 people. Lined up on the antitotalitarian side there were in the world at that time, roughly 1,625,000,000 people. Today, only six years later, there are 800,000,000 people under the absolute domination of Soviet Russia—an increase of over 400 percent. On our side, the figure has shrunk to around 500,000,000. In other words, in less than six years, the odds have changed from 9 to 1 in our favor to 8 to 5 against us. . . .

The reason why we find ourselves in a position of impotency is . . . because of the traitorous actions of those who have been treated so well by this

Nation. It has not been the less fortunate, or members of minority groups, who have been traitorous to this Nation, but rather those who have had all the benefits that the wealthiest Nation on earth has had to offer . . . the finest homes, the finest college education and the finest jobs in government we can give. This is glaringly true in the State Department. There the bright young men who are born with silver spoons in their mouths are the ones who have been most traitorous. . . .

I have here in my hand a list of 205 . . . a list of names that were made known to the Secretary of State as being members of the Communist Party and who nevertheless are still working and shaping policy in the State Department. . . .

As you know, very recently the Secretary of State proclaimed his loyalty to a man guilty of what has always been considered as the most abominable of all crimes—being a traitor to the people who gave him a position of great trust—high treason. . . .

He has lighted the spark which is resulting in a moral uprising and will end only when the whole sorry mess of twisted, warped thinkers are swept from the national scene so that we may have a new birth of honesty and decency in government.

Source: History Matters: The U.S. Survey Course on the Web. "Speech of Senator Joseph McCarthy, Wheeling, West Virginia, February 9, 1950." Available online. URL: http://historymatters.gmu.edu/d/6456. Downloaded November 23, 2006.

Two Opinions in *Jacobellis v. Ohio*: Justice William Brennan for the Majority and Chief Justice Earl Warren Dissenting (June 22, 1964)

Jacobellis *was a landmark case in that the Supreme Court made important statements about obscenity and the First and Fourteenth Amendments, community standards, and the idea of community. The dispositions of other cases, notably* Grove Press v. Garstein, *which made it possible to publish Henry Miller's* Tropic of Cancer *in the United States, were based on this decision.*

Nico Jacobellis was a movie theater owner who was arrested, convicted, and fined twice for showing a French film Les Amants (The Lovers)*, said to be obscene. The convictions were upheld on appeal. The case was first argued before the Supreme Court on March 26, 1963, reargued on April 1, 1964, and decided on June 22, 1964. So important were the issues of obscenity, judging* *what is obscene, and whether the Constitution covers such material that six justices saw fit to write opinions. In addition to Justice Brennan's opinion for the Court, Justices Hugo Black, Potter Stewart, and Arthur Goldberg wrote separate, concurring opinions. Chief Justice Earl Warren and Justice John Marshal Harlan wrote dissenting opinions.*

Ellipses refer to case references except in Justice Brennan's quote of Pennekamp v. Florida *and the first ellipsis in his quote of Judge Learned Hand.*

> ... The dispositive question is whether the state courts properly found that the motion picture involved, a French film called "Les Amants" ("The Lovers"), was obscene and [378 U.S. 184, 187] hence not entitled to the protection for free expression that is guaranteed by the First and Fourteenth Amendments. We conclude that the film is not obscene and that the judgment must accordingly be reversed.
>
> Motion pictures are within the ambit of the constitutional guarantees of freedom of speech and of the press.... But in *Roth v. United States* and *Alberts v. California*... we held that obscenity is not subject to those guarantees. Application of an obscenity law to suppress a motion picture thus requires ascertainment of the "dim and uncertain line" that often separates obscenity from constitutionally protected expression.... It has been suggested that this is a task in which our Court need not involve itself. We are told that the determination whether a particular motion picture, book, or other work of expression is obscene can be treated as a purely factual judgment on which a jury's verdict is all but conclusive, or that in any event the decision can be left essentially to state and lower federal courts, with this Court exercising only a limited review such as that needed to determine whether the ruling below is supported by "sufficient evidence." The suggestion is appealing, since it would lift from our shoulders a difficult, recurring, and unpleasant task. But we cannot accept it. Such an abnegation of judicial ... supervision in this field would be inconsistent with our duty to uphold the constitutional guarantees. Since it is only "obscenity" that is excluded from the constitutional protection, the question whether a particular work is obscene necessarily implicates an issue of constitutional law.... Such an issue we think, must ultimately be decided by this Court. Our duty admits of no "substitute for facing up to the tough individual problems of constitutional judgment involved in every obscenity case...."
>
> In other areas involving constitutional rights under the Due Process Clause, the Court has consistently recognized its duty to apply the applicable rules

of law upon the basis of an independent review of the facts of each case.... And this has been particularly true where rights have been asserted under the First Amendment guarantees of free expression. Thus in *Pennekamp v. Florida*... the Court stated:

"The Constitution has imposed upon this Court final authority to determine the meaning and application of those words of that instrument which require interpretation to resolve judicial issues. With that responsibility, we are compelled to examine for ourselves the statements in issue and the circumstances under which they were made to see whether or not they... are of a character which the principles of the First Amendment, as adopted by the Due Process Clause of the Fourteenth Amendment, protect."

We cannot understand why the Court's duty should be any different in the present case, where Jacobellis has... been subjected to a criminal conviction for disseminating a work of expression and is challenging that conviction as a deprivation of rights guaranteed by the First and Fourteenth Amendments. Nor can we understand why the Court's performance of its constitutional and judicial function in this sort of case should be denigrated by such epithets as "censor" "or "super-censor." In judging alleged obscenity the Court is no more "censoring" expression than it has in other cases "censored" criticism of judges and public officials, advocacy of governmental overthrow, or speech alleged to constitute a breach of the peace. Use of an opprobrious label can neither obscure nor impugn the Court's performance of its obligation to test challenged judgments against the guarantees of the First and Fourteenth Amendments and, in doing so, to delineate the scope of constitutionally protected speech. Hence we reaffirm the principle that, in "obscenity" cases as in all others involving rights derived from the First Amendment guarantees of free expression, this Court cannot avoid making an independent constitutional judgment on the facts of the case as to whether the material involved is constitutionally protected....

The question of the proper standard for making this determination has been the subject of much discussion and controversy since our decision in *Roth* seven years ago. Recognizing that the test for obscenity enunciated there—"whether to the average person, applying contemporary community standards, the dominant theme of the material taken as a whole appeals to prurient interest,"... —is not perfect, we think any substitute would raise equally difficult problems, and we therefore adhere to that standard. We would reiterate, however, our recognition in *Roth* that obscenity is excluded from the constitutional protection only because it is "utterly without redeeming social importance," and that "the portrayal of sex, e. g., in art, literature and scientific works, is not itself sufficient reason to deny material the constitutional protection of freedom of speech and press." . . . It follows that material dealing with sex in a manner that advocates ideas, *Kingsley Int'l Pictures Corp. v. Regents*, . . . or that has literary or scientific or artistic value or any other form of social importance, may not be branded as obscenity and denied the constitutional protection. Nor may the constitutional status of the material be made to turn on a "weighing" of its social importance against its prurient appeal, for a work cannot be proscribed unless it is "utterly" without social importance. . . . It should also be recognized that the *Roth* standard requires in the first instance a finding that the material "goes substantially beyond customary limits of candor in description or representation of such matters." This was a requirement of the Model Penal Code test that we approved in Roth . . . , and it is explicitly reaffirmed in the . . . more recent Proposed Official Draft of the Code. In the absence of such a deviation from society's standards of decency, we do not see how any official inquiry into the allegedly prurient appeal of a work of expression can be squared with the guarantees of the First and Fourteenth Amendments. . . .

It has been suggested that the "contemporary community standards" aspect of the *Roth* test implies a determination of the constitutional question of obscenity in each case by the standards of the particular local community from which the case arises. This is an incorrect reading of *Roth*. The concept of "contemporary community standards" was first expressed by Judge Learned Hand in *United States v. Kennerley* . . . , where he said:

"Yet, if the time is not yet when men think innocent all that which is honestly germane to a pure subject, however little it may mince its words, still I scarcely think that they would forbid all which might corrupt the most corruptible, or that society is prepared to accept for its own limitations those which may perhaps be necessary to the weakest of its members. If there be no abstract definition, such as I have suggested, should not the word 'obscene' be allowed to indicate the present critical point in the compromise between candor and shame at which the community may have arrived here and now? . . . To put thought in leash to the average conscience of the time is perhaps tolerable, but to fetter it by the . . . necessities of the lowest and least capable seems a fatal policy.

"Nor is it an objection, I think, that such an interpretation gives to the words of the statute a varying meaning from time to time. Such words as these do not embalm the precise morals of an age or place; while they presuppose that some things will always be shocking to the public taste, the vague subject-matter is left to the gradual development of general notions about what is decent. . . ."

It seems clear that in this passage Judge Hand was referring not to state and local "communities," but rather to "the community" in the sense of "society at large; . . . the public, or people in general." Thus, he recognized that under his standard the concept of obscenity would have "a varying meaning from time to time"—not from county to county, or town to town.

We do not see how any "local" definition of the "community" could properly be employed in delineating the area of expression that is protected by the Federal Constitution. MR. JUSTICE HARLAN pointed out in *Manual Enterprises, Inc. v. Day,* supra . . . , that a standard based on a particular local community would have "the intolerable consequence of denying some sections of the country access to material, there deemed acceptable, which in others might be considered offensive to prevailing community standards of decency." It is true that *Manual Enterprises* dealt with the federal statute banning obscenity from the mails. But the mails are not the only means by which works of expression cross local-community lines in this country. It can hardly be assumed that all the patrons of a particular library, bookstand, or motion picture theater are residents of the . . . smallest local "community" that can be drawn around that establishment. Furthermore, to sustain the suppression of a particular book or film in one locality would deter its dissemination in other localities where it might be held not obscene, since sellers and exhibitors would be reluctant to risk criminal conviction in testing the variation between the two places. It would be a hardy person who would sell a book or exhibit a film anywhere in the land after this Court had sustained the judgment of one "community" holding it to be outside the constitutional protection. The result would thus be "to restrict the public's access to forms of the printed word which the State could not constitutionally suppress directly. . . ."

It is true that local communities throughout the land are in fact diverse, and that in cases such as this one the Court is confronted with the task of reconciling the rights of such communities with the rights of individuals. Communities vary, however, in many respects other than their toleration of alleged obscenity, and such variances have never been considered to require or justify a varying standard for application of the Federal Constitution. The Court has regularly been compelled, in reviewing criminal convictions challenged under the Due Process Clause of the Fourteenth Amendment, to reconcile the conflicting rights of the local community which brought the prosecution and of the individual defendant. Such a task is admittedly difficult and delicate, but it is inherent in the Court's duty of determining whether a particular conviction worked a deprivation of rights guaranteed by the Federal Constitution. The Court has not shrunk from discharging that duty in other areas, and we see no reason why it should do so here. The Court has explicitly refused to tolerate a result whereby "the constitutional limits of free expression in the Nation . . . would vary with state lines," *Pennekamp v. Florida . . .* ; we see even less justification for allowing such limits to vary with town or county lines. We thus reaffirm the position taken in *Roth* to the effect that the constitutional status of an allegedly obscene work must be determined on the basis of a national standard. It is, after all, a national Constitution we are expounding.

We recognize the legitimate and indeed exigent interest of States and localities throughout the Nation in preventing the dissemination of material deemed harmful to children. But that interest does not justify a total suppression of such material, the effect of which would be to "reduce the adult population . . . to reading only what is fit for children." *Butler v. Michigan. . . .* State and local authorities might well consider whether their objectives in this area would be better served by laws aimed specifically at preventing distribution of objectionable material to children, rather than at totally prohibiting its dissemination. Since the present conviction is based upon exhibition of the film to the public at large and not upon its exhibition to children, the judgment must be reviewed under the strict standard applicable in determining the scope of the expression that is protected by the Constitution.

We have applied that standard to the motion picture in question. "The Lovers" involves a woman bored with her life and marriage who abandons her husband and family for a young archaeologist with whom she has . . . suddenly fallen in love. There is an explicit love scene in the last reel of the film, and the State's objections are based almost entirely upon that scene. The film was favorably reviewed in a number of national publications, although disparaged in others, and was rated by at least two critics of national stature among the best films of the year in which it was produced. It was shown in approximately 100 of the larger cities in the United States, including Columbus and Toledo, Ohio. We have viewed the film, in the light of the

record made in the trial court, and we conclude that it is not obscene within the standards enunciated in *Roth v. United States* and *Alberts v. California,* which we reaffirm here.
Reversed.

THE CHIEF JUSTICE, with whom MR. JUSTICE CLARK joins, dissenting.
In this and other cases in this area of the law, which are coming to us in ever-increasing numbers, we are faced with the resolution of rights basic both to individuals and to society as a whole. Specifically, we are called upon to reconcile the right of the Nation and of the States to maintain a decent society and, on the other hand, the right of individuals to express themselves freely in accordance with the guarantees of the First and Fourteenth Amendments. Although the Federal Government and virtually every State has had laws proscribing obscenity since the Union was formed, and although this Court has recently decided that obscenity is not within the protection of the First Amendment, neither courts nor legislatures have been able to evolve a truly satisfactory definition of obscenity. In other areas of the law, terms like "negligence," although in common use for centuries, have been difficult to define except in the most general manner. Yet the courts have been able to function in such areas with a reasonable degree of efficiency. The obscenity problem, however, is aggravated by the fact that it involves the area of public expression, an area in which a broad range of freedom is vital to our society and is constitutionally protected.

Recently this Court put its hand to the task of defining the term "obscenity" in *Roth v. United States.* . . . The definition enunciated in that case has generated much legal speculation as well as further judicial interpretation by state and federal courts. It has also been relied upon by legislatures. Yet obscenity cases continue to come to this Court, and it becomes increasingly apparent that we must settle as well as we can the question of what constitutes "obscenity" and the question . . . of what standards are permissible in enforcing proscriptions against obscene matter. This Court hears cases such as the instant one not merely to rule upon the alleged obscenity of a specific film or book but to establish principles for the guidance of lower courts and legislatures. Yet most of our decisions since Roth have been given without opinion and have thus failed to furnish such guidance. Nor does the Court in the instant case—which has now been twice argued before us—shed any greater light on the problem. Therefore, I consider it appropriate to state my views at this time.

For all the sound and fury that the *Roth* test has generated, it has not been proved unsound, and I believe that we should try to live with it—at least until a more satisfactory definition is evolved. No government—be it federal, state, or local—should be forced to choose between repressing all material, including that within the realm of decency, and allowing unrestrained license to publish any material, no matter how vile. There must be a rule of reason in this as in other areas of the law, and we have attempted in the *Roth* case to provide such a rule.

It is my belief that when the Court said in *Roth* that obscenity is to be defined by reference to "community standards," it meant community standards—not a national standard, as is sometimes argued. I believe that there is no provable "national standard," and perhaps there should be none. At all events, this Court has not been able to enunciate one, and it would be unreasonable to expect local courts to divine one. It is said that such a "community" approach may well result in material being proscribed as obscene in one community but not in another, and, in all probability, that is true. But communities throughout the Nation are in fact diverse, and it must be remembered that, in cases such as this one, the Court is confronted with the task of reconciling conflicting . . . rights of the diverse communities within our society and of individuals.

We are told that only "hard core pornography" should be denied the protection of the First Amendment. But who can define "hard core pornography" with any greater clarity than "obscenity"? And even if we were to retreat to that position, we would soon be faced with the need to define that term just as we now are faced with the need to define "obscenity." Meanwhile, those who profit from the commercial exploitation of obscenity would continue to ply their trade unmolested.

In my opinion, the use to which various materials are put—not just the words and pictures themselves—must be considered in determining whether or not the materials are obscene. A technical or legal treatise on pornography may well be inoffensive under most circumstances but, at the same time, "obscene" in the extreme when sold or displayed to children.

Finally, material which is in fact obscene under the *Roth* test may be proscribed in a number of ways—for instance, by confiscation of the material or by prosecution of those who disseminate it—provided always that the proscription, whatever it may be, is imposed in accordance with constitutional standards. If the proceeding involved is criminal, there must be a right to a jury trial, a right to counsel, and all the other safeguards necessary to assure due process of law. If the proceeding is civil in nature, the constitutional requirements applicable in such a case must also be observed. There has been . . . some tendency in dealing with this area of the law for enforcement agencies to do only that which is easy to do—for instance, to seize and destroy books with only a minimum of protection. As a result, courts are often presented with procedurally bad cases and, in dealing with them, appear to be acquiescing in the dissemination of obscenity. But if cases were well prepared and were conducted with the appropriate concern for constitutional safeguards, courts would not hesitate to enforce the laws against obscenity. Thus, enforcement agencies must realize that there is no royal road to enforcement; hard and conscientious work is required.

In light of the foregoing, I would reiterate my acceptance of the rule of the *Roth* case: Material is obscene and not constitutionally protected against regulation and proscription if "to the average person, applying contemporary community standards, the dominant theme of the material taken as a whole appeals to prurient interest. . . ." I would commit the enforcement of this rule to the appropriate state and federal courts, and I would accept their judgments made pursuant to the Roth rule, limiting myself to a consideration only of whether there is sufficient evidence in the record upon which a finding of obscenity could be made. If there is no evidence in the record upon which such a finding could be made, obviously the material involved cannot be held obscene. . . . But since a mere modicum of evidence may satisfy a "no evidence" standard, I am unwilling to give the important constitutional right of free expression such limited protection. However, protection of society's right to maintain its moral fiber and the effective administration of justice require that this Court not establish itself as an ultimate censor, in each case reading the entire record, viewing the accused material, and making an independent de novo judgment on the question of obscenity. Therefore, . . . once a finding of obscenity has been made below under a proper application of the Roth test, I would apply a "sufficient evidence" standard of review—requiring something more than merely any evidence but something less than substantial evidence on the record [including the allegedly obscene material] as a whole . . . . This is the only reasonable way I can see to obviate the necessity of this Court's sitting as the Super Censor of all the obscenity purveyed throughout the Nation

While in this case, I do not subscribe to some of the State's extravagant contentions, neither can I say that the courts below acted with intemperance or without sufficient evidence in finding the moving picture obscene within the meaning of the *Roth* test. Therefore, I would affirm the judgment.

Source: FindLaw for Legal Professionals. "U.S. Supreme Court, *Jacobellis v. Ohio*, 378 U.S. 184 (1964)." Available online. URL: http://caselaw.lp.findlaw.com/scripts/getcase.pl?court=us&vol=378&invol=184. Downloaded November 24, 2006.

Justice William Brennan's Opinion for the Supreme Court in *New York Times Co. v. Sullivan* (March 9, 1964) (excerpts)

On March 29, 1960, the New York Times *published a paid advertisement by the Committee to Defend Martin Luther King and the Struggle for Freedom in the South. The ad was titled "Heed Their Rising Voices," and it summarized harassment of Dr. Martin Luther King and various racial confrontations, notably in Montgomery, Alabama. The ad specifically mentioned police harassment in that city.*

L. B. Sullivan, police commissioner for Montgomery, thereupon sued the Times, *claiming he was defamed in the advertisement, although his name was never mentioned. He contended that the* Times *engaged in malicious libel because some of the allegations in the ad were incorrect. Sullivan won his lawsuit in civil court and on appeal in the Alabama courts. The New York Times Company then petitioned the Supreme Court to hear arguments in the case, contending that the suit was a violation of the First and Fourteenth Amendments, and that Sullivan was never directly referred to in the ad.*

The case was heard on January 6, 1964, and decided on March 9, 1964. The Court voted 9-0 to reverse the lower court rulings and remanded the case (sent it back to be reheard). The following are excerpts from Justice William Brennan's opinion for the Court. After discussing the relevance of the Fourteenth Amendment to the case Brennan continued:

> The second contention is that the constitutional guarantees of freedom of speech and of the press are inapplicable here, at least so far as the *Times* is concerned, because the allegedly libelous statements were published as part of a paid, "commercial" advertisement. . . .
>
> The publication here was not a "commercial" advertisement. . . . It communicated information, expressed opinion, recited grievances, protested claimed abuses, and sought financial support on behalf of a movement whose existence and objectives are matters of the highest public interest and concern . . . . That the *Times* was paid for publishing the advertisement

is as immaterial in this connection as is the fact that newspapers and books are sold.... Any other conclusion would discourage newspapers from carrying "editorial advertisements" of this type, and so might shut off an important outlet for the promulgation of information and ideas by persons who do not themselves have access to publishing facilities—who wish to exercise their freedom of speech even though they are not members of the press.... The effect would be to shackle the First Amendment.... To avoid placing such a handicap upon the freedoms of expression, we hold that if the allegedly libelous statements would otherwise be constitutionally protected from the present judgment, they do not forfeit that protection because they were published in the form of a paid advertisement....

Respondent relies heavily, as did the Alabama courts, on statements of this Court to the effect that the Constitution does not protect libelous publications. Those statements do not foreclose our inquiry here. None of the cases sustained the use of libel laws to impose sanctions upon expression critical of the official conduct of public officials.... In deciding the question now, we are compelled by neither precedent nor policy to give any more weight to the epithet "libel" than we have to other "mere labels" of state law.... Like insurrection, contempt, advocacy of unlawful acts, breach of the peace, obscenity, solicitation of legal business, and the various other formulae for the repression of expression that have been challenged in this court, libel can claim no talismanic immunity from constitutional limitations. It must be measured by standards that satisfy the First Amendment....

... The First Amendment, said Judge Learned Hand, "presupposes that right conclusions are more likely to be gathered out of a multitude of tongues, than through any kind of authoritative selection. To many this is, and always will be, folly; but we have staked upon it our all." ... Mr. Justice Brandeis, in his concurring opinion in *Whitney v. California*, ... gave the principle its classic formulation:

"Those who won our independence believed ... that public discussion is a political duty; and that this should be a fundamental principle of the American government. They recognized the risks to which all human institutions are subject. But they knew that order cannot be secured merely through fear of punishment for its infraction; that it is hazardous to discourage thought, hope and imagination; that fear breeds repression; that repression breeds hate; that hate menaces stable government; that the path of safety lies in the opportunity to discuss freely supposed grievances and proposed remedies; and that the fitting remedy for evil counsels is good ones. Believing in the power of reason as applied through public discussion, they eschewed silence coerced by law—the argument of force in its worst form. Recognizing the occasional tyrannies of governing majorities, they amended the Constitution so that free speech and assembly should be guaranteed."

Thus we consider this case against the background of a profound national commitment to the principle that debate on public issues should be uninhibited, robust, and wide-open, and that it may well include vehement, caustic, and sometimes unpleasantly sharp attacks on government and public officials.... The present advertisement, as an expression of grievance and protest on one of the major public issues of our time, would seem clearly to qualify for the constitutional protection. The question is whether it forfeits that protection by the falsity of some of its factual statements and by its alleged defamation of respondent.

Authoritative interpretations of the First Amendment guarantees have consistently refused to recognize an exception for any test of truth—whether administered by judges, juries, or administrative officials—and especially one that puts the burden of proving truth on the speak[er].... The constitutional protection does not turn upon "the truth, popularity, or social utility of the ideas and beliefs which are offered." *N. A. A. C. P. v. Button*, ... As Madison said, "Some degree of abuse is inseparable from the proper use of every thing; and in no instance is this more true than in that of the press" ...

That erroneous statement is inevitable in free debate, and that it must be protected if the freedoms of expression ... are to have the "breathing space" that they "need ... to survive," *N. A. A. C. P. v. Button* ... was also recognized by the Court of Appeals for the District of Columbia Circuit in *Sweeney v. Patterson*....

Injury to official reputation affords no more warrant for repressing speech that would otherwise be free than does factual error ....

If neither factual error nor defamatory content suffices to remove the constitutional shield from criticism of official conduct, the combination of the two elements is no less inadequate. This is the lesson to be drawn from the great controversy over the Sedition Act of 1798, which first crystallized a national awareness of the central meaning of the First Amendment.... The Act allowed the defendant the defense of truth, and provided that the jury were to be judges both of the law and the facts. Despite these qualifications, the Act was vigorously condemned as unconstitutional in an attack joined in by Jefferson and Madison....

... [I]n a debate in the House of Representatives, Madison had said: "If we advert to the nature of Republican Government, we shall find that the censorial power is in the people over the Government, and not in the Government over the people." ...

A rule compelling the critic of official conduct to guarantee the truth of all his factual assertions—and to do so on pain of libel judgments virtually unlimited in amount—leads to a comparable "self-censorship." Allowance of the defense of truth, with the burden of proving it on the defendant, does not mean that only false speech will be deterred. Even courts accepting this defense as an adequate safeguard have recognized the difficulties of adducing legal proofs that the alleged libel was true in all its factual particulars.... Under such a rule, would-be critics of official conduct may be deterred from voicing their criticism, even though it is believed to be true and even though it is in fact true, because of doubt whether it can be proved in court or fear of the expense of having to do so.... The rule thus dampens the vigor and limits the variety of public debate. It is inconsistent with the First and Fourteenth Amendments....

We hold today that the Constitution delimits a State's power to award damages for libel in actions brought by public officials against critics of their official conduct. Since this is such an action, the rule requiring proof of actual malice is applicable. While Alabama law apparently requires proof of actual malice for an award of punitive damages, where general damages are concerned malice is "presumed." Such a presumption is inconsistent ... with the federal rule....

As to the *Times*, we similarly conclude that the facts do not support a finding of actual malice. The statement by the *Times'* Secretary that, apart from the padlocking allegation, he thought the advertisement was "substantially correct," affords no constitutional warrant for the Alabama Supreme Court's conclusion that it was a "cavalier ignoring of the falsity of the advertisement [from which] the jury could not have but been impressed with the bad faith of the *Times*, and its maliciousness inferable therefrom." The statement does not indicate malice at the time of the publication; even if the advertisement was not "substantially correct"—although respondent's own proofs tend to show that it was—that opinion was at least a reasonable one, and there was no evidence to impeach the witness' good faith in holding it....

Finally, there is evidence that the *Times* published the advertisement without checking its accuracy against the news stories in the *Times'* own files. The mere presence of the stories in the files does not, of course, establish that the *Times* "knew" the advertisement was false, since the state of mind required for actual malice would have to be brought home to the persons in the *Times'* organization having responsibility for the publication of the advertisement. With respect to the failure of those persons to make the check, the record shows that they relied upon their knowledge of the good reputation of many of those whose names were listed as sponsors of the advertisement.... There was testimony that the persons handling the advertisement saw nothing in it that would render it unacceptable under the *Times'* policy of rejecting advertisements containing "attacks of a personal character"; their failure to reject it on this ground was not unreasonable. We think ... the evidence against the *Times* supports at most a finding of negligence in failing to discover the misstatements, and is constitutionally insufficient to show the recklessness that is required for a finding of actual malice....

We also think the evidence was constitutionally defective in another respect: it was incapable of supporting the jury's finding that the allegedly libelous statements were made "of and concerning" respondent. Respondent relies on the words of the advertisement and the testimony of six witnesses to establish a connection between it and himself.... There was no reference to respondent in the advertisement, either by name or official position....

... Raising as it does the possibility that a good-faith critic of government will be penalized for his criticism, the proposition relied on by the Alabama courts strikes at the very center of the constitutionally protected area of free expression. We hold that such a proposition may not constitutionally be utilized to establish that an otherwise impersonal attack on governmental operations was a libel of an official responsible for those operations. Since it was relied on exclusively here, and there was no other evidence to connect the statements with respondent, the evidence was constitutionally insufficient to support a finding that the statements referred to respondent.

The judgment of the Supreme Court of Alabama is reversed and the case is remanded to that court for further proceedings not inconsistent with this opinion.

Reversed and remanded.

Source: FindLaw for Legal Professionals. "U.S. Supreme Court *New York Times Co. v. Sullivan,* 376 U.S. 254 (1964)." Available online. URL: http://caselaw.lp.findlaw.com/scripts/getcase.pl?court=us&vol=376&invol=254. Downloaded November 24, 2006.

Justice Hugo Black's Opinion in *New York Times Company v. United States* (June 30, 1971) (excerpts)

In March 1971, Daniel Ellsberg, an analyst for the California think tank Rand Corporation, passed to journalist Neil Sheehan of the New York Times *a copy of a government report titled,* United States-Vietnam Relations, 1945–67. *Among other things, the report detailed the history of U.S. involvement in Vietnam's struggle for independence and support for various dictatorial but anticommunist puppet regimes in the south.*

The New York Times *began publishing excerpts of the report, along with analysis, on June 13, 1971. There were to be 10 installments, but the Justice Department intervened when it sought a restraining order against the newspaper. Judge Murray Gurfein granted the order in a New York federal court.*

Meanwhile Ellsberg also gave a copy of the report to the Washington Post, *which quickly published an excerpt and just as quickly became another newspaper censored by prior restraint. While a Washington, D.C., appeals court lifted the* Post's *restraining order, an appeals court in New York upheld the order against the* Times. *Eventually the two separate battles between the Justice Department and the newspapers made their way (in a combined case) to the Supreme Court. The Court decided to affirm the decision of the Washington, D.C., appeals court and vacate the New York appeals court decision. In other words, the newspapers won.*

What follows is the concurring opinion of Justice Hugo Black.

I adhere to the view that the Government's case against the *Washington Post* should have been dismissed and that the injunction against the *New York Times* should have been vacated without oral argument when the cases were first presented to this Court. I believe that every moment's continuance of the injunctions against these newspapers amounts to a flagrant, indefensible, and continuing violation of the First Amendment. Furthermore, after oral argument, I agree completely that we must affirm the judgment of the Court of Appeals for the District of Columbia Circuit and reverse the judgment of the Court of Appeals for the Second Circuit for the reasons stated by my Brothers DOUGLAS and BRENNAN. In my view it is unfortunate that some of my Brethren are apparently willing to hold that the publication of news may sometimes be enjoined. Such a holding would make a shambles of the First Amendment.

Our Government was launched in 1789 with the adoption of the Constitution. The Bill of Rights, including the First Amendment, followed in 1791. Now, for the first time in the 182 years since the founding of the Republic, the federal courts are asked to hold that the First Amendment does not mean what it says, but rather means that the Government can halt the publication of current news of vital importance to the people of this country.

In seeking injunctions against these newspapers and in its presentation to the Court, the Executive Branch seems to have forgotten the essential purpose and history of the First Amendment. When the Constitution was adopted, many people strongly opposed it because the document contained no Bill of Rights to safeguard certain basic freedoms. They especially feared that the new powers granted to a central government might be interpreted to permit the government to curtail freedom of religion, press, assembly, and speech. In response to an overwhelming public clamor, James Madison offered a series of amendments to satisfy citizens that these great liberties would remain safe and beyond the power of government to abridge. Madison proposed what later became the First Amendment in three parts, two of which are set out below, and one of which proclaimed: "The people shall not be deprived or abridged of their right to speak, to write, or to publish their sentiments; and the freedom of the press, as one of the great bulwarks of liberty, shall be inviolable." The amendments were offered to curtail and restrict the general powers granted to the Executive, Legislative, and Judicial Branches two years before in the original Constitution. The Bill of Rights changed the original Constitution into a new charter under which no branch of government could abridge the people's freedoms of press, speech, religion, and assembly. Yet the Solicitor General argues and some members of the Court appear to agree that the general powers of the Government adopted in the original Constitution should be interpreted to limit and restrict the specific and emphatic guarantees of the Bill of Rights adopted later. I can imagine no greater perversion of history. Madison and the other Framers of the First Amendment, able men that they were, wrote in language they earnestly believed could never be misunderstood: "Congress shall make no law . . . abridging the freedom . . . of the press. . . ." Both the history and language of the First Amendment support the view that the press must be left free to publish news, whatever the source, without censorship, injunctions, or prior restraints.

In the First Amendment the Founding Fathers gave the free press the protection it must have to fulfill its essential role in our democracy. The press was to serve the governed, not the governors. The Government's power to censor the press was abolished so that the press would remain forever free to censure the Government. The press was protected so that it could bare the secrets of government and inform the people. Only a free and unrestrained press can effectively expose deception in government. And paramount among the responsibilities of a free press is the duty to prevent any part of the government from deceiving the people and sending them off to distant lands to die of foreign fevers and foreign shot and shell. In my view, far from deserving condemnation for their courageous reporting, the *New York Times*, the *Washington Post*, and other newspapers should be commended for serving the purpose that the Founding Fathers saw so clearly. In revealing the workings of government that led to the Vietnam war, the newspapers nobly did precisely that which the Founders hoped and trusted they would do.

The Government's case here is based on premises entirely different from those that guided the Framers of the First Amendment. The Solicitor General has carefully and emphatically stated:

"Now, Mr. Justice [BLACK], your construction of . . . [the First Amendment] is well known, and I certainly respect it. You say that no law means no law, and that should be obvious. I can only [403 U.S. 713, 718] say, Mr. Justice, that to me it is equally obvious that 'no law' does not mean 'no law,' and I would seek to persuade the Court that is true. . . . [T]here are other parts of the Constitution that grant powers and responsibilities to the Executive, and . . . the First Amendment was not intended to make it impossible for the Executive to function or to protect the security of the United States."

And the Government argues in its brief that in spite of the First Amendment, "[t]he authority of the Executive Department to protect the nation against publication of information whose disclosure would endanger the national security stems from two interrelated sources: the constitutional power of the President over the conduct of foreign affairs and his authority as Commander-in-Chief."

In other words, we are asked to hold that despite the First Amendment's emphatic command, the Executive Branch, the Congress, and the Judiciary can make laws enjoining publication of current news and abridging freedom of the press in the name of "national security." The Government does not even attempt to rely on any act of Congress. Instead it makes the bold and dangerously far-reaching contention that the courts should take it upon themselves to "make" a law abridging freedom of the press in the name of equity, presidential power and national security, even when the representatives of the people in Congress have adhered to the command of the First Amendment and refused to make such a law. To find that the President has "inherent power" to halt the publication of news by resort to the courts would wipe out the First Amendment and destroy the fundamental liberty and security of the very people the Government hopes to make "secure." No one can read the history of the adoption of the First Amendment without being convinced beyond any doubt that it was injunctions like those sought here that Madison and his collaborators intended to outlaw in this Nation for all time.

The word "security" is a broad, vague generality whose contours should not be invoked to abrogate the fundamental law embodied in the First Amendment. The guarding of military and diplomatic secrets at the expense of informed representative government provides no real security for our Republic. The Framers of the First Amendment, fully aware of both the need to defend a new nation and the abuses of the English and Colonial governments, sought to give this new society strength and security by providing that freedom of speech, press, religion, and assembly should not be abridged. This thought was eloquently expressed in 1937 by Mr. Chief Justice Hughes—great man and great Chief Justice that he was—when the Court held a man could not be punished for attending a meeting run by Communists. . . .

Source: FindLaw for Legal Professionals. "U.S. Supreme Court, *New York Times Co. v. United States,* 403 U.S. 713." Available online. URL: http://caselaw.lp.findlaw.com/scripts/getcase.pl?court=us&vol=403&invol=713. Downloaded November 24, 2006.

USA PATRIOT Act (October 26, 2001) (excerpts)

One and a half months after the terrorist attacks of September 11, 2001, on New York City and Washington, D.C., Congress swiftly passed, and President George W. Bush signed, the Uniting and Strengthening America by Providing Appropriate Tools Required to Intercept and Obstruct Terrorism Act, *generally known by its acronym the USA PATRIOT Act.*

The USA PATRIOT Act was promulgated to fight the war on terrorism, but critics have charged that it also infringes on rights guaranteed by the First Amendment. Furthermore, they charge, the broad powers given to the Justice Department, which is within the executive branch of the federal government, tips the balance of powers as set out by the Founding Fathers.

The act itself is not a completely new law or set of laws but is a series of amendments to the U.S. Code. The act is divided into two sections; section one is further divided into 10 titles, or chapters. Each title is subdivided into sections, which are themselves subdivided according to the number of emendations in each. What follows are excerpts from the USA PATRIOT Act and the sections of the U.S. Code (U.S.C.) to which each excerpt refers.

SEC. 204. CLARIFICATION OF INTELLIGENCE EXCEPTIONS FROM LIMITATIONS ON INTERCEPTION AND DISCLOSURE OF WIRE, ORAL, AND ELECTRONIC COMMUNICATIONS

Section 2511(2)(f) of title 18, United States Code, is amended—

(1) by striking 'this chapter or chapter 121' and inserting 'this chapter or chapter 121 or 206 of this title'; and

(2) by striking 'wire and oral' and inserting 'wire, oral, and electronic'.

U.S.C. Title 18, Section 2511. Interception and disclosure of wire, oral, or electronic communications prohibited

[(2)](f) Nothing contained in this chapter or chapter 121 or 206 of this title, or section 705 of the Communications Act of 1934, shall be deemed to affect the acquisition by the United States Government of foreign intelligence information from international or foreign communications, or foreign intelligence activities conducted in accordance with otherwise applicable Federal law involving a foreign electronic communications system, utilizing a means other than electronic surveillance as defined in section 101 of the Foreign Intelligence Surveillance Act of 1978, and procedures in this chapter or chapter 121 and the Foreign Intelligence Surveillance Act of 1978 shall be the exclusive means by which electronic surveillance, as defined in section 101 of such Act, and the interception of domestic wire, oral, and electronic communications may be conducted.

SEC. 210. SCOPE OF SUBPOENAS FOR RECORDS OF ELECTRONIC COMMUNICATIONS.

Section 2703(c)(2) of title 18, United States Code, as redesignated by section 212, is amended—

(1) by striking 'entity the name, address, local and long distance telephone toll billing records, telephone number or other subscriber number or identity, and length of service of a subscriber' and inserting the following: 'entity the—

'(A) name;

'(B) address;

'(C) local and long distance telephone connection records, or records of session times and durations;

'(D) length of service (including start date) and types of service utilized;

'(E) telephone or instrument number or other subscriber number or identity, including any temporarily assigned network address; and

'(F) means and source of payment for such service (including any credit card or bank account number),

of a subscriber'; and

(2) by striking 'and the types of services the subscriber or customer utilized,'.

SEC. 212. EMERGENCY DISCLOSURE OF ELECTRONIC COMMUNICATIONS TO PROTECT LIFE AND LIMB.

(a) DISCLOSURE OF CONTENTS— . . .

U.S.C. Title 18, Sec. 2703. Required disclosure of customer communications or records

(B) in subsection (c) by redesignating paragraph (2) as paragraph (3);

(C) in subsection (c)(1)–

(i) by striking '(A) Except as provided in subparagraph (B), a provider of electronic communication service or remote computing service may' and inserting 'A governmental entity may require a provider of electronic communication service or remote computing service to';

(ii) by striking 'covered by subsection (a) or (b) of this section) to any person other than a governmental entity.

'(B) A provider of electronic communication service or remote computing service shall disclose a record or other information pertaining to a subscriber to or customer of such service (not including the contents of communications covered by subsection (a) or (b) of this section) to a governmental entity' and inserting')';

(iii) by redesignating subparagraph (C) as paragraph (2);

(iv) by redesignating clauses (i), (ii), (iii), and (iv) as subparagraphs (A), (B), (C), and (D), respectively;

(v) in subparagraph (D) (as redesignated) by striking the period and inserting '; or'; and

(vi) by inserting after subparagraph (D) (as redesignated) the following:

'(E) seeks information under paragraph (2).'; and

(D) in paragraph (2) (as redesignated) by striking 'subparagraph (B)' and insert 'paragraph (1)'.

(2) TECHNICAL AND CONFORMING AMENDMENT—The table of sections for chapter 121 of title 18, United States Code, is amended by striking the item relating to section 2703 and inserting the following:

'2703. Required disclosure of customer communications or records.'.

U.S.C. Section 2703. Required disclosure of customer communications or records

(a) Contents of Wire or Electronic Communications in Electronic Storage.—A governmental entity may require the disclosure by a provider of electronic communication service of the contents of a wire or electronic communication, that is in electronic storage in an electronic communications system for one hundred and eighty days or less, only pursuant to a warrant issued using the procedures described in the Federal Rules of Criminal Procedure by a court with jurisdiction over the offense under investigation or equivalent State warrant. A governmental entity may require the disclosure by a provider of electronic communications services of the contents of a wire or electronic communication that has been in electronic storage in an electronic communications system for more than one hundred and eighty days by the means available under subsection (b) of this section.

(b) Contents of Wire or Electronic Communications in a Remote Computing Service.

(1) A governmental entity may require a provider of remote computing service to disclose the contents of any wire or electronic communication to which this paragraph is made applicable by paragraph (2) of this subsection—

(A) without required notice to the subscriber or customer, if the governmental entity obtains a warrant issued using the procedures described in the Federal Rules of Criminal Procedure by a court with jurisdiction over the offense under investigation or equivalent State warrant; or

(B) with prior notice from the governmental entity to the subscriber or customer if the governmental entity—

(i) uses an administrative subpoena authorized by a Federal or State statute or a Federal or State grand jury or trial subpoena; or

(ii) obtains a court order for such disclosure under subsection (d) of this section; except that delayed notice may be given pursuant to section 2705 of this title.

(2) Paragraph (1) is applicable with respect to any wire or electronic communication that is held or maintained on that service

(A) on behalf of, and received by means of electronic transmission from (or created by means of computer processing of communications received by means of electronic transmission from), a subscriber or customer of such remote computing service; and

(B) solely for the purpose of providing storage or computer processing services to such subscriber or customer, if the provider is not authorized to access the contents of any such communications for purposes of providing any services other than storage or computer processing.

(c) Records Concerning Electronic Communication Service or Remote Computing Service

(1) A governmental entity may require a provider of electronic communication service or remote computing service to disclose a record or other information pertaining to a subscriber to or customer of such service (not including the contents of communications) only when the governmental entity—

(A) obtains a warrant issued using the procedures described in the Federal Rules of Criminal Procedure by a court with jurisdiction over the offense under investigation or equivalent State warrant;

(B) obtains a court order for such disclosure under subsection (d) of this section;

(C) has the consent of the subscriber or customer to such disclosure; or (!1)

(D) submits a formal written request relevant to a law enforcement investigation concerning telemarketing fraud for the name, address, and place of business of a subscriber or customer of such provider, which subscriber or customer is engaged in telemarketing (as such term is defined in section 2325 of this title); or

(E) seeks information under paragraph (2).

(2) A provider of electronic communication service or remote computing service shall disclose to a governmental entity the—

(A) name;

(B) address;

(C) local and long distance telephone connection records, or records of session times and durations;

(D) length of service (including start date) and types of service utilized;

(E) telephone or instrument number or other subscriber number or identity, including any temporarily assigned network address; and

(F) means and source of payment for such service (including any credit card or bank account number),

of a subscriber to or customer of such service when the governmental entity uses an administrative subpoena authorized by a Federal or State statute or a Federal or State grand jury or trial subpoena or any means available under paragraph (1).

(3) A governmental entity receiving records or information under this subsection is not required to provide notice to a subscriber or customer.

(d) Requirements for Court Order.

A court order for disclosure under subsection (b) or (c) may be issued by any court that is a court of competent jurisdiction and shall issue only if the governmental entity offers specific and articulable facts showing that there are reasonable grounds to believe that the contents of a wire or electronic communication, or the records or other information sought, are relevant and material to an ongoing criminal investigation. In the case of a State governmental authority, such a court order shall not issue if prohibited by the law of such State. A court issuing an order pursuant to this section, on a motion made promptly by the service provider, may quash or modify such order, if the information or records requested are unusually voluminous in nature or compliance with such order otherwise would cause an undue burden on such provider.

(e) No Cause of Action Against a Provider Disclosing Information Under This Chapter.

No cause of action shall lie in any court against any provider of wire or electronic communication service, its officers, employees, agents, or other specified persons for providing information, facilities, or assistance in accordance with the terms of a court order, warrant, subpoena, statutory authorization, or certification under this chapter.

(f) Requirement To Preserve Evidence.

(1) In general.—A provider of wire or electronic communication services or a remote computing service, upon the request of a governmental entity,

shall take all necessary steps to preserve records and other evidence in its possession pending the issuance of a court order or other process.

(2) Period of retention.—Records referred to in paragraph (1) shall be retained for a period of 90 days, which shall be extended for an additional 90-day period upon a renewed request by the governmental entity.

(g) Presence of Officer Not Required.

Notwithstanding section 3105 of this title, the presence of an officer shall not be required for service or execution of a search warrant issued in accordance with this chapter requiring disclosure by a provider of electronic communications service or remote computing service of the contents of communications or records or other information pertaining to a subscriber to or customer of such service.

SEC. 213. AUTHORITY FOR DELAYING NOTICE OF THE EXECUTION OF A WARRANT.

Section 3103a of title 18, United States Code, is amended—

(1) by inserting '(a) IN GENERAL-' before 'In addition'; and

(2) by adding at the end the following:

'(b) DELAY—With respect to the issuance of any warrant or court order under this section, or any other rule of law, to search for and seize any property or material that constitutes evidence of a criminal offense in violation of the laws of the United States, any notice required, or that may be required, to be given may be delayed if—

'(1) the court finds reasonable cause to believe that providing immediate notification of the execution of the warrant may have an adverse result (as defined in section 2705);

'(2) the warrant prohibits the seizure of any tangible property, any wire or electronic communication (as defined in section 2510), or, except as expressly provided in chapter 121, any stored wire or electronic information, except where the court finds reasonable necessity for the seizure; and

'(3) the warrant provides for the giving of such notice within a reasonable period of its execution, which period may thereafter be extended by the court for good cause shown.'.

U.S.C. Section 3103a. Additional grounds for issuing warrant

(a) In General.—In addition to the grounds for issuing a warrant in section 3103 of this title, a warrant may be issued to search for and seize any property that constitutes evidence of a criminal offense in violation of the laws of the United States.

(b) Delay.—With respect to the issuance of any warrant or court order under this section, or any other rule of law, to search for and seize any property or material that constitutes evidence of a criminal offense in violation of the laws of the United States, any notice required, or that may be required, to be given may be

delayed if—

(1) the court finds reasonable cause to believe that providing immediate notification of the execution of the warrant may have an adverse result (as defined in section 2705);

(2) the warrant prohibits the seizure of any tangible property, any wire or electronic communication (as defined in section 2510), or, except as expressly provided in chapter 121, any stored wire or electronic information, except where the court finds reasonable necessity for the seizure; and

(3) the warrant provides for the giving of such notice within a reasonable period of its execution, which period may thereafter be extended by the court for good cause shown.

SEC. 412. MANDATORY DETENTION OF SUSPECTED TERRORISTS; HABEAS CORPUS; JUDICIAL REVIEW.

(b) HABEAS CORPUS AND JUDICIAL REVIEW—

'(1) IN GENERAL—Judicial review of any action or decision relating to this section (including judicial review of the merits of a determination made under subsection (a)(3) or (a)(6)) is available exclusively in habeas corpus proceedings consistent with this subsection. Except as provided in the preceding sentence, no court shall have jurisdiction to review, by habeas corpus petition or otherwise, any such action or decision.

'(2) APPLICATION—

'(A) IN GENERAL—Notwithstanding any other provision of law, including section 2241(a) of title 28, United States Code, habeas corpus proceedings described in paragraph (1) may be initiated only by an application filed with—

'(i) the Supreme Court;

'(ii) any justice of the Supreme Court;

'(iii) any circuit judge of the United States Court of Appeals for the District of Columbia Circuit; or

'(iv) any district court otherwise having jurisdiction to entertain it.

'(B) APPLICATION TRANSFER—Section 2241(b) of title 28, United States Code, shall apply to an application for a writ of habeas corpus described in subparagraph (A).

'(3) APPEALS—Notwithstanding any other provision of law, including section 2253 of title 28, in habeas corpus proceedings described in paragraph (1) before a circuit or district judge, the final order shall be subject to review, on appeal, by the United States Court of Appeals for the District of Columbia Circuit. There shall be no right of appeal in such proceedings to any other circuit court of appeals.

'(4) RULE OF DECISION—The law applied by the Supreme Court and the United States Court of Appeals for the District of Columbia Circuit shall be regarded as the rule of decision in habeas corpus proceedings described in paragraph (1).

SEC. 505. MISCELLANEOUS NATIONAL SECURITY AUTHORITIES.
(a) TELEPHONE TOLL AND TRANSACTIONAL Records—Section 2709(b) of title 18, United States Code, is amended—

(1) in the matter preceding paragraph (1), by inserting 'at Bureau headquarters or a Special Agent in Charge in a Bureau field office designated by the Director' after 'Assistant Director';

(2) in paragraph (1)—

(A) by striking 'in a position not lower than Deputy Assistant Director'; and

(B) by striking 'made that' and all that follows and inserting the following: 'made that the name, address, length of service, and toll billing records sought are relevant to an authorized investigation to protect against international terrorism or clandestine intelligence activities, provided that such an investigation of a United States person is not conducted solely on the basis of activities protected by the first amendment to the Constitution of the United States; and'; and

(3) in paragraph (2)—

(A) by striking 'in a position not lower than Deputy Assistant Director'; and

(B) by striking 'made that' and all that follows and inserting the following: 'made that the information sought is relevant to an authorized investigation to protect against international terrorism or clandestine intelligence activities, provided that such an investigation of a United States person is not conducted solely upon the basis of activities protected by the first amendment to the Constitution of the United States.'.

(b) FINANCIAL Records--Section 1114(a)(5)(A) of the Right to Financial Privacy Act of 1978 (12 U.S.C. 3414(a)(5)(A)) is amended—

(1) by inserting 'in a position not lower than Deputy Assistant Director at Bureau headquarters or a Special Agent in Charge in a Bureau field office designated by the Director' after 'designee'; and

(2) by striking 'sought' and all that follows and inserting 'sought for foreign counter intelligence purposes to protect against international terrorism or clandestine intelligence activities, provided that such an investigation of a United States person is not conducted solely upon the basis of activities protected by the first amendment to the Constitution of the United States.'.

(c) CONSUMER REPORTS—Section 624 of the Fair Credit Reporting Act (15 U.S.C. 1681u) is amended—

(1) in subsection (a)—

(A) by inserting 'in a position not lower than Deputy Assistant Director at Bureau headquarters or a Special Agent in Charge of a Bureau field office designated by the Director' after 'designee' the first place it appears; and

(B) by striking 'in writing that' and all that follows through the end and inserting the following: 'in writing, that such information is sought for the conduct of an authorized investigation to protect against international terrorism or clandestine intelligence activities, provided that such an investigation of a United States person is not conducted solely upon the basis of activities protected by the first amendment to the Constitution of the United States.';

(2) in subsection (b)—

(A) by inserting 'in a position not lower than Deputy Assistant Director at Bureau headquarters or a Special Agent in Charge of a Bureau field office designated by the Director' after 'designee' the first place it appears; and

(B) by striking 'in writing that' and all that follows through the end and inserting the following: 'in writing that such information is sought for the conduct of an authorized investigation to protect against international terrorism or clandestine intelligence activities, provided that such an investigation of a United States person is not conducted solely upon the basis of activities protected by the first amendment to the Constitution of the United States.'; and

(3) in subsection (c)—

(A) by inserting 'in a position not lower than Deputy Assistant Director at Bureau headquarters or a Special Agent in Charge in a Bureau field office designated by the Director' after 'designee of the Director'; and

(B) by striking 'in camera that' and all that follows through 'States.' and inserting the following: 'in camera that the consumer report is sought for the conduct of an authorized investigation to protect against international terrorism or clandestine intelligence activities, provided that such an investigation of a United States person is not conducted solely upon the basis of activities protected by the first amendment to the Constitution of the United States.'.

U.S.C. Section 2709. Counterintelligence access to telephone toll and transactional records

(a) Duty to Provide.—A wire or electronic communication service provider shall comply with a request for subscriber information and toll billing records information, or electronic communication transactional records in its custody or possession made by the Director of the Federal Bureau of Investigation under subsection (b) of this section.

(b) Required Certification.—The Director of the Federal Bureau of Investigation, or his designee in a position not lower than Deputy Assistant Director at Bureau headquarters or a Special Agent in Charge in a Bureau field office designated by the Director, may

(1) request the name, address, length of service, and local and long distance toll billing records of a person or entity if the Director (or his designee) certifies in writing to the wire or electronic communication service provider to which the request is made that the name, address, length of service, and toll billing records sought are relevant to an authorized investigation to protect against international terrorism or clandestine intelligence activities, provided that such an investigation of a United States person is not conducted solely on the basis of activities protected by the first amendment to the Constitution of the United States; and

(2) request the name, address, and length of service of a person or entity if the Director (or his designee) certifies in writing to the wire or electronic communication service provider to which the request is made that the information sought is relevant to an authorized investigation to protect against international terrorism or clandestine intelligence activities, provided that such an investigation of a United States person is not conducted solely upon the basis of activities protected by the first amendment to the Constitution of the United States.

(c) Prohibition of Certain Disclosure.

No wire or electronic communication service provider, or officer, employee, or agent thereof, shall disclose to any person that the Federal Bureau of Investigation has sought or obtained access to information or records under this section.

(d) Dissemination by Bureau.—The Federal Bureau of Investigation may disseminate information and records obtained under this section only as provided in guidelines approved by the Attorney General for foreign intelligence collection and foreign counterintelligence investigations conducted by the Federal Bureau of Investigation, and, with respect to dissemination to an agency of the United States, only if such information is clearly relevant to the authorized responsibilities of such agency.

(e) Requirement That Certain Congressional Bodies Be Informed.

On a semiannual basis the Director of the Federal Bureau of Investigation shall fully inform the Permanent Select Committee on Intelligence of the

House of Representatives and the Select Committee on Intelligence of the Senate, and the Committee on the Judiciary of the House of Representatives and the Committee on the Judiciary of the Senate, concerning all requests made under subsection (b) of this section.

Source: Electronic Privacy Information Center. "H.R. 3162 in the Senate of the United States, October 24, 2001." Available online. URL: http://www.epic.org/privacy/terrorism/hr3162.html. Downloaded, December 1, 2006. Findlaw for Legal Professionals. "Laws: Cases and Codes: U.S. Code." Available online. URL: http://caselaw.lp.findlaw.com/casecode/uscodes/toc.html. Downloaded December 1, 2006.

5

International Documents

The documents in this chapter are of a less historical character than those in the previous chapter, being primarily from the last quarter of the 20th century and the first years of the 21st century. Two exceptions are quotes of Mao Zedong and excerpts from Nikita Khrushchev's secret speech. Both of these are included to provide context as both China and Russia have undergone economic, and, in the case of Russia, political changes in the past two decades.

Otherwise, the documents are arranged in chronological order by country. Collectively, they provide a glimpse of the extent of censorship in each of the four countries. The documents excerpt various laws and regulations that are the basis of censorship in the four foreign case-study countries, and a nongovernmental agency report that covers the range of intimidation of the Egyptian press; they are arranged in chronological order by country. Collectively, they provide a glimpse of the extent of censorship in each of the four countries.

CHINA

Mao Zedong

The following quotes from Mao Zedong, while not directly dealing with censorship, illustrate his attitude toward the roles of citizens, particularly writers and artists, in shaping a Communist society. During his lifetime Mao's dicta were commonly known as "Mao Zedong thought" and often taken as guiding principles when formulating policy in the People's Republic of China (PRC). Anyone seen as stepping outside the norms of PRC policy was (and is) liable to fall victim to censorship, at the very least.

The final quote illustrates Mao's thinking at the onset of the Hundred Flowers Campaign, which many scholars have come to regard as a method Mao used to purge his enemies within the Party and those who were not fully committed to the revolution.

"Talks at the Yenan Forum on Literature and Art" (May 1942) (excerpts)

Our literary and art workers must . . . gradually move their feet over to the side of the workers, peasants and soldiers, to the side of the proletariat, through the process of going into their very midst and into the thick of practical struggles and through the process of studying Marxism and society. Only in this way can we have a literature and art that are truly for the workers, peasants and soldiers, a truly proletarian literature and art.

In literary and art criticism there are two criteria, the political and the artistic. . . . [W]hat is the relationship between the two? Politics cannot be equated with art, nor can a general world outlook be equated with a method of artistic creation and criticism. . . . What we demand is the unity of politics and art, the unity of content and form, the unity of revolutionary political content and the highest possible perfection of artistic form. Works of art which lack artistic quality have no force, however progressive they are politically. Therefore, we oppose both the tendency to produce works of art with a wrong political viewpoint and the tendency towards the "poster and slogan style" which is correct in political viewpoint but lacking in artistic power. On questions of literature and art we must carry on a struggle on two fronts.

Source: Mao Tse Tung Internet Archive (Marxists.org) 2000. "Quotations from Mao Tse Tung, Chapter 32: Culture and Art." Available online. URL: http://www.marxists.org/reference/archive/mao/works/red-book/ch32.htm. Downloaded October 20, 2006.

"On the Correct Handling of Contradictions Among the People" (February 27, 1957) (excerpt)

In their political activities, how should our people judge whether a person's words and deeds are right or wrong? On the basis of the principles of our Constitution, the will of the overwhelming majority of our people and the common political positions which have been proclaimed on various occasions by our political parties, we consider that, broadly speaking, the criteria should be as follows:

(1) Words and deeds should help to unite, and not divide, the people of all our nationalities.

(2) They should be beneficial, and not harmful, to socialist transformation and socialist construction.

(3) They should help to consolidate, and not undermine or weaken, the people's democratic dictatorship.

(4) They should help to consolidate, and not undermine or weaken, democratic centralism.

(5) They should help to strengthen, and not shake off or weaken, the leadership of the Communist Party.

(6) They should be beneficial, and not harmful, to international socialist unity and the unity of the peace-loving people of the world.

Of these six criteria, the most important are the socialist path and the leadership of the Party.

Letting a hundred flowers blossom and a hundred schools of thought contend is the policy for promoting the progress in the arts and sciences and a flourishing socialist culture in our land. Different forms and styles in art should develop freely and different schools in science should contend freely. We think that it is harmful to the growth of art and science if administrative measures are used to impose one particular style of art or school of thought and to ban another. Questions of right and wrong in the arts and science should be settled through free discussion in artistic and scientific circles and through practical work in these fields.

Source: Selected Works of Mao Tse Tung (Marxists.org). "On the Correct Handling of contradictions Among the People." Available online. URL: http://www.marxists.org/reference/archive/mao/selected-works/volume-5/mswv5_58.htm. Downloaded October 20, 2006.

Measures on the Regulation of Public Computer Networks and the Internet (1996)

One of the earliest laws to regulate the Internet in the PRC, it was issued by the Ministry of Post and Telecommunications and adopted in 1996. The key article with regard to censorship is Article 10, which liberally interpreted can ban a lot of activity and documents.

Article 2. China Public Computer Network (i.e. Chinanet), refers to the interconnecting network built, operated and managed by China's General Bureau of Posts and Telecommunications (GBPT). This network connects computers to the Internet and is responsible for general service.

Article 3. Chinanet is divided into network management centers and information service centers.

Article 10. No unit or individual may use the Internet to engage in criminal activities such as harming national security or disclosing state secrets. No unit or individual may use the Internet to retrieve, replicate, create, or transmit information that harms national security, threatens social stability and promotes sexually suggestive material. Discoveries of the aforementioned criminal activities and harmful information should be reported to related supervisory units in a timely fashion.

Article 12. Connecting network units, entry point units and users must cooperate with the state's legitimate efforts to monitor and inspect Internet information security, and they should provide necessary information and conditions. . . .

Source: Novexcn.com. "Measures on the Regulation of Public Computer Networks and the Internet." Available online. URL: http://www.novexcn.com/pub_comput_netwrosk_intern.html. Downloaded October 26, 2006.

Measures for Managing Internet Information Services (October 1, 2000) (excerpts)

The PRC had been promulgating numerous Internet regulations to enhance government control since the mid-1990s, amending them to adapt to the ever-changing technology. These excerpted regulations, which have become part of what is now known as the "Great Firewall of China," were issued on October 1, 2000, by the State Council.

Article 1: These measures are drawn up for the purpose of regulating Internet information services (IIS) and promoting the healthy and orderly development of such services.

Article 4: The state requires that commercial IIS be licensed and that non-commercial IIS report their services for the official records. No one may provide IIS without a license or without reporting its services.

Article 5: Prior to applying for an operating license or reporting IIS services for the record, an IIS provider whose services relate to information, the publishing business, education, medical and health care, pharmaceuticals, and medical apparatus; and whose services require the concurrence of the relevant supervisory authorities in accordance with the law, with administrative regulations, or with other relevant state laws, must first obtain the approval of the relevant supervisory authorities.

Article 9: An IIS provider planning to provide e-announcements shall submit a special application, or special request for the record, in accordance with relevant state regulations when it applies for a commercial IIS license, or when it reports its special request to provide non-commercial IIS for the record.

Article 14: An IIS providing services related to information, the publishing business, and e-announcements shall record the content of the information, the time that the information is released, and the address or the domain name of the Web site.

An Internet service provider (ISP) must record such information as the time that its subscribers accessed the Internet, the subscribers' account numbers, the addresses or domain names of the Web sites, and the main telephone numbers they use.

An IIS provider and the ISP must keep a copy of their records for 60 days and furnish them to the relevant state authorities upon demand in accordance with the law.

Article 15: IIS providers shall not produce, reproduce, release, or disseminate information that contains any of the following:

1. Information that goes against the basic principles set in the constitution;

2. Information that endangers national security, divulges state secrets, subverts the government, or undermines national unity;

3. Information that is detrimental to the honor and interests of the state;

4. Information that instigates ethnic hatred or ethnic discrimination, or that undermines national unity;

5. Information that undermines the state's policy towards religions, or that preaches the teachings of evil cults or that promotes feudalistic and superstitious beliefs;

6. Information that disseminates rumors, disturbs social order, or undermines social stability;

7. Information that spreads pornography or other salacious materials; promotes gambling, violence, homicide, or terrorism; or instigates crimes;

8. Information that insults or slanders other people, or infringes upon other people's legitimate rights and interests; or

9. Other information prohibited by the law or administrative regulations.

Article 16: When an IIS provider discovers that the information its Web site provides is clearly of a type listed under Article 15, it should immediately stop transmission, keep the relevant records, and report the situation to the relevant state authorities.

Article 21: For those who fail to meet the obligations prescribed in Article 14, the telecommunications administration of the relevant province, autonomous region, or municipality under the central government's direct jurisdiction will order them to mend their ways. If the cases are serious, these administrations will order them to suspend their operations pending rectification of the acts, or shut down their Web sites temporarily.

Source: Novexcn.com. "Measures for Managing Internet Information Service." Available online. URL: http://www.novexcn.com/internet_law_2000.html. Downloaded October 26, 2006.

Decision of the Standing Committee of the National People's Congress on Banning Heretical Cult Organizations, Preventing and Punishing Cult Activities (October 1999) (excerpts)

This decision was implemented in October 1999. Since it does not specifically state what constitutes a "heresy" other than to "disturb social order and jeopardize people's lives and property and economic development" the inference is that religions (or cults) that question the government or the Communist Party or their policies would find themselves in jeopardy. One such religion, Falun Gong, was banned in 2000.

To maintain social stability, protect the interests of the people, and guarantee the smooth progress of reform and opening and the socialist modernization drive, it is imperative to ban heretical cult organizations, and to prevent and punish cult activities. In line with the Constitution and relevant laws, the following decision is hereby made:

1. Heretical cult organizations shall be resolutely banned according to the law, and all of their criminal activities shall be dealt with severely. Heretical cults, operating under the guise of religion, qigong or other forms, employ various means to disturb social order and jeopardize people's lives and property and economic development, and they must be banned according to the law and punished resolutely. People's courts, people's procuratorates, public security, national security, and judicial and administrative organs shall fulfill their respective duties and cooperate in carrying out these tasks. Persons who do the following will be dealt with severely according to the law: those who organize and take advantage of cult organizations to violate national laws and administrative regulations, who gather a crowd to make trouble, who disrupt social order, and who deceive others, cause deaths, rape women, swindle people out their money and property, or commit other crimes using superstition and heresy.

3. The long-term, comprehensive publicity of and education about the Constitution and laws shall be carried out among all citizens, and the knowledge of science and culture shall be popularized. Banning heretical cult organizations and punishing heretical cult activities according to the law is conducive to protecting normal religious activities and the citizens' freedom of religious belief. The masses of people should be fully aware of the inhumane and anti-social nature of heretic cults so that they can knowingly oppose and resist the influences of cult organizations, enhance their awareness of the law and abide by national laws.

Source: Novexcn.com. "Decision of the Standing Committee of the National People's Congress on Banning Heretical Cult Organizations, Preventing and Punishing Cult Activities." Available online. URL: http://www.novexcn.com/stand_comit_cult_activ.html. Downloaded October 28, 2006.

Regulations on Broadcasting and Television Administration (September 1, 1997) (excerpts)

The Regulations on Broadcasting and Television Administration, enacted to control television and radio broadcasts in the People's Republic of China, came into force on September 1, 1997. The excerpts below highlight the extent of censorship in the Chinese broadcast industry.

Article 1 These Regulations are formulated for the purpose of enhancing broadcasting and television administration, developing the cause of broadcasting and television and promoting the building of socialist spiritual civilization and material civilization.

Article 2 These Regulations shall be applicable to such activities as the establishment of broadcasting stations and television stations and gathering and editing, making, broadcasting and transmitting broadcasting and television programs within the territory of the People's Republic of China.

Article 3 The cause of broadcasting and television should adhere to the orientation of serving the people and socialism and persevere in correct media guidance.

Article 20 Broadcasting and television transmitting stations and relay stations should transmit and relay broadcasting and television programs in accordance with the relevant provisions of the department of broadcasting and television administration under the State Council. . . .

Article 21 No broadcasting and television transmitting station and relay station shall broadcast self-sponsored programs or insert advertisements without authorization.

Article 24 No unit or individual shall broadcast any program via a network of cable broadcasting and television transmission coverage without approval.

Article 32 Broadcasting stations and television stations should improve the quality of broadcasting and television programs, increase the number of excellent Chinese programs and ban the production and broadcast of programs containing any of the following contents:

(1) that which endangers the unity, sovereignty and territorial integrity of the country;

(2) that which endangers state security, honor and interests;

(3) that which instigates nationality separation or disrupts nationality solidarity;

(4) that which divulges state secrets;

(5) that which slanders or insults others;

(6) that which propagates obscenity, superstition or plays up violence; and

(7) other contents prohibited under provisions of laws and regulations.

Article 33 Broadcasting stations and television stations should conduct pre-broadcast censorship and rebroadcast censorship over the contents of their respective broadcasting and television programs pursuant to the provisions of Article 32 of these Regulations.

Article 35 . . . Control measures for television opera production and broadcast shall be formulated by the department of broadcasting and television administration under the State Council.

Article 37 . . . Broadcasting and television stations set up by villages and townships shall not run their own television programs.

Article 39 External films and television operas to be used for broadcast by broadcasting stations and television stations must be subject to the examination and approval of the department of broadcasting and television administration under the State Council. Other external broadcasting and television programs to be used for broadcast by broadcasting stations and television stations must be subject to the examination and approval of the department of broadcasting and television administration under the State Council or its authorized agencies.

Article 43 The department of broadcasting and television administration under the State Council may, under extraordinary circumstances, make a decision to suspend the broadcast, change a particular program or designate the relay of a particular program.

Source: China Legislative Information Network System. "Regulations on Broadcasting and Television Administration." Available online. URL: http://www.chinalaw.gov.cn/jsp/jalor_en/disptext.jsp?recno=10&&ttlrec=58. Downloaded October 28, 2006.

Regulations on Administration of Films (July 1, 1996)

Thirty years after Jiang Qing helped launch the Cultural Revolution in China with film reviews that emphasized Mao Zedong thought, the State Council issued a decree that promulgated regulations covering what was and was not acceptable in the film industry. The regulations went into effect on July 1, 1996.

Article 1 These Regulations are formulated for the purposes of strengthening the administration of the film industry, developing and promoting film undertakings, satisfying the needs of the people for cultural life and promoting the construction of socialist material and spiritual civilization.

Article 2 These Regulations shall apply to activities of the production, import, export, distribution and projection, etc., of feature films, documentary films, science and educational films, films of special subjects, cartoons and puppet films, etc., within the territory of the People's Republic of China.

Article 3 Activities concerning films such as film production, import, export, distribution and projection, etc., must persevere in the direction of serving the people and socialism.

Article 4 The administrative department of radio, film and television of the State Council shall take charge of the nationwide work of films.

Administrative department for films of people's governments at and above the county level shall, in accordance with these Regulations, be responsible for the administration of films within their respective regions.

Article 23 The state shall adopt a film examination system.

Films that have not been examined and approved by the film examination organ of the administrative department of radio, film and television of the State Council may not be distributed, projected, imported or exported.

Article 24 Films are forbidden to have the following contents:

(1) Those endangering the unity, sovereignty and territorial integrity of the state;

(2) Those harming the security, honor and interests of the state;

(3) Those inciting national splitism and disrupting the unity of nationalities;

(4) Those divulging state secrets;

(5) Those publicizing obscenity or superstitions or playing up violence;

(6) Those libeling or insulting other people; or

(7) Other contents prohibited by the state.

Films shall be up to the national standards in terms of technological quality.

Article 26 Film studios shall, after the completion of a film production, submit the film to the film examination organ for examination and pay the examination fee in accordance with relevant provisions of the state. Units engaging in film import shall, after going through the formalities for the temporary import of a film, submit the film to the film examination organ for examination and pay the examination fee.

The schedule of fees for film examination shall be fixed by the financial department and price department of the State Council together with the administrative department of radio, film, and television of the State Council.

Article 29 Import of films shall be managed by units approved by the administrative department of radio, film and television of the State Council for engaging in film import; without approval, no other units or individuals may engage in film import.

Article 30 . . . Films imported for public projection shall be examined by the film examination organ; those having passed the examination shall be issued a Permit for Film Projection and documents approving the import. Only by producing the documents approving the import may the unit engaging in film import go through the formalities for import with the customs.

Article 36 For holding a Sino-foreign film exhibition or international film festival or participating in foreign-related film exchange activities such as film exhibition or film festival held abroad, an application shall be submitted to the administrative department of radio, film and television of the State Council for approval, and the films to be involved in the exchanges shall be submitted to the administrative department of radio, film and television of the State Council for examination; only with the approval can the formalities for temporary import or export of films be handled with the customs.

Article 45 The ratio of time spent on the projection of domestic films and that spent on the projection of the imported films shall be consistent with stipulations.

The time spent every year by a film projection unit on the projection of domestic films may not be less than two thirds of the total time spent annually by the same projection unit on film projection.

Article 56 Units of film production, import, distribution and projection established without approval shall be banned by the administrative department for films of the local people's government at or above the county level with the illegal articles and earnings confiscated and a fine from five to ten times the illegal earnings.

Source: China Legislative Information Network System. "Regulations on Administration of Films." Available online. URL: http://www.chinalaw.gov.cn/jsp/jalor_en/disptext.jsp?recno=6&&ttlrec=22. Downloaded October 28, 2006.

Circular of the State Council on Authorizing the Xinhua News Agency to Exercise within Its Jurisdiction Administration over the Release of Economic Information by Foreign News Agencies and Their Affiliated Information Offices within the Territory of China (1995)

This regulation is one of the earliest in a set that gave China's Xinhua News Agency power over foreign news agencies working in China. It went into force in 1995.

This and subsequent regulations and laws served not only to control the flow of information in and out of the PRC, but they also boosted Xinhua's standing, since news outlets had to do business with the agency.

With a view to defending state sovereignty, protecting the legitimate rights and interests of internal consumers of economic information and promoting the healthy development of the economic information undertakings, the State Council authorizes the Xinhua News Agency to exercise administration within its jurisdiction over the release of economic information by foreign news agencies and their affiliated information offices within the territory of China. Relevant matters are notified as the following:

I. Foreign news agencies and their affiliated information offices shall apply with the Xinhua News Agency for opening economic information business. The Xinhua News Agency shall according to the present Circular and relevant regulations vet the applier and the categories of economic information intended [for] release before authorizing them to do so.

II. The Xinhua News Agency shall in a unified manner reach every agreement on the release of economic information within the territory of China and settle the standards for charges with those foreign news agencies and their affiliated economic information offices that have been vetted and authorized.

III. Foreign news agencies and their affiliated information offices may not directly develop economic information consumers and may not do so in the form of joint ventures, ventures with solely foreign investment or agent companies.

IV. If a foreign news agency or its affiliated information office has by way of releasing information to its Chinese consumers committed actions that are not permitted by Chinese laws or regulations, or has included in the information released to its Chinese consumers contents that defame or slander China or damage the state interests of China, the Xinhua News Agency shall jointly with other relevant departments handle the case according to law.

V. Any government department at different levels, any enterprise or institution who wants to subscribe for economic information of foreign news agencies or their affiliated information offices shall go through registration procedure with the Xinhua News Agency. No department or unit may directly subscribe for economic information with foreign news agencies or their affiliated information offices.

VI. The Xinhua News agencies after being authorized to exercise within its jurisdiction administration over the release of economic information by foreign news agencies or their affiliated information offices within the territory of China, shall adopt substantial and effective measures to ensure the timely provision and reliability of the economic information received by consumers.

VII. Foreign News agencies or their affiliated information offices who have already developed consumers within the territory of China before the publication of the present Circular shall within three months from the publication of the present Circular go through procedures for vetting and authorization with the Xinhua News Agency retroactively.

VIII. The departments and units who have already subscribed for economic information with foreign news agencies or their affiliated information offices shall within three months after publication of the present Circular go through the registration procedure with the Xinhua News Agency retroactively.

IX. Release of economic information within the territory of China by news agencies or their affiliated information offices of Taiwan, Hong Kong or Macau regions shall also be brought under the administration of the Xinhua News Agency within its jurisdiction in light of the above stipulations.

X. Detailed rules for the implementation of the present Circular shall be formulated and promulgated by the Xinhua News Agency according to the present Circular and relevant state regulations.

Source: China Legislative Information Network System. "Circular of the State Council on Authorizing the Xinhua News Agency to Exercise Within Its Jurisdiction Administration Over the Release of Economic Informations by Foreign News Agencies and Their Affiliated Information Offices Within the Territory of China." Available online. URL: http://www.chinalaw.gov.cn/jsp/jalor_en/disptext.jsp?recno=1&&ttlrec=5. Downloaded October 29, 2006.

Regulations on the Administration of the Printing Industry (1997) (excerpts)

These 1997 laws were promulgated to control printed matter, including advertisement. In a sense their purpose was to serve as a further means of censorship should publishers dare defy the strict laws that remained in placed after the Cultural Revolution. Distribution laws were also put in place as yet another backup control.

Article 1 These Regulations are formulated with a view to strengthening the administration of the printing industry, safeguarding the legitimate rights and interests of the operators of the printing industry and the public interest of society and promoting socialist material civilization and spiritual civilization.

Article 2 These Regulations apply to the printing operations of publications, printed matters for packaging and decoration and other printed matters.

The publications referred to in these Regulations include newspapers, periodicals, books, maps, new year paintings, pictures, calendars, pictorial albums as well as the decorative covers of audio-visual products and electronic publications.

The printed matters for packaging and decoration referred to in these Regulations include trademark signs, color packaging boxes (bags), paper packages, printed iron cans and advertising publicity materials with introduction of products as their contents, etc.

The other printed matters referred to in these Regulations include documents, materials, diagrams and tables, vouchers and name cards, etc.

The printing operations referred to in these Regulations mean type setting, plate making, printing, binding and mounting, duplicating, photocopying and typing, etc.

Article 3 Operators of the printing industry must comply with the relevant laws, regulations and other rules of the State concerning the administration of the printing industry, improve quality and continuously satisfy the requirements of society.

Printing of publications, printed matters for packaging and decoration and other printed matters containing reactionary, obscene and superstitious contents and such other contents the printing of which are categorically prohibited by the orders of the State is banned.

Article 6 The State practices licensing system of printing operations. Any unit and individual shall not engage in printing operations without approval.

Article 20 The printing enterprises of publications shall not print publications the publication of which are categorically prohibited by the State and print publications published by non-publishing units.

Article 37 Printing of religious articles shall be handled in accordance with the provisions of the State concerning the administration of religious printed matters.

Article 43 Any printing enterprise or individual printing publications, printed matters for packaging and decoration or other printed matters which contain reactionary, obscene and superstitious contents or other contents the printing of which are categorically forbidden by the order of the State, illegally printing publications the publication of which are categorically forbidden by the order of the State or publications published by non-publication units, or illegally printing such other printed matters as identity cards, documents and vouchers and coupons with value, shall be penalized in accordance with relevant laws and regulations.

Source: China Legislative Information Network System. "Regulations on the Administration of the Printing Industry." Available online. URL: http://www.chinalaw.gov.cn//jsp/jalor_en/disptext.jsp?recno=1&&ttlrec=1. Downloaded November 1, 2006.

Law of the PRC on Assemblies, Processions, and Demonstrations (October 31, 1989) (excerpts)

Less than five months after the riots following the 1989 demonstrations in Tiananmen Square in Beijing, the following law was enacted. Although Article 1 announces that the law's purpose is to "safeguard" citizens' rights to public assembly, as the following excerpts show it can also be used to curtail those rights.

Article 1. Pursuant to the Constitution, this Law is enacted to safeguard citizens' exercise of their right to assembly, procession and demonstration according to law and to maintain social stability and public order.

Article 2. This Law shall apply to assemblies, processions and demonstrations held within the territory of the People's Republic of China. . . . This Law shall not apply to recreational or sports activities, normal religious activities or traditional folk events.

Article 4. In exercising their right to assembly, procession and demonstration, citizens must abide by the Constitution and the laws, shall not oppose the cardinal principles specified in the Constitution and shall not impair state, public or collective interests or the lawful freedoms and rights of other citizens.

Article 8. . . . For the holding of an assembly, a procession or a demonstration for which an application has to be made under this Law, the responsible person(s) must submit an application in writing to the competent authorities five days prior to the date of the activity. The application shall specify the purposes of the assembly, procession or demonstration, how it is going to be conducted, the posters and slogans to be used, the number of participants, the number of vehicles, the specifications and quantities of the sound facilities to be used, the starting and finishing time, the places (including places where the participants assemble and disperse), the route, and the name(s), occupation(s) and address(es) of the person(s) responsible for the assembly, procession or demonstration.

Article 10. If an application is made for an assembly, a procession or a demonstration which will press for the settlement of specific issues, the competent authorities may, after receiving the application, inform the departments or units concerned to resolve such issues through consultation with the person(s) responsible for the assembly, procession or demonstration, and may also postpone for five days the starting date specified in the application.

Article 11. If the competent authorities are of the opinion that the holding of an assembly, a procession or a demonstration at the time or place or along the route specified in the application will seriously affect traffic and public order, they may, upon or after granting permission, change the time, place or route and inform the responsible person(s) of the change in good time.

Article 12. No permission shall be granted for an application for an assembly, a procession or a demonstration which involves one of the following circumstances:

(1) opposition to the cardinal principles specified in the Constitution;

(2) harming the unity, sovereignty and territorial integrity of the state;

(3) instigation of division among the nationalities; or

(4) the belief, based on sufficient evidence, that the holding of the assembly, procession or demonstration that is being applied for will directly endanger public security or seriously undermine public order.

Article 15. No citizens shall, in a city other than his place of residence, start, organize or participate in an assembly, a procession or a demonstration of local citizens.

Article 16. No functionary of a state organ shall organize or participate in an assembly, a procession or a demonstration which contravenes the functions and obligations of functionaries of state organs as prescribed in relevant laws and regulations.

Article 20. In order to ensure the progress of a procession held in compliance with law, the people's police responsible for keeping traffic order may temporarily exercise flexibility in their execution of the relevant provisions of traffic regulations.

Article 21. If it becomes impossible for a procession to follow the permitted route because of unexpected circumstances occurring on the way, the chief police officer present at the scene shall have the authority to change the route of the procession.

Article 22. If an assembly, a procession or a demonstration is held in or passes by places where state organs, military organs, radio stations, television stations or foreign embassies or consulates are located, the competent authorities may, with a view to keeping order, establish temporary security lines, which shall not be crossed without permission by the people's police.

Article 23. No assembly, procession or demonstration shall be held within a peripheral distance of 10–300 metres from the following places, with the exception of those approved by the State Council or the people's governments of provinces, autonomous regions and municipalities directly under the Central Government:

(1) premises of the Standing Committee of the National People's Congress, the State Council, the Central Military Commission, the Supreme People's Court and the Supreme People's Procuratorate;

(2) places where state guests are staying;

(3) important military installations; and

(4) air harbors, railway stations and ports. . . .

Article 24. The time for holding an assembly, a procession or a demonstration shall be limited to 6 A.M.–10 P.M., with the exception of those held by decision or approval of the local people's governments.

Article 25. An assembly, a procession or a demonstration shall be conducted in accordance with the purposes, manners, posters, slogans, starting and finishing time, places, routes and other matters for which permission has been granted. . . .

Article 27. The people's police shall stop an assembly, a procession or a demonstration that is being held, if it involves one of the following circumstances:

(1) failure to make an application in accordance with the provisions of this Law or to obtain permission for the application;

(2) failure to act in accordance with the purposes, manners, posters, slogans, starting and finishing time, places and routes permitted by the competent authorities; or

(3) the emergence, in the course of the activity, of a situation which endangers public security or seriously undermines public order.

Article 28. . . . The public security organ may punish by warning or by criminal detention of not more than 15 days the responsible person(s) and the person(s) who is directly responsible, if an assembly, a procession or a demonstration that is being held involves one of the following circumstances:

(1) failure to make an application in accordance with the provisions of this Law or to obtain permission for the application; or

(2) failure to act in accordance with the purposes, manners, posters, slogans, starting and finishing time, places, and routes permitted by the competent authorities, and disregard of instructions to stop acting without permission.

Article 33. If a citizen, in a city other than his place of residence, starts or organizes an assembly, a procession or a demonstration by local citizens, the public security organ shall have the authority to detain him or send him back by force to his place of residence.

Article 34. This Law shall apply to assemblies, processions and demonstrations held by foreigners within the territory of China. Foreigners in the territory of China may not, without approval by the competent authorities, participate in an assembly, a procession or a demonstration held by Chinese citizens.

Source: China Society for Human Rights Studies. "Laws of the PRC on Assemblies, Processions, and Demonstrations." Available online. URL: http://www.humanrights-china.org/zt/03102410/2003120031127111557.htm. Downloaded November 1, 2006.

Regulations on Publication Administration (February 1, 1997) (excerpts)

These laws to regulate publication went into effect on February 1, 1997. They cover every aspect of the industry, including importation of material to be translated. In addition, they also cover distribution of various printed materials in the PRC. Listed below are some of the important articles of the law dealing with the wide approach to censorship that the PRC takes in this area. Also note Article 7, in which self-censorship is expected, though even that is not left to the publishers' discretion.

Article 2 These Regulations shall be applicable to activities of publication within the territory of the People's Republic of China.

The activities of publication referred to in these Regulations include the publication and printing of publications or the duplication and distribution thereof.

The publications referred to in these Regulations mean newspapers, periodicals, books, audiovisual products and electronic publications, etc.

Article 3 The publication industry must persevere in the orientation of serving the people and socialism, persevere in taking Marxism-Leninism, Mao Zedong Thought and the theory of building socialism with Chinese characteristics as guidance, disseminate and accumulate any science, technology, culture and knowledge instrumental to the improvement of the quality of the nation, economic development and all-round progress of the society, develop and make the best possible use of fine national culture, promote international cultural exchanges and enrich and improve people's spiritual life.

Article 6 The department of publication administration under the State Council shall practice supervision over and administration of activities of publication throughout the country. Other departments of administration concerned under the State Council shall, in accordance with the division of responsibilities determined by the State Council, supervise and administer related activities of publication....

Article 7 National societies of the publication industry shall practice self-disciplined management in accordance with their respective constitutions under the guidance of the department of publication administration under the State Council.

Article 19 The annual publication plans and major subject (topic) selections involving national security and societal stability of book publishing houses, audiovisual publishing houses and electronic publication publishing houses shall be reported by the departments of publication administration of the people's governments of provinces, autonomous regions and municipalities directly under the Central Government in which they are located to the department of publication administration under the State Council for the record. Specific measures shall be worked out by the department of publication administration under the State Council.

Article 25 No publication shall contain the following contents:

(1) anything that goes against the basic principles determined by the Constitution;

(2) anything that endangers the unification, sovereignty and territorial integrity of the country;

(3) anything that endangers state security, reputation and interests;

(4) anything that instigates national separatism, infringes on the customs and habits of minority nationalities and disrupt solidarity of nationalities;

(5) anything that discloses state secrets;

(6) anything that publicizes pornography and superstition or plays up violence, endangers social ethics and the fine traditions of national culture;

(7) anything that insults or slanders others; and

(8) any other contents prohibited by the provisions of laws and regulations.

Article 26 Publications with juveniles as targets must not contain contents which induce juveniles to imitate acts against social ethics and illegal criminal acts and must not contain contents of terror and cruelty which impair the physical and mental health of juveniles.

Article 31 ... No printing of newspapers, periodicals and books and no duplication of audiovisual products and electronic publications shall be undertaken without being granted permission and entering into registration in compliance with law.

Article 32 ... No printing or duplicating units shall engage in the printing and circulation of newspapers, periodicals and books, or the duplication and distribution of audio-visual products and electronic publications without authorization.

Article 33 ... The contents of publications to be printed or duplicated for external trust shall go through the examination and verification of the departments of publication administration of the people's governments of provinces, autonomous regions and municipalities directly under the Central Government....

Article 35 Distribution units engaging in general distribution business of newspapers, periodicals and books shall, with the permission granted upon examination and verification by the department of publication administration under the State Council, obtain business licenses in accordance with law from the department of industry and commerce administration before they can operate the general distribution business of newspapers, periodicals and books.

Distribution units engaging in wholesale business of newspapers, periodicals and books shall, with the permission granted upon examination and verification by the departments of administration concerned prescribed by the people's governments of provinces, autonomous regions and municipalities directly under the Central Government, obtain business licenses in accordance with law from the department of industry and commerce administration before they can operate the wholesale business of newspapers, periodicals and books.

Distribution of newspapers and periodicals by postal enterprises shall be processed in accordance with the provisions of the Postal Law.

Article 36 Units and individuals engaging in retail business of newspapers, periodicals and books shall, with the approval of the departments of administration concerned of the people's governments at the county level prescribed by the people's governments of provinces, autonomous regions and municipalities directly under the Central Government, obtain business licenses in accordance with law from the department of industry and commerce administration before they can run the retail business of publications.

Article 38 Printing or duplicating units and distribution units shall not print or duplicate and distribute publications having any of the following circumstances:

(1) those containing the contents banned under Articles 25 and 26 of these Regulations;

(2) those which have been illegally imported;

(3) those with forged or imitated names of publication units or with forged or imitated names of newspapers and periodicals;

(4) those bearing no names of publication units;

(5) middle school and primary school textbooks without examination and finalization in accordance with law; and

(6) those which infringe on others' copyrights.

Article 45 Establishment of publication units without approval and authorization or running the business of publication, printing or duplication and distribution of publications without authorization shall be banned, their publications, major special tools and equipment for the illegal activities and illegal income shall be confiscated, and a fine of more than two times and less than ten times of the illegal income shall be imposed; where an offence constitutes a crime, criminal responsibility shall be investigated according to law.

Article 54 . . . Specific control measures for electronic publications shall be worked out by the department of publication administration under the State Council in accordance with the principles of these Regulations.

Source: China Legislative Information Network System. "Regulations on Publication Administration." Available online. URL: http://www.chinalaw.gov.cn//jsp/jalor_en/disptext.jsp?recno=7&&ttlrec=7. Downloaded November 2, 2006.

EGYPT

The Press and Publication Law (1996) (excerpts)

The Press and Publication Law that is excerpted below took effect in 1996. Most of the wording of the law appears benign, if not beneficial to Egyptian society, however open-ended interpretations of the various articles can be used to legalize censorship. Examples of this can be found in Article 20, where even criticism of censorship decisions of the al-Azhar Islamic Research Council can be construed as antireligious, and Article 21, which severely restricts investigative reporting of public officials. Article 22 has prompted numerous protests by rights groups in Egypt.

Chapter Three: Obligations of journalists

Article 18—Journalists shall commit in what they publish, to the principles and values embodied in the constitution and the provisions of the law, to uphold in their work honor, integrity and honesty and to respect ethics and traditions to preserve community values, and abstain from violating the rights of citizens or affecting their freedoms.

Article 19—Journalists shall fully commit to the Code of Ethics of the Press and they shall be disciplined if they transgress their duties as set forth in said law or code.

Article 20—Journalists shall refrain from endorsing racist calls which express contempt for religions or hatred or invitations to vilify others' beliefs or promote prejudice or contempt towards any confessions within the community.

Article 21—Journalists, as well as [others] shall not be permitted to expose private lives of citizens and shall not be permitted to address the conduct of a public official, a deputy [in the parliament] or someone entrusted with a public mission unless it [address/article] is closely related to their tasks and benefits the public interest.

Article 22—Anyone who violates the provisions of the two previous articles shall be subject to a jail sentence that shall not exceed one year, and a fine that shall not be less than five thousand Egyptian Pounds and shall not exceed ten thousand Egyptian Pounds or one of said two punishments.

Article 23—Newspapers shall not publish news related to investigations or trials conducted by the authorities and which affect the conduct of the investigation or the trial, or affect the situations of [those] being investigated or tried. Newspapers commit to publish the decisions of the public prosecution [office of the Attorney General) and Courts' decisions issued in the cases addressed by the newspaper during the investigation or the trial, and a summary of the facts if the charges were dropped, a decision of no prima facie was issued or the [defendant] was found innocent.

Source: Harvard Law School Library. *Qānūn raqm 96 li-sanat 1996 bi-sha'n tanẓīm al-ṣiḥāfah wa-lā'iḥ atuhu al-tanfīdhīyah / i'dād wa-murāja'at al-Idārah al-'āmmah lil-Shu'ūn al-Qānūnīyah bi-al-Hay'ah. al-Qāhirah : al-Hay'ah al-'Āmmah li-Shu'ūn al-Maṭābi' al-Amīrīyah, 1998.* Translated by Tarek Dachraoui, 2007.

Arab Press Freedom Watch's Annual Report on Press Freedom in Egypt (2006) (excerpts)

The following excerpts from the Arab Press Freedom Watch report cover the monitoring period April 2005–April 2006. This particular section focuses on censorship and banning of newspapers as well as censorship, harassment, and physical brutality against individual journalists.

APFW Annual Report on Press Freedom in Egypt 2006: Escalation of Attacks Against Egyptian Journalists in the Year of Parliamentary Election and Amendments to the Constitution (excerpts)

(. . .)

Violations against Press Institutions

1- Al-Sha'ab Newspaper

The continuation of the ban imposed on the newspaper, though it has obtained 13 judicial judgments reversing the ban. (. . .)

5- Afaq Arabia Suspension

Following a disagreement between journalists [belonging to a] a religious group and Mohamed Atyea, editor-in-chief of the newspaper, the latter . . . suspended the newspaper for about a month. He then reissued it without its [former] journalists and without observing any publishing rules. (. . .)

Violations against Journalists

Police Investigations

There are continuous investigations under the supervision of the attorney general and state security. Almost every week a journalist is under investigation by the public prosecution or state security, including 11 cases in which ten journalists were investigated. (. . .)

Arrests

Two arrest cases took place against nine Al-Jazeera journalists, photographers and technicians in Cairo who were on their way to cover a meeting of judges and a conference on human rights in one of Cairo hotels.(. . .)

Publishing Prohibition

Ayman Nour, the leader of Alghad Party and the second highest vote-getter in the presidential election, was prohibited from sending an article for publication from his prison through his lawyer. Though Egyptian law allows for the exchange of documents between a prisoner and his lawyer, prison authorities prohibited Ayman from giving his lawyer the article, which contained criticism of the regime and direct criticism of the president, his family, and a number of high profile figures in the regime. (. . .)

Threats: Resorting to the method of "swords against pens"

Last year, many threats against journalists and writers were recorded. (. . .)

Physical Abuse

Forty-four physical-abuse cases were recorded, including five cases against members on the syndicate board, three cases of sexual abuse against female journalists, and 35 cases in the bloody massacre of Alwafd. (. . .)

General Analytical View on Monitoring

There were many violations against the Egyptian press by abusing its basic structure, which includes newspapers, journalists and the headquarters of the Press Syndicate as follows:

There a was direct link between . . . [certain] violations and the urgent emergencies in the political arena, such as: a constitutional amendment, referendum day, presidential elections, parliamentary elections, and the issue of presidential succession. May 2005 and April 2006, respectively, witnessed the majority of these violations.

The majority of the violations were done by ministers and officials, at the top of which the former Deputy Prime Minister and Minister of Agriculture . . . and former Minister of Housing . . . who [between them] filed 35 lawsuits against journalists . . . The Egyptian press has faced all types of violations and abuses. Egyptian journalists were sentenced to prison, fined, beaten, sexually harassed, physically abused, prohibited from publishing, threatened, and arrested. This showed a press under siege, whose heroes are facing bullets, obligatory silence, and prison.

Unfair laws regulating the press profession, that allows journalists' imprisonment in publishing cases, and at the same time doesn't protect them thanks to the very limited authorities of press institutions including the Press Syndicate and the Supreme Council for Press. Thus, anyone who faces accusations of corruption may file a suit to prison or fine the journalist who discovers his corruption under the plea of slander. Most of these suits ended with sentences against the journalists that were settled only through reconciliation bargains and under unfair conditions against the journalists.

The religious institutions still exercises their authority and undermine the freedom of opinion and expression in the press, media, and cinema in particular.

Source: Arab Press Freedom Watch. "APFW Annual Report on Press Freedom in Egypt 2006: Escalation of Attacks Against Egyptian Journalists in the Year of Parliamentary Election and Amendments to the Constitution." Available online. URL: http://www.apfw.org/indexenglish.asp?fname=report\english\2007\01\spe1101.htm. Downloaded August 15, 2007.

RUSSIA

Nikita Khrushchev's "Secret Speech" (February 25, 1956) (excerpts)

In the mid-1950s, Nikita Khrushchev emerged victorious from the power struggle that ensued following the death of Soviet leader Josef Stalin in 1953. By early 1956, when delegates of the Communist Party of the Soviet Union (CPSU) gathered in Moscow for the Twentieth Party Congress, Khrushchev was sure enough of his positions within the party and the government to denounce Stalin and the cult of personality that had arisen around him—albeit in a secret speech that was not made public until many years later. Khrushchev was, himself, deposed in 1964 and replaced by the neo-Stalinist Leonid Brezhnev.

For a brief period after Khrushchev's speech the Soviet Union experienced a "thaw"—a period in which writers, especially, were able to extend the boundaries of what was permissible. During this thaw writers such as the poets Yevgeny Yevtushenko and Andrei Vosnesensky and the novelist Alexandr Solzhenitsyn first gained acclaim. Many consider the thaw to have ended with the arrests and subsequent trial of Andrei Sinyavsky and Yuli Daniel in the mid-1960s, but by the time of their arrests the so-called freedoms were already on the wane.

CENSORSHIP

Comrades, in the report of the Central Committee of the party at the 20th Congress, in a number of speeches by delegates to the Congress, as also formerly during the plenary CC/CPSU sessions, quite a lot has been said about the cult of the individual and about its harmful consequences. . . .

Allow me first of all to remind you how severely the classics of Marxism-Leninism denounced every manifestation of the cult of the individual. In a letter to the German political worker, Wilhelm Bloss, Marx stated: "From my antipathy to any cult of the individual, I never made public during the existence of the International the numerous addresses from various countries which recognized my merits and which annoyed me. I did not even reply to them, except sometimes to rebuke their authors. Engels and I first joined the secret society of Communists on the condition that everything making for superstitious worship of authority would be deleted from its statute. . . ."

[Vladimir Ilyich] Lenin had always stressed the role of the people as the creator of history, the directing and organizational role of the party as a living and creative organism, and also the role of the central committee. . . .

While ascribing great importance to the role of the leaders and organizers of the masses, Lenin at the same time mercilessly stigmatized every manifestation of the cult of the individual, inexorably combated the foreign-to-Marxism views about a "hero" and a "crowd" and countered all efforts to oppose a "hero" to the masses and to the people. . . .

Fearing the future fate of the party and of the Soviet nation, V. I. Lenin made a completely correct characterization of Stalin, pointing out that it was necessary to consider the question of transferring Stalin from the position of Secretary General . . . Vladimir Ilyich [Lenin] said: ". . . I propose that the comrades consider the method by which Stalin would be removed from this position and by which another man would be selected for it, a man, who above all, would differ from Stalin in only one quality, namely, greater tolerance, greater loyalty, greater kindness, and more considerate attitude toward the comrades, a less capricious temper, etc." . . .

Stalin acted not through persuasion, explanation, and patient cooperation with people, but by imposing his concepts and demanding absolute submission to his opinion. . . . Stalin originated the concept enemy of the people. This term automatically rendered it unnecessary that the ideological errors of a man or men engaged in a controversy be proven; this term made possible the usage of the most cruel repression, violating all norms of revolutionary legality, against anyone who in any way disagreed with Stalin, against those who were only suspected of hostile intent, against those who had bad reputations. This concept, enemy of the people, actually eliminated the possibility of any kind of ideological fight or the making of one's views known on this or that issue, even those of a practical character. In the main, and in actuality, the only proof of guilt used, against all norms of current legal science, was the confession of the accused himself, and, as subsequent probing proved, confessions were acquired through physical pressures against the accused. . . .

Considering the question of the cult of an individual we must first of all show everyone what harm this caused to the interests of our party. . . . In practice Stalin ignored the norms of party life and trampled on the Leninist principle of collective party leadership. . . .

When we look at many of our novels, films, and historical scientific studies, the role of Stalin in the patriotic war appears to be entirely improbable. Stalin had foreseen everything. The Soviet Army, on the basis of a strategic plan prepared by Stalin long before, used the tactics of so-called active defense, i.e., tactics which, as we know, allowed the Germans to come up to Moscow and Stalingrad. Using such tactics, the Soviet Army, supposedly, thanks only to Stalin's genius, turned to the offensive and subdued the enemy. The epic victory gained through the armed might of the land of the Soviets, through our heroic people, is ascribed in this type of novel, film, and scientific study as being completely due to the strategic genius of Stalin.

We have to analyze this matter carefully because it has a tremendous significance, not only from the historical but especially from the political, educational, and practical point of view. . . .

During the war and after the war, Stalin put forward the thesis that the tragedy which our nation experienced in the first part of the war was the result of the unexpected attack of the Germans against the Soviet Union. But, comrades, this is completely untrue. As soon as Hitler came to power in Germany he assigned to himself the task of liquidating communism. . . .

Comrades, the cult of the individual acquired such monstrous size chiefly because Stalin himself, using all conceivable methods, supported the glorification of his own person. This is supported by numerous facts.

One of the most characteristic examples of Stalin's self-glorification and of his lack of even elementary modesty is the edition of his Short Biography, which was published in 1948.

This book is an expression of the most dissolute flattery, an example of making a man into a godhead, of transforming him into an infallible sage, "the greatest leader," "sublime strategist of all times and nations." Finally no other words could be found with which to lift Stalin up to the heavens....

We should in all seriousness consider the question of the cult of the individual. We cannot let this matter get out of the party, especially not to the press. It is for this reason that we are considering it here at a closed congress session. We should know the limits; we should not give ammunition to the enemy; we should not wash our dirty linen before their eyes. I think that the delegates to the congress will understand and assess properly all these proposals. [Tumultuous applause.]

Comrades, we must abolish the cult of the individual decisively, once and for all; we must draw the proper conclusions concerning both ideological-theoretical and practical work....

In this connection we will be forced to do much work in order to examine critically from the Marxist-Leninist viewpoint and to correct the widely spread erroneous views connected with the cult of the individual in the sphere of history, philosophy, economy, and of other sciences, as well as in the literature and the fine arts. It is especially necessary that in the immediate future we compile a serious textbook of the history of our party which will be edited in accordance with scientific Marxist objectivism, a textbook of the history of Soviet society, a book pertaining to the events of the civil war and the Great Patriotic War....

We are absolutely certain that our party, armed with the historical resolutions of the 20th Congress, will lead the Soviet people along the Leninist path to new successes, to new victories. [Tumultuous, prolonged applause.]

Long live the victorious banner of our party—Leninism. [Tumultuous, prolonged applause ending in ovation. All rise.]

Source: from the Congressional Record: Proceedings and Debates *of* the 84th Congress, 2nd Session *(May 22, 1956–June 11, 1956), C11, Part 7 (June 4, 1956), pp. 9389–9403.*

On Mass Media (1991)

Russia's mass media law was enacted within days of the dissolution of the Union of Soviet Socialist Republics in December 1991. However, throughout the 1990s and early 2000s, it was amended more than 10 times. While Article 3 explicitly bans censorship, subsequent articles of the law open the door for censorship, including Article 33 which discusses electronic jamming. Article 47 discusses the rights of journalists, but many of those rights have been suspended for individual journalists. And the government has certainly not lived up to its guarantees of the final clause of Article 48, regarding the protection of journalists' lives—many have been murdered while investigating corruption stories.

Article 3 Inadmissibility of Censorship

No provision shall be made for the censorship of mass information, that is, the demand made by officials, state organs, organization, institutions or public associations that the editor's office of a mass medium shall get in advance agreement on a message and materials (except for the cases when the official is an auditor or interviewee) and also for the suppression of the dissemination of messages and materials and separate parts thereof.

No provision shall be made for the creation and financing of organizations, institutions, organs or offices whose functions include the censorship of mass information.

Article 4 Inadmissibility of Misuse of the Freedom of Mass Communication

No provision shall be made for the use of mass media for purposes of committing criminally indictable deeds, divulging information making up a state secret or any other law-protective secret, the performance of extremist activities, and also for the spreading of broadcasts propagandizing pornography or the cult of violence and cruelty.

It shall be prohibited to use-in the television, video and cinema programs, in documentary and feature films, and also in information computer files and in the programs of the processing of information texts belonging to special mass information media concealed in-sets influencing the subconscious of human beings and/or affecting their health.

It shall be prohibited to disseminate in mass media, as well as in via computer networks information on the means, methods of development, production and use, places of trade of narcotics, psychotropic substances and their precursors, propagating of any advantages of use of separate narcotics, psychotropic substances, their analogues and precursors with the exception of advertising of narcotic means and psychotropic substances, included in lists II and III in accordance with the Federal Law "On Narcotic Means and Psychotropic Substances",—in mass media, targeted for the medical and pharmaceutical workers, as well as any other information, dissemination of which is prohibited by federal laws.

Article 4 of the present Law was changed by Federal Law No. 114-FZ of July 19, 1995.

The third paragraph was added by Federal Law No. 90-FZ of June 20, 2000. The first paragraph was changed by Federal Law No. 112-FZ of July 2002.

Article 7 Founders

An individual, association of individuals, enterprise, institution, organization or a state body may be a founder (co-founded) a mass medium.

The following persons and bodies may not act as founders: . . .

an association of private citizens, enterprise, institution and organization whose activity is banned by law; . . .

Article 16 Termination or Suspension of Activity

The functioning of a mass medium may be terminated or suspended only by decision of its founder or by a court of law in civil proceedings at the suit filed by the registration body or the Ministry of the Press and Information of the Russian Federation.

The founder shall have the right to terminate or suspend the functioning of a mass medium exclusively in cases and in the order envisaged by the statutes of the editorial office or the agreement concluded between the founder and the editorial office (editor-in-chief).

Repeated (during twelve months) breaches by the editorial office of the requirements of Article 4 of the present Law, on whose occasion the registration body or the Ministry of the Press and Information of the Russian Federation has made written warnings to the founder and (or) the editorial office (editor-in-chief) and likewise the non-execution of the court's ruling on the suspension of the mass medium shall be grounds for the termination of the activity of the mass medium by the court of law.

The functioning of a mass medium may also be terminated in the order and on the grounds provided for by the Federal Law "On Counteraction to Extremist Activities".

Only the need for the security for a suit, envisaged by the first part of this Article may serve as a ground for the suspension by a court of law of the activity of a mass medium.

The termination of the functioning of a mass medium shall entail the invalidity of the certificate of its registration and the statutes of the editorial office.

The fourth paragraph was added by Federal Law No. 112-FZ of July 25, 2002.

Article 16.1 Suspension of the Activity of a Mass Medium for Breach of the Law of the Russian Federation on Elections and Referenda

If within the period of an election campaign or a referendum campaign after the entry into force of a court decision on bringing the editor-in-chief or the editorial board of a radio or TV program, of a periodical or of other organization engaged in the production of a mass medium (hereinafter referred to as organization engaged in the production of a mass medium) to administrative responsibility for violating the law of the Russian Federation on elections and referenda, this editor-in-chief or this organization repeatedly violates the law of the Russian Federation on elections and referenda, the Central Election Commission of the Russian Federation and, if the products of a mass medium are intended for dissemination on the territory of a subject of the Russian Federation, likewise the election commission of the appropriate subject of the Russian Federation, shall be entitled to address the federal executive body in charge of registration of mass media with a proposal to suspend the activity of a mass medium used for the purpose of committing said offences. Said federal executive body within a five-day term from such an address, but at latest on the day, preceding the ballot day—while if such an address takes place on the day preceding the ballot day and on the ballot day, then immediately—shall verify with the participation of the interested parties the facts stated in the address and shall file with a court of law an application for suspension of the activity of the mass medium used for committing said violations or shall direct to the appropriate election commission a reasoned refusal to file said an application with a court of law. A reasoned refusal to file an application with court for suspension of the activity of a mass medium shall not impede taking other punitive measures provided for by law of the Russian Federation, including a warning, against the organization engaged in producing said mass medium. . . .

The activity of a mass medium shall be suspended by a court of law, for the reasons provided for by this Article, until the time when the poll at the elections or at a referendum is over, or the time, when a recurring poll is over, if a recurring poll is held.

For the purposes of this Article, as a breach by the editor-in-chief or by the organization, engaged in the production of a mass media, of the law of the Russian Federation on elections and referenda shall be understood the violation by this editor-in-chief or by this organization of the procedure, established by these law for informing voters and referendum participants or for waging an election campaign or a referendum campaign, which are punished by the law on administrative offences. . . .

Article 16.1. was added by Federal Law No. 94-FZ of July 4, 2003.

Article 28 Total Circulation

The total circulation of a periodical printed publication, an audio-, video- and newsreel program shall be determined by the editor-in-chief by agreement with the publisher.

The confiscation and also the destruction of the circulation or the part thereof shall be allowed only by the decision of a court of law that has entered into force.

A circulation fee shall be instituted for mass media specializing in the production of advertising or erotic products and collected in the order determined by the Government of the Russian Federation.

Article 33 Radio and Television Jamming

The creation of jamming that prevents the sure reception of radio and TV programs, that is, the spread of radio, TV and other technical signals in the frequency band in which broadcasts are made under the license, shall entail responsibility in keeping with the legislation of the Russian Federation.

Industrial jamming arising during the operation of technical devices in the course of economic activity shall be removed at the expense of the persons owning or managing the source of this jamming.

Article 47 The Rights of the Journalist

The journalist shall have the right:

1. to look for, inquire, receive and spread information;

2. to visit state organs and organizations, enterprises and institutions, the press organs or press services of public associations;

3. to be received by officials in connection with the inquiry of information;

4. to get access to documents and materials, with the exception of their fragments containing information comprising a state, commercial or any other specially law-protected secret;

5. to copy, publish, announce or reproduce by any other method documents and materials subject to the observance of the requirements of the first part of Article 42 of the present Law;

6. to make recordings with the use of audio- and video-equipment, photography and cine-photography, except for the cases provided for by law;

7. to visit specially protected places of natural disasters, accidents and catastrophes, mass disorders and mass gatherings, and also localities where a state of emergency is declared; to attend meetings and demonstrations;

8. to verify the authenticity of the information he or she has received;

9. to set forth his or her personal judgements and assessments in reports and materials intended for dissemination under his or her signature;

10. to refuse to prepare under his or her signature reports and materials inconsistent with his or her convictions;

11. to remove his or her signature put under the report or material whose content was distorted, in his or her opinion, in the process of editorial preparations or to ban or stipulate in any other way the conditions and character of using this report or material in keeping with the first part of Article 42 of the present Law;

12. to spread reports and materials he or she prepared under his or her signature, under pseudonym or without any signature.

The journalist shall enjoy other rights granted to him by the legislation of the Russian Federation on mass media.

Article 48 Accreditation

The editorial office shall have the right to file its application with a state organ, organization, and the organ of a public association for the accreditation of its journalists to them.

State organs, organizations, institutions and organs of public associations shall accredit said journalists, provided the editorial offices observe the accreditation rules established by these organs, organizations, and institutions.

The organs, organizations, and institutions which accredited journalists shall be obliged to notify them in advance about their meetings, conferences and other events, to supply them with verbatim reports, minutes and other documents, and to create favorable conditions for making entries.

The accredited journalist shall have the right to attend the meetings, conferences and other events held by the accrediting organs, organizations, and institutions, except for the cases when decisions have been taken to hold closed gatherings.

The journalist may be deprived of his or her accreditation, if he or she and the editorial office have infringed the accreditation rules or information which denigrates the honor and dignity of the organization that accredited the journalist and which runs counter to the reality, which fact has been confirmed by the court's decision that has entered into legal force.

The mass media offices' own correspondents shall be accredited in keeping with the requirements of this Article.

In his professional activities the journalist shall be obliged to respect the rights, lawful interests, the honor and dignity of private citizens and organizations.

The State shall guarantee for the journalist, who carries on his professional activities, the protection of his honor, dignity, health, life and property as a person discharging his civil duty.

Source: © Translation, the Moscow Media Law and Policy Institute, 2004. "Law of the Russian Federation 'On Mass Media.'" Available online. URL:http://www.medialaw.ru/e_pages/laws/russian/massmedia_eng/massmedia_eng.html. Downloaded December 4, 2006.

On the Freedom of Conscience and Religious Associations (1997, amended 2004) (excerpts)

In 1997, President Boris Yeltsin signed a new law regarding religion and beliefs. This law declared null and void (in the final provision omitted here) all previous Russian laws on the subject. The law was also subsequently amended in the 21st century during President Vladimir Putin's administration.

The fact that such a law exists belies any pronouncements of freedom of belief. In fact the second provision of Article 3 (below) can be interpreted to contravene Article 2. Other, more technical, restrictions are also listed in the law that appear harmless, but which can also be used by government entities to restrict religious freedom, including censoring publications.

Article 2 Laws on the Freedom of Conscience, Faith and Religious Associations

3. Nothing contained in the legislation on the freedom of conscience and faith and religious associations shall be interpreted in the sense of impairment or infringement upon the rights of man and citizen to the freedom of conscience and faith guaranteed by the Constitution of the Russian Federation or ensuing from international agreements of the Russian Federation.

Article 3 The Right to the Freedom of Conscience and Faith

2. The right of man and citizen to the freedom of conscience and faith may be restricted under the Federal law only in so far as it is required for purposes of protection of the basics of the constitutional regime, morals, health, rights and legitimate interests of man and citizen, insurance of the defenses of the country and the security of the state.

3. The establishment of privileges, restrictions or any other forms of discrimination depending on one's attitude to religion shall not be allowed.

6. The prevention of exercise of rights to the freedom of conscience and faith, including that associated with violence against person, the intentional hurting of feelings of citizens in connection with their attitude to religion, the propaganda of religious supremacy, the [destruction] of or damage to the property or a threat of commission of such actions shall be prohibited and prosecuted in accordance with the Federal law. Conducting public events, putting up texts and images that may hurt the religious feelings of citizens close to projects of religious worship shall be prohibited.

Article 4 The State and Religious Associations

3. The state shall effect regulation in granting to religious organisations tax and other exemptions, extend financial, material and other assistance to religious organisations in the restoration, maintenance and protection of buildings and projects being monuments of history and culture as well as in arranging the teaching of general educational subjects at educational establishments set up by religious organisations as is envisaged under the laws of the Russian Federation on education.

Article 7 Religious Group

1. Religious group under this Federal Law shall mean any voluntary association of citizens set up with the objective of joint profession and dissemination of faith, carrying on its activities without the registration with the state authorities and without the acquisition of capacity of a legal entity. The premises and property required for the activities of the religious group shall be provided for use by such a group by its members.

Article 8 Religious Organization

1. Religious organisation shall mean a voluntary association of citizens of the Russian Federation, other persons, residing permanently and legally in the territory of the Russian Federation, set up for purposes of joint profession and dissemination of faith that has been duly registered as a legal entity.

3. Local religious organisation shall mean a religious organisation consisting of no less than ten persons not younger than 18 years old that permanently reside in the same locality or the same town or village settlement.

6. The religious organisation shall also mean an agency or an organisation set up by the centralized religious organisation in accordance with its charter that pursue the objective and possesses the features specified under Item 1 of Article 6 hereof, including a governing or coordinating body or agency as well as the establishment of a professional religious formation.

Article 11 Registration of Religious Organizations with State Authorities

1. Religious organizations shall be subject to state registration in compliance with the Federal Law on State Registration of Legal Persons and Individual Businessmen, subject to the special procedure for state registration of religious organizations established by this Federal Law.

A decision on state registration of a religious organization shall be rendered by the federal executive body authorised in the sphere of the state registration of public associations (hereinafter referred to as the federal organ of state registration) or by a territorial agency thereof. An entry to the Unified State Register of Legal Entities of data on establishment, reorganization and liquidation of religious organizations, as well as of other data, provided for by federal laws, shall be made by the authorized registering body on the basis of a decision on a relevant state registration rendered by the federal body of state registration or by a territorial agency thereof. With this, a procedure for interaction of the federal body of state registration and of territorial agencies thereof with the authorized registering body with regard to state registration of religious organizations shall be determined by the Government of the Russian Federation.

2. A decision on state registration of a local religious organization, as well as of a centralized religious organization having local religious organizations

located on the territory of one subject of the Russian Federation, shall be rendered by a territorial agency of the federal body of state registration in an appropriate subject of the Russian Federation.

3. The federal body of state registration shall render a decision on state registration of a centralized religious organization having local religious organizations on the territories of two and more subjects of the Russian Federation.

4. A decision on state registration of religious organisations formed by a centralized religious organisations in accordance with Item 6 of Article 8 hereof, shall be effected by the body which has rendered a decision on state registration of an appropriate religious organization.

5. For purposes of government registration of a local religious organisation, the founders shall submit to the respective a territorial agency of the federal body of state registration as follows:

—application for registration;

—list of persons setting up a religious organisation, indicating their citizenship, place of residence, date of birth;

—charter of religious organisation;

—minutes of the constituent assembly;

—document confirming the existence of a religious group in the given territory within no less than 15 years, issued by the body of local administration or confirming its membership in the centralized religious organisation, issued by its governing centre;

—data on the basic principles of religious teachings and the corresponding practice, including about the history of origin of religion and the given association, the forms and methods of its activity, the attitude to family and marriage, education, peculiarities of attitude to the health by the followers of the given religion, restrictions imposed on the members and clergymen of the organisation as regards their civic rights and duties;

—data on the address (location) of a standing governing body of a newly-formed religious organization which is used for contacting the religious organization;

—document confirming payment of the state duty.

6. In the event a superior governing body (centre) of the newly formed religious organisation is located outside the Russian Federation, it is required to submit besides the documents specified under Item 5 hereof, according to the prescribed procedure also the charter or any other basic document of a foreign religious organisation to be certified by the government body of the country of location of the said organisation.

12. A state duty for state registration of a religious organization and the amendments introduced to the charter thereof shall be collected in the procedure and in the amount stipulated by the laws of the Russian Federation.

Article 12 Refusal to Effect Government Registration of Religious Organization

1. The government registration may be refused to a religious organisation whenever:

—the objectives and activities of a religious organisation run counter to the Constitution of the Russian Federation and the laws of the Russian Federation—by reference to specific articles of the laws;

—the given organisation has not been recognized as a religious organisation;

—the charter and other submitted documents do not meet the requirements of the laws of the Russian Federation or the data contained therein are not true;

—the organisation with the same name has already been registered in the unified state register of legal entities;

—the founder (founders) is legally incompetent.

Federal Law No. 31-FZ of March 21, 2002 amended Item 2 of Article 12 of this Federal Law. The amendments shall enter into force as of July 1, 2002

2. In case of refusal of government registration of a religious organisation the decision taken shall be communicated in writing to an applicant (applicants) by indicating the reasons for refusal. The refusal for reasons of inexpediency

of setting up a religious organisation shall not be permitted. The refusal of government registration of a religious organisation as well as its evasion from such registration may be protested against in court of law.

Article 13 The Representations of Foreign Religious Organizations

1. Foreign religious organisation shall mean an organisation set up outside the Russian Federation in accordance with the laws of a foreign state.

2. Foreign religious organisation may be granted the right to open its representative office in the territory of the Russian Federation.

The representation of a foreign religious organisation may not engage in the activities of worship and other religious activities and shall not enjoy the status of a religious association as established hereunder.

3. The procedure for registration, establishment and closure of a representative office of a foreign religious organisation shall be prescribed by the government of the Russian Federation in keeping with the laws of the Russian Federation.

Regulations for the Order of the Registration, Opening and Closing of the Representative Offices of Foreign Religious Organizations in the Russian Federation was approved by the Decision of the Government of the Russian Federation No. 130 of February 2, 1998

4. In the event of taking a decision in favour of the registration of a representative office of a foreign religious organisation, its representative shall be given a certificate after the form set by the Government of the Russian Federation.

5. The Russian religious organisation shall be entitled to have under it a representative office of a foreign religious organisation.

Federal Law No. 58-FZ of June 29, 2004 amended Article 14 of this Federal Law

Article 14 Suspension of the Activity of a Religious Association, the Liquidation of a Religious Organization and the Prohibition of the Activity of a Religious Association, if They Violate the Legislation;

1. Religious organisations may be liquidated:

—by decision of their founders or a body authorized thereto by the charter of a religious organisation;

—by court decision in the event of repeated or gross violations of the rules of the Constitution of the Russian Federation, this federal law and other federal laws or in the event of systematic performance by a religious organisation of activities running counter to the objectives of its creation (statutory objectives).

2. The grounds for liquidation of a religious organisation, banning the activities of a religious organisation or a religious group by due course of law shall comprise as follows:

—the breach of public security and public order;

—acts aimed at the performance of an extremist activity;

—forcing to break the family;

—encroachments on the personality, rights and freedoms of citizens;

—infliction of damage established under the law to morals, health of citizens, including the use in connection with their religious activity of narcotic drugs and psychotherapeutic agents, hypnosis, the commission of acts of perversion and other unlawful actions;

—inducement to suicide and refusal for reasons of religion to give medical aid to persons in a state endangering their life and health;

—preventing a citizen by using a threat of damage to his life, health, or property, provided there is a real danger of realization of same, or a threat of violence or by other illegal actions from withdrawing from a religious associations;

—preventing from getting compulsory education;

—forcing members and followers of religious associations and other persons to alienate their property in favour of religious associations;

—encouraging citizens to refuse to perform the civil duties established under the law and to commit other wrongful acts.

3. The bodies of the prosecutor's office of the Russian Federation, the federal body of state registration or territorial agencies thereof, as well as bodies of local administration shall have the right to file applications to the court requesting the liquidation of religious organisation or the ban on the activity of a religious organisation or a religious group.

4. State registration of a religious organization in connection with liquidation thereof shall be carried out in the procedure provided for by the Federal Law on State Registration of Legal Persons and Individual Businessmen subject to the peculiarities of such registration established by this Federal Law.

The data and documents required for carrying out state registration of a religious organization in connection with liquidation thereof shall be submitted to the body that has rendered a decision on state registration of this religious organization, when established.

The federal body of state registration or a territorial agency thereof upon the adoption of a decision on state registration of a religious organization in connection with liquidation thereof shall direct to the authorized registering body the data and documents required for exercising by this body the functions related to keeping the Unified State Register of Legal Entities.

On the basis of said decision, rendered by the federal body of state registration or a territorial agency thereof, and the required data and documents, submitted by them, the authorized registering body in five working days at latest, as of the date of receiving the required data and documents, shall make an appropriate entry to the Unified State Register of Legal Entities and shall inform about it the body, that has rendered said decision, at latest in one working day, next following the date of making an appropriate entry.

A procedure for interaction of the federal body of state registration and territorial agencies thereof with the authorized registering body with regard to state registration of religious organizations in connection with liquidation thereof shall be determined by the Government of the Russian Federation.

State registration of a religious organization in connection with liquidation thereof shall be carried out in ten working days at latest, as of the date of submitting all the documents drawn up in the established procedure.

7. The activity of a religious association may be suspended, a religious organization may be liquidated and the activity of a religious association, which is not a religious organization, may be prohibited in the order and on the grounds, envisaged in the Federal Law on the Counteraction to an Extremist Activity.

Article 25 Exercise of Supervision and Control

Federal Law No. 31-FZ of March 21, 2002 amended Item 2 of Article 25 of this Federal Law. The amendments shall enter into force as of July 1, 2002

2. The organ that has rendered a decision on state registration of a religious organization shall exercise control over the compliance thereby with the charter as regards the objectives and procedure for its activities.

Article 27 Final Provisions

3. The charters and other constituent documents of religious organisations set up prior to entry into effect of this Federal Law, shall be brought into line with this Federal Law. The charters and other constituent documents of religious organisations before they have been brought into accord with this Federal Law shall be effective only in the part that does not conflict with this Federal Law.

The new registration of religious organisations concerning which there are grounds for their liquidation or banning their activities, specified under Item 2 of Article 14 hereof, shall not be required. Upon refusal to re-register for the said reasons, the body of registration shall pass the materials over to the court.

Religious organisations that do not have a document confirming their existence in the corresponding territory within not less than 15 years shall have the right of a legal entity provided they are re-registered annually till the expiration of the said 15-years' term. . . .

Federal Law No. 45-FZ of March 26, 2000 amended Item 4 of Article 27 of this Federal Law

4. The government re-registration of religious organisations set up prior to the entry into effect of this Federal Law, shall be carried out not later than December 31, 2000 in accordance with the requirements of this Federal law.

Upon the expiry of the indicated date the religious organisations that have not been reregistered shall be subject to liquidation judicially by demand of the body carrying out the state registration of religious organisations.

President of the Russian Federation
B. Yeltsin
Moscow, the Kremlin

Source: OSCE Office for Democratic Institutions and Human Rights. "Federal Law No.125-FZ on Freedom of Conscience and Religious Associations (1997, amended 2004)." Available online. URL:Legislationline.org, http://www.legislationline.org/legislation.php?tid=2&lid=584&less=false. Downloaded December 3, 2006.

On the State of Emergency (2001, amended 2005) (excerpts)

In 2001, President Vladimir Putin signed into law a new set of provisions covering all aspects of a state of emergency should one be declared. Among those aspects are censorship powers over the media and restriction of political activity. The law has subsequently been amended twice.

Article 1 State of Emergency

1. The State of Emergency means a special legal regime of operation of the bodies of state authority, bodies of local self-administration, organizations regardless of their organizational form, legal status and forms of ownership, of their officials and societal associations, introduced in accordance with the Constitution of the Russian Federation and this Federal Constitutional Law throughout the territory of the Russian Federation or within its individual localities which allows for individual restrictions of the rights and freedoms of citizens of the Russian Federation, foreign citizens, persons without citizenship, the rights of organizations and societal associations and also the placing on them of additional obligations.

2. The introduction of the State of Emergency is a temporary measure applied exclusively to ensure the security of citizens and the protection of the constitutional system of the Russian Federation.

Article 4 Introduction of the State of Emergency

1. The State of Emergency throughout the territory of the Russian Federation or within its individual localities shall be introduced by a decree of the Presi-

dent of the Russian Federation by giving an immediate notification thereon to the Federation Council of the Federal Assembly of the Russian Federation and the State Duma of the Federal Assembly of the Russian Federation.

2. The decree of the President of the Russian Federation on the introduction of the State of Emergency shall be immediately submitted for approval to the Federation Council of the Federal Assembly of the Russian Federation.

Article 11 Measures and Temporary Restrictions Imposed Upon the Introduction of a State of Emergency

The Decree of the President of the Russian Federation on the introduction of a state of emergency may for an effective period of the state of emergency provide for the imposition of the following measures and temporary restrictions, viz.:

f) ban on or restriction of meetings, rallies, demonstrations, marches, picketing and other mass events;

g) ban on strikes or other methods of suspension or termination of activities of organizations;

Article 12 Measures and Temporary Restrictions Imposed in the Conditions of a State of Emergency Introduced In the Presence of Circumstances Specified under Item "a" of Article 3 of this Federal Constitutional Law

In the event of introduction of a state of emergency in the presence of circumstances specified under Item "a" of Article 3 of this Federal Constitutional Law, the Decree of the President of the Russian Federation on the introduction of a state of emergency may provide, over and above the measures and temporary restrictions specified in Article 11 hereof, with respect to the territory in which the state of emergency is introduced, also for the following measures and temporary restrictions, viz.:

b) restriction of freedom of the press and other media of mass information by introduction of prior censorship, indicating conditions and procedure for carrying out of same and also temporary confiscation or arrest of printed matter, radio-transmitting, sound-amplifying technical facilities, duplicating machines, establishment of a special procedure for the accreditation of journalists;

c) suspension of the activities of political parties and other societal associations that may hamper the elimination of circumstances which served as grounds for the introduction of the state of emergency;

Article 15 Suspension of Legal Acts of State Authorities of the Subjects of the Russian Federation and Acts of Local Self-Administration Bodies

The President of the Russian Federation shall have the right to suspend any legal acts of state authorities of the subjects of the Russian Federation, legal acts of local self-administration bodies that are valid in the territory where the state of emergency is introduced, in the event those acts contradict the decree of the President of the Russian Federation on the introduction of a state of emergency within the given territory.

Article 28 Limits of Application of Measures and Temporary Restrictions in the Conditions of a State of Emergency

1. Measures applied in the conditions of a state of emergency entailing the alteration (limitation) of powers of federal executive authorities, legislative (representative) and executive bodies of authority of the subjects of the Russian Federation, local self-administration bodies, the rights of organizations and societal associations, the rights and freedoms of people and citizens established by the Constitution of the Russian Federation, federal laws and other statutory acts of the Russian Federation shall be carried out within such limits as may be required by the seriousness of a given situation.

2. Measures specified in Part One of this Article shall correspond to the international obligations of the Russian Federation ensuing from international agreements of the Russian Federation in the field of human rights and shall not entail any discrimination against individual persons or groups of the population exclusively on the basis of sex, race, nationality, language, origin, property and official position, place of residence, attitude towards religion, convictions, affiliation with societal associations and also by virtue of other circumstances.

President of the Russian Federation
V. Putin
Moscow, the Kremlin

Source: OSCE Office for Democratic Institutions and Human Rights. Legislationline.org.. "Federal Constitutional Law No.3-FKZ On the State of Emergency (2001, as amended 2005)." Available onlione. URL:http://www.legislationline.org/legislation.php?tid=46&lid=601&less=false. Downloaded December 5, 2006.

On Rallies, Meetings, Demonstrations, Marches, and Picketing (June 19, 2004)

On June 4, 2004, the Duma, the lower house of Russia's parliament, passed a federal law on public assembly; it was endorsed by the Federation Council, the upper house, on June 9, 2004, and signed into law by President Vladimir Putin on June 19, 2004. While it is not nearly as harsh as previous Soviet laws on public assembly, the clauses below are either restrictive (article 5, section 2, paragraph 2) or can be interpreted in a more restrictive manner than they appear on paper, such as in article 13, section 1, paragraph 2.

This federal law is aimed at ensuring realization of the constitutionally mandated right of citizens of the Russian Federation to peaceful assembly without weapons, to hold rallies, meetings, demonstrations, marches and picketing.

Article 1 Legislation of the Russian Federation on rallies, meetings, demonstrations, marches and picketing

2. The holding of rallies, meetings, demonstrations, marches and picketing with a view to election campaigning, agitation related to the issues of a referendum shall be regulated under this federal law and the legislation of the Russian Federation on elections and referenda. The holding of religious rites and ceremonies shall be regulated under Federal Law No. 125-FZ of September 26, 1997 On the Freedom of Conscience and On Religious Associations.

Article 5 Organization of the public event

2. The following persons may not act as promoters of a public event, viz.:

2) a political party, other public and religious association, their regional branches and other structural subdivisions whose activity has been either suspended or banned or that have been liquidated according to the procedure established under the law.

Article 13 Rights and obligations of the authorized representative of the executive power body of the subject of the Russian Federation or the local self-government body

1. The authorized representative of the executive power body of the Subject of the Russian Federation or the body of local self-government shall have the right:

2) to take a decision to suspend or terminate public events by a manner and on the grounds envisaged under this Federal Law.

Article 15 Grounds and procedure for suspension of a public event

1. When and if, there occurs, during the holding of a public event, through the fault of its participants violation of law and order not entailing a threat to the life and health of its participants, the authorized representative of the executive power body of the subject of the Russian Federation or the local self-government body shall have the right to demand that the promoter of the public event either on his own or jointly with the authorized representative of the internal security body make good such violation.

2. In the case of failure to obey the demand to make good a violation mentioned under Part 1 of this Article, the authorized representative of the executive power body of the Subject of the Russian Federation or the local self-government body shall have the right to suspend the public event for the period fixed by him to make good the detected violation. Upon remedying the violation, the public event may, by agreement between the promoter of the public event and respective authorized representative, be continued.

3. When the violation was not made good upon the expiration of the period fixed by the authorized representative of the executive power body of the subject of the Russian Federation or the local self-government body, the public event shall be terminated according to the procedure envisaged under Article 17 of this federal law.

Article 16 Grounds for termination of a public event

The grounds to terminate the public event shall be as follows:

1) creation of a real threat to the life and health of citizens and also to the property of individuals and legal persons;

2) perpetration by participants in the public event of illegal actions and deliberate violation by the promoter of the public event of the provisions of this federal law concerning the procedure for holding the public event.

President of the Russian Federation
V. Putin
Moscow, the Kremlin
June 19, 2004

Source: OSCE Office for Democratic Institutions and Human Rights. Legislationonline.org. "Federal Law on Assemblies, Meetings, Demonstrations, Processions and Pickets (19 June 2004)." Available online. URL:http://www.legislationline.org/legislation.php?tid=200&lid=633&less=false. Downloaded December 6, 2006.

ZIMBABWE

The Public Order and Security Act (2002) (excerpts)

The Public Order and Security Act (POSA) was adopted in 2002 by the government of Zimbabwe to replace the Law and Order Maintenance Act (LOMA), promulgated in 1960—20 years before independence. African nationalist politicians and human rights experts considered LOMA to be perhaps Rhodesia's harshest law, but POSA turned out to be equally harsh, if not worse in some areas. Articles 12 and 16 are comparable to U.S. Espionage and Sedition laws.

12 Causing disaffection among Police Force or Defence Forces
If any person

(a) causes, or attempts to cause, or does any act calculated to cause, disaffection amongst the members of the Police Force or Defence Forces with the result that any member of the Police Force or Defence Forces withholds his services, loyalty or allegiance or commits breaches of discipline, or causes, or attempts to cause, or does any act calculated to cause such disaffection with the intention of bringing about such result; or

(b) induces, or attempts to induce, or does any act calculated to induce, any member of the Police Force or Defence Forces to withhold his services, loyalty or allegiance or to commit breaches of discipline; he shall be guilty of an offence and liable to a fine not exceeding level seven or to imprisonment for a period not exceeding two years, or to both such fine and such imprisonment.

16 Undermining authority of or insulting President
(1) In this section—
"publicly", in relation to making a statement, means—

(a) making the statement in a public place or any place to which the public or any section of the public have access;

(b) publishing it in any printed or electronic medium for reception by the public; "statement" includes any act or gesture.

(2) Any person who publicly and intentionally—

(a) makes any false statement about or concerning the President or an acting President knowing or realising that there is a risk or possibility of—

(i) engendering feelings of hostility towards; or

(ii) causing hatred, contempt or ridicule of;

the President or an acting President, whether in person or in respect of his office; or

(b) makes any abusive, indecent, obscene or false statement about or concerning the President or an acting President, whether in respect of his person or his office; shall be guilty of an offence and liable to a fine not exceeding level six or to imprisonment for a period not exceeding one year or to both such fine and such imprisonment.

19 Gatherings conducing to riot, disorder or intolerance

(1) Any person who, acting together with one or more other persons present with him in any place or at any meeting—

(a) forcibly—

(i) disturbs the peace, security or order of the public or any section of the public; or

(ii) invades the rights of other people;

intending to cause such disturbance or invasion or realising that there is a risk or possibility that such disturbance or invasion may occur; or

(b) performs any action, utters any words or distributes or displays any writing, sign or other visible representation that is obscene, threatening, abusive or insulting, intending thereby to provoke a breach of the peace or realising that there is a risk or possibility that a breach of the peace may be provoked; or

(c) utters any words or distributes or displays any writing, sign or other visible representation—

(i) with the intention to engender, promote or expose to hatred, contempt or ridicule any group, section or class of persons in Zimbabwe solely on account of the race, tribe, nationality, place of origin, national or ethnic origin, colour, religion or gender of such group, section or class of persons; or

(ii) realising that there is a risk or possibility that such behaviour might have an effect referred to in subparagraph (i); shall be guilty of an offence and be liable to a fine not exceeding level ten or to imprisonment for a period not exceeding ten years or to both such fine and such imprisonment.

(2) An offence under subsection (1) is committed whether the action constituting it is spontaneous or concerted, and whether the place or meeting where it occurred is public or private.

25 Regulation of public gatherings

(1) If a regulating authority, having regard to all the circumstances in which a public gathering is taking or is likely to take place, has reasonable grounds for believing that the public gathering will occasion—

(a) public disorder; or

(b) a breach of the peace; or

(c) an obstruction of any thoroughfare;

he may, subject to this section, give such directions as appear to him to be reasonably necessary for the preservation of public order and the public peace and preventing or minimising any obstruction of traffic along any thoroughfare.

(2) Without derogation from the generality of subsection (1), directions under that subsection may provide for any of the following matters—

(a) prescribing the time at which the public gathering may commence and its maximum duration;

(b) prohibiting persons taking part in the public gathering from entering any public place specified in the directions;

(c) precautions to be taken to avoid the obstruction of traffic along any thoroughfare;

(d) prescribing the route to be taken by any procession;

(e) requiring the organiser to appoint marshals to assist in the maintenance of order at the public gathering.

...

(7) The noting of an appeal in terms of this subsection shall not have the effect of suspending the direction appealed against.

(8) A police officer may order the persons taking part in any public gathering to disperse if—

(a) any direction given under subsection (1) in relation to that gathering has been violated; or

(b) the police officer has reasonable grounds for believing that public order is likely to be endangered if the gathering continues.

26 Prohibition of public gatherings to avoid public disorder
(1) Without derogation from section *twenty-five*, if a regulating authority believes on reasonable grounds that a public gathering will occasion public disorder, he may by notice in terms of subsection (3) prohibit the public gathering.

27 Temporary prohibition of holding of public demonstrations within particular police districts
(1) If a regulating authority for any area believes on reasonable grounds that the powers conferred by sections *twenty-five* and *twenty-six* will not be sufficient to prevent public disorder being occasioned by the holding of public demonstrations or any class thereof in the area or any part thereof, he may issue an order prohibiting, for a specified period not exceeding one month, the holding of all public demonstrations or any class of public demonstrations in the area or part thereof concerned.

Source: Veritas Trust. Kubatana.net. "Public Order and Security Act [Chapter 11:17]." Available online. URL:http://www.kubatana.net/docs/legisl/posa060203.pdf. Downloaded January 11, 2007.

The Access to Information and Protection of Privacy Act (2002) (excerpts)

The Access to Information and Protection of Privacy Act (AIPPA) was also put into force in 2002. As with many censorship laws in most countries, its name belies its intent. The law actually establishes and makes use of governmental apparatus to stifle dissent in the media against the regime of President Robert Mugabe. AIPPA not only regulates what can be said in the media, but who is allowed to say it. This ensures reports favorable to the government and fosters a docility among those who have been granted such a favored position. However AIPPA's reach does not extend to Internet sites based outside Zimbabwe.

38 Establishment of Media and Information Commission
(1) For the purposes of this Act, there is hereby established a Commission, to be known as the Media and Information Commission, which shall be a body corporate capable of suing and being sued in its own name and, subject to this Act, of performing all acts that bodies corporate may by law perform.

39 Functions and Powers of Commission
(1) Subject to this Act, the powers and functions of the Commission shall be—

(b) to receive and act upon comments from the public about the administration and performance of the mass media in Zimbabwe; and

(d) to comment on the implications of automated systems for collection, storage, analysis or transfer of information or for access to information or protection of privacy; and

(f) to engage in or commission research into anything affecting the achievement of the purposes of this Act; and

(h) to advise the Minister on the adoption and establishment of standards and codes relating to the operation of mass media; and

(i) to receive, evaluate for accreditation and consider applications for accreditation as a journalist; and

(j) to enforce professional and ethical standards in the mass media; and

(l) to bring to the attention of the head of a public body any failure to meet the prescribed standards for fulfilling the duty to assist applicants; and

(m) to authorise a public body, at the request of its head, to disregard requests that would unreasonably interfere with the operations of the public body; and

(n) to accredit journalists; and

(o) to monitor the mass media and raise user awareness of the mass media; and

(p) to register mass media in Zimbabwe; and

(q) to investigate and resolve complaints against any mass media service in terms of the provisions of this Act.

64 Abuse of freedom of expression

A person registered in terms of this Part who makes use, by any means, of a mass media service for the purposes of publishing—

(a) information which he or she intentionally or recklessly falsified in a manner which—

(i) threatens the interests of defence, public safety, public order, the economic interests of the State, public morality or public health; or

(ii) is injurious to the reputation, rights and freedoms of other persons; or

(b) information which he or she maliciously or fraudulently fabricated; or

(c) any statement—

(i) threatening the interests of defence, public safety, public order, the economic interests of the State, public morality or public health; or

(ii) injurious to the reputation, rights and freedoms of other persons; in the following circumstances—

A. knowing the statement to be false or without having reasonable grounds for believing it to be true; and

B. recklessly, or with malicious or fraudulent intent, representing the statement as a true statement; shall be guilty of an offence and liable to a fine not exceeding level fourteen or to imprisonment for a period not exceeding three years.

66 Registration of mass media services

(1) Subject to section *sixty-eight*, a mass media owner shall carry on the activities of a mass media service only after registering and receiving a certificate of registration in terms of this Act.

(2) An application for the registration of a mass media service whose products are intended for dissemination in Zimbabwe shall be submitted by its owner to the Commission in the form and manner prescribed and accompanied by the prescribed fee.

(4) A mass media service shall be registered when it is issued with a certificate of registration by the Commission.

69 Refusal of registration of mass media service

(1) The Commission may not refuse to register a mass media service unless—

(a) it fails to comply with the provisions of this Act ; or

(b) the information indicated in an application for registration is false, misleading or contains any misrepresentation; or

(c) that mass media service seeks to be registered in the name of an existing registered mass media service;

and the Commission shall forward a written notification of the refusal of registration, stating the grounds upon which such refusal is based.

(2) An appeal shall lie to the Administrative Court against any decision made or action taken by the Commission in terms of this section.

71 Suspension, cancellation and enforcement of registration certificates

(1) Subject to this section, the Commission may, whether on its own initiative or upon the investigation of a complaint made by any interested person against the mass media service, suspend or cancel the registration certificate of a mass media service if it has reasonable grounds for believing that—

(a) the registration certificate was issued in error or through fraud or there has been a misrepresentation or non-disclosure of a material fact by the mass media owner concerned; or

(b) a mass media service concerned does not publish or go on air within twelve months from the date of registration; or

(c) the mass media service concerned has contravened sections *sixty-five, seventy-five, seventy-six, seventy-seven* or *eighty-nine* of this Act

(6) Without derogation from its powers in terms of subsection (1), where the Commission is satisfied that a mass media service is contravening, has contravened or is likely to contravene any of the provisions of this Act, the Commission may serve upon the mass media service an order—

(a) requiring the mass media owner to do, or not to do, such things as are specified in the order for the purpose rectifying or avoiding any contravention or threatened contravention of this Act; and

(b) stipulating the period within which any requirement referred to in paragraph (a) shall be commenced and completed.

74 News agencies

(1) Subject to this Act, no person shall carry on or operate a news agency without a valid registration certificate issued in terms of this Part.

(4) In addition to any fine imposed in terms of subsection (2) and without derogation from any of its powers granted under any enactment, a court convicting a person of contravening subsection (1) may declare forfeited to the State any equipment or apparatus used for the purpose of or in connection with the offence.

(5) The proviso to subsection (1) and subsections (3), (4), (5) and (6) of section 62 of the Criminal Procedure and Evidence Act shall apply, *mutatis mutandis*, in relation to a declaration in terms of subsection (3).

77 Obligatory reports

A mass media service shall, if ordered to do so by the Commission, publish, free of charge the full particulars or a summary approved by the Commission of the substance of a decision of a court or the Commission pertaining to its mass media service that has come into effect—

(a) on the front page or centrespread, if it is a newspaper; or

(b) if it is an electronic mass media service, on three consecutive occasions during prime time;

or in such other manner as the Commission may prescribe.

79 Accreditation of journalists

(1) No journalist shall exercise the rights provided in section *seventy-eight* in Zimbabwe without being accredited by the Commission.

(2) Subject to subsection (4), no journalist shall be accredited who is not a citizen of Zimbabwe, or is not regarded as permanently resident in Zimbabwe by virtue of the Immigration Act.

(3) Any person who wishes to be accredited as a journalist shall make an application to the Commission in the form and manner and accompanied by the fee, if any, prescribed:

Provided that a mass media service or news agency may file an application for accreditation on behalf of journalists employed by such mass media service or news agency.

(4) A journalist who is not a citizen of Zimbabwe, or is not regarded as permanently resident in Zimbabwe by virtue of the Immigration Act may be accredited for any period specified by the Commission not exceeding thirty days:

Provided that the Commission may, for good cause shown or for the purpose of enabling the journalist to work for the duration of any event he or she is accredited to cover, extend the period by a specified number of days.

(6) Every news agency that operates in Zimbabwe, whether domiciled inside or outside Zimbabwe, shall in respect of its local operations not employ or use the services of any journalist other than an accredited journalist who is a citizen of Zimbabwe, or is regarded as permanently resident in Zimbabwe by virtue of the Immigration Act:

Provided that the news agency may employ or use the services of a journalist referred to in subsection (4) for the duration of that journalist's accreditation.

80 Abuse of journalistic privilege

A journalist who abuses his or her journalistic privilege by publishing—

(a) information which he or she intentionally or recklessly falsified in a manner which—

(i) threatens the interests of defence, public safety, public order, the economic interests of the State, public morality or public health; or

(ii) is injurious to the reputation, rights and freedoms of other persons; or

(b) information which he or she maliciously or fraudulently fabricated; or

(c) any statement—

(i) threatening the interests of defence, public safety, public order, the economic interests of the State, public morality or public health; or

(ii) injurious to the reputation, rights and freedoms of other persons; in the following circumstances—

A. knowing the statement to be false or without having reasonable grounds for believing it to be true; and

B. recklessly, or with malicious or fraudulent intent, representing the statement as a true statement;

shall be guilty of an offence and liable to a fine not exceeding level seven or to imprisonment for a period not exceeding two years.

82 Roll of journalists

The Commission shall maintain a roll of all journalists and shall issue to every person whose name is entered in the roll, a certificate of accreditation in the prescribed form.

83 Prohibition against practice by, or in association with, unaccredited journalists

(1) No person other than a accredited journalist shall practise as a journalist nor be employed as such or in any manner hold himself out as a journalist.

(2) No person who has ceased to be a accredited journalist as a result of the deletion of his name from the roll, or who has been suspended from practising as a journalist, shall, while his name is so deleted, or is so suspended, continue to practice directly or indirectly as a journalist, whether by himself or in partnership or association with any other person, nor shall he, except with the written consent of the Commission, be employed in any capacity whatsoever connected with the journalistic profession.

90 Representative offices of foreign mass media services

(1) A representative office of a foreign mass media service shall not be set up or operated in Zimbabwe except with the permission of the Commission.

Source: The NGO Network Alliance Project. Kubatana.net. "Access to Information and Protection of Privacy Act (showing forthcoming amendments to be made by act 5/2003)." Available online. URL: http://www.kubatana.net/docs/legisl/aippaamd030611.pdf. Downloaded January 11, 2007.

Censorship and Entertainments Control Act (1979, 2004) (excerpts)

This law dates from the end of Rhodesia's unilateral independence, and has remained on the books throughout the years of the Mugabe government. The version of the act from which these excerpts are taken dates from May 1, 2004, and incorporates amendments that went into effect in 1997 and 2002.

3 Board of Censors

(1) The Minister shall appoint a board, to be known as the Board of Censors, to perform the functions entrusted to it under this Act.

(2) The Board shall consist of not less than nine members who shall be appointed for a period of not more than three years.

(3) The Minister may appoint an alternate member to any member of the Board.

(4) A retiring member and an alternate member shall be eligible for reappointment as a member or as an alternate member.

(5) The Minister shall designate one member as chairman of the Board and one member as vice-chairman of the Board.

(6) If the chairman is prevented by illness, absence from Zimbabwe or other cause from exercising his functions on the Board or committees of the Board, the vice-chairman shall exercise the functions and powers and perform the duties of the chairman.

(9) A decision of the majority of the members present at a meeting of the Board shall be the decision of the Board:

Provided that in the event of an equality of votes the person presiding at the meeting shall have a casting vote in addition to his deliberative vote.

4 Functions of Board

The functions of the Board shall be—

(a) to examine any article or public entertainment submitted to it;

(b) to make such inquiries as it may consider necessary in regard to any publication, picture, statue, record or public entertainment which is

alleged to be or which the Board has reason to believe is of a nature contemplated in section *seventeen*;

(*c*) to advise the Minister in regard to any matter arising out of the application of any provision of this Act which the Minister may refer to the Board;

(*d*) to perform any other function assigned to it by this Act or any other enactment.

9 Prohibition of unapproved films

(1) Subject to this Part, no person shall—

(*a*) distribute, televise or publicly exhibit any film; or

(*b*) exhibit to any person, other than a person referred to in subsection (2), any film which—

(i) is intended to be exhibited in public; or

(ii) though recorded in such a manner as to be incapable of being exhibited in public, is wholly or substantially a copy or recording of a film intended to be so exhibited; or

(*c*) publish any film advertisement;

unless the film or copy or recording or film advertisement, as the case may be, has been approved by the Board in terms of section *ten*.

(2) A film referred to in paragraph (*b*) of subsection (1) may be exhibited to—

(*a*) any person concerned in the making of the film; or

(*b*) any person in the course of his business as a distributor or exhibitor of films; or

(*c*) any person or class of persons exempted from that paragraph by the chairman of the Board;

without the film having been approved by the Board.

10 Powers of Board in respect of films

(1) The Board shall have power to examine any film or film advertisement and—

(*a*) subject to subsection (2), to approve the film or film advertisement either unconditionally or subject to any one or more of the conditions set out in subsection (3); or

(*b*) to reject the film or film advertisement; or

(*c*) in accordance with sectior *twelve*, to declare the film to be prohibited.

(2) The Board shall not approve any film or film advertisement which in its opinion—

(*a*) depicts any matter that is indecent or obscene or is offensive or harmful to public morals; or

(*b*) is likely to be contrary to the interests of defence, public safety, public order, the economic interests of the State or public health; or

(*c*) depicts any matter in a manner that is indecent or obscene or is offensive or harmful to public morals.

(3) In approving any film or film advertisement, the Board may impose one or more of the following conditions—

(*a*) in the case of a film intended to be televised, that it shall not be televised except—

(i) between such hours as may be specified;

(ii) after notices, indicating that the film is considered unsuitable for viewing by persons of such class as may be specified, have been televised at such times and after such intervals as may be specified;

(iii) after any specified portion has been excised therefrom;

(*b*) in the case of a film other than a film referred to in paragraph (*a*) or in the case of a film advertisement, that it shall not be distributed, exhibited or published, as the case may be—

(i) to persons of a specified age or sex;

(ii) except after any specified portion has been excised therefrom;

(*c*) any other condition designed to ensure that the film or film advertisement is not distributed, exhibited or published, as the case may be, to any person or class or persons.

(5) Subject to subsection (6), no person shall—

(*a*) where the Board has approved a film or film advertisement subject to the excision of any portion therefrom, exhibit or televise such film or publish such film advertisement after the excision of such portion therefrom unless the film or film advertisement has thereafter been submitted to the Board for further examination:

Provided that the Board may authorize the exhibition or televising of the film or publication of the film advertisement without further examination; or

(*b*) without the approval of the Board, distribute, televise or exhibit any film or publish any film advertisement which, after having been approved by the Board, has been in any way altered or modified; or

(*c*) contravene any condition imposed by the Board in terms of subsection (3):

Provided that no condition imposed in relation to a film in terms of subparagraph (i) of paragraph (*b*) of subsection (3) shall be contravened in respect of a person who—

(i) is required to be present at the exhibition of such film in the course of his employment; or

(ii) sees such film while he is outside the place to which persons are admitted for the purpose of witnessing the exhibition of such film; or

(*d*) televise or publicly exhibit any film approved by the Board, without signifying in the prescribed manner the Board's approval thereof.

12 Prohibited films

(1) After examining any film, the Board may, if it considers that—

(*a*) the film is of a nature described in subsection (2) of section *ten*; and

(*b*) it is necessary or expedient in the public interest to do so; declare the film to be prohibited.

(5) No person shall import any recorded video or film material on which is recorded a film that the Board has declared to be prohibited in terms of subsection (1).

(5a) Any person who contravenes subsection (5) shall be guilty of an offence and liable to a fine not exceeding level seven or to imprisonment for a period not exceeding two years or to both such fine and such imprisonment.

13 Prohibition of importation, production and dissemination of undesirable publications, pictures, statues and records

(1) No person shall—

(*a*) import, print, publish, manufacture, make or produce, distribute, display, exhibit or sell or offer or keep for sale any publication, picture, statue or record; or

(*b*) publicly play any record;

which is undesirable or which has, under section *fourteen* or *fifteen*, been declared by the Board to be undesirable:

Provided that, where a person has imported such a publication, picture, statue or record, nothing in paragraph (*a*) shall prevent him from re-exporting it to the source from which he imported it or to such other place as the Board may approve.

(2) A publication, picture, statue or record shall be deemed to be undesirable if it or any part thereof—

(*a*) is indecent or obscene or is offensive or harmful to public morals; or

(*b*) is likely to be contrary to the interests of defence, public safety, public order, the economic interests of the State or public health; or

(*c*) discloses, with reference to any judicial proceedings—

(i) any matter which is indecent or obscene or is offensive or harmful to public morals or any indecent or obscene medical, surgical or physiological details the disclosure of which is likely to be offensive or harmful to public morals; or

14 Power of Board to examine publications, pictures, statues and records and to declare them undesirable or to declare publication or record prohibited

(1) The Board shall have power to examine any publication, picture, statue or record and to declare whether or not it is, in the opinion of the Board, undesirable.

(2) The Board may, if it considers it necessary or expedient in the public interest to do so, declare any publication, picture, statue or record which has been declared undesirable under subsection (1) or section *thirteen* to be prohibited.

15 Future periodical publications

(1) Subject to this section, where—

(*a*) four or more consecutive editions of any publication which is published periodically have, under subsection (1) of section *fourteen*, been declared by the Board to be undesirable; and

(*b*) every subsequent edition of that publication is, in the opinion of the Board, likely to be undesirable;

the Board may declare all editions of that publication subsequent to the date of the declaration to be undesirable.

(8) Any publication imported after the Board has, under subsection (1), declared it to be undesirable shall be liable to forfeiture and shall be disposed of as the Board may direct.

16 Prohibition of public entertainments unless approved

(1) Subject to this section, no person shall perform in or give or permit the giving of any public entertainment unless such public entertainment has been approved by the Board.

(3) When the Board approves of any public entertainment it shall signify such approval by means of a certificate given in the form and manner prescribed:

Provided that the Board may in its discretion give such certificate in respect of any public entertainment without requiring such public entertainment to be submitted to it for approval.

(4) There shall be paid for every certificate given by the Board such fees as are prescribed.

(7) No person shall—

(*a*) without the approval of the Board, perform in any public entertainment or give or permit the giving of any public entertainment which, after having been approved by the Board, has in any way been altered or modified; . . .

17 Prohibition of certain exhibitions and entertainments

(1) Notwithstanding anything to the contrary in this Act, the Board may, by notice in writing addressed to any person who is or is believed by the Board to be in charge of—

(*a*) the public exhibition or intended exhibition of any publication, picture, statue or record or the public playing or intended playing of any record; or

(*b*) the public exhibition or intended exhibition, or the televising or intended televising, of any film in respect of which an exemption in terms of subsection (3) of section *nine* is in force or which has been approved in terms of subsection (4) of section *ten*; or

(*c*) the giving or intended giving of any public entertainment in respect of which an exemption under subsection (2) of section *sixteen* is in force or a certificate has been given under the proviso to subsection (3) of that section;

prohibit the same, or permit it subject to such conditions as the Board may in its discretion impose, if the Board has reason to believe that the said publication, picture, statue or record is undesirable. . . .

33 Determination of what is indecent or obscene or offensive or harmful to public morals

For the purposes of this Act a matter or thing, or the manner in which any matter or thing is depicted, as the case may be, shall be deemed to be—

(*a*) indecent or obscene if—

(i) it has the tendency to deprave or corrupt the minds of persons who are likely to be exposed to the effect or influence thereof or it is in any way subversive of morality; or

(ii) whether or not related to any sexual content, it unduly exploits horror, cruelty or violence, whether pictorial or otherwise;

(*b*) offensive to public morals if it is likely to be outrageous or disgustful to persons who are likely to read, hear or see it;

(*c*) harmful to public morals if it deals in an improper or offensive manner with criminal or immoral behavior.

Source: The NGO Network Alliance Project. Kubatana.net. "Censorship and Entertainments Control Act." Available online. URL: http://www.kubatana.net/html/archive/legisl/040501cecact.asp?orgcode=par001&range_start=31. Downloaded January 14, 2007.

PART III

Research Tools

6

How to Research Censorship

DEFINING THE TOPIC

There are numerous ways to cover a broad topic such as censorship. To help narrow the scope and define the topic, it is best to begin a research project by creating an outline. The outline should describe what the project is about and how it will be presented. The outline is a work-in-progress: As the research evolves it may be necessary to eliminate some things from the outline and expand or even add others. Some of the narrower censorship themes on which one might focus include:

- Specific areas of censorship. There is an enormous amount of material in library reference sections, in newspapers and magazines, or through the Internet on the censorship of books, films, music, the Internet, and the press. Because there is so much material, the best options are to either focus on one type of censorship in a particular country or compare (book censorship, for instance) in two countries. In these cases it may be helpful to research the historical background to be able to place the current censorship into context.
- Another area of focus is type of censorship. Censorship can be for political, religious, or social reasons, though the latter tends to blend in with the other two. Since politics and religion are the two classic controversial issues, it is essential to maintain a sense of balance; otherwise it might appear as though one political ideology or religion is being demonized. A good approach might be to illustrate the censorship actions of opposing political ideologies or religious faiths. Examples from this volume include book denunciations from both the right and left wings of the political spectrum in the United States and comparing censorship in the United States, a capitalist society, to China, a communist one.

- A third aspect of censorship worth examining is wartime and military censorship and censorship during a state of emergency. At a glance, these may seem like the same thing, but they are not. Military censorship can extend beyond the military to those journalists covering war zones. Wartime censorship is generally civilian censorship during times of war. This may be part of censorship during a state of emergency, but the latter term is usually used during peacetime and has become a political tool for repression. Of the case-study countries examined in this volume, Egypt and Zimbabwe have been under a state of emergency for many years.

The researcher can narrow the focus even further to topics such as "music censorship in the United States," "newspaper censorship in Russia," or "Internet censorship in China." One thing the researcher should keep in mind when searching for information on a particular country is that some countries have undergone name changes. Using the case-study nations of this book as an example: For 70 years in the 20th century Russia was the most important constituent republic of the Union of Soviet Republics, also called the Soviet Union or simply the USSR. For a time in the late 1950s and early 1960s, Egypt (along with Syria) was part of the United Arab Republic. And prior to its independence from Great Britain in 1980, Zimbabwe was known as Rhodesia, before that Southern Rhodesia.

GATHERING MATERIAL

Access to a home, library, or school computer will make the initial research easier since public and university libraries often post their catalogues online at their Web sites. Some public libraries have two types of computers for public use: one contains only the library's catalogue (and perhaps the catalogues of affiliated libraries) and the other is for general use—browsing the Internet or creating documents and files. If that is the case, both computers will be needed, but either way multiple searches will have to be employed. It is always better to have gathered more research material than not enough, but not such an amount that it bogs down the project.

Using This Book as a Starting Point

There are several sections in this book that offer good ways to begin research on censorship:

- Organization and agencies. These Web sites often provide information on current censorship activity and the laws that bolster such activity.

Links often found on the sites may provide even more detailed information. Agency telephone and fax numbers and e-mail addresses serve as points of contact for clarification of material posted on the site.

- Key players and the chronology. The listed names can be divided into three categories: those who instigate censorship, those who are victims of censorship, and those who fight it. These can provide both historical and contemporary frames of reference for a particular area of censorship—book banning, for example.
- The annotated bibliography is an important reference tool. The researcher can use the descriptions of various books, articles, and Web documents to pinpoint important source materials and, just as important, weed out what is not needed for the project.
- Historical documents. Some of the primary source documents in this book may be useful in providing the legal underpinning of certain areas of censorship; the source locations for these documents may also lead to other primary source materials.

Books

Whether using a school, public, college, or university library, it makes sense to check to see if the library is part of a consortium (a group whose members share resources). If it is, all the better, but even if it is not, access to books in other libraries can be gained through interlibrary loan. Remember to check all of the branches of your public library when searching the computer catalogue; some town libraries also have the school libraries linked to the online catalogue.

A good way to begin the library search is with the titles of those books from the annotated bibliography of this volume that seem useful for the project. The library's computer will list the books that are immediately available and their locations within the library. The books are shelved by call numbers that make them generally easy to find, though you may have to ask a librarian for assistance. The computer catalogue will also provide information about books not on the shelf such as when they are due back or what branch library they can be found in.

Other books on the subject in the library's collection are probably shelved nearby, but not necessarily. To find additional books on the topic, type in the keywords of the topic such as "film censorship" or "music censorship." Be sure to select the word "subject" under search options to avoid books in which the topic words appear in the titles of books of fiction or poetry or any other book that may be inappropriate for the project. Write down titles, authors, and call numbers of all that you think are appropriate for the project. The reason for writing down the titles and authors is because if the book is unavailable the researcher can search for it in another library; note that not all libraries use the same filing system—especially college and university libraries.

Deciding which books to use will save unnecessary trips to the library and help in arranging the structure and content of the writing project. Check the following in each book:

- The year of publication on the copyright page. If the book is too old it will be good for historical purposes but not contemporary censorship. For example, a book on music censorship published in the 1980s or 1990s will have little or no information about online downloading and the Napster controversy. On the other hand, a recently published book might not have some of the historical background information the project needs.
- The table of contents. The chapter titles should provide some clues as to whether or not the book is necessary for the project. Skimming a prospective chapter would also help.
- The index. An index is an alphabetically arranged list of topics discussed in the books, with page numbers indicating where the topic appears in the book. More so than the chapter titles, this will give some indication whether or not the particular book is right for the project and how deeply it discusses the project topic. The index may also spark interest in other matters that the researcher had considered peripheral to the project. As with the chapters, it is a good idea to look up a few subjects from the index to see how they are covered. A sentence or two in a 300-page book is obviously inadequate, but an entire chapter or even a few pages would probably be very helpful. If the book has no index then definitely skim a few chapters from the table of contents.
- The bibliography. Most bibliographies will not be annotated; nevertheless the bibliography can lead the researcher to other books, not necessarily in the library's holdings. If there is no bibliography listed then be wary of the book's facts.

Once the researcher has collected all of the books necessary for the project, from various libraries if need be—including interlibrary loan—and taken them home, the project may suddenly seem daunting. However one thing to remember is that the researcher does not need to read all of these books in their entirety. Read completely those that will potentially give the best grounding in the subject area. They are not necessarily the longest books, but the ones that best fit the project's overall thesis. The rest can be skimmed for the vital information. Here again the researcher will make use of the books' tables of contents and the indexes. Whether reading an entire book or skimming over to particular chapters or sections the researcher will need to take notes. These notes will help further to organize thoughts and the text of the project. Post-it notes to mark places in the books are also helpful.

Articles

There are more ways to search for newspaper and magazine articles than there are for books, but using the Internet is the easiest and most time-saving way to go about it. The quickest way is to search either LexisNexis or Factiva. These are electronic databases of magazine and newspapers, divided into different categories dating back to the 1970s. It is more common for a college or university library to have access to at least one of these databases than a public library, and the college or university library may also be part of a consortium of other college and university libraries. If access to these databases is unavailable, an alternative is to access individual newspapers and magazines through the library computer; libraries often have links to major newspapers and journals. A last resort is to visit the Web sites of various newspapers and magazines. However, some Web sites provide only the first few sentences of an article (called the "stub") for free and require payment for the entire article. If that is the case then another tactic is to research each newspaper and magazine online using the same keywords as you did for the book search and any others that you have come across in your reading that you think might be helpful. Then search for the articles in print or on microfilm at the library.

Some U.S. newspapers to search include: the *New York Times, Boston Globe, Washington Post, Chicago Tribune, Los Angeles Times, St. Louis Post-Dispatch, Atlanta Journal-Constitution,* and *Portland Oregonian.* U.S. magazines include *Time, Newsweek, U.S. News and World Report,* the *Nation,* the *National Review,* the *Smithsonian* (for historical perspective), the *New Republic,* the *New Yorker,* the *New York Review of Books,* and the *Wilson Quarterly.* There are also foreign newspapers and magazines such as the *International Herald Tribune, Toronto Star,* the *Times* of London, *Manchester Guardian,* the *Independent* (London), *Economist,* and the *Times Literary Supplement.* Journals in political science, history, human rights, and possibly sociology and ethics might also prove helpful.

Accessing an electronic database, the researcher can modify the search by looking at major English-language newspapers, foreign-language newspapers, and magazines by typing in particular words that might appear in the headline or in the text, which is particularly good when searching newspapers. The focus of the search can be on certain publications, a particular timeframe, or both. Chances are the researcher will need to focus a newspaper search to a narrow timeframe to avoid getting a message window that says that the request has returned more than 1,000 responses—which is daunting enough. (LexisNexis tops out at 1,000.)

Most libraries will also have electronic versions of encyclopedias and many other specific reference databases. The amount of electronic reference material almost seems overwhelming, but with a project outline in hand the researcher will be able to zero in on specifics fairly quickly.

Online Sources

Essentially, almost anything can be found on the Web, including the above-mentioned electronic databases. These, however, would charge the individual researcher a prohibitive site license fee, which is why usually only college and university libraries have them. Despite that, there are many more research opportunities on the Web. The abundance of material to be found and the ease with which it can be accessed has made the Internet the most popular research tool. However, scholars use it with caution.

The common search engines used for research are Google, Yahoo! AltaVista, AOL, MSN Search, and Ask Jeeves. In addition many of these are combined in meta-search engines such as Dogpile. (However, as noted in chapter 3, some of these search engines have their own issues with censorship.)

Online sources, excluding the Web sites of well-known newspapers, periodicals, and news services such as CNN or the BBC, are tricky because it is difficult to gauge the correctness of an article that appears either anonymously or unfootnoted. Some of the articles that appear in online encyclopedias are too short; others have not been fact-checked. Many online postings are too subjective to be reliable, especially Web logs, commonly called blogs. Unless the researcher is positive about the reliability of the blogger's information these should be avoided even if they support the project. If quoted or paraphrased the researcher should identify the material as being opinion. (The same goes for newspaper editorials, which are also reprinted online.)

The best approach to take when it comes to researching online sources for information on censorship is to go to the Web sites of those organizations that are involved in monitoring censorship, such as those listed in this book. These organizations frequently post press alerts, lists of offending countries, articles on serious violations, and their own counterstrategies. Furthermore they usually archive their past articles so a researcher can check on the censorship history of a particular country or individual.

Good online sources of information on censorship include the Web sites of newspapers and magazines published in the country (or countries) you are researching. Many sites, if they emanate from non-English speaking countries, maintain parallel English-language pages. In addition, most offer links to other sites of similar interest such as newspapers and nongovernmental organizations. Like most organizations, online newspapers and magazines archive their material, though if a particular periodical predates the Internet then much of its early material might not be archived online.

The easiest way for the researcher to move back and forth between online information is to bookmark the various Web sites or save them as "favorite places" on the computer. It is best to bookmark anything that looks promising (in effect, placing electronic Post-it notes on the web pages).

EVALUATING MATERIAL

As discussed in the section on books, the age of the material is important. Not only should the researcher be aware of the copyright date of any books being used, but also when newspaper, magazine, and other journal articles were published. Censorship laws and government policies change often and thus the more current a resource the better.

Objectivity is important, but so is correctness. Just because a piece may sound objective does not mean it necessarily is. The researcher has to be like a lawyer in that corroborating evidence is needed. Corroboration is when more than one source is in agreement on a specific point of fact. If, for example, a magazine article lists a certain book or film as having been banned or censored it is a good idea to see if any other publication has also mentioned this. The researcher need not mention every piece of corroborating evidence, though it can be included in the bibliography. Here, an electronic database such as LexisNexis is very helpful because it lists more than one newspaper published on a given date. Thus, if some important censorship action has been taken, more than one newspaper (or magazine) is bound to have reported on it; the researcher can corroborate the fact quickly. Of course the story itself might be wrong, but so big that it gets wide play. The CIA's report on weapons of mass destruction in Iraq is one such example.

A second aspect of objectivity is that the researcher has to be aware of the agenda of the author or the publication (and in doing so become more aware of the agenda of the researcher's own project). Questions to keep in mind are:

- For whom was this article or book written?
  If the book or article seems as if the author were "preaching to the converted" then that is probably the case. This does not make the text worthless, actually the opposite is more likely true. However, a good reader and researcher needs to be aware of a text's intent. When it comes to books and articles on censorship the vast majority are from opposing viewpoints. The texts are written to enlighten readers to the circumstances in a particular country, not to convince them about the negativity of censorship. Almost all of the remainder will be cleverly disguised defenses of a censorship action.
- What point does it make and does it do so clearly?
  A straightforward news article about censorship in schools is unlikely to muddy the issue, but it may still have a slant—remember to keep in mind the author's "agenda." Despite the pro or con slant, it can still be a valuable resource as a record of censorship or as a record of the battle of censorship. A feature article (such as those found in general interest magazines) may (intentionally or not) confuse the issue in the reader's mind by trying to fit the facts to support a preconceived conclusion.
- Does the article or book engage in hyperbole (exaggeration)? What is the tone?
  Be careful of this; hyperbole is not always easy to spot. The author may use a lot of meaningless facts to build a case. In general, political magazines across the spectrum are more likely to engage in hyperbole; scholarly magazine are less likely to.

Examining the bibliography of a book or the "sources" or "further reading" sections of articles is another way of evaluating the material. (Newspaper articles do not have these sections, but many good magazine articles do, and all scholarly articles have them.) Footnotes and/or endnotes should also be checked as they will say a lot about the material's credibility. In the text who does the author quote or paraphrase? Do these people seem credible with regard to the material?

COMMON PITFALLS

Becoming sidetracked is a pitfall of any research project, and, with the enormous amount of material available on censorship, this can easily happen. Therefore it is best to prioritize the research material as it pertains to the project outline. The further it gets from the outline, the less important it is to the project. While it is acceptable to alter the outline (or the approach the researcher takes), it is unwise to do so too drastically. The researcher must also keep in mind the length of the project. Making too many points in a short paper will dilute from the overall effectiveness; making too few points in a long paper can leave the reader underwhelmed.

It is best to avoid material that is subjective. It takes a skilled researcher (or reader) to be able to separate the author's agenda from the facts. Furthermore, too much subjective material to bolster an argument or text makes for a weak foundation. Forgetting to check provenance (the origin of the material) can lead to problems later on. What may seem objective can turn out to be the opposite, or worse—propaganda. As one might expect, government Web sites are poor sources for information on censorship. In fact it would be amazing to find any country's government site that lists its censorship laws. They generally all post their constitutions online—and all constitutions include provisions guaranteeing various human rights—but not the laws that may contradict those provisions. As we have seen, though, some constitutional articles can be interpreted to contradict one another with regard to censorship. These provide the basis for the actual laws that legalize censorship in authoritarian countries. Laws from such countries are often posted (and translated) by dissident expatriates—citizens who live abroad, or by a monitoring agency. However, this is not always the case. For example, at the time of this writing no English translations (from Arabic) of the Egyptian censorship laws were available online. Nor were they in the two most important repositories of Arabic-language law in the United States—the Library of Congress and the Harvard Law Library. However, secondary sources abound, especially on the Web sites of various human rights organizations.

Since censorship is an ongoing process, it is impossible for the research to be completely up to date on what is happening. Often it is a hard enough task to discover what is happening. Not even the Internet provides censorship news in real time (what newsrooms refer to as a "breaking story"). Furthermore, censorship laws and people's attitudes change. What was considered scandalous 50 years ago is quite common now. What does not change are the reasons for censorship. Thus, censorship continues, but even in the most authoritarian societies new methods have evolved that make it harder to prove its illegality. Laws are written with ambiguous language that on face value may have nothing to do with censorship (such as registering for a radio or television broadcast permit). The researcher has to give careful readings to these laws as they can be so easily overlooked.

A final, but very important, thing the researcher must be on guard against is his or her own attitude toward the material and toward the subjects of the material. It is good to be skeptical, especially when there is no corroborating material to support an assertion of censorship or one of non-censorship, but it is dangerous to be too skeptical as this can lead to cynicism. A cynical researcher can easily become judgmental, and a judgmental researcher of such a seemingly clear-cut issue as censorship might, in the end, unwittingly promote the sort of attitude he or she opposes.

7

Key Players A to Z

The following is an alphabetical listing of important figures throughout history whose lives were, or are, linked with censorship—either as instigators, victims, or opponents of it. In some cases the last two categories overlap.

ABDÜLHAMID II (1842–1918) Sultan (ruler) of the Ottoman Empire in the late 19th and early 20th centuries. He was a study in contrasts: A reformer who modernized the school system and during whose reign the first Ottoman constitution was written, and an autocrat who suspended the same constitution and dismissed his parliament. His rule became more and more despotic, relying heavily on a vast network of secret police and severe censorship to subdue dissenters. He was eventually deposed.

JOHN ADAMS (1735–1826) Second president of the United States and de facto leader of the Federalist Party. In 1798, he signed into law the Sedition Act claiming an impending war with France made it necessary to ensure public order. In reality, the law was used to stifle dissent, and Federalists in various states used it to prosecute and imprison Democratic-Republicans. The law had a sunset clause, and it expired on the final day of Adams's term of office, thus ensuring that it would not be used against the Federalists.

ANNA AKHMATOVA (1889–1966) Pseudonym of Anna Andreevna Gorenko, a 20th-century Russian poet widely considered one of the premier poets of Russian literature. After World War II, she was denounced by the Communist Party's Central Committee and by Soviet cultural boss ANDREI ZHDANOV. She was barred from publishing—a collection of poems set for distribution was destroyed. This phase of her censorship lasted until 1950 when she wrote a number of poems praising Stalin in order to gain the release of her son from prison. After Stalin's death she was gradually "rehabilitated."

JOHN ASHCROFT (1942–) First attorney general in the administration of President George W. Bush. As head of the Justice Department, he was one of the key administration figures in drafting the USA PATRIOT Act and presenting it to Congress in the initial days of the War on Terror. The act gave extensive powers of detainment, arrest, and search to the Justice Department, which is under the aegis of the executive branch of the federal government.

MIGUEL ANGEL ASTURIAS (1899–1974) Guatemalan writer, politician, diplomat, and winner of the 1967 Nobel Prize for Literature. His political activities sent him into exile on two occasions—the second time, U.S.-backed dictator Carlos Castillo Armas stripped him of his citizenship. In the mid-1950s, his novels were branded subversive and burned. Among them were *El Señor Presidente* (*The President*), which had to wait more than a decade for publication because of an earlier authoritarian regime; *Viento Fuerto* (*Strong Wind*), *El Papa Verde* (*The Green Pope*), and *Los Ojas de Los Enterrados* (*Eyes of the Interred*). The last three novels make up Asturias's "Banana Trilogy," an examination of U.S. imperialism in Guatemala.

ANDREI BABITSKY (1964–) Russian journalist for the U.S.-funded Radio Liberty. Reporting on the Second Chechen War, he was detained by Russian forces in January 2000. Later, he was handed over to Chechen forces and subsequently released back to Russian security. An international outcry eventually forced Russia's hand, though for a time he was unable to travel outside of Russia. Babitsky and his family eventually immigrated to Prague.

ROGER BACON (c. 1214–1292) English philosopher and Franciscan monk. His writings and lectures at Oxford, dealing with mathematics and physics, placed him at odds with his order and the church. He was sent to Paris, where he was imprisoned for 10 years and forbidden to publish his writing. During that time he wrote his three major works: *Opus Majus, Opus Minus,* and *Opus Tertium* under the protection of Pope Clement IV. After Clement's death, his books were banned and he was imprisoned for the last 14 years of his life.

BORIS BEREZOVSKY (1946–) Russian businessman whose shady dealings made him the richest of the oligarchs in the late 1990s. He also controlled various holdings in television and the print media. As an adviser to President BORIS YELTSIN, he helped engineer the ailing leader's resignation. Never a favorite of Yeltin's successor, VLADIMIR PUTIN, he embarked on a campaign of opposition and was eventually stripped of his media holdings and forced into exile in Great Britain.

JUDY BLUME (1938–) American author of young adult and adult fiction. She probably holds the distinction of being the most widely read writer of young adult fiction as well as the most challenged by those who censor school reading lists in the United States. Five of her books were on the American Library Association's list of the 100 most challenged books for the years 1990–2000. The books are challenged because of the way they deal with characters' notions about sex, parents, peers, school, responsibility, and a host of other issues that preteens and adolescents struggle with.

LENNY BRUCE (1925–1966) American comic. Often thought of as a "sick" comic, he was arrested in numerous cities in the 1960s for public obscenity during his performances, which featured satires of established religions, historical and contemporary religious figures, politicians, as well as forays into modern sociological ills. Toward the end of his career, his act dealt more and more with his legal troubles as he pled his case of abridgement of his First Amendment rights before the court of public opinion.

GIORDANO BRUNO (1548–1600) Italian philosopher who denied Roman Catholic teachings regarding Moses, the Scriptures, Christ, and God. He lectured in various middle European cities, but was arrested by the Inquisition upon his return to Italy. He spent two years in prison before being burned alive for the crime of heresy.

WILLIAM JENNINGS BRYAN (1860–1925) Three-time Democratic nominee for president and former secretary of state who volunteered his services for the prosecution in the 1925 trial of JOHN T. SCOPES for teaching evolution. In a famous exchange with defense attorney CLARENCE DARROW in which he testified as a witness, Bryan reiterated his belief in the truth of the Bible, though not such a literal belief as a later play and film based on the trial characterized it. After the verdict and sentenced were pronounced, Bryan offered to pay Scopes's fine.

ANTHONY COMSTOCK (1844–1915) Leader of the New York Society for the Suppression of Vice. He succeeded in lobbying Congress to pass the Act for the Suppression of Trade in, and Circulation of, Obscene Literature and Articles for Immoral Use, known as the Comstock Act. Then, Comstock expanded his role by becoming a postal inspector, empowered with seizing these materials. By his own account, he seized approximately 160 tons of material during his career.

WILLIAM COSBY (1690–1736) Royal governor of the colony of New York from 1732–36. After an anonymously written article criticizing Cosby appeared in JOHN PETER ZENGER'S *Weekly Journal* in October 1734 he ordered copies of the newspaper burned in public. The following month, he had Zenger arrested for seditious libel. The subsequent trial became the first blow for freedom of the press in the New World. COSBY was soon replaced as royal governor.

FATHER CHARLES COUGHLIN (1891–1979) Roman Catholic priest whose popular radio broadcasts in the 1930s and early 1940s attacked President Franklin D. Roosevelt's New Deal policy. A rabid anti-Communist, his praise of the fascist dictatorships of Mussolini and Hitler and his anti-Semitic rants drew the attention of the federal government after the United States entered World War II in December 1941. The government convinced his ecclesiastical superior to pressure Father Coughlin to abandon all political activity or face being defrocked as a priest. Father Coughlin acceded to the bishop's demand in 1942.

YULI DANIEL (1925–1988) Soviet writer who along with ANDREI SINYAVSKY was tried and sentenced to five years' hard labor in the mid-1960s. In the 1950s and early 1960s, he wrote under the pseudonym Nikolai Arzhak, and many of his satirical short stories were published abroad. After serving his sentence, he chose to remain in the Soviet Union where he worked as a translator, though for a time he was blacklisted and had to publish his translations under the name of his friend, the bard Bulat Okudzhava. He also published *Prison Poems.*

CLARENCE DARROW (1857–1938) One of the defense lawyers in the trial of JOHN T. SCOPES for teaching evolution in the state of Tennessee. Darrow's tactic of challenging the authenticity of the Bible's version of creation has had reverberations that have lasted into the 21st century. His examination of prosecution attorney WILLIAM JENNINGS BRYAN, though highly unorthodox, is considered the central debate of the trial.

EUGENE DEBS (1855–1926) Five-time presidential candidate for the Socialist party, he ran his last campaign while imprisoned under the Espionage Act of 1917 and yet still garnered over 900,000 votes. Debs was arrested following a speech he made in Ohio where he had gone to visit other Socialists imprisoned under the Espionage Act. He was released on Christmas Day 1923 on the executive order of President Warren G. Harding.

DENG XIAOPING (1904–1997) Chinese Communist revolutionary who was purged during the Cultural Revolution (1966–76). He was rehabilitated in the 1970s, but again purged after the death of Zhou Enlai and MAO ZEDONG. His second rehabilitation came in the late 1970s, and by the early 1980s Deng was the supreme leader of China, although he held no important leadership post. Though a reformist, Deng was the person most responsible for the massacre of the demonstrators at Tiananmen Square in 1989.

FYODOR DOSTOEVSKY (1821–1881) Russian novelist and short-story writer. As a young man, he joined a group of utopian socialists that had been infiltrated by an agent of the secret police. He was arrested and sentenced to death, which was commuted to hard labor in Siberia. He served four years and upon his release was assigned to the army. While serving his sentence, he had an epiphany of sorts and became a monarchist and fervent believer in the Russian Orthodox Church. These views, especially the latter, imbued his later fiction with a sense of morality and the notion of redemption.

DANIEL ELLSBERG (1931–) Harvard-educated analyst for the Rand Corporation, a defense-oriented think tank. In 1969, he made copies of the secret 7,000-page report: "History of U.S. Decision-Making Process on Vietnam Policy, 1945–1967," commonly known as the Pentagon Papers. In 1971, in an effort to end the Vietnam War, he began leaking the Pentagon Papers to the *New York Times* and then to the *Washington Post.* In an effort to discredit Ellsberg, federal agents broke into his psychiatrist's office.

FANG LIZHI (1936–) Former physics professor at the University of Science and Technology in Hefei and a longtime agitator for intellectual freedom. Two days after the Chinese government tanks rolled into Tiananmen Square to break up the demonstrations in June 1989, for which Fang and other dissident leaders were held responsible, Fang and his wife sought asylum in the U.S. embassy. By September, still holed up in the embassy, they were numbers one and two on China's most wanted list. In 1990, they migrated to the United Kingdom and from there made their way to the United States.

JAMES FRANKLIN (1697–1735) Boston printer and older half-brother of Benjamin Franklin who founded the *New England Courant* in 1721. It was Boston's third newspaper but the first truly independent one, somewhat patterned after London's *The Spectator.* The newspaper's contributors criticized the colonial political and religious establishment, which in turn came down hard on Franklin. For a time, he handed over editorial control to his apprentice, his brother Benjamin, in order to continue publishing as he was under an arrest warrant for contempt. The government forced the newspaper to submit to prior restraint (prepublication censorship) and banned it in 1723.

GALILEO GALILEI (1564–1642) Italian Renaissance natural philosopher and early astronomer. His use of a more powerful telescope enabled him to empirically support the theory of Polish astronomer Nicolas Copernicus, who had proposed that the Earth revolved around the Sun. This violated Ptolemaic theory, supported by the church, that the Earth was the center of the universe. Galileo's published support in book form made it past the Florentine censor, but upset the pope. He was found guilty by the Inquisition, sentenced to life imprisonment, and forced to recant his scientific belief.

NIKOLAI GOGOL (1809–1852) Russian short story writer, novelist, and playwright in Russia's Golden Age. His work was fantastic and satirical, and his most famous work, the play *The Inspector General,* enjoyed success during his lifetime. However, after Gogol's death, Czar NICHOLAS I and others eventually found the play to be subversive and banned it. At its lowest point Gogol's reputation was such that praising him in public, especially in print, was cause for arrest.

EMMA GOLDMAN (1869–1940) Russian-born anarchist who immigrated to the United States at the end of the 19th century. Her writing was censored by ANTHONY COMSTOCK among others. She served two years in jail for speaking out against military conscription and, after her release in 1919, she was deported to Russia. She was later expelled from the Soviet Union.

BETTE GREENE (1934–) Award-winning American writer of children's and adolescent literature. She is best known for the novels *Summer of My German Soldier* and *The Drowning of Stephan Jones,* both of which were on the American Library Association's list of the 100 most frequently challenged books from 1990 to 2000. The challenges to the former range from depictions of anti-Semitism and child abuse to unacceptable language. The second book was challenged because of its sympathetic portrayal of a homosexual relationship. Language was another concern.

GEORGE GROSZ (1893–1959) German artist whose expressionist style combined with his political outlook caused him to be arrested and censored many times during the 1920s. His work ran afoul of the army and established religion. His drawings were also seized in London in 1929. He left Germany in 1933 but did not escape castigation by the Nazis. He lived most of the last 26 years of his life in the United States, but returned to Germany in May 1959 and died two months later. In the decade after his death, his work continued to cause problems for art gallery curators in the United States and Italy.

VLADIMIR GUSINSKY (1952–) Russian media and banking mogul in the post-Soviet era of the 1990s. He was also one of the original "oligarchs"—men who managed to manipulate Russia's privatization program and shaky capitalism to their benefit. His media holdings included NTV television station, the newspaper *Segodyna,* and the Echo Mosvy radio station. In the early

2000s, he ran afoul of President Vladimir Putin and subsequently turned his media properties into opposition voices. He eventually lost control of holding company Media-Most to the government and went into exile.

LEARNED HAND (1872–1961) United States judge whose legal thinking in free speech cases influenced later Supreme Court opinions. During World War I, he granted an injunction that stopped the U.S. government from barring the socialist magazine *Masses* from the mails as per the Espionage Act of 1917. Hand's argument was that the law was not meant to impinge on the First Amendment and stifle opinion. His decision was reversed on appeal by the federal government. More than 30 years later, while sitting on a court of appeals, Hand devised a formula for the "clear and present danger" model used by the Supreme Court: the amount of danger of a particular advocated action and the likelihood of the act being committed.

WILL HAYS (1879–1954) Indiana politician, Republican National Committee chairman, and Postmaster General in the cabinet of President Warren G. Harding. In the latter post, he enforced the blocking of sending obscene material through the mail. In 1922, he became president of the newly created Motion Picture Producers and Distributors of America, which became known as the Hays Office. His job was to clean up and "police" the industry, which at the time was scandal ridden. By 1930, the Hays Office had also produced the Production Code, which imposed censorship on films made in Hollywood.

OLIVER WENDELL HOLMES, JR. (1841–1935) United States Supreme Court justice whose opinion for a 1919 unanimous Court decision in *Schenck vs. United States* upheld the government position: "The most stringent protection of free speech would not protect a man in falsely shouting fire in a crowded theater, and causing a panic. . . ." Throughout the next decade, Holmes moved toward a more liberal First Amendment position as he and Justice Louis Brandeis, and later incoming justices, slowly shifted the Court's thinking on First Amendment issues to the "clear and present danger" model.

CHENJERAI HOVE (1956–) Zimbabwean novelist, poet, essayist, radio playwright, and journalist. One of Zimbabwe's most prominent writers, he is best known for his novel *Bones,* which won the 1988 Zimbabwe Publishers' Award and the 1989 NOMA Award. He has also published four books of poetry, but his political writings—a former supporter of Robert Mugabe, he eventually took to criticizing the regime's corruption—have caused the government the most consternation. He and his family fled to Norway after receiving threats.

JIANG QING (1914–1991) Former stage and film actress and third wife of MAO ZEDONG and one of the principal instigators of the Cultural Revolution. She was also a member of a small radical clique, known as the Gang of Four, that held a great deal of power in China during Mao's declining years. After his death Jiang and other members of the Gang of Four were arrested for their roles in inciting the Cultural Revolution. She was sentenced to death, but the sentence was commuted to life imprisonment. Jiang allegedly committed suicide in 1991.

DMITRI KHOLODOV (1967–1994) Investigative journalist for the Russian newspaper *Moskovsky Komsomolets* who was killed when a booby-trapped briefcase exploded. The briefcase, which he had picked up at a train station locker, was thought to contain irrefutable evidence of illegal arms deals. At the time of his death, he was investigating military corruption and planning to testify before the Duma concerning illegal arms trading. Prior to his death he had received threatening letters and telephone calls. Six men were brought to trial for the killing and acquitted twice before the statute of limitations in effect at the time of the murder ran out.

EVGENI KISELYEV (1956–) Russian television and print journalist whose weekly news show, *Itogi,* was one of the most popular television programs in Russia in the 1990s. The show was broadcast on NTV, part of the media empire of VLADIMIR GUSINSKY. After VLADIMIR PUTIN's ascension to the Russian presidency, NTV began broadcasting criticisms and news stories that were unflattering to the Kremlin. Kiselyev himself criticized the new president, commented on the BABITSKY affair, and continued to broadcast uncensored news from Chechnya. After Gusinsky lost NTV, Kiselyev and some of his colleagues moved over to TV-6, which itself was hounded off the air.

PAUL KLEBNIKOV (1963–2004) American-born journalist and editor of *Russian Forbes* magazine. In July 2004, he was shot to death while leaving his Moscow office. Much of his writing dealt with financial and political corruption in Russia, including his book: *Godfather of the Kremlin: Boris Berezovsky and the Looting of Russia.* During his brief stint as editor of *Russian Forbes,* he advertised the disparity in Russian society between the rich and poor, though he felt that Russia's economy had turned a corner and that better times lay ahead for the average person.

LAO SHE (1899–1966) Chinese novelist and playwright. His best-known work, *Cat Country,* is a satire on Chinese society during the early stages of the civil war between the Communists and the Nationalists. As a member of the Chinese Communist party, he held numerous important cultural posts, all of which were taken away during the Cultural Revolution. Like many other writers and intellectuals he was denounced and imprisoned. He eventually committed suicide.

ANATOLY LUNACHARSKY (1875–1933) First commissar for education in the Soviet Union. Prior to the October Revolution, he had switched back and forth between the Bolshevik and the Menshevik factions, but joined the Bolsheviks in time to help overthrow the provisional government. As commissar, he oversaw the rise in literacy in the Soviet Union, but also the inculcation of Marxism-Leninism into the general population.

MATTHEW LYON (1749–1822) Republican (forerunner of the modern Democratic Party) congressman and newspaper and magazine publisher from Vermont who became the first person jailed under the Sedition Act of 1798. A major critic of President JOHN ADAMS in the House of Representatives and within his home state, he was indicted for sedition on October 5, 1798. At his trial, he argued the unconstitutionality of the Sedition Act, but his argument was rejected by the presiding judge. He was found guilty, sentenced to prison, and fined $1,000. He spent four months in prison during which time he won reelection to Congress. His supporters also helped defray the cost of the fine.

JAMES MADISON (1751–1836) Fourth president of the United States and primary author of the Bill of Rights, comprising the first 10 amendments to the U.S. Constitution. Madison also served as secretary of state during the presidency of his predecessor, Thomas Jefferson. His opposition to the Alien and Sedition Acts of 1798 inspired his coauthorship, with Jefferson, of the Virginia Resolutions that were adopted by Virginia and Kentucky. These called for the rights of states to declare on the constitutionality of federal legislation.

NAGUIB MAHFOUZ (1911–2006) Egyptian writer and winner of the 1988 Nobel Prize for Literature—the first writer in Arabic to win the prize. His Cairo Trilogy—*Palace Walk, Palace of Desire,* and *Sugar Street*—made him famous throughout the Arab world and subsequently the rest of the world. Despite his stature, his 1959 novel, *Children of the Alley,* was banned throughout his life. Seven months before his death he had petitioned the government to have the book published.

MAO ZEDONG (1893–1976) Leader of the People's Republic of China from 1949 until his death in 1976. He came to prominence in the Chinese Communist Party after the Long March of 1934–35. As Party chairman, he held the reins of power and managed to outwit and defeat his opponents through a series of gambits. The best-known of such tactics was the Cultural Revolution, during which young fanatics, inspired by Mao and others, humiliated, beat, tortured, and murdered thousands who were deemed traitors to the revolution.

THOMAS MAPFUMO (1945–) Zimbabwean musician and longtime voice of protest. He began his career singing songs in opposition to the white Rhodesian government of IAN SMITH, but after Zimbabwe's independence he became disenchanted with the regime of ROBERT MUGABE. His anti-Mugabe music has been banned from radio and television in his homeland, and he lives in exile in the United States.

JOSEPH McCARTHY (1908–1957) Republican senator from Wisconsin who in a 1950 speech in Wheeling, West Virginia, claimed to have a list of 205 names of Communists employed by the State Department. This claim was later proved wrong. McCarthy also took on Voice of America and the U.S. Army, the latter proved his undoing when the hearings were televised and the nation was able to witness his bullying tactics. He was condemned by the Senate in 1954 and a virtual nonentity for the last two years of his second and final term in office.

HENRY MILLER (1891–1980) American writer whose novel *Tropic of Cancer* was still deemed obscene in the United States long after it had been published elsewhere. In a landmark 1964 decision, in which the Supreme Court referenced *Jacobellis v. State of Ohio,* a case that had been decided the same day, the Court reversed lower court decisions and declared the book was not obscene. The two Court decisions paved the way for the U.S. publication of many works of 20-century literature and the showing of many foreign films, which were not subject to Hollywood's production code.

JOHN MILTON (1608–1674) English poet and essayist, best known for his epic poem *Paradise Lost.* His essay *Areopagitica,* directed at Parliament, argued for an end to prepublication censorship during the English Civil War. The law remained on the books for another 50 years, but the work is considered a classic defense of freedom of the press.

HOSNI MUBARAK (1928–) President of Egypt who came to power upon the assassination of his predecessor ANWAR SADAT in 1981. After winning reelection for the second time in 1993, he began cracking down on opposition groups such as the Muslim Brotherhood, especially those individuals who had planned to run for office in Egypt's parliament. Political dissent was further stifled over the next 12 years. In 2005, Mubarak was reelected for the fourth time with more than 85 percent of the vote, and there was talk that his son would eventually succeed him as president of Egypt.

ROBERT MUGABE (1924–) Leader of Zimbabwe since its independence in 1980. He originally won election as a Marxist, but over the years has shed many of his leftist views while ruling with a more authoritarian hand. Early on he tried to establish a one-party state, but was defeated. Nevertheless, Mugabe's tight control of the media has allowed for his ZANU-PF Party to dominate every parliamentary election, as well as enabled his numerous reelections. His current term is set to expire in 2008, and in 2007, he was chosen as his party's presidential candidate in the upcoming election.

GAMAL ABDEL NASSER (1918–1970) Egyptian army colonel who took part in the 1952 Free Officers coup d'état that overthrew King Faruq and his prime minister. Within four years, he became president of the Arab Republic of Egypt and declared it a socialist state. He deflected domestic problems with a hardline anti-Israel stance and a dream of pan-Arabism. Within Egypt, he retained power through censorship of the media, expanding the police and other security organizations, and arresting political opponents.

NICHOLAS I (1796–1855) Czar of Russia following the death of his brother Alexander I. Early in his reign he faced an uprising from the Decembrists, a group of nobles and military officers who balked at his authoritarianism. Though their revolt was a failure, Nicholas became more resolute regarding limiting freedom of speech and of the press. New censorship laws were enacted in 1828, some of which empowered the secret police to act in an extralegal manner.

BORIS PASTERNAK (1890–1960) Soviet poet, novelist, and translator. His first brush with censorship came in the 1930s and 1940s when he was unable to publish his poetry because it did not adhere to the tenets of socialist realism. Though best known in the literary world for his poetry, he received the 1958 Nobel Prize in Literature for his novel *Dr. Zhivago,* which was banned in Russia, but published in Italy and elsewhere. The announcement of his winning the prize heightened cold war tensions. He was denounced in Russia, expelled from the Writers Union, and refused a visa to travel abroad. *Dr. Zhivago* was finally published in the Soviet Union in the late 1980s.

ANNA POLITKOVSKAYA (1958–2006) Russian investigative journalist shot to death in 2006 in the elevator of her Moscow apartment building. Her article for the newspaper *Novaya gazeta* focused on abuses of civilians in Chechnya during the Second Chechen War. In 2001, she fled Russia after receiving death threats. At the time of her death she was preparing a story on civilian torture in Chechnya.

OTTO PREMINGER (1906–1986) Iconoclastic expatriate Austrian who was one of the first Hollywood directors to defy the Production Code in the 1950s. In succession, he directed *The Moon Is Blue* (1953), a comedy denied the Code's seal of approval because of risqué language; *The Man with the Golden Arm* (1955), based on Nelson Algren's novel about heroin addiction; and *Anatomy of a Murder* (1959), a courtroom drama that was one of his most popular films.

VLADIMIR PUTIN (1952–) Second president of Russia following the dissolution of the Soviet Union. He quickly moved to strengthen the power of the presidency and to silence critics in the media through the use of legal, though questionable, tactics. He broke the media power of the oligarchs VLADIMIR GUSINSKY and BORIS BEREZOVSKY by turning their television channels into quasi-government entities, driving some of their other holdings out of business, or simply making them irrelevant. This action hastened the self-imposed exiles of both men.

WILLIAM PYNCHON (1590–1662) Cofounder of Springfield (Massachusetts) Colony, writer, and theologian whose book *The Meritorious Price of Our Redemption* became the first book publicly burned in the New World English colonies. The book criticized Puritanism; Pynchon ultimately returned to England.

QIN SHI HUANGDI (YING ZHENG, 259–210 B.C.E.) First emperor of the Qin (Ch'in) dynasty in China. Ordered the destruction of thousands of books in what became possibly the largest act of book burning in antiquity. Among the works destroyed were those of Confucius. The reason for the destruction was to create a new "history" that would begin with the Qin rulers. The dynasty was short lived and the mass destruction was unable to claim all prohibited works—thus, Confucius's works not only survived but eventually became the mainstay of Chinese thought.

FRANÇOIS RABELAIS (1494–1553) French writer and physician. One of the premier satirists of world literature, his book *Pantagruel,* published in 1533 without his knowledge, was immediately placed on the University of Paris Index. Two years later a papal bull (a decree) defended him, but this did not stop the banning of his work completely by the Tridentine Index. In the United States, his works were banned until 1930, and South Africa banned his work completely in 1938.

DIEGO RIVERA (1886–1957) Mexican painter and avowed Communist who was expelled from the Mexican Communist Party. His controversial 1933 mural for the RCA Building in Rockefeller Center in New York City was never completed because he refused to remove a portrait of Vladimir Lenin, first leader of the Soviet Union. The unfinished mural was later removed. Three years later in Mexico City his work on display in the Hotel Reforma was distorted over his protests. He also practiced self-censorship on at least one occasion in order to have his work viewed publicly.

BARNEY ROSSET (1922–) American publisher whose Grove Press initially gained fame by introducing European avant-garde writer to readers in the United States. He also published the first uncensored U.S. edition of D. H. Lawrence's *Lady Chatterley's Lover.* He followed this with work by William S. Burroughs (*Naked Lunch*) and Hubert Selby (*Last Exit to Brooklyn*) and other writers whose work was considered groundbreaking or at the very least daring. By the 1960s and 1970s, Rosset had made Grove Press the premier imprint for outsider literature in the United States.

ANWAR SADAT (1918–1981) President of Egypt who came to power after the death of President Nasser. Though best known for his groundbreaking treaty with Israel, that same treaty sparked domestic unrest and criticism of Sadat. As a result the Press Law and the Law on Protecting Values from Shameful Conduct were passed in 1980, which infringed on the freedoms of the press and speech. These laws were followed by mass arrests in 1981, the same year Sadat was assassinated.

ANDREI SAKHAROV (1921–1989) Soviet physicist, father of the Soviet hydrogen bomb program, and winner of the 1975 Nobel Peace Prize. An early supporter of human rights in the Soviet Union, in the 1960s he publicly opposed Soviet measures to test hydrogen bombs, criticized the government repression, and called for bilateral nuclear arms reductions. In the 1970s, his continued anti-Soviet discourse combined with his high international profile marked him as the leading dissident in the USSR. After the 1979 invasion of Afghanistan, he called for a boycott of the 1980 Moscow Olympics, which in turn brought him internal exile in the city of Gorky, where he and his wife, rights activist Yelena Bonner, spent most of the 1980s.

MARGARET SANGER (1879–1966) The foremost advocate for birth control, a term she coined, and women's health during the first half of the 20th century. She began her career as a nurse on New York's Lower East Side, but eventually quit nursing to devote herself full time to birth control and women's health issues. Her newspaper, *The Woman Rebel,* published birth control information, which caused Sanger to run afoul of the Comstock Laws. She cofounded the American Birth Control League (which later became Planned Parenthood) and served as its first president.

FRA GIROLAMO SAVONAROLA (1452–1498) Florentine monk whose name is synonymous with the excesses of censorship. He was opposed to most literature, paintings, and music for what they represented in his eyes—luxury. In the mid-1490s, as de facto leader of Florence, he instituted the Bonfires of the Vanities in which books, manuscripts, artwork, tapestries, musical instruments, and other prohibited objects (such as mirrors) were tossed into the periodic flames. In the end, he was arrested on orders of Pope Alexander VI and burned as a heretic, ironically with his own writings.

JOHN T. SCOPES (1900–1970) Eponymous defendant in the famous 1925 Tennessee trial, charged with teaching evolution, at the time a violation of the law. Scopes's trial was actually a test case to try and have the law overturned and as such it drew nationwide attention. Two nationally known figures, CLARENCE DARROW and WILLIAM JENNINGS BRYAN, squared off for the defense and the prosecution, respectively. Scopes was found guilty, but his conviction was later overturned on a technicality. One of the interesting contradictions of the case was that Scopes had taught evolution from a state-approved textbook.

ANDREI SINYAVSKY (1925–1997) Soviet novelist, short story writer, and critic, who wrote under the name Abram Tertz. His satirical work, which did not conform to the tenets of socialist realism and was published abroad, ruffled the feathers of the Soviet government. In 1966 he went on trial, along with friend and fellow writer YULI DANIEL, and was sentenced to hard labor. After his release from prison in 1971, he immigrated to France. In the mid-1990s, he criticized Russian President BORIS YELTSIN's ordering of the military's firing on the White House—the building where Russia's upper chamber of parliament meets—during a political standoff.

IAN SMITH (1919–2007) Prime minister of Rhodesia in that country's last all-white minority-ruled government. In 1965, his government issued a Unilateral Declaration of Independence from the United Kingdom, which the latter rejected. In subsequent years, he authorized the arrests and internal exiles of numerous dissident African Natioalist leaders and the banning of the Nationalist newspaper *Daily News*. By the late 1970s, Smith gave in to the external and internal pressures and a majority government took over.

SOCRATES (c. 470–399 B.C.E.) Ancient Greek philosopher whose ideas have been transmitted through the writings of his "students," notably Plato.

Socrates never considered himself a teacher, despite the fact that he attracted a good number of Athens's youth to his philosophical outlook. His method was simply to question anyone and everyone to help them understand their ignorance. His trial and death are the most notable instance of censorship in the ancient world. He was accused of blasphemy for not worshiping the municipal gods and of corrupting the Athenian youth and condemned to die.

ALEXANDER SOLZHENITSYN (1918–) Soviet and Russian writer and winner of the 1970 Nobel Prize for Literature whose most notable work is *The Gulag Archipelago.* In the 1960s, after the fall of Nikita Khrushchev, his work either went unpublished or was censored. From 1971 on he began publishing his work abroad. When *Gulag* was published in 1973, he was arrested and charged with treason. The following year he was deported from the USSR, living first in Switzerland and then in the United States. He returned to Russia in the mid-1990s after the fall of the Soviet Union.

WOLE SOYINKA (1934–) Nigerian writer and winner of the 1986 Nobel Prize for Literature. Beginning in 1961, his works have been censored and he has been subject to imprisonment—he served stretches of three months and 27 months—confiscation of his passport, and finally self-exile. His initial bout with censorship dealt with his radio plays, but in 1984 *The Man Died: The Prison Notes of Wole Soyinka* was banned altogether.

JOSEPH STALIN (1879–1953) Georgian born Soviet dictator whose real name was Josef Dzhugashvili. He instituted widespread repression of political rivals and perceived rivals, as well as any criticism of his government and policies. In the late 1920s, this involved the killing of peasants resistant to collectivization; in the 1930s, Communists and military leaders; in the late 1940s and early 1950s, Jews, whom he distrusted as a group. His policies encouraged the secret police and censorship in all of its forms.

JOHN STEINBECK (1902–1968) American writer and winner of the 1962 Nobel Prize for Literature. His most famous work, *The Grapes of Wrath,* faced censorship problems at the outset of its 1939 publication when towns in Oklahoma and Kansas banned it. A previous novel, *Of Mice and Men,* has faced challenges right down to the 21st century, ranking sixth on the American Library Association's list of the 100 most frequently challenged books from 1990–2000. In 1953, *The Wayward Bus* was placed on the House of Representatives' Select Committee on Pornographic Materials. That same year all Steinbeck's works were banned in Ireland.

HOWARD STERN (1954–) Controversial radio personality who was one of the first to be called a "shock jock." He has been cited by the Federal

Communications Commission (which oversees broadcast television and radio) for obscenity—between 1990 and 2004 over $2 million in fines were levied against his show. This total was more than half of all FCC fines during that period. In 2004, under government pressure, the Howard Stern Show was temporarily dropped by the largest U.S. radio broadcaster, Clear Channel Communications. Stern later jumped to censorship-free satellite radio.

EDGAR TEKERE (1937–) Controversial Zimbawean politician and former guerrilla fighter. He was one of the original leaders in ZANU-PF who served in the newly independent Zimbabwean government as a member of Prime Minister ROBERT MUGABE's cabinet. He was also secretary-general of ZANU-PF until 1981, Critical of government corruption and Mugabe's plan to make Zimbabwe a one-party state, he eventually broke with ZANU and founded the Zimbabwe Unity Movement. In 1990, he ran for president against Mugabe, but lost decisively. His public retirement afterward prompted rumors that his campaign was merely a plant to give the election a democratic appearance.

J. PARNELL THOMAS (1895–1970) Republican congressman from New York who became chairman of the House Committee for Un-American Activities (HUAC) in 1947, following Republican electoral gains in the 1946 election. Under his chairmanship, HUAC investigated Hollywood for Communist infiltration. The committee interviewed 41 "friendly witnesses" and 10 unfriendly witnesses, known collectively as the Hollywood Ten. During his tenure, Thomas made HUAC synonymous with the early cold war suppression of First Amendment and Fifth Amendment rights.

HARRY S. TRUMAN (1884–1972) Thirty-third president of the United States who ascended to the presidency upon the death of Franklin D. Roosevelt. Considered a pragmatist, he took a tough stance against Communism abroad. But bowing to pressure from the congressional majority Republicans, he instituted the federal loyalty program, which he later regretted. The loyalty program, intended to root out Communists, called for investigations of every federal worker followed by hearings for those whom the investigations turned up suspicious evidence. It had the unintended effect of stifling free speech and was actually a failure in its intended task.

CLEMENT VALLANDIGHAM (1820–1871) Democratic politician from Ohio who opposed Lincoln's handling of the Union war effort during the Civil War. In 1863, he decided to challenge the legality of General Order No. 38, issued by General Ambrose Burnside, that curtailed freedom of speech in Ohio regarding the war. The challenge came in the form of a two-hour speech and resulted in Vallandigham's arrest. Tried before a military commission, he was found guilty and sentenced to prison. President Lincoln ordered the sentence commuted to exile to the Confederacy. While in exile he was nominated a Democratic candidate for governor of Ohio but lost the election. It took him about a year to make his way back to his home state where he was given a hero's welcome.

ROGER WILLIAMS (C. 1603–1683) Colonial preacher born in London. He was an early advocate for freedom of religion and speech in the colonies. Having run afoul of the Puritans in Massachusetts, he escaped first to the southern boundary of Plymouth Colony and then to what is now Providence, Rhode Island, which he founded. He became the first governor of Providence Plantations: Providence, Newport, and Portsmouth; an expert on Native Americans; and a successful trader. His unwavering stance on religious freedom ensured the growth of the colony.

WOODROW WILSON (1856–1924) Twenty-eighth president of the United States whose second term was marked by the United States' entry into World War I, suppression of antiwar dissent, failure of his postwar policy in Congress, and illness. In 1917, he demanded from Congress a strict law to stifle dissent and criticism of his policy. What he received was the Espionage Act of 1917 and the Sedition Act of 1918. The government used both of these laws, though primarily the first, to suppress and imprison antiwar dissenters. Though some judges, notably LEARNED HAND, ruled against the laws' constitutionality, they were upheld by the Supreme Court at the time.

BORIS YELTSIN (1931–2007) First president of Russia after the dissolution of the Soviet Union. He presided over a period of economic chaos and internal military conflict in Russia, but also a period in which freedom of the press flowered like no other time in the nation's history. Newspapers, magazines, and television and radio channels independent of government influence and proclaiming different views from the government and from each other sprang up. Toward the end of his second term his relationship with the media grew more strained.

NASSER ABU ZAYD (1943–) Egyptian academic accused of apostasy and forced to emigrate with his wife to the Netherlands. The declaration was eventually lifted. His book *Discourse and Interpretation* was banned by the al-Azhar Islamic Research Council. Prior to fleeing Egypt, he had advocated an historical and linguistic approach to interpreting the Koran. In 2005, he was awarded the Ibn Rushd-Prize for Freedom of Thought.

JOHN PETER ZENGER (1697–1746) Colonial New York City newspaper publisher whose *Weekly Journal* printed an article critical of Governor

William Cosby. Zenger was arrested and spent nine months in jail before going to trial, whereupon the jury found him not guilty, though it had been advised by the judge that the truth or falsity of the article was irrelevant to the case. The trial struck a blow for freedom of the press that resonated through the First Amendment and later Supreme Court rulings right down to present-day attitudes.

LEONARD ZHAKATA (1966–) Zimbabwean musician whose protest music is banned from radio and television, but who nevertheless enjoys a huge following. His songs of everyday life in Zimbabwe focus on how various hardships such as price increases and power and water cuts affect the people.

ANDREI ZHDANOV (1896–1948) Former Communist Party boss of Leningrad who after World War II as Stalin's cultural boss established a cultural policy in the Soviet Union known as Zhdanovism (*Zhdanovshchina* in Russian). He was originally concerned with bringing literature back into the socialist realist fold, but eventually his policy of repression extended to most walks of life. In the months prior to his death, he initiated a campaign against "cosmopolitans," a term meant to describe those in opposition to his policy of art for the sake of Soviet ideology but also a code word for Jews.

8

Organizations and Agencies

This chapter contains a list of U.S. and international organizations and agencies that monitor and publicize censorship activity, provide legal assistance, and develop counterstrategies. More detailed information about each organization's activities can be found at the particular Web site.

African Free Media Foundation
URL: http://www.freemediafoundation.org
P.O. Box 70147
00400-Tom Mboya Street
Nairobi, Kenya
Phone: 254-66-51118

Founded in Harare, Zimbabwe, in 1993, but now based in Kenya, the organization was originally called Network for the Defence of Independent Media in Africa. AFMF promotes professionalism in publishing and defends the publishing industry against government takeover and other quasi-legal maneuvers. It also trains journalists, promotes freedom of expression, monitors elections in Africa while focusing on the media's role in the election, works to repeal unjust laws, and sponsors educational and cultural radio and television programs.

American Civil Liberties Union (ACLU)
URL: http://www.aclu.org
125 Broad Street, 18th Floor
New York, NY 10004
Phone: (212) 549-2500

The premier civil rights advocacy group in the United States, with chapters in nearly every state, the ACLU was founded in 1920 in the days of the first Red Scare. The ACLU provides legal assistance to plaintiffs, and in many instances is lead plaintiff. Free speech is one of the numerous civil liberties issues on the organization's Web site drop-down menu. ACLU news briefs and current actions accompany each particular issue.

Amnesty International
URL: http://www.amnesty.org.uk
International Secretariat
1 Easton Street
London
WC1X 0DW
United Kingdom
Phone: 44-20-741-35500

U.S. Office
URL: http://www.amnestyusa.org
5 Penn Plaza
New York, NY 10001
Phone: (212) 807-8400

Founded in 1961 by delegates from the UK, US, Belgium, France, Ireland, and Switzerland, Amnesty International is the largest human rights organization in the world with offices in more than 150 countries. It deals with such issues as the death penalty, refugees, violence against women, arms dealing, and political prisoners.

Arab Press Freedom Watch
URL: http://www.apfw.org
Chytel House
160-164 Mile End Road
London E1 4LJ
United Kingdom
Phone: 44-7821-120-158

APFW monitors violations of press freedoms in 20 countries in the Middle East and northern Africa and publicizes these violations and works toward censorship elimination. The organization publishes a newsletter and an "annual record of freedom of expression in the Arab world." It works closely with similar orgaizations to effect new media legislations in the Middle East.

Article 19
URL: http://www.article19.org/index.html

6-8 Amwell Street
London
EC1R 1UQ
England
Phone: 44-20-7278-9292

Founded in 1987, Article 19 takes its name from Article 19 of the Universal Declaration of Human Rights. Among its actions the organization engages in advocacy, monitoring, litigation, lobbying, and policy development. It advocates on behalf of censorship victims and engages in various freedom of expression campaigns with national partners throughout the world.

Association for Progressive Communications
URL: http://www.apc.org/english/index.shtml
P.O. Box 29755
Melville 2109
South Africa
Phone: 27-11-726-1692

Since its founding in 1990, APC has focused on "Internet and ICT (information communication technology) social justice and development" with a goal of empowering people through a free communications technology. Among its endeavors is the Wireless Connectivity Project, based in Africa. This helps to bypass the traditional means of communication and, to a certain extent, censorship.

Cartoonists Rights Network, International
URL: http://www.cartoonistrights.com
P.O. Box 7272
Fairfax Station, VA 22039
Phone: (703) 543-8727

This is an international organization dedicated to protecting editorial and social cartoonists. It supports those at risk and trains cartoonists in various free speech issues and laws—both local and international. Additionally, CRNI helps provide assistance to the families of those cartoonists in jail or forced to flee because of the threat of prison or who have otherwise been harmed because of their work.

Center for Democracy & Technology
URL: http://www.cdt.org
1634 Eye Street NW #1100

Washington, D.C. 20006
Phone: (202) 637-9800

CDT staff has expertise in law and technology as it works to expand constitutional liberties in digital telecommunications. Free expression tops the organization's list of issues, which also include privacy, security, copyright, data mining, etc. The Web site includes sections on policy briefs, reports, articles, issues, and congressional bills dealing with the Internet and digital communications.

Center for Journalism in Extreme Situations (CJES)
URL: http://www.cjes.ru
Zubovsky Bulvar 4, # 101
Moscow, Russia 119992
Phone: 7-495-637-7626 / 7-495-637-3550

Founded in 2000 during the Second Chechen War, CJES monitors journalists' rights in Russia and other countries of the Commonwealth of Independent States (CIS) and investigates serious violations of those rights. It also offers legal assistance to journalists, conducts training seminars for journalists, and studies media legislation throughout the CIS and offers recommendations.

The Center for Public Integrity
URL: http://www.publicintegrity.org/default.aspx
910 17th Street, NW, 7th Floor
Washington, D.C. 20006
Phone: (202) 466-1300

Since its founding in 1989, CPI has conducted numerous campaigns of "investigative journalism in the public interest." One of these projects, "Well Connected," traces corporate ownership of the U.S. media, its political influence, and how all of this plays out in Congress and in the various state legislatures. The CPI Well Connected Web page also has a "Media Tracker" that lists corporate media ownership within a given zip code or city.

Committee to Protect Journalists
URL: http://www.cpj.org
330 Seventh Avenue, 11th Floor
New York, NY 10001
Phone: (212) 465-1004

Founded by U.S. foreign correspondents, the goal of CPJ is to protect journalists. It monitors and publicizes attacks, abductions, censorship, legal actions against journalists (such as withholding registration), imprisonment, expeling of journalists, and the killing of journalists. The Web site reproduces articles from newspapers and magazines around the world detailing press abuses.

Derechos Human Rights
URL: http://www.derechos.org
46 Estabrook Street
San Leandro, CA 94577
Phone: (510) 483-4005

Using the Internet as its medium of choice for communication and research, Derechos Human Rights investigates abuses, contributes to developing international human rights law, assists human rights NGOs, as well as activists and victims. It also works in partnership with an international network of organizations and activists.

The Egyptian Organization for Human Rights
URL: http://www.eohr.org
8/10 Mathaf El-Manial Street, 10th Floor
Manyal El-roda
Cairo, Egypt
Phone: 20-2-363-6811

Founded in 1985, EOHR is one of Egypt's oldest NGOs with provincial branches throughout the country. Its stated goal is to promote freedoms of the press, speech, and religion in Egypt. It also seeks to reform Egyptian law and prisons and guarantee fair trials. The organization provides legal aid to prisoners whose freedom of expression has been violated, sends out fact-finding missions, publicizes human rights violations, promotes human rights, and pressures Egyptian government agencies as well as NGOs to take action to resolve human rights violations.

Electronic Frontier Foundation
URL: http://www.eff.org
454 Shotwell Street
San Francisco, CA 94110
Phone: (415) 436-9333

Founded in 1990, EFF defends privacy issues, bloggers' rights, free speech, file sharing, and fair use. The free speech section of the EFF Web site contains summaries and analyses of important U.S. court cases affecting free speech and the Internet, a subdirectory listing more than a dozen topics of censorship, and numerous articles and other documents chronicling the free speech battle on the Internet.

First Amendment Center/Vanderbilt University
URL: http://www.firstamendmentcenter.org/default.aspx
1207 18th Ave. S.
Nashville, TN 37212
Tel: (615) 727-1600
Fax: (615) 727-1319
E-mail: info@fac.org

First Amendment Center/Arlington
1101 Wilson Blvd.
Arlington, VA 22209
Tel: (703) 528-0800
Fax: (703) 284-2879

The First Amendment Center works to preserve and protect First Amendment freedoms through information and education. The center serves as a forum for the study and exploration of free expression issues, including freedom of speech, the press, and religion, and the rights to assemble and to petition the government.

Inter American Press Association
URL: http://www.sipiapa.org
1801 S.W. 3rd Avenue
Edificio Jules Dubois
Miami, FL 33129
Phone: (305) 634-2465

IAPA's mission is to defend freedom of the press and freedom of expression throughout the Western Hemisphere. The organization represents newspapers the length and breadth of the two continents, from Alaska to Patagonia, whose combined circulation exceeds 40 million. It also has two autonomous affiliates: the IAPA Press Institute and the IAPA Scholarship Fund.

International Crisis Group
URL: http://www.crisisgroup.org/home/index.cfm?l=1
149 Avenue Louise
Level 24
B-1050 Brussels

Belgium
Phone: 32-2-502-90-38

U.S. Offices
420 Lexington Avenue, Suite 2640
New York, NY 10170
Phone: (212) 813-0820
1629 K Street NW, Suite 450
Washington, D.C. 20006
Phone: (202) 785-1601

Working on five continents to advocate for the resolution and prevention of conflicts, ICG uses field analysts either in country or as near as possible to a particular hot spot. The organization publishes white papers and reports and its board of distinguished politicians, diplomats, and businesspeople helps to ensure that the reports are taken seriously. ICG also publishes a monthly newsletter.

International Federation of Journalists
URL: http://www.ifj.org/
IPC-Residence Palace, Bloc C
Rue de la Loi 155
B-1040 Brussels
Belgium
Phone: 32-2-235-22-00

Founded in 1926, the IFJ has been in its present form since 1952. It has more than 500,000 members in over 100 countries. While remaining politically neutral, the IFJ nevertheless promotes freedom of the press, social justice, and unionism among journalists. It is also the representative organization for journalists at the United Nations and within the international trade union movement. The IFJ publishes reports and sponsors World Press Freedom Day and a safety fund.

International Federation of Library Associations and Institutions
URL: http://www.ifla.org
P.O. Box 95312
2509 CH The Hague
Prins Wilhelm-Alexanderhof 5
2595 BE The Hague
Netherlands
Phone: 31-70-314-0884

Founded in Edinburgh in 1927, IFLA has expanded to 150 countries. It promotes library services, the understanding of those services, and the interests of its members worldwide. IFLA endorses Article 19 of the Universal Declaration of Human Rights and freedom of access to information, ideas, and expression of ideas. IFLA runs committees on Free Access to Information and Freedom of Expression (FAIFE) and covers legal matters such as copyrights, preservation and conservation work, and a joint steering committee with the International Publishers' Association.

International Freedom of Expression Exchange
URL: http://www.ifex.org/en
555 Richmond Street W.
P.O. Box 407
Toronto, Ontario
Canada M5V 3B1
Phone: 1-416-515-9622

IFEX, a consortium of 71 organizations from more than 40 countries, was founded in 1992. It maintains an Action Alert Network in which member organizations report freedom of expression violations in their geographical regions that are in turn circulated throughout the world, does outreach and development in the developing world, and publishes a weekly electronic bulletin, *IFEX Communiqué.*

International PEN
URL: http://www.internationalpen.org.uk/index.php?pid=2
Brownlow House
50/51 High Holborn
London
WC1V 6ER
England
Phone: 44-20-7405-0339

Founded in London in 1921, International Pen is made up of 144 autonomous PEN centers in 101 countries. The international secretariat maintains the PEN Emergency Fund and the PEN Foundation. There are committees to deal with writers in prison, those in exile, and translation and linguistic rights. There are also committees on women writers and writers for peace.

International Press Institute
URL: http://www.freemedia.at
Spiegelgasse 2, A-1010

Vienna
Austria
Phone: 43-1-512-90-11

An international network of journalists, editors, and media executives, IPI defends and promotes freedom of the press and journalists' safety, carries out investigations where such freedom is endangered, engages in formal protests to government and organizations that hinder press freedom, publishes studies of government pressure on media, and publishes quarterly and annual reports on the state of press freedom throughout the world.

International Publishers' Association
URL: http://www.ipa-uie.org
3, avenue de Miremont
Ch-1206, Geneva
Switzerland
Phone: 41-22-346-30-18

Founded in 1896, the IPA is represented in 66 countries. It provides technical and legal assistance, monitors and, where possible, takes actions against violations of publishers' and writers' freedoms, monitors Internet free expression, and promotes and monitors the ratification and enforcement of the UNESCO Florence Agreement on the Importation of Educational, Scientific, and Cultural Materials.

Media Institute of Southern Africa
URL: http://www.misa.org/index.html
21 Johann Albrecht Street
Private Bag 13386
Winhoek, Namibia
Phone: 264-61-232-975

MISA's chapters in 11 southern African countries focus on such issues as freedom of expression, broadcasting diversity, and legal support. It conducts research into free speech violations advocacy on behalf of the victims. It also facilitates news exchange and publishes specialized reports on free press, gender media studies, and democracy in the region. It was founded in 1992.

Media Watch
URL: http://www.mediawatch.com/welcome.html
P.O. Box 618

Santa Cruz, CA 95061
Phone: (831) 423-6355

Founded in 1984, Media Watch challenges abusive and biased images found in the media. The group's main concerns are the (sometimes subtly) discriminatory and violent techniques used in the corporate media. It conducts protests, produces videos and newletters, and its members write opinion pieces.

The Middle East Media Research Institute
URL: http://memri.org/index.html
P.O. Box 27837
Washington, D.C. 20038
Phone: (202) 955-9070

Founded in 1998, MEMRI provides translations from Arabic and Turkish language media into English, German, Hebrew, Italian, French, Spanish, and Japanese. The Web site lists eight subjects of research, each with related translated documents from Abrabic and Turkish media.

National Coalition Against Censorship
URL: http://www.ncac.org/censorship_news
275 Seventh Avenue
New York, NY 10001
Phone: (212) 807-6222

The coalition, founded in 1974, consists of 50 nonprofit literary, artistic, religious, educational, professional, labor, and civil liberties organizations that oppose censorship. Its advocacy includes censorship in the arts, with regard to science, in schools, and with sexual matters. The coalition also sponsors the Youth Free Expression Network. The Web site lists numerous coalition actions and activities and available resources.

Open Democracy
URL: http://www.opendemocracy.net/home/index.jsp
23-25 Great Sutton Street
London EC1V 0DN
United Kingdom
Phone: 44-20-7608-2000

Open Democracy is a Web-based organization that promotes open discussion and debate on its site. Hundreds of writers address global issues centered on eight main themes, one of which is media and the Net. On this page, 21st-century media challenges are discussed, ranging from media distortion to copyright protection in the digital age. Open Democracy is exactly what it claims to be: a free-access site where one can read and debate the issues facing the world.

PEN American Center
URL: http://www.pen.org
588 Broadway, Suite 303
New York, NY 10012
Phone: (212) 334-1660

The largest of the constituent centers that make up International PEN, it is involved in many of the umbrella organization's activities as well as sponsoring forums, developing literacy programs, defending writers, and providing grants and loans to writers. PEN American Center is also leading the effort to halt the domestic intimidation of U.S. journalists.

People for the American Way
URL: http://www.pfaw.org/pfaw/general
2000 M Street NW, Suite 400
Washington, D.C. 20036
Phone: (202) 467-4999 or (800) 326-7329

PFAW is a progressive organization that performs legal work on the state and federal level, monitoring, and advocacy in such general areas as constitutional liberties, civil and equal rights, religious freedom, and public education. In particular, its actions cover free speech (including the Internet), dissent, and banned books.

Reporters Without Borders (Reporters sans frontières)
URL: http://www.rsf.org/
5, rue Geoffrey-Marie
75009
Paris, France
Phone: 33-1-44-83-8484

One of the best-known advocates for press freedom and journalists' safety in the world, Reporters Without Borders monitors press violations, provides legal assistance to journalists who have been victimized and/or intimidated, provides financial support to journalists under intimidation or in prison, and works to improve journalists' safety, especially in war zones. The organization also publishes regular and special reports. Since 2002, it has published an annual Worldwide Press Freedom Index, which it posts on its Web site.

9

Annotated Bibliography

The following annotated bibliography is divided into six sections, grouped by the five case-study countries presented in this book and a general section. Each is subdivided into books, articles, and Web documents.

GENERAL

Books

Bald, Margaret. *Literature Suppressed on Religious Grounds,* Revised Edition. New York: Facts On File, 2006. A survey of more than 100 banned books that includes the Bible, the Quran, the Talmud, the writings of Martin Luther and Charles Darwin, and contemporary authors such as Nikos Kazantzakis, Naguib Mahfouz, Salmon Rushdie, and J. K. Rowling. Texts are presented in alphabetical order with original date and place of publication and literary genre. Each text is summarized after which its censorship history is presented. There are also quotes from censored authors and brief profiles of the authors whose works are discussed in the book.

Bush, Douglas, ed. *The Portable Milton.* New York: The Viking Press, 1969. Contains the most important poems and essays of John Milton, including *Areopagitica,* in which he argues for free political discussion and an end to censorship. The introduction, written by the editor, gives a background into Milton's life and the political circumstances that brought him to write *Areopagitica.*

Green, Jonathon, and Nicholas J. Karolides, reviser. *Encyclopedia of Censorship,* New Edition. New York: Facts On File, 2005. A comprehensive look at censorship around the world and throughout history. More than 800 articles cover prominent figures and organizations on both sides of the issue, laws, censored works, countries, and court cases.

Karolides, Nicholas J. *Literature Suppressed on Political Grounds,* Revised Edition. New York: Facts On File, 2006. A survey of works by writers such as Karl Marx, George Orwell, Thomas Paine, Edward Said, Agnes Smedley, Alexander Solzhenitsyn, John Steinbeck, Harriet Beecher Stowe, Jonathan Swift, and Richard Wright among others. Texts are presented in alphabetical order with original date and place of publication and literary genre. Each text is summarized after which its censorship history is presented. There are also brief profiles of the authors whose works are discussed in the book.

Mitchell, Sally, ed. *Victorian Britain: An Encyclopedia.* New York, London: Garland Publishing, 1988. Hundreds of articles examine virtually every aspect of the Victorian Era: customs and mores; important personalities and their influences; laws; political, social, and artistic movements; recreation; technology; and numerous other characteristics of British society in the 19th and early 20th centuries.

Sova, Dawn B. *Banned Plays: Censorship Histories of 125 Stage Dramas.* New York: Facts On File, 2004. Each selection includes a plot summary and a censorship history as well as the play's original production date and location, character list, and film versions (if any). Three appendices provide profiles of the playwrights whose works are discussed, group the plays according to the reason(s) they were banned (sexual, social, political, or religious), and list an additional 100 plays that have been challenged, censored, or banned outright.

———. *Literature Suppressed on Social Grounds,* Revised Edition. New York: Facts On File, 2006. One hundred fifteen books by such writers as Mark Twain, Allen Ginsberg, William S. Burroughs, Sir Arthur Conan Doyle, Geoffrey Chaucer, William Faulkner, Alexandre Dumas, *fils*, J. D. Salinger, Studs Terkel, and Lesléa Newman are examined. As with the other books in this series, texts are presented in alphabetical order with original date and place of publication and literary genre. Each text is summarized, after which its censorship history is presented. There are also brief profiles of the authors whose works are discussed in the book.

Web Documents

Canada, Mark. "Journalism." Colonial America, 1607–1783. All American: Literature, History, and Culture. 2000. Available online. URL: http://www.geocities.com/markcanada_uncp/period.html. Accessed August 2, 2007. Provides an overview of the origins and growth of newspapers in the English colonies of North America and the content they published, which in some cases led to them being banned. Also notes their impact.

"Censorship." Ancient Civilizations. 2000. Available online. URL: http://library.thinkquest.org/C004203/political/political05.htm. Accessed August 2, 2007. Discussion of censorship in ancient China, Greece, and Rome. It also touches on the Inquisition.

Guibovich, Pedro. "The Lima Inquisition and Book Censorship, 1570–1820: Study and Annotated Bibliography." Available online. URL: http://www.beaconforfreedom.org/about_database/peru.html. Accessed August 2, 2007. A history and critical study of the Peruvian Inquisition that discusses the reasons for its existence, its methods, and its success and failures.

"Index of Prohibited Books." New Advent Catholic Encyclopedia. 2006. Available online. URL: http://www.newadvent.org/cathen/07721a.htm. Accessed August

2, 2007. Article on the history of the Index of Prohibited Books, promulgated by the Roman Catholic Church. Discusses what caused a book to be put on the Index.

Kemerling, Garth. "Socrates (469–399 B.C.E.)." Available online. URL: http://www.philosophypages.com/ph/socr.htm. Accessed August 2, 2007. An assessment of Socrates' life and influence. Highlights Socrates' character in different works of Plato.

Linder, Douglas. "The Zenger Trial: An Account." Famous Trials. 1995–2007. Available online. URL: http://www.law.umkc.edu/faculty/projects/ftrials/zenger/zenger.html. Accessed August 2, 2007. A very good account of the events leading up to the trial and the trial itself. The Web page has ancillary material to the trial, such as letters, and a discussion of the trial's impact.

Stearns, Peter N. et al. *Encyclopedia of World History: Ancient, Medieval, and Modern.* Sixth Edition. 2001. Available online. URL: http://www.bartleby.com/67/. Accessed August 2, 2007. More than 20,000 entries cover the history of the world from prehistoric times to 2000.

UNITED STATES

Books

Delfattore, Joan. *What Johnny Shouldn't Read: Textbook Censorship in America.* New Haven, London: Yale University Press, 1992. Primarily an examination of the textbook wars in the United States during the 1980s, it also discusses other books (generally fiction) that were banned in various school districts as a result of criticisms from both extremes of the political spectrum. Court cases, the politicizing of school boards, textbook purchasing, and test laws are also discussed.

Finan, Christopher M. *From the Palmer Raids to the Patriot Act: A History of the Fight for Free Speech in America.* Boston: Beacon Press, 2007. Since it really covers a little more than 80 years, this book, despite its subtitle, is not actually a complete history of the free-speech struggle in the United States. It does a fine job of presenting the 20th-century history of the attack on free speech and its extension into the 21st century.

Fribourg, Marjorie G. *The Bill of Rights: Its Impact on the American People.* Philadelphia: Macrae Smith Company, 1967. Divided into six sections, each one is prefaced by a brief explanation of the rights and issues dealt with in that particular section. Various Supreme Court cases are analyzed for the short- and long-term effects on American society.

Haiman, Franklyn S. *Speech and Law in a Free Society.* Chicago, London: The University of Chicago Press, 1981. Examines the problem of when free speech clashes with other rights guaranteed in American society—such as the right to a fair trial—and how the courts have resolved these clashes as American law evolves. Both the notion of speech in our society and the complexity of the problem are dissected in the book's first two sections.

Hentoff, Nat. *The War on the Bill of Rights and the Gathering Resistance.* New York: Seven Stories Press, 2003. Concentrates on the erosion of civil rights in the United States in the 21st century, particularly free speech, free press, and habeas corpus. The book argues that the blame can squarely be placed on the George W. Bush administration, with particular emphasis on the Justice Department and the USA PATRIOT Act.

Hutchison, E. R. *Tropic of Cancer on Trial: A Case History of Censorship.* New York: Grove Press, Inc., 1968. Examines the political and legal atmospheres leading up to and postdating the publication of *Tropic of Cancer* in the 1960s, including the landmark 1964 Supreme Court ruling that set a major precedent in the struggle against censorship.

Jensen, Carl, and Project Censored. *20 Years of Censored News.* New York: Seven Stories Press, 1997. Covering the years 1976–1995, each chapter begins by listing the top 10 news stories of its particular year then goes on to present the top 10 censored stories of that year. A synopsis of each censored story, sources, and an update (current to 1997) is given.

Johnson, John W., ed. *Historic U.S. Court Cases, 1690–1990: An Encyclopedia.* New York, London: Garland Publishing, 1992. Colonial court, U.S. Supreme Court, and lower court cases are outlined and briefly analyzed by scholars for the judicial thinking behind the opinions. The case are arranged chronologically by various areas of the law.

McCullough, David. *John Adams.* New York: Simon & Schuster, 2001. Examines the life and political career of the second president of the United States, including his stormy relations with the opposition. Although the author takes care to cover the issues, the book suffers a bit from being hagiographic.

———. *Truman.* New York: Simon & Schuster, 1992. A more even presentation than the author's *John Adams.* This biography of the 33rd president of the United States takes care not to skirt the tough issues of Truman's presidency, including his faults and weaknesses.

Peck, Robert S. *Libraries, the First Amendment, and Cyberspace: What You Need to Know.* Chicago: ALA Editions, 2000. Geared toward librarians, it nevertheless provides useful information on the rights, responsibilities, and restrictions of libraries. One drawback is that it predates the USA PATRIOT Act.

Stone, Geoffrey R. *Perilous Times: Free Speech in Wartime from the Sedition Act of 1798 to the War on Terrorism.* New York, London: W. W. Norton & Company, 2004. Examines how and why exceptions to the First Amendment have been sanctioned during wartime or even under threat of war, and how the federal government, particularly the executive branch, has used those exceptions to stifle challenges to its policies. The evolution of judicial thought concerning the First Amendment is also discussed, as are various challenges to the exceptions.

Truman, Harry S. *Memoirs,* 2 vol. Garden City, N.Y.: Doubleday & Co., 1955. Volume 1, *Year of Decisions,* recounts the momentous year 1945 when the author succeeded to the presidency upon the death of Franklin D. Roosevelt and led the country to the conclusion of World War II. Truman also recalls his decision to deploy nuclear weapons on Hiroshima and Nagasaki. Volume 2, *Years of Trial and Hope,* discusses Truman's foreign and domestic policies as president, including the Federal Loyalty Program.

Articles

Barringer, Felicity. "A Nation Challenged: The Broadcast; State Dept. Protests Move by U.S. Radio." *New York Times,* September 26, 2001, p. B3. Brief article that gives a State Department perspective on why it tried to censor a Voice of America interview with a Taliban leader two weeks after the terrorist attacks on New York City and Washington, D.C.

Grier, Peter. "How the Patriot Act Came in from the Cold." *Christian Science Monitor,* March 3, 2006, p. 1. Discusses the USA PATRIOT Act's renewal just prior to the vote. Also discusses certain civil liberty guarantees made by the Bush administration to appease the Senate Democrats.

Nakashima, Ellen. "Broadcast with Afghan Leader Halted: State Department Pressures Voice of America Not to Air 'Voice of the Taliban.'" *Washington Post,* September 23, 2001, p. A9. Presents State Department and Voice of America views concerning an interview with a Taliban leader. Also shows steps taken by Congress to make Voice of America more independent.

Neal, June Sandra. "A Patriotic Act: How Four Connecticut Librarians Faced down the Government to Protect Their Patrons' Constitutional Rights." *NE Magazine* (Sunday *Hartford Courant*), September 24, 2006, p. 4. Presents in detail the case of four librarians served with a national security letter to release computer data; the gag order that accompanied the letter; their recruitment of the ACLU, and the case's aftermath.

Web Documents

Electronic Frontier Foundation. Available online. URL: http://www.eff.org/. Accessed August 2, 2007. Provides numerous resources and links. Two of EFF's more important activities are the FOIA (Freedom of Information Act) Litigation for Accountable Government (FLAG) Project and the Legal Guide for Bloggers.

FindLaw for Legal Professionals. Available online. URL: http://lp.findlaw.com. Accessed August 2, 2007. One of the best legal reference sites online. It covers nearly all aspects of U.S. law including the U.S. Code and U.S. Supreme Court decisions. The latter are listed by case number or chronologically by year. Users will need to register for access, but registration is free.

Linder, Douglas. "Tennessee v. John T. Scopes: The 'Monkey Trial' 1925." Famous Trials. 1995–2007. Available online. URL: http://www.law.umkc.edu/faculty/projects/FTrials/scopes/scopes.htm. Accessed August 2, 2007. Provides background and discussion of the trial and its aftermath. It also included the statute Scopes was charged with violating, excerpts from the trial transcript, H. L. Mencken's account of the trial, and a number of other background details.

"The Motion Picture Production Code of 1930 (Hays Code)." ArtsReformation.com. 2006. Available online. URL: http://www.artsreformation.com/a001/hays-code.html. Accessed August 2, 2007. Presents the Production Code in its original 1930 form.

Nuzum, Eric. "A Brief History of Banned Music in the United States." 2003. Available online. URL: http://ericnuzum.com/banned/. Accessed August 2, 2007. Presents a time line of music censorship in the United States arranged by decade, beginning with the 1950s. The site also includes resources (links to other Web sites) and articles dealing with music censorship.

"The 100 Most Frequently Challenged Books, 1990–2000." ALA-American Library Association. 2006. Available online. URL: http://www.ala.org/ala/oif/bannedbooksweek/bbwlinks/100mostfrequently.htm. Accessed August 2, 2007. Presents the complete list of the 100 most frequently challenged books of the decade. There are also links to non-ALA Web sites that deal with First Amendment issues.

"'The Shadow of Incipient Censorship': The Creation of the Television Code of 1952." Available online. URL: http://www.historymatters.gmu.edu/d/6558/. Accessed August 2, 2007. Provides a brief history and discussion of the television code and a synopsis, in outline form, of what the code demanded. Also mentions testimony concerning the code given to the Senate Subcommittee to Investigate Juvenile Delinquency.

"U.S. Supreme Court Opinions." Findlaw for Legal Professionals. Available online. URL: http://caselaw.lp.findlaw.com/scripts/getcase.pl?court=us&navby=year. Accessed August 2, 2007. Lists all Supreme Court opinions by year, beginning with 1893; cases are listed in alphabetical order by year.

CHINA

Books

Fang Lizhi. *Bringing Down the Great Wall: Writings on Science, Culture, and Democracy in China.* New York: Alfred A. Knopf, 1991. The writings of the famous Chinese dissident and physicist over an 11-year period. In the nonscientific writings of this collection, Fang discusses the vague place reserved for the intellectual in post–Cultural Revolution Chinese society and argues for political and intellectual reform.

Spence, Jonathan D. *The Search for Modern China.* New York, London: W. W. Norton and Company, 1990. History of China from the Ming Empire to the suppression of the demonstrations in Tiananmen Square in 1989, with a concentration on the 20th century and the results of the social programs of the Communist Party.

Wang, Ban. *Illuminations from the Past: Trauma, Memory and History in Modern China.* Palo Alto, Calif.: Stanford University Press, 2004. A cultural history of modern China that examines various genres, from film and literature to political and cultural writing as it reveals intellectuals and writers' reactions to the events of their country that have shaped them personally as well as Chinese society as a whole.

Articles

"The Great Firewall of Modern China: Beijing's New Internet Rules Suggest Anxiety, not Strength." *Financial Times,* September 27, 2005, p. 14. Brief article reviews new Chinese restrictions of Chinese Web sites and discusses the Internet vis-à-vis other media in China.

Kahn, Joseph. "China Tightens Its Restrictions for News Media on the Internet." *New York Times,* September 26, 2005, p. A9. Discusses recently imposed restrictions on Chinese Web sites, including rules that prohibit private commentary from being posted and the registration of individuals and organizations.

Mufson, Steven. "Chinese Impose Strict Controls over Financial News Agencies." *Washington Post,* January 17, 1996, p. 2. Discusses new law that orders foreign financial news agencies to register with the Xinhua news agency and bars Chinese companies from direct subscription to foreign financial news agencies. It also discusses penalties for violations of the new rules.

Web Documents

Belt, Dave. "Chinese Government Cracks Down on Internet Free Speech." Newshour Extra, October 19, 2005. Available online. URL: http://www.pbs.org/newshour/extra/features/july-dec05/china_10-19.pdf. Accessed August 2, 2007. Discusses Internet options for Chinese citizens, such as what is blocked (BBC) and what is open (CNN) at the time of the writing. It also reports on the steps Internet users have to take to get online at Internet cafes, which are extremely popular.

"China's Internet Censorship." CBSnews.com, December 3, 2002. Available online. URL: http://www.cbsnews.com/stories/2002/12/03/tech/main531567.shtml. Accessed August 2, 2007. Reports on a Harvard Law School study that examined more than 200,000 Web sites using Chinese Internet Service Providers and Chinese proxies between May and November 2002. Discusses which sites were most frequently blocked by the Chinese government.

History of China. Available online. URL: http://www-chaos.umd.edu/history/toc.html. Accessed August 2, 2007. This is the table of contents page for the whole site. From here one can click on separate eras of Chinese history or individual dynastic periods within a particular era. The history runs from the pre–dynastic period to 1988.

Kurtenbach, Elaine. "China Tightens Controls on Foreign News." boston.com, September 10, 2006. Available online. URL: http://www.boston.com/news/world/asia/articles/2006/09/10/china_tightens_controls_on_foreign_news/. Accessed August 2, 2007. Associated Press report that details new Chinese press laws that affect foreign news agencies such as AP and Reuters. The laws make the Chinese news agency, Xinhua, even more an arbiter of what is permissible than previous laws had done. Provides analysis of the laws and quotes.

"List of People Detained for Internet-related Offences in China." Amnesty International, November 2002. Available online. URL: http://web.amnesty.org/web/content.nsf/pages/gbrimages7/$FILE/China_internet_list.pdf. Accessed August

2, 2007. Lists 33 individuals who were tried between 2000–02 for Internet offenses. Details, where known, are arranged under the following categories: name, (year) born, gender, (date) detained, accusation, (date) tried, sentence, province, occupation, and notes. The last category gives prisoner's status (if known) as of November 2002 and other information such as religious or political affiliation.

MacKinnon, Rebecca. "Yahoo! Helped Jail Another Chinese Cyberdissident." RConversation, February 8, 2006. Available online. URL: http://rconversation.blogs.com/rconversation/2006/02/yahoo_helped_ja.html. Accessed August 2, 2007. Cites Reporters Without Borders story of the case of Chinese cyberdissident, Li Zhi, who was given an eight-year prison sentence by the Chinese government based on information supplied by Yahoo! There are links to other news Web sites, which also detail the story.

McLaughlin, Andrew. "Google in China." Google Blog, January 27, 2006. Available online. URL: http://googleblog.blogspot.com/2006/01/google-in-china.html. Accessed August 2, 2007. A Google senior counsel explains Google's rationale for accepting China's strict censorship terms as the price of doing business in that country.

Yu, Peter K. "The Sweet and Sour Story of Chinese Intellectual Property Rights." Available online. URL: http://72.14.209.104/search?q=cache:_wBxxCL3jbsJ:www.peteryu.com/sweetsour.pdf+%22Tang+Code%22+censorship&hl=en&gl=us&ct=clnk&cd=6. Accessed August 2, 2007. Scholarly article that discusses the T'ang and Song codes, and some of the censorship each prescribed.

EGYPT

Books

Abdo, Geneive. *No God but God: Egypt and the Triumph of Islam.* Oxford, New York: Oxford University Press, 2000. Discussing the longstanding split between Egypt's official recognition of sharia as the basis of civil law and the leadership's determination to limit Islamist influence. Also discusses censorship stemming from al-Azhar and various Islamist organizations.

Abdulla, Rasha A. *The Internet in the Arab World: Egypt and Beyond* (Digital Formations V. 43). Berlin, New York, Oxford: Peter Lang Publishing, 2007. An examination of Internet use throughout the Arab World, primarily in Egypt. It also examines online censorship in the Middle East.

Collins, Robert O., and Robert L. Tignor. *Egypt & Sudan.* Englewood Cliffs, N.J.: Prentice-Hall, Inc., 1967. Though this book is dated, its final chapter provides interesting background information on Nasser's domestic and foreign policies. The stifling of free speech and a free press under Nasser, the authors contend, is an attempt to extend the revolution which the Free Officers had begun.

Mahfouz, Naguib. *Children of the Alley,* tr. by Peter Theroux. New York: Doubleday, 1996. The novel by the Nobel Prize–winning author that has been banned in his own country since 1959. Symbolic novel about the history of an alley (or side-street), its people, and their struggles, told by one of its inhabitants.

Articles

Bradley, John R. "Tuning in to the Bloggers' Wavelength." The *Straits Times* (Singapore), September 6, 2005. Discusses blogging throughout the Mideast. The section on Egyptian bloggers discusses political bloggers, who use the Internet to get around the censorship of the traditional mass media.

Diehl, Jackson. "The Freedom to Describe Dictatorship." *Washington Post,* March 27, 2006, p. A15. Profile of the opposition newspaper, *al-Masri al-Tom,* and it publisher, Hisham Kassem. Discusses the limited freedom and how it came about.

Epstein, Jack. "Fundamentalist Fears: Egyptian Artists Worry about Growing Islamic Fervor in a Nation Long Known for Being a Cultural and Secular Center in the Arab World." *San Francisco Chronicle,* July 15, 2006, p. E1. Article discusses intimidation of a female film director, increasing scrutiny of works of art, conflict between Muslims and Coptic Christians. There are interviews with people on both sides of the question, and a brief description of contemporary Egyptian society in comparison to those of other Middle Eastern countries.

Hardaker, David. "Egypt's Nobel Winner Asks Islamists to Approve Book." The *Independent* (London), January 28, 2006, p. 34. Describes how 94-year-old Naguib Mahfouz began a campaign to have one of his books published. The book had been banned since 1959. The article also details the various points of view surrounding Mahfouz's campaign and quotes his friend and translator, Raymond Stock.

Levinson, Charles. "Egypt's Growing Blogger Commuity Pushes Limit of Dissent." *Christian Science Monitor,* April 24, 2005, p. 7. Reports on Egypt's political blogger scene from the inside and from the perspective of an American political science professor. A list of Egyptian blogs is presented at the end of the article.

Menezes, Gabrielle. "Cairo Sheikhs Find Book Bans Tougher." *Christian Science Monitor,* December 10, 2003, p. 16. Describes how the Al Azhar Islamic Research Council was overruled when it tried to ban a book in 2003. Various viewpoints for the overruling are given, as is a brief background on Al Azhar censorship.

Saville, Guy. "Egypt Draws Veil over Top Pop Star; Egypt's Favourite Pop Star Banned." *The Independent* (London), January 14, 2002, p. 11. Describes the national radio censorship campaign against an Egyptian pop star and the political undertones involved in the censorship. Also reports on the parliamentary debate surrounding his censorship, with various viewpoints including the singer's.

Schemm, Paul. "Book Banning in Egypt Targets a Muslim Moderate." *Christian Science Monitor,* September 22, 2004, p. 11. Interviews and details the plight of writer Gamal al-Banna whose book, *The Responsibility for the Failure of the Islamic State,* was banned in August 2004. The book outlined various Islamic reforms the author believes ought to be undertaken. Also gives a bookseller's point of view on the censorship.

Tuinstra, Jacqueline. "V-Day Comes to Cairo—Very Carefully." *Globe and Mail* (Canada), February 19, 2004, p. R1. Describes the steps taken to perform Eve Ensler's *The Vagina Monologues* at American University in Cairo. The production had to be put on without the university's sanction and with a by-invitation-only audience so as to avoid censorship. Also mentions various changes in staging and text to make the play more compatible to Egyptian culture.

Wax, Emily. "Literary Agents of Change; A New Generation Finds Power in Prose, Poetry." *Washington Post,* May 14, 2003, p. C1. Describes the early 21st century renascent literary scene in Cairo. Interviews with novelists, poets, and academics show the power of literature on the youth of Egypt's capital, and their various dilemmas as they seek to transcend their personal and cultural problems by the power of the word.

Whitaker, Brian. "Egyptian Censors Block Magazine." *Guardian* (London), August 12, 2005. Brief article describing the plight of *Cairo* magazine, an English-language journal that was removed from the newsstands because of a cover photo that showed "plainclothes security forces preparing to attack pro-democracy demonstrators." The magazine's previous run-ins with the censors are given as well as a brief interview with the editor and a representative for the organization Article 19.

Web Documents

"Egypt: State Censorship Committee Bans Music Videos." FREEMUSE: Freedom of Musical Expression. Available online. 2005. URL: http://www.freemuse.org/sw9979.asp. Accessed August 2, 2007. Brief news report that discussing intransigence of the Egyptian Censorship Committee in refusing to allow scenes to be cut from videos in lieu of outright banning.

"Gamal Abdel Nasser." CNN Cold War. Available online. URL: http://www.cnn.com/SPECIALS/cold.war/kbank/profiles/nasser/. Accessed August 2, 2007. Profile of the Egyptian leader, concentrating on his time in power. Of particular interest is that the article mentions Nasser's antidemocratic policies and the various forms of censorship he authorized.

"History of Egypt." Available online. URL: http://www.touregypt.net/ehistory.htm. Accessed August 2, 2007. A good site for Egyptian history. It begins with the prehistoric era and goes on to list all of the dynasties and ruling periods up to the British occupation. In turn each dynasty and ruling era can be accessed.

"Reading between the 'Red Lines': The Repression of Academic Freedom in Egyptian Universities." Human Rights Watch Publications, June 2005 Vol. 17, No. 6(E). Available online. URL: http://hrw.org/reports/2005/egypt0605/. Accessed August 2, 2007. The report is laid out in outline form with each section and subsection available for browsing and reading. The main topics include: a definition and legal protections of academic freedom, government repression, non-state attacks on academic freedom, self-censorship, institutional restrictions, and proposed reforms.

"The Right to Freedom of Expression." The Egyptian Organization for Human Rights, 2002. Available Online. URL: http://www.eohr.org/annual/wr02/ar8.htm. Accessed August 2, 2007. Report breaks down Egyptian censorship into the following classifications: journalists arrested for doing their jobs and the dispositions of their cases in court, censorship in Egypt, and freedom of thought and belief. There are subsections under each classification.

Youssef, Nelly. "Internet Police on the Nile." Qantara.de, December 12, 2005. Available online. URL: http://www.qantara.de/webcom/show_article.php/_c-476/_nr-501/i.html. Accessed August 2, 2007. Article describes Egypt's growing censorship of the Internet. In addition to political activists, those targeted include homosexuals; e-mail is monitored, opposition Web sites are banned, and Internet cafes are under surveillance.

RUSSIA

Books

King, David. *The Commissar Vanishes: The Falsification of Photographs and Art in Stalin's Russia.* New York: Metropolitan Books/Henry Holt and Company, Inc., 1997. The text is accompanied by photos from the author's collection showing how, during the period of Josef Stalin's rule, censors in the Soviet Union took great care to eliminate the photo record of those Communists who had been purged from the Party and in most cases imprisoned or executed. Comparison "before" and "after" photos show how individuals were airbrushed out of photos, sometime replaced by architectural or landscape features, but often not. In a few rare cases the individuals were rehabilitated and added back in post-Stalin versions of the photo.

Mickiewicz, Ellen. *Split Signals: Television and Politics in the Soviet Union.* Oxford, New York: Oxford University Press, 1988. Covering the late Soviet Union during the years of its final two leaders, it examines how the medium of television was used to manipulate the audience. The book also compares Soviet and U.S. television of the period.

Nikitenko, Alexandr. *The Diary of a Russian Censor,* tr. by Helen Saltz Jacobson. Amherst, Mass.: The University of Massachusetts Press, 1975. A look at 19th-century Russia's literary and political scenes from a consummate insider. The diary covers more than 50 years, spanning Russia's golden age of literature from Pushkin and Lermontov to Dostoevsky and Turgenev.

Politkovskaya, Anna. *Putin's Russia: Life in a Failing Democracy.* New York: Owl Books, 2007. An indictment of Russian government and society under the second post-Soviet government by Russia's foremost investigative journalist. This book was originally published in English in 2005, and Politkovskaya was murdered the next year.

Shatz, Marshall S. *Soviet Dissent in Historical Perspective.* Cambridge, London, New York: Cambridge University Press, 1980. Concentrates on Soviet dissent in the 1960s and 1970s with an examination of how it fits into the overall pattern of dissent throughout Russian history. Particular attention is paid to dissent in the Khruschev period and the Sinyavsky and Daniel trial.

Shevtsova, Lilia. *Putin's Russia.* Washington, D.C.: Carnegie Endowment for International Peace, 2003. Discusses the meteoric rise to power of Vladimir Putin from virtual unknown to president of Russia and the various policies he enacted to make the presidency the strong position Russians supposedly crave. An examination of Putin's background, the circumstances of Kremlin intrigue, and the chaotic drift of Russian society point toward an authoritarianism constrained only by the economic system.

Swayze, Harold. *Political Control of Literature in the USSR, 1946–1959.* Cambridge, Mass.: Harvard University Press, 1962. A concise but clear elucidation of censorship in Soviet literature that covers the last seven years of Stalin's life to the heyday of Khrushchev's power, when Boris Pasternak was not allowed to accept the Nobel Prize. Chapters cover the imposition of socialist realism and Zhdanovism, and the bureaucratic structure, including the writers union, that contributed to the climate of censorship.

Articles

Chivers, C. J. "Journalist Critical of Chechen War Is Shot Dead in Moscow." *New York Times,* October 7, 2006, p. 16. Reports on the murder of journalist Anna Politkovskaya in her Moscow apartment building. The article discusses her past and most recent work and quotes colleagues who speculate as to the reason for her murder.

Myers, Steven Lee. "Russia Fines Museum Aides for Art Said to Ridicule Religion." *New York Times,* March 28, 2005. Discusses the background and outcome of a case stemming from the exhibition, "Caution! Religion," at the Andrei Sakharov Museum that was condemned by the Russian Orthodox Church. The article also presents quotes from both sides of the argument.

Rodriguez, Alex. "Attacks on Russian Journalists Often Unexamined, Unsolved." *Chicago Tribune,* October 24, 2006. Discusses the murders of various journalists, in Moscow and elsewhere in Russia, and how these murders have by and large gone unsolved. Recounts various attacks, police apathy, and official corruption surrounding crimes against journalists in Russia's provinces.

Web Documents

"Alexander Radishchev, *Journey from St. Petersburg to Moscow.* 1790." Documents in Russian History. Seton Hall University. Available online. URL: http://artsci.shu.edu/reesp/documents/radishchev.htm. Accessed August 2, 2007. A brief profile of Radishchev's life precedes an English translation (by Nathaniel Knight) of an excerpt of *Journey from Saint Petersburg to Moscow.*

"Ancient Russia." History and Culture of Russia. Available online. URL: http://www.geographia.com/russia/rushis02.htm. Accessed August 2, 2007. Overview (with time line) of Russian history from the ancients to the Soviet period. There are links within each section that cover various matters in more detail.

Coalson, Robert. "Babitsky's 'Crime' and Punishment." CPJ Special Reports from around the World, February 28, 2000. Available online. URL: http://www.cpj.org/Briefings/2000/Babitsky/main.html. Accessed August 2, 2007. Reports on the plight of Radio Liberty journalist Andrei Babitsky who went missing early in Putin's reign and then was handed over to Chechen rebels in an exchange. The article also details then acting president Putin's reaction to the affair and government press controls at that time.

Curtis, Glenn E., ed. "Russia: A Country Study." Russiansabroad.com. Available online. URL: http://www.russiansabroad.com/russian_history_1.html. Accessed August 2, 2007. A good in-depth examination of Russia's history from ancient times to the present. It includes a chronology, a discussion of Russia's geography, and overviews of its society, economy, transportation and telecommunications systems, government and politics, and national security. Good sections on censorship, both historical and in contemporary Russia.

"Journalists Killed: Statistics and Archives." Committee to Protect Journalists. Available online. URL: http://www.cpj.org/killed/killed_archives/stats.html. Accessed August 2, 2007. Statistics on all journalists killed from the years 1992–2006, inclusive. The top 20 countries list shows Russia ranks third during that time period. Each year is highlighted at the top of the Web page and clicking on them gives the circumstances of each journalist's murder that year, in alphabetical order by country.

"Soviet Predecessor Organizations, 1917–1954." FAS (Federation of American Scientists), May 1989. Available online. URL: http://www.fas.org/irp/world/russia/intro/su0510.htm. Accessed August 2, 2007. Article covers intelligence organizations that preceded the KGB. Covers the various name changes, the powers each organization held, the roles they played in establishing the Soviet Union and maintaining, especially the Red Terror and the Show Trials of the late 1930s.

ZIMBABWE

Books

Blake, Robert. *A History of Rhodesia.* New York: Alfred A. Knopf, 1978. Straightforward narrative history that includes the prehistoric record and tribal histories, but concentrates on the British invasion and rule, and the "self-rule" of white Rhodesians. Published during the period between minority-ruled Rhodesia's Unilateral Declaration of Independence and the majority-ruled independence of Zimbabwe.

Chan, Stephen. *Robert Mugabe: A Life of Power and Violence.* Ann Arbor, Mich.: The University of Michigan Press, 2003. A critical examination of the career of the man whose authoritarian leadership of Zimbabwe (as its only ruler in its first three decades) played on tribal differences and anti-European backlash to bring his country to the brink of ruin.

Meldrum, Andrew. *Where We Have Hope: A Memoir of Zimbabwe.* New York: Atlantic Monthly Press, 2004. Written by the first journalist tried in court for violating AIPPA and the last foreign journalist to write from inside Zimbabwe before he was deported in 2003. The book exposes the abuses of the Mugabe regime from firsthand accounts. The author spent 23 years in Zimbabwe and was an eyewitness to the consolidation of power and the destruction of democracy in that country.

Nyagumbo, Maurice. *With the People.* London: Allison & Busby, Ltd., 1980. A political autobiography by the man who became minister of mines in Robert Mugabe's first government. The author describes his growing political awareness and the nationalist struggle within Rhodesia, despite the censorship and the outlawing of various African nationalist parties by the minority government.

Tamarkin, M. *The Making of Zimbabwe: Decolonization in Regional and International Politics.* London: Frank Cass & Co. Ltd., 1990. A history of the events of the 1970s when internal and external pressures resulted in the transformation of Rhodesia into Zimbabwe. The author examines the conferences, squabbles, alliances, and setbacks that occurred in the country and which finally brought majority rule and independence.

Vambe, Lawrence. *An Ill-Fated People: Zimbabwe before and after Rhodes.* Pittsburgh, Penn.: University of Pittsburgh Press, 1972. A written account taken from the oral tradition, by which history had been passed down from one generation to the next in Zimbabwe. Vambe's history is national, tribal, familial, and personal. The author is a mission-educated grandson of a tribal chief and therefore able to dispute many European historical claims and rationalizations for the wreckage done to African society in that area.

Articles

Cauvin, Henri E. "Zimbabwe Arrests Editor, Raising Fears of Wider Crackdown." *New York Times,* November 9, 2001, p. 14. Reports on the second arrest within three months of the editor of Zimbabwe's only privately owned daily newspaper and the fallout the arrest has had on Zimbabwe's journalism community.

Howden, Daniel. "Zimbabwe Journalist Murdered Over Leaked Tsvangirai Pictures." *Independent* (London), April 4, 2007, p. 22. Describes the murder of a photojournalist who allegedly had ties to the Zimbabwean opposition. Discusses how photos of opposition leader Morgan Tsvangirai lying on a hospital bed with a fractured skull may have led to the murder.

Meldrum, Andrew. "Mugabe Introduces New Curbs on Internet." *Guardian,* June 3, 2004, p. 17. Describes how the Zimbabwean government is trying to bypass the law by using a new contract with Internet service providers to censor any information it deems "anti-national."

Rees, Jasper. "Drama in a Land of Fear." *Daily Telegraph,* February 4, 2003, p. 19. Discusses theatrical censorship in Zimbabwe.

Shillinger, Kurt. "In Wartorn Africa, Governments Target Media Institutes, See Violations of Press Freedoms." *Boston Globe,* December 1, 1999, p. A2. Describes press censorship and imprisonment of journalists in various African countries, including Zimbabwe. Also describes Mugabe's actions toward and attitude concerning the media.

Smith, Alex Duval. "Clampdown Hounds Out Foreign Journalists." *Independent* (London), August 17, 2001, p. 10. Discusses the alternative means of newsgathering employed by the local and foreign press in Zimbabwe in the wake of government actions against journalists and news organizations.

"Zimbabwe's Music Sings the Message of Dissidents." *Globe and Mail,* February 2, 2002, p. A12. Describes popular musicians and their work, the threat of their being banned by the government, and how banning their music from radio and stores makes them more popular. The article was written by an anonymous Zimbabwean correspondent whose name was withheld by the newspaper for that person's protection.

Web Documents

"Chronology for Europeans in Zimbabwe." Available online. URL: http://www.cidcm.umd.edu/mar/chronology.asp?groupId=55201. Accessed August 2, 2007. Chronological list of European incursions and activities in Zimbabwe (and, early on, South Africa) from 1837, when Afrikaners attacked Ndebele, to 1999, when the Mugabe government instituted its program of land reform and resettlement. Each item listed in the chronology is culled from a news source.

"History of Zimbabwe." History of Nations, 2004. Available online. URL: http://www.historyofnations.net/africa/zimbabwe.html. Accessed August 2, 2007. Historical overview of Zimbabwe and Rhodesia that begins with the prehistoric evidence and ends with Robert Mugabe's election victory in March 2002. The article primarily concentrates on the events from 1965–2002, following Rhodesia's Unilateral Declaration of Independence, the isolation of the minority government, the rise of African nationalism in Rhodesia, the struggle for Zimbabwean independence, and Mugabe's reign.

"History of Zimbabwe, The." Bulawayo1872.Com. Available online. URL: http://www.bulawayo1872.com/history/zimhistory.htm. Accessed August 2, 2007. Overview of Zimbabwe/Rhodesia history from the decline of Great Zimbabwe to the end of the 20th century. Concentrates on British colonization and Rhodesian politics.

"Jamming of Radio Stations Extended to VOA." Reporters Without Borders, July 6, 2006. Available online. URL: http://www.rsf.org/print.php3?id_article=18218. Accessed August 2, 2007. RFS report that affirms that VOA broadcasts into Zimbabwe have been jammed since mid-June 2006. Also mentions that VOP (Voice of the People), owned by a private Dutch corporation, has had its broadcasts jammed since December 2005. Article quotes a Zimbabwean official who concurs. It also asserts that Zimbabwe is receiving technological assistance from China.

Kwinika, Savious. "Over 150 Women Charged under Draconian Law of POSA in Zimbabwe." PeaceWomen: Women's International League for Peace and Freedom. Available online. URL: http://www.peacewomen.org/news/Zimbabwe/Nov06/Women_Charged.html. Accessed August 2, 2007. Details how women marching from the post office to the Reserve bank of Zimbabwe in Bulawayo were arrested. Discusses what provision of the POSA law they were charged with violating and mentions the forms of torture some endured while in custody.

"Public Order and Security Act (POSA), Sokwanele Comment: 20 August 2004." Sokwanele Civic Action Support Group. Available online. URL: http://www.sokwanele.com/articles/sokwanele/POSA_20aug2004.html. Accessed August 2, 2007. An analysis of the Public Order and Security Act that includes background and commentary on the Zimbabwe African National Union and Robert Mugabe. The analysis concentrates on parts II, III, and IV.

"Street Actors Beaten Up for Satirising Crisis." ZimOnline, December 1, 2006. Available online. URL: http://www.zimonline.co.za/Article.aspx?ArticleId=553. Accessed August 2, 2007. Reports on the plights of four street actors who were arrested in Bulawayo for performing a play titled, *Indlala* (Hunger). The four were arrested for violating POSA by "inciting people to revolt. . . ." The actors discuss their treatment and torture at the hands of the police. The article also mentions other Zimbabwean artists who have been censored.

"Zimbabwe: An Opposition Strategy." International Crisis Group. ZimOnline, September 14, 2006. Available online. URL: http://www.zimonline.co.za/Article.aspx?ArticleId=96. Accessed August 2, 2007. A very detailed report prepared by the Crisis Group that covers the state of affairs in Zimbabwe, such as the country's economy and the fragility and breakdown of its political infrastructure, and offers scenarios for a post-Mugabe Zimbabwe and strategies for restoring democracy to the country.

"Zimbabwe." Encyclopedia of the Nations. Available online. URL: http://www.nationsencyclopedia.com/Africa/Zimbabwe-HISTORY.html. Accessed August 2, 2007. Overview of Zimbabwe/Rhodesia history that also mentions prehistoric evidence and ancient Shona migrations. The final half of the article deals with Zimbabwe since independence. The Web page also contains a link to a biographical article on Robert Mugabe.

"Zimbabwe: Supreme Court Strikes down Repressive Media Legislation." Committee to Protect Journalists. May 7, 2003. Available online. URL: http://www.cpj.org/news/2003/Zim07may03na.html. Accessed August 2, 2007. Brief article from CPJ that discusses a Zimbabwean Supreme Court decision striking down a clause of the Access to Information and Protection of Privacy Act (AIPPA) as unconstitutional. The article mentions that both AIPPA and the Public Order and Security Act have been used to prosecute journalists.

Chronology

The chronology below gives an overview of how rulers, leaders, and even criminals in all types of societies throughout history have used censorship to promote their agendas and bar contradictory ideas from entering peoples' discussions. The practice continues to this day.

443 B.C.E.

- The position of censor is established in Rome during the republican period. The censor's duties were originally confined to taking the census, but the position acquired more power as time passed. Regulating citizens' morals was one of those new responsibilities.

399 B.C.E.

- Trial of Socrates in Athens for blasphemy and corrupting the youth. Considered the father of Greek philosophy, Socrates challenged people's beliefs through intense questioning. The account of his trial and his death are found in Plato's *Apology.*

221 B.C.E.

- Emperor Qin Shi Huangdi, first emperor of the Qin dynasty, orders the destruction of history and philosophy books, including the writings of Confucius. Books dealing with mathematics, science, and oracles were spared.

Fourth Century C.E.

- Roman emperor Constantine legalizes Christianity, but does not make it the state religion. However, he does order the destruction of certain books of Greek philosophy.

Sixteenth Century

- During the Spanish conquest of the New World, Catholic missionaries, working to gain converts, banned the Mayan religion. Nearly all Mayan writing was destroyed with the exception of four books now known as the Dresden Codex, the Paris Codex, the Grolier Codex, and the Madrid Codex.

1559

- During the reign of Pope Paul IV, the General Inquisition issues the *Index librorum prohibitorum,* or *Index of Prohibited Books.* The Index bans all books that the Inquisition considers heretical or obscene. Limits were placed on other books, with new books having to receive approval before they were published. Authors of banned books faced excommunication.

1568

- The Peruvian Inquisition is introduced during the reign of Spain's King Philip II. Peruvian booksellers, located primarily in Lima, are required to list their inventories with the Inquisition and also notify authorities if private collectors own forbidden books, when evaluating those collections. Despite the harshness of the law, it isn't until the 18th century, and particularly the latter half, that the Inquisition cracks down on the importation of forbidden books.

1597

- Sentenced by the Inquisition, Italian philosopher Giordano Bruno is burned alive for heresy, after having spent two years in prison for declaring that the Scriptures were fictitious, that Christ was not the messiah, and that the worship of God was superstition.

1633

- Italian astronomer and natural philosopher Galileo Galilei is found guilty of supporting the Copernican heliocentric theory (that the Sun is the center of the solar system) by the Inquisition and sentenced to house arrest and formally forced to renounce his belief in the theory. The year before he had published *Dialogo sopra I due massimi sistemi del mondo, tolemaico e copernicano* (*Dialogue Concerning Two Great Systems of the World, Ptolemaic and Copernican*).

1643

- King Charles I of Great Britain begins to enforce a 1637 law requiring the registration and prior approval of all published works. Poet and essayist John Milton responds the following year with his eloquent essay *Areopagitica,* which argues against this law. The law is not repealed until 1694.

1650

- *The Meritorious Price of Our Redemption* by theologian William Pynchon, a founder of Massachusetts Colony, is the first book publicly burned in the 13 English colonies for its criticism of Puritanism. Pynchon returns to England.

Chronology

1690

- The first newspaper in the English colonies of North America, *Publick Occurrences, Both Foreign and Domestick,* is published by Benjamin Harris. It lasts one issue before it is closed down for failing to comply with Massachusetts's licensing law.

1721

- The *New England Courant* is founded by James Franklin, the older half brother of Benjamin Franklin. Within two years the newspaper is banned.

1735

- After nine months' imprisonment, newspaper publisher John Peter Zenger is brought to trial, charged with seditious libel for printing an article critical of Governor William Cosby. Zenger is found not guilty by the jury.

1790

- Alexander Radishchev publishes *Journey from Saint Petersburg to Moscow,* an indictment of serfdom in Russia. Catherine the Great is incensed by the book and compares Radishchev to one of the more notorious Caucasian rebels of the period. A court sentences him to death, but Catherine commutes his sentence to 10 years' exile in Siberia. After Catherine, her son Czar Paul I frees Radishchev.

1791

- The Bill of Rights, the first 10 amendments to the U.S. Constitution, is ratified. The First Amendment guarantees U.S. citizens freedom of speech, the press, and religion.

1798

- Using the threat of war with France as a pretext, the Federalist-controlled Congress passes, and President John Adams signs into law, the Sedition Act, which makes it unlawful to criticize the president or the government. The law expires the day Adams's term in office ends.

1801

- The Society for the Suppression of Vice is established in Great Britain. Originally an organization that seeks the punishment of fortune-tellers, those cruel to animals, and panderers, it soon becomes involved with suppressing obscene books and prints.

1815

- ***January-March:*** Just prior to and in the weeks after the Battle of New Orleans, General Andrew Jackson places the city under martial law and suspends habeas corpus. His rationale is that a general has absolute control of his military camp and that New Orleans fell within that jurisdiction.

1821

- Massachusetts declares that John Cleland's 1750 novel, *Memoirs of a Woman of Pleasure,* commonly known as *Fanny Hill,* is obscene.

1825

- ***December:*** Unhappy with the young regime of Czar Nicholas I, a group of nobles and military officers organize a brief, ill-fated revolt. Known as the Decembrists, some are executed though most are sent to Siberia. As a result of their actions, though, Nicholas becomes more autocratic, and censorship in Russia becomes harsher. The Russian secret police, the Third Section, plays an important role in stifling dissent during Nicholas's reign and after.

1832

- Parliament passes the Reform Act of 1832, which makes criticism of the government legal in the United Kingdom. Because of this law the notion of seditious libel is abandoned. It also paved the way for further legal underpinnings for citizens' political rights.

1843

- The Libel Act of 1843 reforms Great Britain's libel laws by allowing for the truth of a matter to be taken into account. Not only is the law of defamatory libel altered, but seditious libel is further weakened.

1863

- During the U.S. Civil War, Union general Ambrose Burnside of the Department of Ohio issues General Order No. 38, which declares martial law and outlaws expression of sympathy for the Confederacy. Under this law, Ohio Democrat Clement Vallandigham is arrested for speaking out against the war, and the *Chicago Times* is temporarily closed down.

1868

- The Hicklin Rule used to determine whether a text is obscene in both the United Kingdom and the United States (and named for a famous British obscenity case *Regina v. Hicklin*) comes into force. Essentially it allows for a jury to declare a text obscene even if only one sentence (or word) is thought to be so. The rule remains in effect until the mid-20th century.
- ***July 9:*** The Fourteenth Amendment to the United States Constitution is ratified. The Supreme Court subsequently interprets this amendment as extend-

ing First Amendment guarantees whereby state and municipal governments are subject to the same standards as the federal government.

1873

- ***March 3:*** President Ulysses S. Grant signs the Act for the Suppression of Trade in, and Circulation of, Obscene Literature and Articles for Immoral Use into law. This law is commonly known as the Comstock Act after its chief supporter, Anthony Comstock. Over the next 42 years, Comstock uses the law to prosecute such people as Victoria Woodhull, Margaret Sanger, and George Bernard Shaw.

1876

- Sultan Abdűlhamid II ascends the throne of the Ottoman Empire. Though something of a reformer, Abdűlhamid nevertheless rules as an autocrat. He makes use of a vast network of secret police, dissolves the national assembly, and stifles free speech and a free press to curb dissent.

1908

- The first banning of films in the United States takes place in Chicago when the chief of police bans *The James Boys in Missouri* and *Night Riders.* The bans were initiated as per a 1907 Chicago municipal law that required the licensing of films shown in the city.

1914

- ***January 10:*** President Yuan Shikai of the Republic of China dissolves the National Assembly, in which the Guomindang held a majority. He also outlaws the Guomindang, forcing the party's leader, Sun Yat-Sen, to flee the country.

1917

- The U.S. Congress passes, and President Woodrow Wilson signs into law, the Espionage Act of 1917. The law is used primarily to stifle dissent in the United States during World War I. Never repealed, it is also used by the federal government more than 50 years later in its attempt to block publication of excerpts of the Pentagon Papers.
- The monthly socialist magazine *The Masses* is barred from the mails by the Postmaster General for violating the Espionage Act. This leads to the magazine going out of business.
- Film producer Robert Goldstein is jailed under the Espionage Act for his film *The Spirit of '76.* The film is actually a patriotic depiction of the American Revolution, but is found to violate the new law in its portrayal of British soldiers—Great Britain being a wartime ally—as cruel.

CENSORSHIP

1918

- President Wilson signs the Sedition Act of 1918 (actually an amendment to section three of the Espionage Act) into law. Used at first against wartime dissenters and critics of the government's policies, the law plays an even greater role in prosecuting so-called Reds and anarchists during the Red Scare years of 1919–20. The law is eventually repealed on December 13, 1920.
- Vladimir Lenin signs a decree ordering press censorship in Russia and the territory controlled by the Communists during the Civil War. Though it was only a temporary authorization, the decree remains in place when the war is over.

1922

- Will Hays becomes the first head of the Motion Picture Producers and Distributors of America, responsible for Hollywood censorship. At first he mainly serves a public relations purpose, but by the end of the decade he issues a list of "Don'ts" and "Be Carefuls."

1925

- John T. Scopes is tried in Dayton, Tennessee, for the crime of teaching evolution. The trial is an ACLU test case to overturn Tennessee's antievolution law, but the jury finds Scopes guilty. The trial's most notable incident was Clarence Darrow's examination of William Jennings Bryan. On appeal, the guilty verdict was overturned on a technicality.

1930

- The Hays Office issues a Production Code of film standards. These standards apply to domestic films and to imports. The code goes unenforced for four years until pressure is applied by the National Legion of Decency (formerly the Catholic Legion of Decency). With some revisions, the Code will remain in place for more than 30 years, though its hold on Hollywood producers and directors will begin to weaken in the 1950s.

1933

- ***April 11:*** The Gestapo raids and temporarily closes the Bauhaus, arresting some of the students, though the leading mentors had already fled Germany. The Bauhaus is officially closed down in August.
- ***May 10:*** Approximately 20,000 books are burned by students in a bonfire in a square opposite the University of Berlin. Simultaneous book burnings take place in other German cities and are repeated at later dates.
- In a test case brought about to have the ban on James Joyce's novel *Ulysses* lifted (*United States v. One Book Entitled* Ulysses), Federal District Court Judge John M. Woolsey decides in favor of the book. The decision is upheld on appeal.

Chronology

1934

- During the convocation of the First Writers' Conference in the Soviet Union, author Maxim Gorky and politicians Nikolai Bukharin and Andrei Zhdanov unveil the artistic aesthetic of socialist realism. The concept, whose main goal is to portray communism in a positive light, eventually spreads from literature to encompass all artistic endeavors. Its heyday comes in the years just after World War II when Zhdanov was able to impose his artistic views on the country in what has become known as Zhdanovism.

1936

- More than 20 years after Margaret Sanger was arrested for using the U.S. mails to distribute birth control literature, the Comstock Act is amended to make such distribution legal.

1937

- ***July 19:*** The exhibition *Entartete Kunst* (Degenerate Art) opens in Munich, Germany. It is an exhibition of modern art banned by the Nazi regime. The intention of the exhibition is to show the links between modern art, Judaism, communism, and the decadent democracies. More than 650 paintings, sculptures, prints, books, and manuscripts of musical notation are exhibited. Ironically, 2 million viewers saw it in Munich and another 1 million saw it when the exhibition went on tour in Germany and Austria.

1947

- ***January:*** J. Parnell Thomas takes over as chairman of the House Committee on Un-American Activities (HUAC) following the Republican victory in the midterm congressional elections. HUAC soon begins investigating communist influence in Hollywood. Eventually hundreds working in films, television, and radio are blacklisted.
- ***March 21:*** President Harry S. Truman signs Executive Order No. 9835, which establishes the Federal Employees Loyalty and Security Program. Within four years, over 3 million federal employees are investigated, resulting in thousands of resignations and the employment of 212 being terminated. No one was indicted.

1950

- ***February 9:*** During a speech in Wheeling, West Virginia, Senator Joseph McCarthy claims that he has a list containing the names of 205 employees of the State Department who are or were members of the Communist Party. Although the claim is proven wrong, it nonetheless launches McCarthy's career as a communist hunter.

CENSORSHIP

1951

- ***February:*** The government of the People's Republic of China issues Regulations for the Suppression of Counterrevolutionaries. Dissidents are the first victims of the new law, followed by intellectuals, writers, artists, composers, and actors. Many are forced to undergo "reeducation" and practice self-criticism.

1952

- As chairman of the Senate Permanent Subcommittee on Investigations, Senator Joseph McCarthy is responsible for the State Department's banning of more than 30,000 books from its offices worldwide because they were written by so-called Communists or fellow travelers.

1954

- The comics code, administered by the Comics Code Authority of the Comics Magazine Association of America, is instituted. The code covers content and advertising. As a direct result, several comics publishers went bankrupt and many artists and writers left the industry because of the censorship.
- Author Nikos Kazantzakis is excommunicated by the Greek Orthodox Church for his 1951 novel, *The Last Temptation of Christ.* The book is also placed on the Roman Catholic Index of Prohibited Books.

1956

- Gamal Abdel Nasser becomes president of Egypt; he had previously served as acting head of state and leader of the nine-member Revolutionary Command Council following the abdication of King Faruq. As president, Nasser declares Egypt a one-party Islamic socialist state. During his reign, Egypt suffers under harsh censorship laws, but he remains popular because of his anti-Israel and pan-Arab positions.

1958

- Boris Pasternak is awarded the Nobel Prize in Literature for his novel *Dr. Zhivago.* The book was rejected by Soviet censors, but published in Italy in 1957. Soviet authorities force Pasternak to reject the award, expel him from the Writers Union, and strip him of his honors.

1960

- White minority government of Southern Rhodesia (later Rhodesia, and Zimbabwe after independence) passes the Law and Order Maintenance Act. Ostensibly meant to suppress antigovernment guerrilla activity, it severely curtails the rights of black Africans in the country.

Chronology

1961

- ***October 4:*** Comedian Lenny Bruce is arrested in San Francisco and charged with obscenity for a performance at the Jazz Workshop. He is found not guilty in March 1962. Over the next five years, Bruce is arrested for obscenity in Los Angeles, Hollywood, Chicago, and New York City.

1964

- Rhodesian prime minister Ian Smith, facing rising insurgency because of his government's refusal to allow majority rule, orders the arrests of African nationalist politicians (and guerrilla leaders) and bans the nationalist newspaper, *Daily News.* He also declares two major nationalist parties, the Zimbabwe African People's Union (ZAPU) and the Zimbabwe African National Union (ZANU) illegal.
- The United States Supreme Court votes unanimously to overturn lower court decisions in *New York Times Company v. Sullivan.* The case concerned the publication of an advertisement that supposedly defamed a Montgomery, Alabama, county police commissioner. The Court's decision strengthened freedom of the press.
- ***June:*** After court cases in various states, the Supreme Court decides that Henry Miller's novel *Tropic of Cancer* is acceptable for Americans to read. The decision paved the way for the publication of a number of 20th-century novels in the United States.

1966

- ***February:*** Mao's wife, Jiang Qing, and her cohorts, later known as the Gang of Four, meet in Shanghai to discuss Mao's cultural writings and attend radical opera performances. What eventually results from their meetings is the Cultural Revolution, another attempt to rid Chinese culture of its bourgeois aspects. The Cultural Revolution lasts 10 years and during its first phase young people denounce their elders with many joining the fanatical Red Guards.
- ***February 10–14:*** Soviet writers Andrei Sinyavsky and Yuli Daniel go on trial, charged with "agitation or propaganda carried out with the purpose of subverting or weakening the Soviet regime . . . dissemination for the said purposes of slanderous inventions defamatory to the Soviet political and social system. . . ." In a smear campaign, the newspaper *Izvestia* claims that they slandered Lenin, Chekhov, and the army. They are found guilty and both serve five years' hard labor.
- One hundred forty-five years after Massachusetts declared it obscene, the Supreme Court declares in *Memoirs v. Massachusetts* that John Cleland's *Memoirs of a Woman of Pleasure* has literary merit.

1967

- ***October 23:*** President Lyndon B. Johnson signs into law the U.S. Commission on Obscenity and Pornography. Almost three years later, the commission released an 874-page report that called for the repeal of 114 state and federal laws that limited citizens' rights to determine what books they could read and films they could view. In October 1970, the Senate rejected the report by a 60-5 vote.

1968

- A film rating system is installed to replace the Production Code. Over the next few decades the ratings system undergoes changes, but remains in place. Essentially the new system lifts restrictions on film producers, directors, and writers while placing the burden of censorship on parents and theater owners.

1970

- ***November:*** Three directors of IT, England's first underground newspaper, are found guilty of conspiring to corrupt public decency and conspiring to corrupt public morals for running gay contact advertising. In an appeal heard in May 1972, the decency charge is reversed, but the morals charge is upheld.

1971

- ***June 13:*** The *New York Times* publishes the first installment of analysis and excerpts from the Pentagon Papers. The federal government acts to have a restraining order granted against the newspaper. The order is granted, and the New York Times Company takes the case to the Supreme Court.
- ***June 18:*** The *Washington Post* begins publishing excerpts from the Pentagon Papers. A temporary restraining order is granted, pending appeal by the justice department. The appellate court rules in favor of the newspaper. The justice department then takes the case to the Supreme Court.
- ***June 26***: The U.S. Supreme Court combines the two cases into *New York Times Company v. United States.* The Court rules 6-3 in favor of the newspaper. Nine separate opinions are handed down and legality of prior restraint is left unsettled.

1980

- After relaxing Egypt's harsh censorship laws, President Anwar al-Sadat oversees the passage of two laws that once again restrict freedom of the press and of speech: the Press Law and the Law on Protecting Values from Shameful Conduct. Both laws make it a crime to criticize Sunni Islam and the government.

Chronology

1981

- ***September:*** Egyptian president Anwar al-Sadat orders the mass arrests of more than 1,000 members of Egypt's political class in response to continuing disaffection that has stemmed from Egypt's treaty with Israel. The following month Sadat is assassinated.
- ***October:*** Egyptian vice president Hosni Mubarak becomes president upon the death of Anwar al-Sadat and immediately declares a state of emergency. According to Article 48 of the Egyptian constitution, "In a state of emergency or in time of war, a limited censorship may be imposed on the newspapers, publications and mass media in matters related to public safety or for purposes of national security in accordance with the law." Mubarak extends the state of emergency in 1988 and never lifts it.

1982

- ***January 5:*** The U.S. District Court for the Eastern District of Arkansas rules against Arkansas's balanced treatment law. The law made it legal to teach creationism alongside evolution. Proponents of the law claim that evolution is part of the religion of secular humanism. Opponents claim it is a violation of the First Amendment's establishment clause.
- ***December 4:*** China adopts a new constitution (amended four times thereafter). Though it guarantees basic civil rights to China's citizens, one of the articles in the constitution declares broadly: "The exercise by citizens of the People's Republic of China of their freedoms and rights may not infringe upon the interests of the state, of society and of the collective, or upon the lawful freedoms and rights of other citizens."

1983

- U.S. military troops invade the Caribbean island nation of Grenada ostensibly to rescue American medical students following a military coup that overthrew and executed Marxist prime minister Maurice Bishop. The military bars the press from reporting the invasion and the American public is allowed only secondhand information, informed speculation, or official reports.

1987

- ***June 19:*** The U.S. Supreme Court affirms a lower court decision that Louisiana's balanced treatment law is unconstitutional. The Court finds that it violates the First Amendment's establishment clause.

1989

- ***February 14:*** Ayatollah Khomeini of Iran issues a fatwa (religious opinion) sentencing author Salman Rushdie to death for blasphemy in his depiction of

Muhammed in the novel *The Satanic Verses*. Rushdie spends the next nine years in hiding until the fatwa is lifted.

- ***March:*** Parental warning stickers are placed on recorded music for sale. The stickers are a result of actions and testimony by the Parents Music Resource Center. Musicians as diverse as Frank Zappa and John Denver testify before Congress that the stickers are another form of censorship.
- ***June 3:*** On orders from Deng Xiaoping, Chinese troops push into Beijing's Tiananmen Square to break up a month-and-a-half-long protest. The demonstrators, initially students but later joined by workers, have been calling for Deng's dismissal and political reforms. During the short battle, hundreds are killed and thousands wounded.

1990s

- The Office for Intellectual Freedom of the American Library Association records more than 6,300 challenges to books during the decade. Since most challenges went unreported, the ALA later estimates that the actual number could be 25,000–30,000. The challenges concern books taught in public schools, or in school and public libraries.

1994

- ***October:*** Moscow journalist Dmitri Kholodov is killed when he opens a suitcase thought to have documents incriminating military officials in a corruption scandal, but instead contains a bomb. Kholodov had been investigating military corruption for the newspaper *Moskovskii Komsomolets*. No one is ever convicted of the murder.

1995

- Cairo University professor Nasser Abu Zayd is declared an apostate because of his views of the Qu'ran. He and his wife are forced to flee Egypt for the Netherlands. The declaration against him is eventually lifted. The al-Azhar Islamic Research Council, which also has censorship powers, later bans Zayd's book, *Discourse and Interpretation*.
- Well-known television journalist Vladislav Listyev is shot to death in the entryway to his apartment building in Moscow. Listev had just become the head of the Russian state television channel one, ORT, and was planning to make changes at the station.

1996

- ***January:*** The People's Republic of China places new restrictions on foreign financial news agencies working in China. The foreign agencies must register with the Chinese Xinhua news agency, which would also act as an intermediary and control subscription rates. China threatens to take action against any foreign financial news agency that "slanders or jeopardizes the national interest of China."

1999

- ***July:*** Police arrest adherents of the Falun Gong religious sect, and the government of the People's Republic of China bans the sect. The action is a reprisal for an April Falun Gong demonstration that protested violence against the sect and a ban on the publishing of their material. It is later ascertained that some Falun Gong members die in custody.
- ***December 2:*** New York Court of Appeals affirms a lower court ruling that Prodigy, an Internet service provider, was not responsible for defamation of character in the case of a fraudulent Internet account in which a person had been slandered. In essence, the court equated ISP with telephone companies and therefore not liable for the communications of their customers.

2001

- Gazprom, the Russian state natural gas monopoly, through its subsidiary Gazprom-Media, takes over television station NTV. The station was part of the media empire of Vladimir Gusinsky, a wealthy critic of President Vladimir Putin. NTV journalists opposed to the Putin administration are forced out. Gusinsky's newspaper, *Sevodnya,* fails and his magazine, *Itogi,* is also stripped of journalists critical of Putin. Only the Moscow radio station Echo Moskvy remains intact. Gusinsky goes into exile.
- ***October 26:*** President George W. Bush signs into law the USA PATRIOT Act of 2001. In the wake of the September 11 terrorist attacks in New York City and Washington, D.C., the law's proponents claim it is a much-needed security measure. Critics argue it is a violation of the Bill of Rights. The bill was introduced into the House of Representatives on October 23 and passed the House the next day by a 357-66 vote. It passed the Senate on October 25 by a 98-1 vote.

2002

- The government of Zimbabwe enacts two restrictive laws: the Public Order and Security Act (POSA) and the Access to Information and Protection of Privacy Act (AIPPA). POSA is basically an anti-sedition law, making it a crime to criticize or insult the president, the military, or law enforcement agencies. AIPPA called for the registration of media companies and tightening of accreditation for journalists.
- ***August 1:*** China issues Interim Regulations on Management of Internet Publishing; the government also launched a campaign titled Public Pledge on Self-Discipline for China's Internet Industry. The regulations promote a strict

censorship of Web sites that might "harm national unity, sovereignty, or territorial integrity, or damage national honor or interests, disturb the social order or damage social stability, or advocate cults."

2004

- ***February:*** A production of Eve Ensler's *The Vagina Monologues* is performed at American University in Cairo. The production is unsanctioned by the university and is not open to the public. Audience members are by invitation only. The private, unsanctioned atmosphere protects the production from being closed down by the censor.
- ***July 9:*** American-born Russian *Forbes* editor, Paul Klebnikov, is shot while leaving his Moscow office building and dies en route to the hospital. Klebnikov's journalism dealt with the confluence of wealth, organized crime, and the war in Chechnya.

2005

- ***March:*** Two curators at the Andrei Sakharov Museum and Public Center in Moscow are found guilty of inciting religious hatred. The charges are brought against them after the Orthodox Church formally complains about a 2003 exhibit in the museum titled, "Caution—Religion." The Church charged that the exhibit was blasphemous.
- ***July:*** Reporter Judith Miller of the *New York Times* is sentenced to jail for contempt of court after refusing to disclose the name of her source regarding the leaking of the name of a CIA agent, a federal crime. Miller serves 12 weeks in jail and is released after her source releases her from her obligation. Her imprisonment sparks a lobbying campaign to have Congress pass a "shield" law that would protect journalists doing their jobs.
- Egyptian censors ban 20 music videos, claiming they are sexually suggestive. They also complain that the songs' lyrics are "meaningless." The following year they ban a music video by the popular Tunisian singer, Najla, as being pornographic.

2006

- Google, Yahoo!, and Microsoft announce they are altering their search engines to comply with Chinese censorship laws in order to do business in China. The three Internet service providers rationalize that getting their feet in the door will help open up the country. Critics contend it is a setback for freedom of speech and of the press in China.
- ***March 9:*** President George W. Bush signs the USA Patriot Improvement and Reauthorization Act of 2005. The new law reauthorizes those provisions of

the USA PATRIOT Act that were about to expire and closes loopholes in the earlier law.

- ***April:*** Russian president Vladimir Putin signs into law a bill that gives the government stricter regulatory power over nongovernmental organizations (NGOs). In addition to making it more difficult for NGOs to register, the government has the right to withhold or revoke registrations from NGOs. The new law is worded vaguely enough to be used for censorship purposes.
- ***September 10:*** China further tightens control of foreign news agencies working in the country making the Xinhua news agency the distributor of foreign news reports in China—thus making the domestic agency a de facto censor.
- ***October:*** The Harry Potter series of children's fantasy books are challenged in a suburban Georgia county. The challenge contends that the books' purpose it to indoctrinate children in the Wicca religion and therefore violate the First Amendment's establishment clause.
- ***October 7:*** Russian investigative journalist Anna Politkovskaya is shot to death in the elevator of her Moscow apartment building. A reporter for the newspaper *Novaya gazeta,* she is murdered two days before she is to publish a story about kidnapping and torture of Chechen civilians by Chechen security forces loyal to Russia.
- ***December 1:*** Four street actors in Bulawayo are arrested and beaten for satirizing Zimbabwe's economy with a play called *Indlala* (Hunger). The actors are also accused of inciting rebellion as members of the opposition group Movement for Democratic Change.
- ***December 28:*** The Venezuelan president Hugo Chávez announces the decision not to renew the broadcasting license of Radio Caracas Television, an opposition channel.

2007

- ***April:*** Journalists at the Russian News Service, Russia's largest radio news network, are told by new managers that at least 50 percent of the news they report must be positive.
- ***April 19:*** Yale University bans the use of realistic-looking prop weapons in university plays in response to the shootings at Virgina Tech. The ban is lifted on April 23.
- ***May:*** Seven journalists from the Russian News Service resign over censorship issues with new management.
- ***August 17:*** The BBC Russian Service is taken off the air by the new owners of the Moscow radio station on which it broadcast, Bolshoye Radio.

- ***August 29:*** Thailand's National Legislative Assembly votes unanimously to annul outdated publication laws that called for police enforcement of censorship.
- ***September:*** The CEO of the state-owned Zimbabwe Broadcasting Holdings testifies before a parliamentary committee that censorship and political interference are rampant.
- ***September 25:*** A news report in the *Christian Science Monitor* states that China has shut down over 18,000 Web sites.
- ***October 16:*** Reporters Without Borders releases its 2007 Worldwide Press Freedom Index, ranking 169 countries according to press freedom for journalists and bloggers. The United States ranks 48; Russia, 144; Egypt, 146; Zimbabwe, 149; China, 163. Iceland and Norway are tied at the first ranking; Eritrea is 169.
- ***October 31:*** The government of Sri Lanka imposes censorship on reporting the strife between government forces and the insurgent Tamil Tigers; security forces had already barred print and photojournalists. The censorship restrictions are lifted two days later.
- ***November 3:*** President Pervez Musharraf of Pakistan declares a state of emergency. Parliament is dissolved, and independent media critical of Musharraf are closed down. Musharraf lifts the state of emergency on December 15; 12 days later his primary political opponent, Benazir Bhutto, is assassinated.
- ***December 30:*** Kenya imposes a ban on live television broadcasting.

2008

- ***January:*** The president of the Montclair State University student government freezes the funds of the student newspaper, the *Montclarion*, following criticism of closed-door student government meetings.
- ***January 1:*** Five Ethiopian journalists, who were freed from prison in 2007, are denied licenses to practice their profession.
- ***January 1:*** Myanmar raises annual license fees for receivers of satellite television from approximately $5 to more than $800, three times the annual salary of a teacher.
- ***January 10:*** Azerbaijan's National Television and Radio Council bans television broadcasts in foreign languages.
- ***January 22:*** Azeri police seize over 500 copies of banned religious books.
- ***January 29:*** The Federation Council, the upper house of Russia's parliament, begins discussion of a new law "On the Internet."

Glossary

Access to Information and Protection of Privacy Act 2002 Zimbabwean law that requires registration of media companies and tightening of accreditation rules for journalists.

affirmative oath also called a positive oath; an oath or affidavit in which a person is asked to affirm belief in something or a willingness to carry out a duty, usually delivered in general terms.

al-Azhar Islamic Research Council an important Sunni institution in Egypt that has the power of CENSORSHIP of anything it finds blasphemous.

anti-Semitism any of a number of manifestations against Jews; in its most virulent form it led to the Holocaust; CENSORSHIP of Jewish writers, intellectuals, and artists has also been a part of programmatic anti-Semitism.

Areopagitica seventeenth-century essay written by the poet John Milton that argues against the English licensing law.

bad tendency a judicial free speech test of the 1920s and 1930s that said that speech does not have to actually incite a criminal or terrorist act, but may do so.

blacklisting a prominent tactic used during the second Red scare to keep Communists and fellow travelers, or those suspected of being such, out of certain industries, notably film and television.

blasphemy spoken or written speech that denigrates the idea, the teachings, or the works of God, thus a crime in theocratic nations.

blog short for "Web log," blogs range from personal musings to political writing to journalism. Since the early 2000s, blogs have moved more and more into the mainstream.

Boy Spies of America one of the numerous World War I era volunteer organizations that helped quell dissent, which was equated with disloyalty, in the United States.

Broadcasting Services Act 2001 Zimbabwean law whose effect is to limit the point of view of radio and television broadcasts, allowing for only one independent station in each medium.

censorship the control of verbal or pictorial information, entertainment, or speech by a group, organization, or government.

chopping military euphemism for the process of censoring information.

clear and present danger a judicial free speech test created by the U.S. Supreme Court in the 1919 case *Schenk v. United States.* The doctrine allowed that certain speech was unprotected if it presented a "clear and present danger" to the general population, especially in wartime.

Comics Code Authority formed in the mid-1950s to police the U.S. comics industry and to purge its products of violence, sex, and horror. The code was revised a number of times, but began to lose its effectiveness by the mid-1980s.

Comstock Act law passed in 1873 that made it illegal to send obscene material through the mail; since obscene was not defined, a broad interpretation was used. Formally called the Act for the Suppression of Trade in, and Circulation of, Obscene Literature and Articles for Immoral Use, but named for its chief supporter, Anthony Comstock.

creationism generally understood as a reconciliation of the biblical account of creation with some aspects of science, however there are various forms of creationism; it stands in general opposition to evolution.

Cultural Revolution period in the People's Republic of China (1966–76) in which young extremists, taking their cues from verbal signals by Communist Party elders, engaged in massive violence and repression against those whom they deemed bourgeois.

defamation libel or slander in which the person making the statement knew or should have known a particular account was wrong.

Entartete Kunst modern art exhibit held in Munich during the Nazi era that strived to portray the art and the artists as abominable according to Nazi ideology; the term means "degenerate art."

Espionage Act of 1917 law passed during World War I that stifled dissent by equating it with disloyalty to the war effort; it is still on the books.

establishment clause the section of the FIRST AMENDMENT that deals with freedom of religion.

Falun Gong Chinese religious sect founded in 1992 and officially banned in 1999; many of its adherents were arrested in 1999; some died in custody.

Federal Loyalty Program a political response to the early cold war Red Scare established March 21, 1947, by President Harry S. Truman to investigate federal workers for communist affiliations.

First Amendment The amendment that guarantees freedom of religion, speech, the press, the right to peaceably assemble and to petition the government.

Fourteenth Amendment The amendment that extends constitutional guarantees and freedoms to the spheres of state and municipal government, as interpreted by the Supreme Court.

Gang of Four name given to those Chinese radical leaders, including Mao's wife Jiang Qing, whose public remarks inspired the Cultural Revolution. All were arrested after Mao's death.

Glavlit Russian contraction for *Glavnoye upravlenie po delam literatury I pechati* (Central Board for Literary and Press Affairs), the main structure of Soviet book and newspaper CENSORSHIP.

Great Firewall of China a combination of outright Internet CENSORSHIP, registrations of e-mailers and online newsgroups, and sophisticated blocking technology used to control information going in and out of China via cyberspace.

habeas corpus Latin phrase that literally means "you have the body"; it is a legal petition for a prisoner to appear before a judge who decides if the person is lawfully imprisoned.

hate speech speech based on hatred of an individual or a group; outlawed in many Western democracies though not banned outright in the United States.

HUAC acronym for the House Un-American Activities Committee (also House Committee on Un-American Activties) that investigated Communists in Hollywood in the late 1940s.

Index expurgatorius an index of passages from books that had to be either deleted or revised according to authorities of the Roman Catholic Church. The Index began in the 16th century and remained until 1966.

Index librorum prohibitorum (*Index of Prohibited Books*) a list issued by the Roman Catholic General Inquisition in 1559 that banned all books that the Inquisition considered obscene or heretical.

Internet filter general term for any computer program that blocks particular Internet sites. In the United States, Internet filters are primarily used to prevent minors from viewing adult material; elsewhere, they are often used for political reasons.

KGB the Committee for State Security, the Soviet internal and external investigation organization during the final 37 years of the USSR; the second and fifth directorates with the organization dealt with suppression of dissidents.

Law and Order Maintenance Act of 1960 the most repressive law enacted in Rhodesia, it reduced the rights of the majority black Africans under the guise of maintaining public order.

Law on Protecting Values from Shameful Conduct 1980 Egyptian law that makes it a crime to criticize Sunni Islam or the Egyptian government.

Libel Act of 1843 British law that allowed the truth of a comment to be taken into account during a trial.

Licensing Order of 1643 law that required prepublication licensing, registration of printed materials, seizure and destruction of books found offensive to the government, and the arrests and imprisonment of writers, publishers, and printers of such books.

magnitizdat A Russian term, based on the Russian word *SAMIZDAT*, which refers to surreptitious recording and distribution of music during the Soviet period.

McCarthyism term coined by Washington, D.C., political cartoonist Herblock to define the atmosphere of anti-Communist baiting and bullying of innocent witnesses in the early 1950s, that led to infringement of First Amendment rights. Named for Senator Joseph McCarthy.

national security letter essentially, a search warrant issued by the FBI that is not subject to a court order and which also has a gag order prohibiting the recipient from disclosing that he or she has even received the letter.

New York Society for the Suppression of Vice organization founded by Anthony Comstock and others in 1873 that targeted a broad range of material as pornographic; in 1947, the organization changed its name to the Society to Maintain Public Decency.

New York Times v. Sullivan landmark 1964 Supreme Court case that decided for the newspaper in a landmark opinion that strengthened the guarantee of freedom of the press.

New York Times v. United States 1971 Supreme Court case that upheld press freedom in two prior restraint cases regarding the PENTAGON PAPERS, but did not put to rest the issue of prior restraint.

nonmailability provision section of the ESPIONAGE ACT OF 1917 that granted the Postmaster General discretionary power to withhold a newspaper or periodical from the U.S. mail because of perceived disloyalty.

obscenity abhorrent to morality or virtue; something calculated to arouse PRURIENT INTEREST; that lacks literary, artistic, political, or scientific intent.

Operation Urgent Fury military code name for the 1982 U.S. invasion of Grenada in which the press was not allowed access to report the combat.

Pentagon Papers common name for a report titled *United States-Vietnam Relations, 1945–67* that was leaked to the press. Its publication and analysis by the *New York Times* and *Washington Post* sparked a Supreme Court battle with the Nixon administration. (See *NEW YORK TIMES V. UNITED STATES*.)

Peruvian Inquisition colonial arm of the Spanish Inquisition, begun in 1568, though less effective. It controlled imports of literature and periodicals into the Spanish New World.

Press Law 1980 Egyptian law that makes it a criminal offense to challenge Sunni Islam and advocate the destruction of state institutions.

prior restraint CENSORSHIP or banning of a text before publication.

Production Code a code of self-censorship enforced by the U.S. film industry from 1930 until 1968. Its heyday was from 1934 to the early 1950s.

prurient interest an unwholesome interest in sex; used as a test of whether or not something is obscene.

Public Order and Security Act 2002 Zimbabwean law that replaced the LAW AND ORDER MAINTENANCE ACT OF 1960, but which made it a crime to criticize the president, limited the right of public assembly, and authorized the police to impose curfews.

ratings system a method of gauging the appropriate age level for a film, television program, or CD. The film version replaced the PRODUCTION CODE.

Red Scare, 1919–20 Widespread fear of a Communist revolution in America following the 1917 Bolshevik revolution in Russia and strikes and bombings in the United States. It resulted in numerous arrests and deportations.

Red Scare, 1945–54 Initially a political tactic used by both major U.S. political parties to garner support in the early years of the cold war, it spread from anti-Communist hunts in government to private industry, directly affecting thousands of people and indirectly affecting millions.

Reform Act of 1832 British law that contributed to the end of seditious libel in that country.

Regulations for the Suppression of Counterrevolutionaries 1951 Chinese law that empowered the police to detain or arrest dissidents and opponents of the Communist Party; the law was also used against intellectuals, writers, artists, and other "culture workers."

samizdat A Russian word that literally means self-publishing house, it was a technique popular during the last three decades of the USSR for surreptitiously distributing censored or likely-to-be censored texts in handwritten, typed, or mimeographed form.

secular humanism a nontheistic belief in the scientific method and rationalism; opponents call it a form of religion but adherents deny it.

sedition speech or writing that opposes a government but is not treasonous.

Sedition Act of 1798 A law passed by the Federalist Congress and signed by President Adams that made it a crime to criticize the government or the president. It expired in 1801.

Sedition Act of 1918 A revised section of the ESPIONAGE ACT OF 1917, passed during World War I, that made criticism of government policy or the military, including uniforms, a crime.

Smith Act of 1940 actual title, the Alien Registration Act of 1940, named for Senator Howard Smith who authored the antisedition portion. Used in the 1950s to prosecute Communists.

socialist realism literary (and later artistic) theory, first espoused by Soviet writer Maxim Gorky and others that literature should reflect soviet ideals; see ZHDANOVISM.

Spanish Inquisition the best-known of the Roman Catholic inquisitions, it lasted from c. 1478–1834; its CENSORSHIP and other activities, designed to stamp out heresy in Spain, were reactions to the Protestant Reformation and the conversions of the Marranos and Moriscos.

Stage Licensing Act 1737 British law dealing with theatrical productions that required plays and actors to be sanctioned beforehand by the lord chamberlain who had extraordinary CENSORSHIP power.

symbolic speech nonverbal, usually political, speech such as flag burning.

tamizdat A Russian term, based on the Russian word *SAMIZDAT*, which refers to work published abroad (*tam* = "there") during the Soviet period.

Tariff Act A 1930 U.S. law that empowered the U.S. Customs Department to seize any material coming into the United States that it deemed obscene. Seized material is then judged by a federal court.

unprotected speech in the United States, speech that is not protected by the First Amendment. This has meant different things at different times, but now generally means DEFAMATION, OBSCENITY, and harassment.

USA PATRIOT Act of 2001 antiterrorist act swiftly passed in both houses of Congress and signed into law by President George W. Bush. Its detractors claim that it infringes on the First, Fourth, Sixth, Eighth, and Fourteenth Amendments.

V-chip a television filter technology in use since mid-1999 that reads encoded information and blocks programs based on a preselected rating.

Voice of America International broadcaster funded by the U.S. government; it has at times been subjected to varying degrees of CENSORSHIP.

ZANU acronym for Zimbabwe African National Union; political party founded in 1963, banned in 1964, engaged in the guerrilla insurgency until it won the 1980 election; led by Robert Mugabe since the 1970s, it has been the leading party of Zimbabwe since the country's independence.

ZAPU acronym for Zimbabwe African People's Union; political party founded in 1961 by Joshua Nkomo, banned in 1962, engaged in the guerrilla insurgency until Zimbabwe's independence. In 1987, it merged with ZANU.

Zhdanovism policy of strict government control of literature and the arts so as to keep it in line with the theories of SOCIALIST REALISM; named for Andrei Zhdanov, it was at its height in the post-World War II years.

Index

Note: page numbers in **boldface** indicate major treatment of a subject. Page numbers followed by *b* indicate biographical entries. Page numbers followed by *c* indicate chronology entries. Page numbers followed by *g* indicate glossary entries.

Index

Index

Index

Index

Index

O

Index

Index

Index

Z